Guidance and Counseling

in the Elementary School

RICHARD C. NELSON
Purdue University

HOLT, RINEHART AND WINSTON, INC.
*New York   Chicago   San Francisco   Atlanta   Dallas
Montreal   Toronto   London   Sydney*

Copyright © 1972 by Holt, Rinehart and Winston, Inc.
All rights reserved
Library of Congress Catalog Card Number: 79–185783
ISBN: 0-03-084848-2
Printed in the United States of America
2 3 4 5   038   9 8 7 6 5 4 3 2 1

TO BETTY

The more I love, the more I can,
The more I can, the more I do,
The more I do, the more I shall,
The more shall I, the more shall you.

To keep your love I give my love,
The giving does receive its due;
The more I give, the more I have,
The more have I, the more have you.

Preface

The writing of this book has been undertaken with a broad audience in mind. My classes in Guidance in the Elementary School have included master's degree candidates in counselor and teacher education, experienced elementary and secondary school counselors, Ed. S. and Ph. D. candidates in teacher and counselor preparation, and an occasional advanced undergraduate student. I find that my own understanding of the field has grown through experiences with children and with this welcome and stimulating diversity of people. Because I have tried to write so as to reach across this wide range of interested individuals, the more widely read educator may appropriately scan or overlook some sections, while the inexperienced person may find the extensive references useful in exploration of topics requiring further discussion.

The comparatively recent national attention upon elementary school guidance is an exciting development that has resulted in a great variety of programs, some carefully and uniquely formulated, others created as downward extensions of secondary school programs, while still others have just grown like Topsy. This text recognizes the need for continuity with secondary school guidance while emphasizing the foundational character of the elementary school and the special needs of its children.

Further, this text acknowledges the interdependence of the counselor and the teacher in the elementary school setting. The counselor is seen as having the task of counseling in one-to-one or group contacts with children, and in support of his counseling he consults with others, coordinates guidance efforts, and is knowledgeable in the area of child development. The teacher is seen as having the primary tasks of providing for group educational experiences in the classroom that are consistent with good mental health practices, and of making additional provisions for children with special needs. The view is taken that maximum effectiveness emerges when a well-trained, personally effective counselor is assigned to one building and works with a concerned and interested group of teachers in an atmosphere of strong administrative support.

An effective guidance program requires breadth and innovation, with the counselor, for example, making play materials available to children, utilizing a variety of group counseling processes in his schedule, and providing a consultation service to teachers and parents; and the teacher incorporating various mental health approaches and exploring careers and life styles with children. Cooperative teacher-counselor functioning increases the likelihood that children who need help will encounter a guidance program in which their various needs are met through an appropriate range of approaches—multidimensionality in the guidance program is frequently the appropriate response to the needs of children.

Here the principle is accepted that guidance and counseling should be truly accessible to all children. While a variety of consultative and educative processes is vital in elementary school guidance, it is most important that there be a developmental, sequential program and accessible adults who take time with children, who listen to them, who treat their ideas and concerns as important, and who demonstrate a caring for them.

R. C. N.

Lafayette, Indiana
March 1972

Contents

Part One

The Need

1

An Introduction

According to the order of nature, all men being equal, their common vocation is the profession of humanity; and whoever is well educated to discharge the duties of a man, cannot be badly prepared to fill up any of those offices that have a relation to him.

JEAN JACQUES ROUSSEAU: Emile

GUIDANCE NEEDS ARE ENCOUNTERED BY ALL CHILDREN AND ADULTS

The elementary school guidance program and counseling service exist to meet the needs of children. All children encounter problems that are the concerns of guidance:

"No one listens to me."
"I wish I had more friends."
"I wish I had deeper friendships."
"I don't feel good about myself."
"Some (or all) of this work is too hard (too easy) for me."
"The kids tell me to do one thing and my parents (or teachers) tell me to do another."
"I get tired of just sitting."
"I worry about things."
"I'm afraid of some things—and I wish I weren't."

Other difficulties include personal disappointment, illness or death of adults in his own life or in the lives of his friends, the lack of a personal

3

sense of meaning, and frightening news headlines. Still other problems may be raised by the desire to explore the trappings of adolescence or adulthood, such as smoking, drinking, sexual activity, drug use, and hair or clothing styles.

The guidance program and the counseling service may also help children by helping the adults in their lives. Many teachers and parents can identify with one or more of the following comments:

From teachers:
"Eric fidgets all the time."
"Sue seems to cry whenever I look at her."
"I don't get any work out of Allen."
"I can't spend all my time with these slow children."
"Too many of these children are below grade level in reading."
"This whole class is about to drive me up a wall."
"Jimmy's parents don't show any interest in him."
And from parents:
"Jimmy is just driving me wild."
"What are you doing to these children that they don't want to go back to school?"
"If only someone could help me keep Louie out of trouble."
"I'm not going to let these kids suffer like I did."
"Those teachers don't know how hard it is nowadays."
"I'll punish him by grounding him for the rest of the year."
"These children have to get good grades or they won't get into a good college later."

Life puts pressures upon the adults in children's lives; the adults in turn may pass these pressures on to their children, and this may well become the source of much anxiety and frustration in these children. Children in their own maturing also experience difficult moments, frustrations, temptations, and special needs.

Modern guidance efforts are directed toward easing some of life's difficult moments for the child; meeting some of his needs; helping him to understand himself, his feelings, his changing personality, the demands placed upon him, and the ways in which he is responded to by others. Modern guidance efforts also are directed toward facilitating the teacher's work with children within and beyond the presentation of academic material, and toward helping parents to understand and live better with the changing child, the changing school, and the changing environment.

THE ONGOING NATURE OF GUIDANCE

Although the attempt to make guidance services available to all children is a comparatively recent phenomenon, guidance has long been a part of education. For many centuries, in their own ways, thousands and perhaps millions of teachers have incorporated principles of guidance into their efforts with children in order to facilitate learning.

In recent years, however, the school has played an increasingly important role in aiding children to cope with some of their needs. This stems in part from the developing awareness of educators that the child's mind cannot be disassociated from the rest of his total person and personality. It stems also from the attempt to educate all of the public—a vital necessity in a democratic society. Educators have recognized the need to help children see the values inherent in education, relate these values to themselves, and evaluate the success with which these objectives are achieved. In general, the modern emphasis on guidance as a clear-cut professional responsibility of the schools has emerged largely in response to perceptions of the inadequate extent to which children's needs have been met in the past.

PANDORA'S BOX

The teacher of the early 1900's may have been fully aware of the disturbance on the face of the girl in the front row and the teasing of the boy in the back, but, except to control the situation in terms of discipline, he tended not to involve himself further. Perhaps he sensed his own inadequacies and the absence of sources of help, should he examine the situation more closely and find that help was needed. After a while he became inured to the problem. He did not open Pandora's box. It is open now, and the cover no longer closes.

Today's teacher may have a minimal background in psychology and sociology, yet be far more aware than yesterday's teacher of children's needs and of the possibilities for assistance. He seeks and expects help and looks for it from the guidance professional and from the administrator.

All manner of pupil-stated, parent-stated, and teacher-stated concerns now mingle in the educational environment. Pandora's box had nothing on the concealed concerns that have swarmed into the atmosphere now that the lid is off.

ELEMENTARY COMPARED WITH
SECONDARY SCHOOL

Full awareness of the need for guidance services may well have hit both elementary and secondary school at the same time, but clearer and more persuasive justification was formulated for the secondary school guidance program. High school dropout statistics, juvenile delinquency, teen-age marriages, problems of entry into college and livelihood, and the like lent greater urgency to initiating the program at that level. Further, the implementation of accrediting standards for guidance programs in secondary schools has hastened development of programs designed to meet the needs of adolescents.

With the development of the secondary school program in guidance has come an awareness that efforts must be made even earlier. Many dropouts are gone before the secondary school guidance program touches them in any way; others are present only physically. Increasingly, technological job requirements and difficulties in college entrance may keep the secondary school counselor involved with students' efforts to reach decisions along these lines. The adolescent who has not learned earlier to discuss and share concerns in the school setting may now show little inclination to let the school enter his life in a personal way; his need to be independent of adults may block his impulse to do so.

On the other hand, elementary school children function more of the time in a self-contained classroom setting, they seem very willing to deal with problems and concerns at their level of understanding, and they appear to be more open than adolescents to assistance from others. Fewer seem to have given up on themselves; fewer have ceased to believe that adults may be found who will care about them, hear them, and help them; and fewer of them have departed from the school setting. Personalized, timely guidance offers more promise here than at the secondary school level, although much worthwhile guidance can occur at any level.

DEFINITIONS

Guidance has been defined in hundreds of ways. In general, it may be thought of as an attempt to help the individual to understand himself and the world about him, or as an attempt to achieve maximum self-realization for the individual. For example:

> Conceptually, guidance involves the utilization of a point of view to help an individual; as an educational construct, it refers to the provision of experiences which assist pupils to help themselves; and as a service, it refers to organized procedures and processes to achieve a helping relationship.[1]

> To assist the immature but growing pupil in a better understanding of himself, to think through with him the meaning of personal choices, to encourage him to optimal academic productivity, to give dignity to his individuality, this is the nature of guidance.[2]

> Guidance is, essentially, an emphasis in the school program seeking to individualize education. It is our effort to bring the total facilities of

[1] Bruce Shertzer and Shelley C. Stone, *Fundamentals of Guidance* (Boston: Houghton Mifflin, 1971), p. 31.

[2] Herman J. Peters, Bruce Shertzer, and William Van Hoose, *Guidance in Elementary Schools* (Skokie, Ill.: Rand McNally, 1965), p. 13.

the school to bear upon the optimum development of the individual child. It is the personalizing of education.[3]

Four key elements are generally inherent in definitions of guidance: (1) guidance involves helping, (2) guidance is personalized, (3) guidance seeks to expand self-understanding, (4) guidance seeks to expand understanding of others. Thus:

Guidance encompasses the full range of personalized assistance given to the individual in seeking to expand his self-understanding and his understanding of others.

GUIDANCE AND EDUCATION

What is the difference between guidance and education? When guidance is considered as an attempt to help the individual to understand himself and the world about him or to achieve maximum self-realization, then certainly, considerable overlap should be expected. The differences are more of focus than of kind. Meeks' view is: "The guidance process complements the instructional process, and together they constitute the educational process in the school setting."[4]

Guidance focuses especially upon the individual as a self, his self-understanding and his understanding of others in relation to himself. Education focuses especially upon the individual as a member of a democratic society, his understanding of the society, its history, traditions, and concepts, and (less centrally) his relationship to that society. It is obvious that the guidance-education overlap is great; Carey[5] points out that counselors and students (and one may suggest teachers also) want education to be sensitive to the individual needs of young people—a guidance objective.

Cautioning that his statement may oversimplify the issue, especially in omitting mention of the counselor's responsibility to children who have problems in learning, Hill makes the following distinction between guidance and education:

If we seek, then, to distinguish between the teaching and guidance function in schools we can make this distinction between "teaching" for that which society insists children learn, and "guiding" for decision-making in areas in which society leaves the individual relatively free. . . .[6]

[3] George E. Hill, *Management and Improvement of Guidance* (New York: Appleton-Century-Crofts, 1965), p. 7.

[4] Anna R. Meeks, *Guidance in Elementary Education* (New York: Ronald, 1968), p. 46.

[5] Richard W. Carey, "Student protest and the counselor," *Personnel and Guidance Journal, 48:* 185 (1969).

[6] Hill, *op. cit.,* p. 11.

COUNSELING

Counseling is both a process and a relationship, as suggested by Stefflre and Matheny and by Combs:

> Counseling may be defined as a professional relationship between a counselor and a client, in which the counselor helps the client to understand himself and his life space in order to make meaningful and informed choices consonant with his essential nature in those areas where choices are available to him.[7]

> There can be little doubt that counseling is, in essence, a learning process. When counseling is successful, the client learns a new and better relationship between himself and the world in which he lives.[8]

Counseling here is regarded as an opportunity for the child to explore his feelings, thoughts, and actions and to learn to mobilize his resources to meet the challenges in his environment. In the elementary school setting, counseling focuses on preventing problems from occurring or from escalating and on anticipating the difficulties that appear in the process of growing and maturing.

In describing counselors who are of greatest help to their clients, Russell has distilled some of the essence of effective counseling. He suggests that counselors who are of greatest help to the child have the following things in common: "(1) they accept him; (2) they listen to him and try to understand him; (3) they are genuinely concerned about his welfare; (4) they are able to convey to him the feeling that they are concerned about his welfare; (5) they help him to capitalize on his strengths and to correct those weaknesses which he can correct with a reasonable effort; (6) they respect him as an individual; (7) they have confidence in his ability to choose what is best for him; and (8) they try to teach him to take increasingly greater responsibility for himself."[9]

COUNSELING AND GUIDANCE

What is the difference between counseling and guidance? Both involve helping that is personalized and that seeks to expand understanding. Counseling, however, is a relationship in which a counselor meets face-to-face with a child (or children) for the purposes of developing understand-

[7] Buford Stefflre and Kenneth B. Matheny, *The Function of Counseling Theory* (Guidance Monograph Series, Boston: Houghton Mifflin, 1968), p. 8.

[8] Arthur W. Combs, "Counseling as a learning process," *Journal of Counseling Psychology, 1:* 31 (1954).

[9] R. D. Russell, "Blacks' perceptions of guidance," *Personnel and Guidance Journal, 48:* 728 (1970).

ing of self and others. Guidance includes counseling as well as all other acts designed to produce these same understandings, whether or not they involve a face-to-face relationship focused on the child.

The term guidance might include such acts as the following: talking with a child about his agony over imminent divorce proceedings between his parents, presenting a film to a classroom for discussion of the meaning of friendship, conferring with a social worker about a particular child's need for financial help to get glasses, or checking that the library has an up-to-date file of career-information materials. Of these acts, only that of talking with the child whose parents are about to be divorced is counseling.

The title of this book includes both guidance and counseling in order to underscore the concept that counseling is a primary activity of the counselor but not his only activity. Where the paired terms, guidance and counseling, are used, the intent is to emphasize both counseling and noncounseling activities within the guidance program. The term guidance, used alone, tends to refer to the noncounseling aspects of the program.

Now that terms have been made more explicit, let us consider the objectives inherent in guidance and counseling.

GUIDANCE AND COUNSELING FOR WHAT?

To what ends are guidance and counseling efforts directed? What values, principles, and points of view are suggested by these efforts?

OBJECTIVES OF GUIDANCE AND COUNSELING

The facilitation of effective living in the present; the development of understandings, concepts, and skills that will result in responsible living in the future; the reduction of undue tensions and anxieties related to or inhibiting learning—in short, reaching the individual child: these are central objectives of guidance and counseling.

Dimick and Huff[10] see the two major objectives of the total guidance program as (1) the prevention of maladjustment, and (2) the development of human potential. Peters and Farwell[11] see the program as assisting the individual toward self-fulfillment, and simultaneously benefiting society. Murphy views the guidance objective not as "by-passing fundamental weaknesses . . . but as discovering capacities for social warmth

---

[10] Kenneth M. Dimick and Vaughn E. Huff, *Child Counseling* (Dubuque, Iowa: William C. Brown Company, Publishers, 1970), pp. 18–21.

[11] Herman J. Peters and Gail F. Farwell, *Guidance: A Developmental Approach* (Skokie, Ill.: Rand McNally, 1967), p. 33.

and outgoingness, capacity to enjoy and work with other people, the capacity to become effective members of the community."[12]

Murphy's accent on social proficiency and outgoingness may be questioned; nonetheless, his general point is valid: that the counselor and teacher must consider and sustain certain values. The alternative, he suggests, is the subordination of the individual to techniques.

In considering objectives, then, the counselor or teacher is considering values. He can emphasize the discovery of capacities for becoming an effective member of the community, if he recognizes that inherent in those capacities must be individuality and self-expression.

VALUES INHERENT IN GUIDANCE

The counselor or teacher is a valuing being. His choice of profession implies his view that people can change, that helping others in the processes of gaining self-understanding and making decisions is both feasible and desirable, that society has an obligation to aid those in need, that the possibility of living well is open to large numbers of people, and that altruism is needed in this world. His presence in the school setting shows an awareness that school is or can be a force for good and that education is, in itself, valuable. Beyond his evident value structure, he tends to value, both for himself and for the children with whom he works, self-control, cooperation, social proficiency, human kindness, idealism, honesty, genuineness, and love.

The counselor's willingness to work with children, parents, and teachers demonstrates a respect for the individual, counseling, his own skills, and the potential that exists in all human beings.

Krumboltz and Varenhorst[13] found that the values of the counselor were quite influential at junior high school level. When statements were attributed to counselors, young people agreed more often than when they were attributed either to parents or to peers (teachers were not included in the study). Zimmerman[14] found that the counselor in a few brief contacts with high school seniors was able to influence either for or against decisiveness in career objectives. These findings suggest that counselor values are important. Part of the task of the counselor may be, first, to determine his own values; second, to ascertain how much these values may be entering into his counseling; and third, to decide whether there is need for change.

[12] Gardner Murphy, "The cultural context of guidance," *Personnel and Guidance Journal, 34:* 7 (1955).

[13] John D. Krumboltz and Barbara Varenhorst, "Molders of pupil attitudes," *Personnel and Guidance Journal, 43:* 443–446 (1965).

[14] Gary Zimmerman, "Decision making and indecision in the vocational development of college-bound males" (unpublished doctoral thesis, Purdue University, Lafayette, Ind., 1970).

Murphy calls for more integration of values in counseling: "Those who can guide boys and girls, men and women, into a life full of zest in pursuing personal interests and at the same time serving the larger needs of a cooperative commonwealth are imposing nothing arbitrary; they are giving their clients a sounder, as well as a richer life."[15]

PHILOSOPHICAL PRINCIPLES

It may be impossible for anyone to construct a totally adequate life philosophy, and, judging by the criticism evoked by recent attempts, it may be impossible for anyone to construct an adequate philosophy of guidance. The attempt needs to be made, however. Four questions are briefly considered here and the views of the writer stated. What is the nature of man? What is the role of meaning in the life of man? What values accrue to the good works of man? What values accrue from meditation and contemplation?

MAN's NATURE   Man, here, is viewed as essentially neither good nor evil. He is open to learning both or either extreme. His perception of the effects of punishment and reward and his awareness of potential gains through either avenue tend to persuade him that his own needs are served well through cooperation and participation. Although man may be inclined toward either good or evil, his capability for development of deep love makes a reasonable argument for viewing him as more good than evil.

Further, man is viewed as essentially neither free nor determined; he is open to functioning in either way. Past events, abilities, limitations, and habits may restrict his perceived freedom, but he is generally freer than he lets himself be. Although man as a creature may be inclined toward either freedom or determinism, his adaptability in stress situations, his creativity, and his ability to set goals and achieve them makes a reasonable argument for viewing him as more free than determined.

The counselor or teacher involved in the guidance of the child is, as we have noted, a valuing person, engaged in assisting the child to learn to serve his needs by considering the immediate situation and the future ramifications of actions chosen. Helping the individual to find common ground between his need for self-fulfillment and the demands of the society is an important aspect of the guidance task.

MEANING   Frankl has made a strong case that man is in a constant search for meaning—not so much to find a preexisting meaning *of* his life, as to locate or generate a meaning *in* his life: "A man who becomes conscious of the responsibility he bears toward a human being who affectionately waits for him, or to an unfinished work, will never be able to throw away his life. He knows the 'why' for his existence, and will be able

---

[15] Murphy, *op. cit.*, pp. 8–9.

to bear with almost any 'how.' "[16] Thus Frankl sees the primary motivational force in life not as power or homeostasis or pleasure, nor anything other than meaning itself: "Man is never driven to moral behavior; in each instance he decides to behave morally. Man does not do so in order to satisfy a moral drive and to have a good conscience; he does so for the sake of a cause to which he commits himself, or for a person whom he loves, or for the sake of his God."[17]

This position is consistent with a school guidance philosophy, and it is as relevant to the child in the elementary school guidance program as it is to the adult philosopher. Meaning does not emerge with adulthood, but must be detected relevant to the life of the child. Perhaps adults who lack a sense of meaning are, in fact, largely those who found little meaning in childhood.

GOOD WORKS   Man seeks meaning in his life in many ways—among others, through good works. Those who detect meaning in their lives—a God to serve, a person to love, a cause that attracts them—may well fulfill that meaning through their acts. Further, those who take the traditional Christian view are enjoined to good works. "What doth it profit, my brethren, though a man say he hath faith and have not works? Can faith save him? . . . by works a man is justified and not by faith only."[18]

Aside from the question of heavenly reward, which may concern many individuals, we are concerned here with the inherent worth of good works in achieving a sense of meaningfulness. Certainly the educator is committed to the view that good works are intrinsically rewarding, and he tends to convey this value in his mode of living. The counselor may deal with these matters more specifically, because his ultimate purposes include helping others to develop a sense of personal worth and value, to discover the potential for meaning in their lives, and to consider ways in which they may express their own uniqueness through good works. These are developmental steps, in that the first may have to be the focus before the second or third can be dealt with extensively. At his own level even the young child is coping with each of these questions, though his attention may be focused primarily on experiencing self-worth.

MEDITATION   Religious men, searchers for meaning, existentialists seek direction, solace, and comfort through contemplation, meditation, or prayer. Meditative activity yields insight into the meaning of one's own life and an understanding of the works that might enhance that meaning.

Counseling has a clear relationship to the meditative process by which human beings seek direction, solace, comfort, and the discovery of

---

[16] Viktor Frankl, *Man's Search for Meaning* (New York: Washington Square Press, 1963), p. 127.

[17] *Ibid.,* p. 158.

[18] *James* 2: 14, 24.

meaning. The participation of the counselor need not change the inherent nature of the process. Many individual concerns may be reduced or understood through counseling, and the meaning of the life under discussion may be directly and appropriately considered.

The value structure of the teacher or counselor is of great importance in guidance and counseling. We have said that we view man here as inherently neither good nor evil, neither totally free nor determined; he may learn behaviors that range from one extreme to the other. Central to the life of man is a search for meaning, which he may discover through contemplation, action, or both. Guidance and counseling efforts may be directed toward the development of understandings or toward the reduction of tensions to facilitate the search for meaning.

PRINCIPLES OF GUIDANCE

Emerging from the views stated above are several principles specifically related to guidance and appropriate at the elementary school level. These principles are offered tentatively, especially in the light of Cribbin's[19] criticism that the term "principle" is inconsistently used, and that it tends to be synonymous with assumption. They will provide us a backdrop for consideration of further specific techniques and understandings relevant to elementary school guidance.

1. GUIDANCE IS, OR SHOULD BE, ACCESSIBLE TO ALL CHILDREN Every child should have the opportunity to consider his personal values, his sense of meaning, and his interaction in the world with a responsible adult, preferably one who, situationally, is not otherwise involved with him. He also may need opportunities to do nothing more than to relate to such an adult. Time limitations may prevent teachers from relating in the relaxed, unhurried way implied here; counselors may encounter children whose concerns are beyond the depth of their training and who should be referred for psychological, medical, or other assistance. Some form of guidance assistance should be accessible to *all* children within the elementary school setting. This does not mean, for example, a parading of all fourth graders through a series of fifteen-minute interviews; rather, it means an availability that is clear to the child and that places him under no obligation to participate.

2. GUIDANCE IS BASED ON THE CONCEPT THAT CHILDREN HAVE A RIGHT TO ASSISTANCE WHEN THEY NEED IT   It is a rare child who passes through his elementary school years without desiring some kind of guidance, support, or understanding beyond that which his parents or teachers can give, either because of their involvement in the concern or

[19] James J. Cribbin, "A Critique of the Philosophy of Modern Guidance," in Gail Farwell and Herman Peters, eds., *Guidance Readings for Counselors* (Skokie, Ill.: Rand McNally, 1960), pp. 78–93.

because of his need to resolve it independent of their assistance. The most understood child may wish to corroborate an opinion with an adult who is able to take the time to listen. The least understood child may desperately need a refuge. While frequently the child is aware of his needs and refers himself for assistance, at other times parents, teachers, and others may encourage him to seek guidance assistance or may refer him for counseling when they perceive the need.

3. GUIDANCE SERVES THE CHILD'S NEEDS IN ORDER TO ENHANCE HIS CHANCES OF REALIZING HIS POTENTIALITIES FOR INDIVIDUAL AND SOCIETAL ENDS   The efforts of those conducting the guidance program, as they look beyond the group toward the individual, may lead to many discoveries. Individual contacts may uncover needs that can be met through medical referrals, through family service agency referrals, through counseling, through individualized teaching, and through minor environmental changes (such as helping a child to understand and manage his aggressive feelings, creating better home study conditions, and so on). The appropriate handling of one or more of these unmet needs may, of course, enhance the likelihood that the child will become a more effective learner or will develop more positive attitudes toward school. The child may then be released to serve more effectively his own immediate and long-term goals as well as those of society.

4. GUIDANCE IS ORIENTED AROUND UNDERSTANDING OF SELF, UNDERSTANDING OF OTHERS, GOAL SEEKING, AND CHOICE MAKING   When self-understanding, understanding of others, goal seeking, and choice making are recognized as fundamental to guidance, it becomes clearer that all students can benefit from guidance in their elementary school years. While no one can be sufficient unto himself or unto another in dealing with these four vital aspects of life, a guidance program, the help of interested teachers, and the services of a counselor can provide some assistance, appropriate to the child's age level.

5. GUIDANCE IS A CONTINUOUS PROCESS AND IS AN INTEGRAL PART OF EDUCATION   Parents, relatives, neighbors, teachers, counselors, school administrators, and various community members—through example, exhortation, and demand—tell the child who they are, who he is, how and what they expect him to be, and what limits they see as appropriate for his behavior. The concept the child holds of himself as a learner is an integral factor in his learning, and his concept is influenced by many of those who are involved in his world. Guidance, whether positive or negative, incidental or organized, clear or unspecified, is indeed continuously operative within the child's education. The development of a formal guidance and counseling program offers the child at least intermittent guidance that is both organized and positive.

6. GUIDANCE IS BOTH PRESENT- AND FUTURE-ORIENTED   It may be said that the most important "job" of childhood is for the child to become an adult. Often this argument is used to rationalize a pushing of the child that, for him, is too rapid. Perhaps the *first* job of the child is to "become" a child. Guidance efforts may be more profitably applied toward helping the child be effective today rather than tomorrow in his work, his play, his social interactions, and his self-acceptance. Take care of today's needs, and often the skills and habits developed will take care of to-morrow's. Yet the long-range impact of behavior and choices *must* be considered, and the need to grow and seek the challenges that the future presents must be acknowledged. Conflict is a by-product, frequently, of the demands and habits of the past, the need for present success, and the pull of the future on the life of the individual.

7. GUIDANCE ATTENDS TO AND RESPONDS TO WEAKNESSES, BUT FOCUSES ON STRENGTHS   This principle may properly be termed a policy or an objective rather than a description of past performance. Children need to be alerted to their weaknesses, certainly, but they may only be able to attend to them insofar as they are also credited with strengths. Some young people, such as those who come from lower socioeconomic environments, need to be appreciated, and to be aware that they are appreciated, for their directness, their candor, their strength of conviction on some matters, and their willingness to stand up for their rights even in the face of punishment. Often they are told only of their reading difficulties and the troubles they cause.

If guidance is to be accessible to all children, it must focus on strengths, and time must be spent in reinforcing these strengths and recognizing children's skills and potentialities. Attention, of course, must also be given to responding to, or at least identifying, many of the children's needs. The person helping a child because of a perceived weakness may be most effective when he also helps the child to recognize and capitalize upon his strengths—when he helps the child to understand what is "right" about himself.

8. GUIDANCE IS A SHARED RESPONSIBILITY   The counselor brings special skills to his work with the child and has the time to see him individually, but the teacher has many more hours in a group setting to use for observation and assistance. The school administrator, the school social worker, the school nurse, the school psychologist, and especially the parent have valuable insights into the child's behavior, his needs, and his environment. Each of these persons need not be consulted concerning every child; nonetheless, the shared nature of the guidance responsibility must be recognized. For the sake of the children, a truly effective guidance program demands well-trained and dedicated professionals, good communication

and cooperation among all those who can contribute, and adequate resources to which children and their families may be referred.

9. GUIDANCE IS DEPENDENT ON ADEQUATE CHILD STUDY   The term "adequate" is emphasized here. The child who is finding sufficient value in relating occasionally to the counselor or teacher as an understanding adult, the child who shows a drawing that pleases him and for whom life is a positively weighted range of events, the child who by the acknowledgement of the teacher and the observation of the counselor seems to be effectively expanding his self-understanding and his understanding of others, may not require intensive study. Adequate child study with such children may involve little more than collecting achievement and intelligence testing data, plus such other information as the sociogram, which is utilized for group study purposes. With other children only intensive psychometric assessment followed by a diagnostic report will be sufficient. The collection of data should fit the concern about the child.

10. GUIDANCE IS DEPENDENT FOR MAXIMUM EFFECTIVENESS ON RESEARCH AND EVALUATION   The field of elementary school guidance badly needs both action research and deeper scientific research—for the benefit of children, for the clarification of guidance policies, and in order to sharpen the foci of guidance efforts. The field depends now on content validation, concentrating efforts where logic and appropriateness to need are evidenced; hard statistical data are needed, however, to validate or invalidate many of these well-meaning efforts. Research in the field has by no means been adequate for this purpose.

The principles of guidance suggested here are the foundation of this text. The teacher or counselor who wishes to serve the needs of children would do well to see that these principles are actualized.

THE HISTORICAL DEVELOPMENT OF GUIDANCE

HISTORY

The modern guidance movement has traditionally been dated from 1908, when Frank Parsons in Boston founded a Vocational Bureau to advise young men in self-assessment, job assessment, and the reasoning required to make vocational choices. Recognition has also been given to Jesse B. Davis of Grand Rapids, Michigan, who even earlier spent much of his time in counseling boys and girls while serving in a school administrative capacity. The beginnings of the psychological measurement efforts of Binet and others, and the social casework movement, also predate by a few years the efforts of Parsons. Regardless of who deserves first credit, the turn of the century saw the beginning of the guidance movement, as identifiable guidance efforts sprang up in many locations.

With the establishment of the National Vocational Guidance Association in 1913 in Grand Rapids, Michigan, the guidance movement began to crystallize. That organization, active today as a division of the American Personnel and Guidance Association, in 1915 began to publish *The Vocational Guidance Bulletin.*

The two World Wars clarified the need for identification of talents and abilities through testing, and for appropriate placement of men in the military services. War needs stimulated much investigation involving the selection of leaders. The depression of the 1930's clarified the need for guidance efforts beyond mere considerations of supply and demand, and such efforts began to be incorporated in the programs of various federal agencies, such as NYA and CCC, as well as state and local agencies. After the second World War, which aroused a national concern for effective use of human as well as economic resources, several legislative acts showed recognition of the need for guidance and counseling services. The George-Barden Act (1946) provided funds (distributed through the U.S. Office of Education) for partial financial support of state supervisors of guidance and for counselor education. Public Laws 11 and 346, which provided financial aid for education, also provided for counseling services through the Veterans Administration. In 1958 the National Defense Education Act strongly encouraged the guidance movement by providing funds for the training of counselors and for the expansion of guidance and testing programs in schools.

Elementary school guidance has enjoyed less support and growth than secondary school guidance, as more immediate manpower and vocational needs have received first attention. However, with the 1964 revision of the NDEA guidelines, which permitted funds to be used for the education of elementary school counselors and the expansion of elementary school guidance programs, and with the Elementary and Secondary Education Act of 1965, elementary school guidance has begun to receive its due recognition. Still trailing badly in numbers of functioning counselors, the elementary school counseling and guidance program is daily being acknowledged as foundational to a truly developmental guidance program.

Legislation is only part of the story, however. The American Personnel and Guidance Association (including as a division the National Vocational Guidance Association) was created in 1952 by the combination of several related and interested personnel organizations and NVGA. Including a current membership of well over 20,000 members, APGA has eight divisions: American College Personnel Association (ACPA), Association for Counselor Education and Supervision (ACES), National Vocational Guidance Association (NVGA), Student Personnel Association for

Teacher Education (SPATE), American School Counselor Association (ASCA), American Rehabilitation Counseling Association (ARCA), Association for Measurement and Evaluation in Guidance (AMEG), and National Employment Counselors Association (NECA).

The American School Counselor Association, responding to the upsurge in interest in elementary school guidance, has given support and encouragement to a previously mimeographed communication; as a result, in 1967 *Elementary School Guidance and Counseling* became a full-fledged journal.

INFLUENCES

Guidance did not emerge in a cultural or social vacuum, and several influences that promoted its development may be identified. Traxler[20] has isolated six such influences: humanitarianism, religion, mental hygiene, social change, pupil study, and nondirective therapy.

HUMANITARIANISM   In the late 1800's a spirit arose that has been characterized as humanitarian. Concern for the worker, the child in the factory, and the immigrant and others in the new slums developed to counterbalance the industrialization within our society and the prevailing low wages and poor working conditions. Child and adult welfare programs emerged through the efforts of humanitarians who believed that society could be improved if those less able to compete were given assistance. Humanitarian efforts influenced the development of child labor laws and school leaving laws. The growth in the school population of those who, in former years, would have been gainfully employed created a clear need, eventually recognized, for the school to consider the vocational guidance of youth.

RELIGION   Religion also has influenced the development of guidance services. The religious man sees great benefits in early training of youth. Since the school has the attention of the child for a great many hours a week, and since it also has a social service purpose, the religious man looks to the school to offer guidance services that will reinforce religious training.

MENTAL HYGIENE   Clifford Beers' book, *A Mind That Found Itself,* led to the Mental Hygiene movement. Concerned at first with conditions endured by persons in mental hospitals, this movement, through the National Committee for Mental Health, began to be interested in preventive mental hygiene. Eventually it brought about the inclusion in school curricula

---

[20] Arthur E. Traxler, *Techniques of Guidance* (New York: Harper & Row, 1957), pp. 3–4.

of subject matter related to mental health. The contribution of this movement was its focus on anticipatory action relative to one's mental or emotional health—its view that one did not have to await the hospitalization level before identifying and dealing with a problem.

SOCIAL CHANGE Such factors as two world wars, a depression, child labor laws, automation, and consequent unemployment have created enormous changes in our society, and these are reflected in our schools. The large number of youth remaining, often unwillingly, in school has created needs for curricular revision and guidance, as has the demand for better educated persons to man the more complex tasks of industry. Many guidance programs were developed to deal with the cumulative effect of these social changes, and much guidance effort today still concerns itself with such problems.

PUPIL STUDY The mental measurement movement, resulting from a need to know pupils as individuals and as group members, has led to more thoroughgoing pupil study. This kind of exploration has influenced the initiation and design of many guidance programs. Cumulative records, testing, case histories, and the like, have been developed and utilized extensively in the schools as this influence has shaped the guidance movement.

NONDIRECTIVE THERAPY Nondirective therapy, client-centered counseling, or, perhaps better, self theory, has made counseling a more manageable, feasible, and appropriate aspect of the school guidance movement. Traxler notes that:

> . . . while it may be questioned whether the guidance program at the school level can or should be strictly nondirective, Rogers and his associates have performed a distinct service in helping to neutralize the highly directive, paternal, authoritarian methods which too often characterized the clumsy efforts at counseling in the earlier stages of guidance in the schools of the United States.[21]

In the same spirit, Shertzer and Stone comment:

> The contributions of Rogerian therapy have made counselors more aware of the unity of personality, of the fact that a counselor counsels people rather than problems, of the fact that problems of adjustment in one segment of life have effects in other sectors, and of the complexity of the process of counseling concerning any type of individual adjustment, whether in the field of occupations, group living, or personal values. Even of greater importance, it has enabled all types of counselors to better understand counseling processes and techniques.[22]

[21] *Ibid.,* p. 4.
[22] Shertzer and Stone, *op. cit.,* p. 50.

SUMMARY

Elementary school counseling is a specific aspect of elementary school guidance, involving a personal relationship and directed toward helping a child understand himself, explore his environment, and cope more adequately with the challenges he faces. Guidance encompasses all assistance provided to children to enable them to develop understanding of themselves and of others. All children are seen as needing guidance assistance during their elementary school years.

Objectives of guidance and counseling include the facilitation of effective living in the present, the providing of a base for responsible future functioning, and the discovery of meaning in the life of the individual. Effective guidance is seen as accessible, oriented to student needs, directed toward exploration of the self and others, continuous, both present- and future-oriented, and focused on strengths. It is considered to be a shared responsibility, dependent on both adequate child study and research and evaluation.

Many and varied influences have shaped and encouraged the development of guidance in our public schools. A tide of interest in providing guidance services has arisen from many different motivations and to serve many needs. At the leading edge of this rising tide of interest is the current development of elementary school guidance, developing from awareness of the foundational character of early guidance for later efforts.

REFERENCES

ACES-ASCA Committee on the Elementary School Counselor. *The Elementary School Counselor in Today's Schools.* Washington, D.C.: American Personnel and Guidance Association, 1969.

Berlin, I. N. "The school counselor: his unique mental health function," *Personnel and Guidance Journal, 41:* 409–414 (1963).

Carey, R. W. "Student protest and the counselor," *Personnel and Guidance Journal, 48:* 185–191 (1969).

Chenault, J. "Help giving and morality," *Personnel and Guidance Journal, 48:* 89–96 (1969).

Combs, A. W. "Counseling as a learning process," *Journal of Counseling Psychology, 1:* 31–36 (1954).

Cottingham, H. F. *Guidance in Elementary Schools.* Bloomington, Ill.: McKnight, 1956.

Cribbin, J. J. "A critique of the philosophy of modern guidance," in Gail Farwell and Herman Peters, eds., *Guidance Readings for Counselors.* Skokie, Ill.: Rand McNally, 1960. Pp. 78–93.

Dimick, K. M., and V. E. Huff. *Child Counseling*. Dubuque, Iowa: William C. Brown Company, Publishers, 1970.

Dinkmeyer, D. C., and C. E. Caldwell. *Developmental Counseling and Guidance*. New York: McGraw-Hill, 1970.

Frankl, V. *Man's Search for Meaning*. New York: Washington Square Press, 1963.

Guidance for Today's Children. Washington, D.C.: Thirty-third Yearbook, Department of Elementary School Principals, NEA, 1954. Pp. 2–10.

Hill, G. E. *Management and Improvement of Guidance*. New York: Appleton-Century-Crofts, 1965. Pp. 1–41.

Krumboltz, J. D., and B. Varenhorst. "Molders of pupil attitudes," *Personnel and Guidance Journal, 43:* 443–446 (1965).

Meeks, A. R. *Guidance in Elementary Education*. New York: Ronald, 1968.

Murphy, G. "The cultural context of guidance," *Personnel and Guidance Journal, 34:* 4–9 (1955).

Nelson, R. C. "An open letter to administrators from a counselor," *Educational Leadership, 23:* 571–577 (1966).

Peters, H. J., and G. J. Farwell. *Guidance: A Developmental Approach*, 2nd ed. Skokie, Ill.: Rand McNally, 1967.

Peters, H. J., B. Shertzer, and W. Van Hoose. *Guidance in Elementary Schools*. Skokie, Ill.: Rand McNally, 1965.

Russell, R. D. "Black perceptions of guidance," *Personnel and Guidance Journal, 48:* 721–728 (1970).

Shertzer, B., and S. C. Stone. *Fundamentals of Guidance*. Boston: Houghton Mifflin, 1971.

Stefflre, B., and K. B. Matheny. *The Function of Counseling Theory*. Guidance Monograph Series, Boston: Houghton Mifflin, 1968.

Traxler, A. E. *Techniques of Guidance*. New York: Harper & Row, 1957.

Ulich, R., ed. *Three Thousand Years of Educational Wisdom*. Cambridge: Harvard University Press, 1954.

Willey, R. DeV. *Guidance in Elementary Education*. New York: Harper & Row, 1960. Pp. 1–33.

Wrenn, C. G. *The Counselor in a Changing World*. Washington, D.C.: American Personnel and Guidance Association, 1962. Pp. 1–10.

Yamamoto, K. "The 'healthy person': a review," *Personnel and Guidance Journal, 44:* 596–603 (1966).

Zimmerman, G. "Decision making and indecision in the vocational development of college-bound males." Unpublished Doctoral thesis, Purdue University, Lafayette, Ind., 1970.

ARTICLES IN BOOKS OF READINGS

Dinkmeyer, D. C. *Guidance and Counseling in the Elementary School: Readings in Theory and Practice*. New York: Holt, Rinehart and Winston, Inc., 1968. Readings beginning on pages 1, 7, 17, 32, 47, 75, 85.

Koplitz, E. D. *Guidance in the Elementary School: Theory, Research and Practice*. Dubuque, Iowa: William C. Brown Company, Publishers, 1968. Readings beginning on pages 5, 12, 45, 54.

Mills, G. D. *Elementary School Guidance and Counseling*. New York: Random House, Inc., 1971. Readings beginning on pages 5, 77, 104.

Peters, H. J., A. C. Riccio, and J. J. Quaranta. *Guidance in the Elementary School: A Book of Readings*. New York: Macmillan, 1963. Readings beginning on pages 3, 21, 34, 52, 168, 295, 304, 315.

2

The Need: Home, School, and Society

Goodbye, proud world! I'm going home:
Thou art not my friend, and I'm not thine.
Long through thy weary crowds I roam;
A river-ark on the ocean brine,
Long I've been tossed like the driven foam;
But now, proud world! I'm going home.

RALPH WALDO EMERSON: "Goodbye"

It is tempting to look from an adult perspective upon the "happy, un-troubled" times of youth and to reflect with a kind of nostalgia upon golden moments of a long ago. An afternoon rolling on a hillside, a secret swimming hole, the thrill of a roller coaster ride, the pact with a real friend—recalling such vignettes can blind us to realities that made us heartsore as children. And if we ourselves did not encounter experiences by which we were sorely troubled, as counselors and educators we cannot well afford to ignore the experiences of others.

Dimick and Huff[1] stated that the average classroom of thirty children includes one or two who are severely neurotic, four who already experience emotional and behavioral problems, seven who will marry and become divorced, one who will become an alcoholic, and three who at some time in the course of their lives will be hospitalized for mental illness.

[1] Kenneth M. Dimick and Vaughn E. Huff, *Child Counseling* (Dubuque, Iowa: William C. Brown Company, Publishers, 1970).

Probably several of these children will come to use drugs of one sort or another, and some will experience addiction.

Such problems may be looked upon as symptomatic of the life experiences of the members of the average class of children. Periods of genuine unhappiness, grief, and depression, feelings of guilt, unworthiness, and low self-esteem are, for a great many children, by-products of living. Those who are fortunate experience these difficulties in a transitory manner; the exceptionally fortunate may escape them altogether.

Many children live basically contented lives, highlighted by beautiful experiences that help them grow toward being the best kind of person they can become. Even adversity may produce growth for these young people because they are helped to understand, to accept their feelings, and to gain strength. Others experience a reality that is diametrically opposite.

In the lives of some, great pressures are caused by the rapid movements within our society, changes in family relationships, population mobility, and conflicting social and ethical values that a child may encounter in his own subculture, his school, his church, and through communication media. Too often the school creates further difficulties, as academic pressures are heaped upon the others that confront the child, and as mounting enrollments reduce individualization in the classroom. Still other special needs, talents, or disabilities appear in the child for which the elementary school is inadequately equipped to make allowance.

This chapter will consider the needs for guidance originating in situations outside the child himself—forces within the home, school, and society that impinge upon him and create the emotional climate in which he grows and with which he must contend. Chapter 3 attends more specifically to the internalization process within the child, to the child's need structure, and to matters relating to his self-concept and development.

Much of this text focuses on what can be done for the child who suffers moderate or severe difficulty arising from his membership in his home, school, or society. This chapter attempts to identify these difficulties. Although solutions are not sought at this point, Seeley's suggestion that "we have more matter, more power, more technique, more know-how at our disposal with less sense of what to do with it or about it . . . than ever before in history,"[2] is both comforting and disturbing.

The discussions that follow here deal with some of the more dramatic evidence that children need assistance. Such evidence is viewed here as symptomatic; that is, these data reflect only the extremes. Whether the issue is child neglect, illiteracy, or poverty, the normal curve suggests

[2] John R. Seeley, "Guidance and the youth culture," *Personnel and Guidance Journal, 41:* 306 (1962).

that there are more children in circumstances tending toward the negative end of these continua than appear in the statistics.

THE HOME AND THE NEED FOR GUIDANCE

Amy comes from an affluent home; love and material goods abound. Her complaint: "My parents don't let me do anything the other kids do. I don't want to do wild things; I just want them to trust me."

John states simply: "I wonder where my dad is. I haven't seen him for two years."

Ted sniffles: "I know mom and dad like the other kids better than me. I try, but they just think I'm dumb."

Marie, inferring that her mother is a prostitute, worries: "I wonder how I'm going to turn out. The other kids say I'm gonna be trash like . . . like . . . ." Tears.

It is folly to assume that all children grow up in basically loving homes, are moderately well cared for, and are treated decently. There are home situations that would break the best of us. Some children live with theft, incest, assault and battery, and murder. Others live in various insidious emotional situations, amidst hate, invective, a total unconcern, or debilitating overprotection. Still others live in conditions that cannot but produce physical or emotional crippling.

Fortunately, many children live around genuine parents whose lives are full, whose feelings are directly related to their actions, who can give and receive affection, who can permit and encourage the independent development of each child, and who can provide necessary limits.

We shall first discuss statistical, then nonstatistical considerations that point up needs for guidance arising in the home; then we shall consider the home and genuineness.

STATISTICAL CONSIDERATIONS

Perhaps 20 percent of the child population shows up in the data that follow on poverty, one-parent families, orphans, delinquents, illegitimate births, and related issues. Data cannot be as effectively mustered on such matters as borderline economic deprivation, nonreported separation and desertion, births of unwanted children, unhappy but unbroken homes, child abuse, and the like. The statistical material that follows, then, should be viewed as symptomatic rather than comprehensive.

Smith, in part using Health, Education, and Welfare Department data, points out the following statistical factors relating directly or indirectly to the home and evidencing need, in some cases, for elementary school guidance:

> In 1964, there were 28.3 million families with related children under 18 years of age. Eighty-nine percent were husband-and-wife families (25.1 million), 11 percent were one-parent families (2.8 million), 4.4 percent of the child population were orphans (3.1 million), and about 60 percent of all divorces involved children. . . . State and local public welfare agencies spent an estimated $313 million in fiscal year 1964 for public child welfare services, a 17 percent increase over 1963. In the past decade juvenile delinquency cases in the United States have doubled while the child population age 10 through 17 has increased by less than 50 percent. In 1964 the courts handled 686,000 delinquency cases, excluding traffic violations, an increase of 14 percent, costing the United States well over a billion dollars a year.
>
> Two-hundred fifty-thousand children are treated each year in psychiatric clinics, and, on any one day, about 19,700 children with serious disorders are in our mental hospitals.[3]

The *Statistical Abstract* for 1970 points out many realities indicating home conditions clearly less than optimum. In 1968, over 141,000 dependency and neglect cases were referred to juvenile courts for some form of neglect or inadequate care by parents or guardians; this amounts to 2.0 per every thousand children.[4] Residents in homes for dependent and neglected children, not including institutions or foster homes, numbered 73,000.[5]

Over 339,000 illegitimate live births occurred in 1968, nearly 10 percent of all live births, indicating that in the decade 1968–1978 well over three million illegitimate live children might be expected to be born. The 1968 rate was 24.1 such births per thousand unmarried women age 15 to 44.[6]

More data, clearly affecting the home, have been associated with societal conditions and will be given in a subsequent section. But one further demonstration of inadequate home support for some children seems appropriate. Table 2–1, taken from material in the 1970 *Statistical Abstract*,[7] demonstrates that there is, indeed, a white-nonwhite contrast in family income, since white adults with an elementary school education nearly match nonwhite adults with a high school education in annual family income.

---

[3] Hyrum M. Smith, "Preventing difficulties through elementary school guidance," *Elementary School Guidance and Counseling, 1:* 10 (1967).

[4] U. S. Bureau of the Census, *Statistical Abstract of the United States: 1970* (Washington, D.C.: U. S. Government Printing Office, 1970), p. 154.

[5] *Ibid.,* p. 40.

[6] *Ibid.,* p. 50.

[7] *Ibid.,* p. 114.

The home in which the black (or other nonwhite) child is reared does not have the same financial support available as does the home in which the white child is reared, even when education is held constant.

Table 2–1 PERCENT DISTRIBUTION OF FAMILIES BY INCOME LEVEL, YEARS OF SCHOOL, RACE OF HEAD, 1968

Income Level	White Elementary School	White High School	White College	Nonwhite Elementary School	Nonwhite High School	Nonwhite College
Less than $3000	19.1	5.7	3.1	31.7	17.2	6.2
$3000 to $4999	18.9	8.5	4.5	26.9	20.1	8.1
$5000 to $6999	17.4	14.5	7.5	16.7	17.7	9.4
$7000 to $9999	21.9	27.4	18.8	13.6	20.7	18.2
$10,000 to $14,000	16.2	30.0	32.6	8.9	17.8	31.9
$15,000 and over	6.3	13.8	33.5	2.2	6.3	26.1
Median income	$6328	$9309	$12,356	$4297	$6432	$10,954

The family, then, which for many children, is a great source of strength, solace, and understanding, is no rock on which all children can depend; and these statistics could be supplemented by data on such other factors as child abuse in the home, infanticide, child desertion, and sexual molestation of children in the home.

NONSTATISTICAL CONSIDERATIONS

While objective evidence can demonstrate the more bizarre acts perpetrated against children and can specify the economic conditions that affect children, there is no effective way to show statistically the number of children who sense they are unwanted, rejected, unloved, overprotected, not trusted, unworthy, or are being used by parents who wish to live through them. This section briefly considers these factors.

Willey[8] suggests a number of home problems for which data are not readily available, including overprotection; overindulgence; poverty and consequent neglect, deprivation, rejection, lack of security, and low self-esteem; poor parent-child communication; parental modeling of violence, conflict, emotional coldness, illegal or antimoral actions; parental rejection, direct or indirect; parental favoritism of one child over another; expectations for the child that are too high or low; abusive punishment processes; and parental use of fear or bribery for motivation.

While guidance may not alter divorce statistics or reduce poverty, it may well be an instrument that can convey society's concern for the

[8] Roy DeVerl Willey, *Guidance in Elementary Education* (New York: Harper & Row, 1960).

well-being of the child who faces difficulties in his home environment by providing specific help where feasible and necessary.

THE HOME AND GENUINENESS

Chapter 3 devotes a section to contrasting genuine and nongenuine behavior, discussing the development of each, and considering patterns of withdrawal behavior. The present section concentrates more specifically on defining genuineness and examining it as a concern of the home.

A substantial majority of homes must escape severe problems of poverty, neglect, illegitimacy, and the like, and provide good to ideal conditions for the nurturance of children. Yet few children experience much encouragement to genuineness.

Genuineness in people, suggests Moustakas, involves trusting ". . . the mystery and wonder in themselves and in the world, . . . an expanding self-awareness and an enlarging reality." It is opposed to saying and doing what is "appraised and adjusted, reacted to and balanced off,"[9] to create the desired impression or to compete for status. Genuineness is a quality of doing for its own sake rather than for effect, of feeling feelings strongly because these feelings *are*, of loving hard and hurting hard.

Perhaps adults feel a subtle threat that causes them to eradicate that which is genuine in children. For surely that is done, in the very cradle, and in every home—in some homes to the point of destroying the individual. Much of the cry of youth may be protest, however well or ill directed, against the nongenuineness that the adult world exhibits, and to which it subjects children and youth.

Frank observes: "Every child suffers to a greater or less extent from . . . denial of his own personal, temperamental individuality, because even the most emancipated parents are not wholly free from the desire to see their children conform to the images they have constructed."[10]

Moustakas views the matter of parents and nongenuineness as follows:

> Ambitious parents set up goals and communicate expectations, indirectly and deviously (so that what they really want and expect from the child registers clearly at subliminal levels regardless of what they actually say). Or, quite openly, parents may program the child's life in such a way that he progresses step by step toward their values, their goals, their expected achievements.
>
> Often the individual is unaware that he, as a unique person, has been cancelled out and in place of his genuine self there is only a concept,

[9] Clark Moustakas, *Creativity and Conformity* (New York: Van Nostrand-Reinhold Company, 1967), p. 127.

[10] L. K. Frank, "The fundamental needs of the child," *Mental Hygiene, 22:* 356 (1938).

a definition of what he should be—and that definition so pieced together that the individual lacks substance and identity. The living qualities of sensitivity and awareness remain hidden, dwarfed and undeveloped.[11]

Nearly every force that the child meets has a potency to encourage or discourage genuineness. By and large, those experiences that most effectively release the child to become a real individual are facilitated by the significant persons, both adults and children, with whom he comes in contact, and the thwarting attempts along this line involve those same persons.

One hypothesis is that the less frequently approval or rejection is dominated by a parent's or other person's needs, the more genuine is the child's behavior. The less frequently the parent says yes or no because he needs to receive social approval through the child, to dominate, or to enhance himself in the child's esteem, the more genuine the child will become as a result of the experience. The child who meets *real* reasons for *wise* limitations by people concerned with *his* welfare is able to learn from these experiences and become a genuine person.

Two points should be made about the home as a source of guidance needs. First, the best efforts of parents, well applied, may still be insufficient response to children's needs for activity that is independent, self-sufficient, self-directed, and yet subtly supported. Second, the consideration of guidance needs should not imply that all homes are poor soil for the growth of the child; of course they are not. The problem is that genuineness in children draws too little awareness or concern. Thus, while the adults in the lives of many children manage to meet all of the physiological needs and most of the psychological needs of the child, at present many remain unaware of the need to encourage the child in the process of becoming a genuine, an authentic, being.

Unfortunately, many guidance programs at all levels contribute little to encouraging or inspiring genuineness. Ways must be found for the guidance counselor and the teacher to nourish genuineness in children, in parents, and in themselves. This text attempts to promote this end.

THE SCHOOL AND THE NEED FOR GUIDANCE

Julie tells a simple story: "My teacher hates me."

Tom's story is different but also disturbing: "I get into trouble 'cause I'm just so bored. I get all my work done and I'm supposed to sit in my seat and wait, or read, but I just can't. Not all the time."

[11] Moustakas, *op. cit.,* p. 128.

Lucy complains: "I've been in this school for two years and they still don't ask me to parties or over to play."

Willie's concern is often heard. He states it emphatically: "I just can't do that schoolwork. I don't know how, I don't like it, and I don't know why I have to do it. Besides I can't think about it with all the trouble at home.

The school may be optimistically viewed as an agent for protection, growth, encouragement, and development of children. In truth it is that— to a degree. Realistically, however, often it is also an agent that discourages, inhibits growth, and retards development, and against which children need protection. Those who "fit," intellectually, emotionally, and socially, are encouraged, enlightened, and occasionally inspired. Many do not fit, and for them school ranges from a challenge to drudgery to an instrument that regularly administers cruel and abusive treatment to the body or the psyche.

STATISTICAL CONSIDERATIONS

Table 2–2, taken from the 1970 *Statistical Abstract*, challenges the assumption of twelve years of free universal education for all. Further, it points up the discrepancy in participation in American education between the nonwhite and white communities.

Table 2–2   YEARS OF SCHOOL COMPLETED BY PERSONS OVER 25 BY RACE, 1969[12]

Education Completed	All Races	Negro
Less than 8 years	15.0%	33.8%
8 years through noncompletion of four years of high school	30.9%	33.9%
4 years of high school	33.5%	22.3%
1–3 years of college	9.8%	5.4%
4 years of college or more	10.7%	4.6%
Median school years completed	12.1	9.6

Peters and Farwell cite an Ohio study of dropouts by Nachman, Getson, and Odgers in which "it was found that approximately 90 percent of the ninth grade dropouts and 66 percent of the tenth grade dropouts were overage for grade."[13] Further: "It is estimated that in the decade of the sixties, more than 7.5 million pupils will drop out before completing high school. Approximately 2.5 million will not go beyond eighth grade."[14]

[12] U. S. Bureau of the Census, *op. cit.,* p. 111.
[13] Herman J. Peters and Gail F. Farwell, *Guidance: A Developmental Approach* (Skokie, Ill.: Rand McNally, 1967), p. 393.
[14] *Ibid.,* p. 393.

Peters and Farwell also cite a statement of implications by Seymour Wolfbein: "It is traditional in this country to count the dropout as a charge against the high school for the young person usually leaves the school system from the secondary school. Yet, our experience with those boys and girls points to this: that the problems which finally result in a dropout begin, and are quite overt, way back in the elementary grades."[15] This, though true, is not the whole story. For many, the cause is in the cradle; for others, in conception. Some wag has said that the cause of divorce is marriage; so we might echo that the cause of dropouts is school. Yet in both areas there are clear and crucial antecedents.

Finding culprits and placing blame, however, is not useful. What matters is the fact that there *is* a school noncompletion problem and that no level of the school can be held blameless, nor can the home. Since literacy and schooling are demands of our society, there is a clear need for dramatically improved school approaches to children.

Kowitz and Kowitz[16] report a study of second graders that did not bear out the assumption of poorer attendance for children with learning or educational problems. If their finding applies to other populations, it has great significance. It suggests that there is a time in the early grades when children with learning difficulties *are* attending school, at least physically. They are giving the school a chance, and their parents presumably are seeing to it that children attend, even if perhaps only to get them out from underfoot. Judging by dropout statistics, the school is not adequately responding to this opportunity.

Illiteracy is certainly related to the school and the need for guidance. Table 2–3 gives evidence of this condition as of 1959, demonstrating again the severity of the problem, especially among nonwhites. The United States has an illiteracy rate of 2.2 percent among those over 14 years of age—over two and one-half million persons unable to read or write in any language. This is probably a small fraction of those for whom reading is anathema—a skill that is available but rejected.

NONSTATISTICAL CONSIDERATIONS

Statistical evidence can be amassed concerning dropouts, school failures, underachievement, and retardation, suggesting persuasively that the school functions for many children as a great social screening mechanism, not an environment in which all succeed and are content. This screening effect is not amenable to charting in a statistical way, nor is the person-

---

[15] Seymour L. Wolfbein, "Transition from school to work: a study of the school leaver," *Personnel and Guidance Journal, 38:* 103 (1959).

[16] Gerald Kowitz and Norma G. Kowitz, "Elementary school attendance as an index of guidance needs," *Personnel and Guidance Journal, 44:* 938–943 (1966).

ality damage done in the schools by well-meaning souls who pound on tables and state their demands for high standards. Children should experience more often than they do, a measurement of themselves against themselves. Millions of children experience a sense of unworthiness, inadequacy, and personal failure as they find they cannot achieve the standards expected. Millions of others feel bored, restrained, and faintly amused at a system that holds them to performance below their abilities.

Table 2–3   ILLITERACY BY SEX AND COLOR AMONG PERSONS OVER AGE 14, 1959[17]

	Total Population	*Illiterate Persons*	Percent Illiterate		
			Total	*White*	*Nonwhite*
Total	121,373,000	2,619,000	2.2	1.6	7.5
Male	58,378,000	1,480,000	2.5	1.7	9.8
Female	62,995,000	1,139,000	1.8	1.4	5.4

Every teacher educated in this century has heard of the spread of individual differences in the average classroom, yet—despite hopeful signs appearing here and there—few give more than lip service to the incorporation of procedures that are truly individual.

The school, perhaps a bit too sensitive to pressures within the society, jumps to popular demands, then often settles back into secure mediocrity. A sputnik goes up and suddenly all students, regardless of their interests or capabilities, or those of their teachers, must be pressured into further study of science. Again, as college admissions become more selective, the high schools promote their students into deeper involvement with "academics." The junior high has given up its role of providing a wide range of exploratory experiences in favor of a preparatory role. As each level "prepares" for the level above, the matters of exploration and personal relevance become less and less important. Booming enrollments create a deepening sense that education is a group phenomenon and that the individual is not really very important in the school setting, unless he can both conform and lead within his conformity. The "make it tough, repetitive, and dull" school of thought remains highly vocal, lest the schools be accused of worrying too much about frills and motivation.

The elementary school, perhaps less susceptible to some of these pressures, responds nonetheless, aiding and abetting the downward movement of aspects of the curriculum, referring constantly to the future and future needs, and generally not daring to present a program that truly re-

[17] U. S. Bureau of the Census, *Pocket Data Book, U.S.A. 1967* (Washington, D.C.: U. S. Government Printing Office, 1967), p. 151.

sponds to present needs of children. Lockstep, one-book, repetitive teaching is often not only sanctioned, but rewarded. The dream of treating the child as an individual, providing for learning at his individual rate, and not alienating him by too early emphasis on evaluation, is still just that—a dream. Here and there—and, one may suspect, in increasing proportions— elementary schools are learning to value themselves as foundational rather than purely preparatory and are deepening their concern for the individual, increasingly recognizing that the needs of large segments of our society remain unmet in areas of responsibility assigned to the schools.

The degree to which third grade marks related to secondary school achievement led de Bottari[18] to suggest that elementary schools need to provide, especially for deprived children, more intensive and stimulating experiences. Tiegland, Winkler, Munger, and Kranzler[19] found that low socioeconomic standing related to elementary school level underachievement. Thus the problem seems to be experienced most intensely by children who are deprived.

Although many school settings seem to be inert, nonetheless, sweeping changes are occurring that may both create and alleviate pressures on children. Programmed instruction, use of television and motion pictures, and curricular innovations may demonstrate that traditional methods that parents tend to reinforce do not meet today's needs, perhaps thereby reducing the resistance to change in American education. As Wrenn observes: "Perhaps in no other societal activity is there so much of a tendency for parents and employers to want schools 'as they were in my days,' to put the brakes on change. Fighting for new ideas is, unfortunately, characteristic only of those who 'stand tall' in the profession. Too many of the others submit weakly to public pressure for no change or carry into their teaching and administration only the perpetuation of their own experience."[20]

Too often in the school setting the child's genuineness is sacrificed. Too little attention is given to helping each child to experience (1) an overall sense of approval by his peers, (2) approval by his teachers and other adults, (3) affection from those about him, (4) a sense of his own competence, and (5) a sense of his growing toward independence. The child who spends six years in the elementary school without feeling these needs met in good measure has been cheated by the school: it did not have to happen.

[18] Linda de Bottari, "Primary school correlates of secondary school achievement," *Personnel and Guidance Journal, 47:* 675–678 (1969).

[19] John J. Tiegland, R. C. Winkler, P. F. Munger, and G. D. Kranzler, "Some concomitants of underachievement at the elementary school level," *Personnel and Guidance Journal, 44:* 950–955 (1966).

[20] C. Gilbert Wrenn, *The Counselor in a Changing World* (Washington, D.C.: American Personnel and Guidance Association, 1962), p. 68.

THE SCHOOL AND GENUINENESS

The school contributes to the encouragement or discouragement of genuineness in the child. In this respect it stands next to the family and peers. There is an especial difficulty in encouraging or facilitating genuineness in the classroom, where some order is required for its own sake. Too often, however, this need for order is used as an excuse to put children "in their place" and keep them there.

EVALUATION CAN MAKE IT DIFFICULT FOR THE CHILD TO MAINTAIN GENUINENESS   Almost habitually, children's responses to questions draw remarks from the teacher, characterizing the child's response as good, bad, or indifferent. Many teachers seem to decree an ever-present day of judgment, always ready to shout: "Off with their heads!" But children need to learn to judge for themselves the adequacy of their responses, teachers need much more to involve children in the planning and evaluation process, and time must be allowed between teaching and evaluating. Harold Taylor once compared our penchant for evaluation to planting seeds and constantly digging them up to see if they are growing.

Baker and Doyle[21] found that teachers tended to increase the number of unsatisfactory marks given to pupils whom they recognized as bright. High performance became an expectation, and when it was not achieved more unsatisfactory marks were given, with no allowance for any emotional factors or personal concerns that might have interfered with achievement.

Roth and Meyersburg[22] suggest that poor achievement, basically, does not result from incapacity to achieve; rather, it is an expression of a student's choice based on his self-concept. That choice affects the way the student prepares for study, and his development or neglect of academic skills. Choice patterns are enduring and do not undergo spontaneous change; they are related to personality organization; and they are amenable to counseling. The assumption made here is that low grades and frequent evaluation merely reinforce the choice, whereas involving children in planning and evaluation may supplement counseling as a way of breaking the cycle.

EXTRINSIC MOTIVATIONS MAY BE STRESSED MORE THAN THE QUEST FOR KNOWLEDGE   In the urgency to move children along, extrinsic motivations are constantly used as substitutes for intrinsically valuable

[21] Robert L. Baker and Roy P. Doyle, "Teacher knowledge of pupil data and marking practices at the elementary school level," *Personnel and Guidance Journal, 37:* 644–647 (1959).

[22] Robert M. Roth and H. Arnold Meyersburg, "The non-achievement syndrome," *Personnel and Guidance Journal, 41:* 535–540 (1963).

educational experiences, dealing genuineness a severe blow. "Learn for a grade" is the outcome. Maintaining the zest for learning is considered infinitely less important than getting everyone moving along at the same rate so that letter grades can be assigned.

INSECURITY MAY UNDERMINE THE TEACHER'S WILLINGNESS TO PERMIT GENUINE EXPRESSION BY ELEMENTARY SCHOOL CHILDREN Many a teacher who wants to create a joyous, active, exciting elementary school learning experience is inhibited by internally felt pressures, which suggest his classroom should not be the noisiest in the school and which reinforce what is orderly above what might be interesting.

It takes a depth of personal security to create an atmosphere that offers children the joy of learning, some choice of experiences, and latitude for activity far beyond that of individual recitation before a motionless total class audience. This is especially true in a highly traditional school setting, where other teachers, much like the union men who pressure a fast worker to keep down production so that quotas don't rise, apply subtle pressures that discourage the higher activity of a freer classroom. Frequently, however, the felt limits that inhibit many teachers from displaying their enthusiasm for learning and from giving latitude in choice and breadth of activity, are imagined limits.

LIMITS IN THE CLASSROOM SHOULD BE FEW, REALISTIC, AND REASONABLY CONSISTENT The teacher who can convey a few limits that are logical, that children help to develop, and that they can accept as promoting their own safety and benefit is well on the road toward facilitating genuineness in his pupils. If these limits are applied with affection, consideration, and occasional good humor, another leg of the journey has been completed. If these limits are applied with reasonable consistency—consistency but not rigidity—the goal insofar as it may be achieved through that teacher is close at hand.

THE COUNSELOR AND TEACHER SHOULD CONTINUALLY STRIVE TO FACILITATE GENUINENESS IN CHILDREN The counselor's job, it has been said, is to put himself "out of business" by aiding those he serves to become self-maximizing individuals. The teacher's job should be to put himself "out of business" by aiding children to assume responsibility for evaluating the products of their own efforts, by creating an environment in which children feel the excitement of learning and thus a motivation to learn, and by aiding children to understand and accept reasonable limits—as a necessary and accepted premise of classroom life. Together, stimulating, encouraging, and supporting each other, teacher and counselor can do much to reverse the present stifling of genuineness in the elementary school.

THE SOCIETY AND THE NEED FOR GUIDANCE

Stan explains: "I was just doing what everyone else was. Only they caught me going out the door with the stuff."

Ray says: "If you ain't black here, you don't have a chance. I hate to come outside in the street. They're always looking for me and beating on me."

Rita says: "I just know my brother will get in trouble again as soon as they let him out. Someday I think he'll just do somethin' real terrible."

Florence complains: "My dad looks for a job every day, but they just won't hire him. Only thing they give him is a sweeping job for a couple of hours. He says, 'Whitey only wants a servant, not a worker.' "

Suburbia, the farm community, the city luxury apartment, and the ghetto present to children vastly different settings in which to grow within our society. For some, every advantage exists; for others, all aspects of society crush in to create an environment offering little but disadvantage. We shall discuss here, first, statistical and nonstatistical considerations in the society that show needs for guidance, and then, in general terms, the society and genuineness.

STATISTICAL CONSIDERATIONS

The *Statistical Abstract* states that in 1960 over one-third of a million persons were in penal institutions[23] and nearly two-thirds of a million persons were inmates of mental institutions.[24] Thus, nearly one million were institutionalized for criminal behavior or mental or emotional difficulty. Over nine hundred thousand delinquency cases, excluding traffic, were handled by juvenile courts in 1968; this figure represents 28.7 court cases per thousand juveniles.[25] Active known narcotic addicts in 1968 numbered sixty-four thousand,[26] a figure that has continued to rise rapidly.

Well over five million total arrests for all causes excluding traffic occurred in 1968, nearly one and one-half million for drunkenness.[27] Suicides numbered over twenty thousand, and homicides over thirteen thousand.[28]

[23] U. S. Bureau of the Census, *Statistical Abstract of the United States: 1968,* p. 156.

[24] *Ibid.,* p. 40.

[25] *Ibid.,* p. 154.

[26] *Ibid.,* p. 80.

[27] *Ibid.,* p. 147.

[28] *Ibid.,* p. 145.

Unemployment statistics demonstrate that the scope of societal difficulties is intensified in the nonwhite (especially black) community; for example, the April 1970 unemployment rate for white male workers was 3.9, for nonwhite males 6.7.[29] Two-fifths of all black children are in homes in which the income is below the poverty level as defined by the January 1965 Social Security Bulletin.

Table 2–4 POOR PERSONS—NUMBER AND INCIDENCE BY COLOR AND FAMILY STATUS, 1968[30]

Family Status and Color	Number of Persons in Millions	Percent of All Persons in Group
All poor persons—white	17.4	10.0%
All poor children under 18—white	6.4	10.7%
All poor persons—nonwhite	8.0	33.5%
All poor children under 18—nonwhite	4.4	41.6%

Another factor of interest is that although nonwhites account for 10 percent of the population in the United States, they account for 25.5 percent of the homes in which females head the household.[31]

Table 2–5 CIVILIAN LABOR FORCE BY OCCUPATION AND COLOR, 1960[32]

	Male		Female	
	Number	Nonwhite Percent	Number	Nonwhite Percent
Professional, technical, and kindred	4,543,000	3.5	2,793,000	7.2
Managers, officials, and kindred	4,695,000	2.0	794,000	3.9
Clerical and kindred workers	3,120,000	6.8	6,497,000	3.6
Salesworkers	3,055,000	2.1	1,746,000	2.8
Craftsmen and skilled workers	8,973,000	4.9	268,000	7.3
Operatives and kindred	9,234,000	11.1	3,612,000	10.6
Service workers except household	2,745,000	21.5	3,020,000	19.5
Farm laborers	1,290,000	24.0	270,000	33.9
Laborers except farm and mine	3,405,000	26.1	—	—
Private household workers	—	—	1,760,000	54.5
Total	45,686,000	9.6	22,304,000	12.8

Perhaps nowhere is the lower opportunity level for blacks more apparent than in labor-force figures (Table 2–5). Only at the lower end of

[29] *Ibid.*, p. 213.
[30] *Ibid.*, p. 328.
[31] *Ibid.*, p. 38.
[32] *Ibid.*, pp 227–228.

this continuum do nonwhites exceed their percentage of the population in employment.

NONSTATISTICAL CONSIDERATIONS

In his landmark publication, *The Counselor in a Changing World*, Wrenn has mentioned[33] numerous trends in American society that may affect the future needs of children. Many of these developments, which the future will see intensified, are present realities. The notes that follow are abstracted from his commentary.

1. Achievement and excellence will be stressed in American education and in society.
2. Rights of minority groups will receive increased attention and recognition.
3. Larger units of political power will become increasingly more important.
4. Material comfort will receive greater national emphasis.
5. Security will occasionally be overvalued at the expense of individualism.
6. Pressures in society will reinforce conforming behavior.
7. Scientific progress will increase the gap between generations and will create a larger gulf than is observed at present between power available and wise use of power.
8. Population pressures will raise anxieties over world food supplies, acceptable methods of controlling population increases, and over the disparity between the "haves" and "have nots."
9. Within the United States, the population increase will intensify problems of personal identity, job competition, and use of leisure time as the face of the nation changes.
10. The job structure of the future will demand increased brain power as simpler jobs are eliminated.
11. Increased educational demands in the world of work will create a deeper sense of alienation in those who are not able to compete.
12. The percentage of women in the labor force will increase, and societal expectations will bend to incorporate this change.
13. Increasing percentages of blacks will complete high school, undergraduate college work, and graduate work, and employment in all echelons of work will be opened to blacks.
14. Services to people will employ proportionately more workers; thus large numbers of new positions will be created in fields of education, health, social work, recreation, and personnel.
15. Personal problems of children will increase as family patterns

[33] Chapter 2.

change toward smaller households, new distributions of authority, increased proportions of working mothers, and cloudier differentiation of husband and wife roles.

16. The megalopolis of the immediate future will create growing pains as neighborhoods change, grow, and fuse.

17. Individual wealth and higher general salary levels will create new markets, new styles of living, and new power structures.

18. Federal and state governmental agencies will act to alleviate old problems and sometimes, inevitably, will create new ones.

Frank has commented: "The fundamental needs of the child are in truth the fundamental needs of society."[34] In a real sense, as the needs of society are met, the needs of children are met also. If one can envision a society that has met the needs suggested by the factors enumerated above, one can see that in the general sense children would have their needs rather well anticipated. This millennium is so remote as to be almost beyond imagination. Yet we cannot turn the clock backward to the agrarian society in which all had a place and knew it. Children will need guidance in order to live with present and future realities.

THE SOCIETY AND GENUINENESS

The Midcentury White House Conference on Children and Youth[35] recognized certain needs of children. Meeting these needs helps greatly in making genuineness possible. These needs are: love, recognition as a worthwhile person, the right to be a separate self, the chance to develop initiative and imagination, the opportunity to satisfy curiosity and develop pride in workmanship, wholesome play, the chance to develop integrity and moral courage, truth, faith, understanding of art, elimination of prejudice and discrimination, an adequate standard of living, rewarding educational opportunities, protection against exploitation and undue hazards, a decent and satisfactory home life, the opportunity for the development of individual potentialities, and improved conditions for all children and youth.

Although these needs are clearly matters of concern to our society, society-at-large does not deal directly with individual children, the contact that encourages or discourages genuineness is made by specific adults. Members of society as a whole can, however, begin by recognizing their own tendency to promote a model for children, to create role concepts and press children into playing those roles, and to limit and eliminate the expressions of genuineness by children. Societal expectations and genuineness on the part of children may be somewhat antithetical.

[34] Frank, *op. cit.*, p. 379.
[35] *Midcentury White House Conference on Children and Youth: Proceedings* (Raleigh, N.C.: Health Publications Institute, 1950).

Seeley[36] suggests that adults ought to be listening to and selectively valuing what is being said by members of the youth culture. For example, traditional values suggest: anything worth doing is worth doing well, the industrious bee and saving squirrel are models, all must enter the "fur-lined rat race"—views emerging from an economy of scarcity. New values suggest: nothing is worth doing if it cannot be shown to be worthwhile, it is best to cultivate one's own little garden, the world is essentially absurd—views emerging from an economy of affluence.

Counselors and teachers are badly needed who can help to interpret the society to children and interpret children to adults in the society. The society can afford to show its concern for the needs of children by providing guidance services. Seeley points out that, at least among adolescents, ". . . guidance people have a definition in the youth culture as emissaries of the adult culture more dangerous even than parents and teachers, veritable Greeks bearing gifts, of whom it is wise to beware. They are the ones, the kids say, who want to weaken you by defining resistance to assimilation as *your* psychological problem instead of *their* social one."[37]

Counselors can ill afford the hypocrisy of being insidious, gentle, loving, and helping individuals who hide their manipulations of children behind a "saving" intention. They can, however, be genuine individuals, promoting genuineness in the children they serve, helping them to understand and cope with societal expectations as well as their own motives and values.

SUMMARY

The home, school, and society give ample evidence of the presses and stresses that beset the child growing up today. The child is rare indeed who does not encounter severe disappointments, grief, and genuine unhappiness on his path toward adolescence. Also readily available are statistical evidences of problems stemming from poverty and related conditions, divorce, child neglect, school failure, imprisonment and commitment to mental institutions, and the like. The normal-curve concept suggests that these data represent only extreme conditions, and that children suffer in still larger numbers from conditions of the same order. Even the home that escapes representation in negative statistics may restrict the genuineness exhibited and permitted to the child. Counseling and guidance are sorely needed, not as a panacea for all of these ills, but as an honest attempt to meet children's emotional needs and, if possible, to prevent or ameliorate some of these expensive and debilitating difficulties. Children are often more

---

[36] Seeley, *op. cit.*, pp. 302–310.
[37] *Ibid.*, p. 309.

amenable to assistance than they will ever be again. The wide range of difficulties posed to the child in the home, school, and society argues that counseling and guidance services be made available to him.

REFERENCES

Baker, R. L., and R. P. Doyle. "Teacher knowledge of pupil data and marking practices at the elementary school level," *Personnel and Guidance Journal, 37:* 644–647 (1959).

Banducci, R. "The effect of mother's employment on the achievement, aspirations, and expectations of the child," *Personnel and Guidance Journal, 46:* 263–267 (1967).

de Bottari, L. "Primary school correlates of secondary school achievement," *Personnel and Guidance Journal, 47:* 675–678 (1969).

Dimick, K. M., and V. E. Huff. *Child Counseling.* Dubuque, Iowa: William C. Brown Company, Publishers, 1970.

Frank, L. K. "The Fundamental Needs of the Child," *Mental Hygiene, 22:* 353–379 (1938).

Hutson, P. W. *The Guidance Function in Education.* New York: Appleton-Century-Crofts, 1968. Chapters 2, 3, 4.

Kowitz, G. T., and N. G. Kowitz. "Elementary school attendance as an index of guidance needs," *Personnel and Guidance Journal, 44:* 938–943 (1966).

Midcentury White House Conference on Children and Youth. *Proceedings.* Raleigh, N.C.: Health Publications Institute, 1950.

Moustakas, C. *Creativity and Conformity.* New York: Van Nostrand-Reinhold Company, 1967.

Munson, H. L. *Elementary School Guidance: Concepts, Dimensions, and Practice.* Boston: Allyn and Bacon, 1970.

NASSP Committee on Curriculum Planning. "The imperative needs of youth of secondary school age." *NASSP Bulletin 145.* Washington: NEA, 1947.

Nelson, R. C. "Counselors in elementary schools: promise and proposal," *Guidance Journal, 2:* 47–57 (1962).

Peters, H. J., and G. F. Farwell. *Guidance: A Developmental Approach.* Skokie, Ill.: Rand McNally, 1967.

Proctor, S. A. "Reversing the spiral toward futility," *Personnel and Guidance Journal, 48:* 707–712 (1970).

Roth, R. M., and H. A. Meyersburg. "The non-achievement syndrome," *Personnel and Guidance Journal, 41:* 535–540 (1963).

Seeley, J. R. "Guidance and the youth culture," *Personnel and Guidance Journal, 41:* 302–310 (1962).

Smith, H. M. "Preventing difficulties through elementary school guidance," *Elementary School Guidance and Counseling, 1:* 8–14 (1967).

Strang, R. "The relation of guidance to the teaching of reading," *Personnel and Guidance Journal, 44:* 831–836 (1966).

Tiegland, J. J., R. C. Winkler, P. F. Munger, and G. D. Kranzler. "Some concomitants of underachievement at the elementary school level," *Personnel and Guidance Journal, 44:* 950–955 (1966).

U. S. Bureau of the Census. *Pocket Data Book, U.S.A., 1967.* Washington, D.C.: U. S. Government Printing Office, 1967.

U. S. Bureau of the Census. *Statistical Abstract of the United States: 1968.* Washington, D.C.: U. S. Government Printing Office, 1968.

Willey, R. DeV. *Guidance in Elementary Education.* New York: Harper & Row, 1960.

Wolfbein, S. L. "Transition from school to work: a study of the school leaver," *Personnel and Guidance Journal, 38:* 98–105 (1959).

Wrenn, C. G. *The Counselor in a Changing World.* Washington, D.C.: American Personnel and Guidance Association, 1962.

————. "The wonderful world we live in," *Personnel and Guidance Journal, 43:* 613–615 (1965).

ARTICLES IN BOOKS OF READINGS

Dinkmeyer, D. C. *Guidance and Counseling in the Elementary School: Readings in Theory and Practice.* New York: Holt, Rinehart and Winston, Inc., 1968. Readings beginning on pages 92, 99, 167, 175, 180.

Koplitz, E. D. *Guidance in the Elementary School: Theory, Research and Practice.* Dubuque, Iowa: William C. Brown Company, Publishers, 1968. Readings beginning on pages 160, 165, 175, 181, 185, 211.

Mills, G. D. *Elementary School Guidance and Counseling.* New York: Random House, Inc., 1971. Readings beginning on pages 41, 52, 89.

Peters, H. J., A. C. Riccio, and J. J. Quaranta. *Guidance in the Elementary School: A Book of Readings.* New York: Macmillan, 1963. Readings beginning on pages 40, 48, 59, 112.

3

The Need: The Child Himself

I exist as I am, that is enough,
If no other in the world be aware I sit content,
And if each and all be aware I sit content.

One world is aware and by far the largest to me and that
*   is myself,*
And whether I come to my own today or in ten thousand or
*   ten million years,*
I can cheerfully take it now, or with equal cheerfulness
*   I can wait.*

WALT WHITMAN: "Song of Myself"

The child is not an innocent bystander who does nothing but receive inputs from home, school, and society, neither is he a mere *tabula rasa* upon which the world makes its imprint. He is a living human individual who selectively receives stimuli from the forces about him and who has a unique personal output. To know the child, it is not enough to look at the world and his environment; we must look at *him*. Meeks[1] suggests making the assumption that the child has a measure of control over some aspects of his environment. Thus, however important the adults in his world may be, counselors and teachers cannot wisely exclude the child himself from the process that is designed to help him.

This chapter considers the child himself as the most important feature in his own development. It discusses, first, children's needs; second,

[1] Anna R. Meeks, *Guidance in Elementary Education* (New York: Ronald, 1968).

the self-concept; third, genuineness, nongenuineness, and alienation; and fourth, four types of guidance needs.

CHILDREN'S NEEDS

Cronbach[2] describes a need as a broad motive that makes specific goals important to the individual. What do children need? Cronbach offers a partial answer by suggesting the following: (1) affection, (2) approval by peers, (3) approval by those in authority, (4) independence, and (5) competence and self-respect.

In an earlier, even more basic exploration, Maslow[3] identified six levels of human needs that motivate and direct behavior: (1) physiological needs, (2) safety needs, (3) love and belonging needs, (4) esteem needs, (5) self-actualization needs, and (6) the need to know and understand.

Physiological needs are those which are necessary to maintain life—needs for oxygen, food, water, and rest, for vitamins, minerals, and the like. A lack of gratification of such needs is almost certain to reduce motivation in other areas—motivation that rekindles once the physiological needs are gratified.

Children show their safety needs by their preference for routine or rhythm rather than disorder, their avoidance of situations in which they perceive danger, and their withdrawal from what is strange and unfamiliar.

The love need is a desire or hunger for a place in the group and for affectionate relations with people in general.

Esteem needs require recognition of the individual as a worthwhile person. Their fulfillment brings feelings of confidence, strength, usefulness, and worth.

The self-actualization need is to be or to become the person one can be, to realize one's own potential.

Desires to know and to understand, according to Maslow, are not as clearly evidenced as the other needs. When they are present, the individual tends to systematize, to analyze, to organize, and to look for relationships.

The order of needs cited by Maslow may be viewed as a pyramidal structure, each successive tier depending to some degree upon fulfillment of more basic needs.

Dember and Earl[4] have also identified a need for exploration and manipulation, and many sources have discussed a need for achievement,

[2] Lee Cronbach, *Educational Psychology* (New York: Harcourt, 1963).

[3] A. H. Maslow, "A theory of human motivation," *Psychological Review,* 50: 370–396 (1943).

[4] W. N. Dember and R. W. Earl, "Analysis of exploratory, manipulatory, and curiosity behaviors," *Psychological Review, 64:* 91–96 (1957).

or an achievement motive. Klausmeier and Goodwin state: "The persistent and varied attempts that children make to learn to ride bicycles, to skate, to read, and to write, suggest that there is a strong need to secure mastery over things and ideas."[5]

Some of the several needs of children arise and can be met only through the home, school, or society; others are more internal and personal. Any review of children's needs suggests that they are many and varied and often remain unmet or only partially met. It is the obligation of the counselor, the teacher, and other school personnel to ascertain and attempt to meet the unmet needs with which the school may suitably contend, or, if the need cannot be filled, to give the child emotional support.

Two needs are central to the discussion in the next two major sections of this chapter. *The need for a positive self-concept* is related to Maslow's need for esteem. *The need for genuineness* is related to Maslow's self-actualization need. These needs are key matters in developing a relevant guidance and counseling effort.

THE SELF-CONCEPT

Much energy and time have been spent in the exploration of the self-concept, its dimensions, the processes through which it develops, and the means by which it may be changed.

Anderson contends that "everyone has an image or concept of himself as a unique person or self, different from every other self."[6] "The self emerges as a consequence of learning experiences with other human beings and the introjection of their values and attitudes,"[7] says Hawk; ". . . an individual's behavior is consistent with his perceptions of himself."[8]

Lecky considered self-consistency so important to the individual that he termed it a theory of personality.[9] Gillham states the same point as follows: "It is hypothesized that when he has decided what kind of person he is, the individual moves through life behaving subconsciously in a certain way so as to evoke the treatment or response to which he has adjusted."[10]

[5] Herbert J. Klausmeier and William Goodwin, *Learning and Human Abilities* (New York: Harper & Row, 1961), p. 430.

[6] Camilla M. Anderson, "The self-image: a theory of the dynamics of behavior," *Mental Hygiene, 36:* 227–228 (1952).

[7] Travis L. Hawk, "Self-concepts of the socially disadvantaged," *Elementary School Journal, 67:* 197 (1967).

[8] *Ibid.*

[9] Prescott Leckey, *Self Consistency: A Theory of Personality* (New York: Island Press, 1945).

[10] Isabel Gillham, "Self concept and reading," *The Reading Teacher, 21:* 271 (1967).

In view of its possible importance, it seems appropriate to examine here briefly the development, aspects, and changing of the self-concept.

DEVELOPMENT OF THE GENERAL SELF-CONCEPT

As the baby grows, he begins to discriminate himself from his environment; in stages he realizes that his mother is a separate being, that those objects waving in front of his eyes belong to him, and that he can propel himself toward things that are separate from him.

He also begins to realize that many of his acts as he reaches out to explore the world are evaluated and reinforced or denied. He aimlessly makes a "dah dah" sound and finds this elicits great excitement and enthusiasm; he chews on a lamp cord or attempts to use the draperies to pull himself along and finds this creates great consternation, perhaps accompanied by a sharp, painful slap. Event piles upon event, day upon day, month upon month, and the child begins to perceive a general reaction toward him: "Things I do make people happy most of the time," or "Most things I do that people let me know about make others unhappy." It is not very far from this generalization to "I'm a good person" or "I'm a bad person."

Anderson states: "In the development of the self image, the first year of life is the most important, each succeeding year becoming of lesser importance until the image is essentially completed before adolescence. This is not due to the fact that the earliest period of life is the most plastic or the most impressionable, but rather to the fact that the helplessness and dependency of the child are maximum in the earliest period, and therefore, his necessity is so much greater."[11]

Generally speaking, the self-concept initially may be considered an "other-concept," a concept assumed by the child as a composite of the feelings conveyed to him by those about him and weighted in relation to the significance of those "others"—a kind of gross "mirror image" of these views of others. *The self-concept initially is general.*

The healthy self-concept is appropriately and reasonably positive, allowing for the child to accept criticism without permanent damage. It requires that the experiences perceived as positive sufficiently outnumber and thus overbalance those perceived as negative. In this sense, the child who feels he can do no wrong and the child who feels he can do no right are both deprived.

Williams and Cole[12] suggest that a positive self-concept is essential to a child's success and happiness. These writers found that self-concept

---

[11] Anderson, *op. cit.,* p. 234.
[12] Robert L. Williams and Spurgeon Cole, "Self concept and school adjustment," *Personnel and Guidance Journal, 46:* 478–481 (1968).

data correlated with conception of school, social status at school, emotional adjustment, mental ability, reading achievement, and mathematical achievement. The findings of Allen, Spear, and Johnson[13] that warmth of experimenters related to performance and perception, taken together with the Williams and Cole data, suggest that warmth of school personnel and parents may, indeed, affect self-concept and performance in many areas of life.

An interesting view of the development of the self-concept, especially as applied to disadvantaged children, is provided by Hawk:

> I submit that the self-concept is formed through assimilation of external labels that are applied to the person. If this proposition is valid, we would expect that counterparts of these external labels would be represented in the self-concepts of children from disadvantaged cultures. In fact, several investigators have found the self-concepts of disadvantaged children to be characterized by low self-esteem, self-deflation and self depreciation.[14]

An interesting related finding by Carpenter and Busse[15] is that black children do not become increasingly more negative than white children in their self-concepts in elementary school, when social status is held constant. White children of low social status, in fact, tended to become more negative over time than black children of low social status.

In the initial phases of self-concept development the mother is generally the key figure. Later the father and siblings enter to modify the view the child holds of himself. The concept held by those "others" tends to reinforce the view conveyed by the mother, though not without exception. It is certainly possible that a father, for example, unable to adjust to the demands the child makes upon the mother's time, may convey a negative impression of the baby. The family members, however, generally develop at least a sense of responsibility for the child, if only because he is their own.

As the child receives more and more input, his self-concept solidifies and he may try to maintain the concept he holds of himself in the face of obstacles. As Jersild points out, he may resist learning if that learning might break down his self-concept: "When a person resists learning that may be beneficial to him, he is, in effect, trying to protect or to shield an unhealthy condition. But, more broadly speaking, he is not actually protecting something unhealthy as such; he is trying to safeguard his picture

[13] Sara A. Allen, Paul S. Spear, and Jerry Johnson, "Experimenter role effects in children's task performance and perception," *Child Development, 40:* 1–9 (1969).

[14] Hawk, *op. cit.,* p. 199.

[15] Thomas R. Carpenter and Thomas V. Busse, "Development of self concept in Negro and white welfare children," *Child Development, 40:* 935–939 (1969).

of himself, his self-concept, the illusions concerning himself which he has built and which give him much trouble."[16]

Often difficulties arise as the child is exposed to the pictures of him held by those outside the home, since the feeling of responsibility that affects the thinking of family members in no way inhibits those whom he meets outside the family. Here the child may encounter his first unvarnished worldly reactions. On the other hand, close supervision of play by many mothers may continue to provide a kind of insulation from reactions by other children; and even among adults it is a rare individual who will give a sincere reaction, such as, "That child surely is spoiled," while a protective mother stands nearby.

If a child has had a great many hours of involvement with other children and has developed successful ways to interact with them, there may be no uniqueness in the interactive aspects of the school situation. The child who has been protected in his involvements with other children, or the child who has not learned to cope successfully with other children, however, may feel thoroughly undermined by the experience of crossing the classroom threshold, having his mother leave him, and gradually learning that others do not automatically give the same positive reaction that he receives at home. There are a great many moments unsupervised by the teacher in which the assessments of other children are clearly conveyed. "Boy, are you dumb," one says, "you can't even button your coat." Another says, "Gee, you sure know how to do somersaults."

However much his new classmates may help modify a child's self-concept, his first teachers tend to be even more important. The power of the teacher in self-concept modification is summed up by Hawk: "If you want a child to feel positive about himself, feel positive about him."[17] This statement emerged from his summary of a Davidson and Lang study in which a $+.82$ correlation was found between children's statements beginning, "My teacher thinks I am . . ." and "I think I am. . . ." This study may be interpreted in at least two ways: first, that children are aware of their teachers' feelings about them, or second, that children believe teachers see them as they see themselves. In either case this suggests that in order to help children who need improved self-concepts, teachers must convey positive feelings to them.

In another study that may bear on the teacher's responsibility, Wright[18] found that experimenters who combined both positive and negative reinforcement were more potent in affecting learning than either

---

[16] A. T. Jersild, *In Search of Self* (New York: Bureau of Publications, Columbia University, 1952), p. 114.

[17] Hawk, *op. cit.,* p. 204.

[18] Derek Wright, "Social reinforcement and maze learning in children," *Child Development, 39:* 177–183 (1968).

positive or negative reinforcers. Masters[19] noted that children who received fewer rewards tended to indulge in high self-reinforcement; one would assume that such children had already possessed moderate to high self-concepts.

The child's very feeling that he is now big enough to go to school—an adventure shared by other children who have status in his eyes—may in itself be self-enhancing. Adults, too, convey a sense of positive significance about school. Some writers have drawn a parallel with the puberty rites of primitive tribes—an experience not entirely positive, but clearly status-giving.

Parenthetically, one might contrast the sense of positive anticipation that accompanies the average child as he ventures into school with a pair of other possible reactions. Jimmy has been told to keep away from the big boys who are rough and will hurt him: he feels quite frightened as he ventures away. Susie's dad talks about how he hated school, was bored by it, and found it a complete waste of time: she knows housework and farm-work have status and would prefer to stay home. Certainly the enhancement that the self-concept may undergo with school entry is far from a universal thing.

In summary, then, a general concept of self arises from other's reactions to the individual—a concept that is modified as the child meets new experiences and other persons. Hopefully the child comes to provide at least some of his own reinforcement, to develop his own concepts as to what is good for him and what is less good. The further he can develop an independent and positive self-concept, and the further he can go in finding his own significance and direction in life, the better he will be able to cope with the difficulties he encounters. Certainly the elementary school teacher and counselor can play important roles in this self-discovery process, both as sounding boards and as guides who can help the child see alternative courses and their ramifications.

SPECIFIC ASPECTS OF THE SELF-CONCEPT

The general concept of himself that the individual holds can be affected by specific concepts. The child may hold the general view that he is a "good" person, but if he also believes it important to be a good athlete, a scholar, and a person who makes friends easily, and if these attributes are somewhat lacking, his self-concept will undergo a reexamination over a period of time. The outcome may be a reduced sense of personal worth, a questioning—"I'm a good person, but good for what?"—that eventually lowers the self-concept. Thus the individual develops a general concept of

[19] John C. Masters, "Social comparison, self-reinforcement, and the value of a reinforcer," *Child Development, 40:* 1027–1038 (1969).

personal "goodness" and gradually modifies this over a period of time as he begins to sort out and compare himself to others in regard to several specific aspects of self-concept.

APPEARANCE   One of the most important areas into which specific self-concepts reach is that of the physical self. In American society, looks play an important role. Neatness, clean-cut physical features, handsomeness, absence of any even slightly outlandish trait, a "proper" walk, all contribute to others' concept of the individual. More important, though, is the concept the individual holds of himself. Counselors and teachers have asked children to stand before a mirror and write or tell what they see.

"I see just me and my ugly old glasses."
"I see a good-looking boy."
"Just a big fat blob."
"Nothing. Nothing worth looking at."
"A pretty girl."
"Ugh!"

The range of personal reactions to the physical self is very great, and it may not coincide at all with the reactions of others. Adults see a pretty little girl and she sees "Just my terrible, ugly braces." Or they see a homely freckle-faced boy and he sees, "Like my dad says, 'all boy.'"

PHYSICAL PROWESS   Prowess is of particular concern to boys, who may feel more aptly judged by this yardstick, while girls are likely to feel judged more by appearance.

Think about yourself on the playground in an active, hard running game. What do you see?
"I'm the strongest boy in the room."
"I don't like boy's games, I'd rather watch."
"Afraid. I can run fast, but I don't like to be hurt."
"I can play as good as the boys. Better than some."
How does it make you feel about yourself when you think about yourself that way?
"Good. Real good."
"O.K. Girls shouldn't play rough anyway."
"Bad. I don't like what I see."
"Fine. But my mom thinks I ought to be more dainty."

Certainly such comments reflect and affect larger considerations in the self-concept, shoring up or tearing down the effects of other characteristics.

COMPETENCE The child tends to have a concept of himself in terms of his competence as a "doer," which emerges from his early attempts to be helpful. The young child who is encouraged by being allowed to help to dry the dishes, to set the table, to cut the lawn, to mop the floor, to hand daddy the tools, and who receives support and commendation for his efforts conceives of himself as a "doer" and a "helper." The child whose efforts are continually rebuffed by a parent—"You're not big enough or old enough"—begins to perceive himself as an inadequate person, often rationalizes that the tasks are hateful anyway, and then associates the task with the rebuff and when he is "big enough" finds the job distasteful. The self-concept of a child as a "doer" or as competent is a matter of great import, of particular importance because of the inclination of the child to live up to the perceptions others hold of him.

SCHOOL ACHIEVEMENT Just as a child may react in one way to his face and another way to his body, or assess himself positively in running or swimming and negatively in body contact games, the academic self-concept may have both positive and negative overtones or may be perceived as a unified whole.

"I'm good in reading, but poor in math. Same as Mom."
"I like all the school subjects and I'm good in them. Thank goodness, because that's about the only thing I am good in."
"Oh, how I wish I could do better."

O'Shea[20] found a significant relationship between high achievement and social activity. Perhaps self-concepts in these areas might correlate well, although certainly not for all children.

SOCIABILITY The interpersonal self-concept becomes increasingly developed throughout the middle childhood period and well past adolescence. New experiences and new situations may serve to undermine or enhance the existing self-concept.

How do you see yourself getting along with people?
"I get along real well."
"Other kids don't seem to like me much, but I try hard."
"Grownups like me, but other kids I'm not sure about."
"Pretty good."
Suppose you had to start in a new school tomorrow. How would you feel about getting along with a new group?

[20] Arthur J. O'Shea, "Peer relationships and male academic achievement: a review and suggested clarification," *Personnel and Guidance Journal, 47:* 417–423 (1969).

"They couldn't be worse than this one."
"I'd do O.K."
"Scared."
"I've done it before. It's not so bad."

OTHER FACTORS IN THE SELF-CONCEPT   The child has concepts of himself regarding his getting up and speaking before groups of people, his effectiveness in art work, his musical talent, his aptitudes for making simple mechanical repairs, and so on through many other areas. Each specific factor has some part to play in the individual's general self-concept; each may adversely affect school performance or attitudes; and any one or more of them may undergo change as a result of counseling efforts.

SELF-CONCEPT AND CHANGE

One of the major concerns of the counselor or teacher regarding particular children may well be the shoring up of damaging self-concepts. He must be aware simultaneously that many children would benefit by change and that nonetheless they may resist it. As Hawk points out: "Self-concepts are relatively stable entities, changing only very slowly through the experiences that are provided. No end product of education is more important, however, than one's concept of self. If an individual can look in the mirror and take pride in what he sees, his chances of success and happiness are good. As the ill effects of social disadvantagement are alleviated, the major advantage will lie in the way individuals view themselves."[21]

Combs has put squarely before teachers and counselors the importance of positive self-concept: ". . . it is people who see themselves as unliked, unwanted, unworthy, unimportant or unable who fill our jails, our mental hospitals, and our institutions."[22] In contrast, according to Barrett,[23] persons with high self-regard seem better able to incorporate new information about themselves and, thus, to change.

Since self-concept formation begins early in the life of the individual, perhaps a child may be most open to viewing himself differently in the early elementary school grades. A hopeful note is sounded by Gillham: "Building and rebuilding of these attitudes toward self . . . is constantly occurring to some extent throughout life."[24] She also maintains, in speaking of the determination to maintain self-image, ". . . that this

[21] Hawk, *op. cit.*, p. 205.

[22] Arthur W. Combs, ed., *Perceiving, Behaving, Becoming* (Washington, D.C.: Association for Supervision and Curriculum Development, 1962), p. 52.

[23] Roger L. Barrett, "Changes in accuracy of self-estimates," *Personnel and Guidance Journal, 47:* 353–357 (1968).

[24] Gillham, *op. cit.*, p. 270.

behavior has been learned, and that learned behavior can be modified and adjusted. The individual who has learned to see himself as stupid and insignificant is enslaved by this self-concept until some significant person or persons in his life help him see himself as capable and worthwhile."[25] Ludwig and Maehr[26] affirm that significant persons may help alter self-concepts, citing several other studies that support this contention.

Blain and Ramirez,[27] in a study of children of low sociometric status, found that unknown, not disliked children of low sociometric standing could have their sociometric rank affected through organized interaction with other children. This, presumably, could benefit children having low self-concepts, as their peers helped them see themselves differently.

However stable the self-concept may be, it may be found to be a structure that can be affected by input. The elementary school counselor or teacher can be encouraged by this prospect. He needs to be aware, too, that the child's development and his self-concept interact. Many social skills are developed with reference to the individual's perception of himself. A mental set that says: "People generally like me and so I'll see if these kids will let me play baseball with them," will produce a very different outcome than a mental set that says: "These kids don't care about me so I'm just going to watch the game and laugh if they do anything stupid."

Just as the self-concept affects some aspects of child development, in the same way aspects of development affect the self-concept. For example, many perceptions of the self are conditioned by the child's maturity of physical development. A child may believe in himself, see other children playing a complex game, enter into it, and change his self-concept as he realizes he does not have the requisite skills for competing. Effective counseling may help the child view himself positively and realistically as well as understand his own personal development.

In a general sense the changing of the self-concept involves the seeking out of the genuineness within an individual. Hawk makes it sound easy, but it is far from easy to meet his objective: "Each person must realize that 'it is all right to let other people see the real *me*.' He does not have to fabricate a *me* for others to see, a *me* that he feels will be more acceptable than the real *me*. An individual must know that he is in a situation in which it is comfortable for him to reveal the real *me* and not have to develop a *me* that he feels others will approve."[28]

[25] *Ibid.*, p. 272.

[26] David J. Ludwig and Martin L. Maehr, "Changes in self concept and stated behavioral preferences," *Child Development, 38:* 453–467 (1967).

[27] Michael J. Blain and Manuel Ramirez, "Increasing sociometric rank, meaningfulness, and discriminability of children's names through reinforcement and interaction," *Child Development, 39:* 949–955 (1968).

[28] Hawk, *op. cit.*, p. 204.

Clearly the self-concept and genuineness are interrelated. We shall now expand our discussion of the need for genuineness, developed in Chapter 2, and relate it more specifically to the individual child.

GENUINENESS, NONGENUINENESS, AND ALIENATION

GENUINENESS

Who is the genuine child? What is he like? What is "genuine" about him?

The child is born genuine. When he is responding to the objects and persons in his environment in the way that he most feels like responding, he is being genuine. As he fondles and mouths objects, as he grows older and eyes them and puzzles about them, and as he attempts to disassemble them in order to understand them, he is being genuine.

His major characteristic is that he does respond, and appropriately, in terms of his own individual development.

He is clearly an emerging, developing, becoming organism who reaches out toward life. He seeks the new; he is readily receptive to the adventure in his environment. He experiences and shows few fears—those demanded for safety of life and limb. He learns to discriminate a few things to fear, others to respect, and the great mass to welcome eagerly.

The genuine child is refreshingly open, sure of himself in ways that demonstrate simple security rather than arrogance, and, as Clark Moustakas says, he is not "programmed."[29] He responds because his inner being demands the response, not because others have programmed him to give it. He is able to laugh delightfully and delightedly, to respond to grief with tears, and to feel anger, love—a whole spectrum of feelings—at deep levels. He is curious, and therefore questioning; he is absorbed by ideas, and therefore attending to them. With all his openness and candidness, he is aware of others and responsible because he has been allowed to be responsible. It might well be noted that this description applies to genuineness in persons well beyond childhood.

Moustakas states: "Every person has within himself the potentiality for creative living, for participating in interhuman experience on an authentic basis, while maintaining a distinctive and unique individuality."[30] Though many children, adolescents, and adults exhibit some of these behaviors, the genuine adult is altogether too rare in our society. Instead of learning to be genuine, the child tends to unlearn his earlier natural genuineness.

[29] Clark Moustakas, *Creativity and Conformity* (New York: Van Nostrand-Reinhold Company, 1967), p. 129.
[30] *Ibid.*, p. 127.

NONGENUINENESS AND ALIENATION

What, by contrast, is the nongenuine child like? What characteristics mark him? How can he be distinguished from the genuine child.

Genuine behavior is spontaneous, natural, and direct; by contrast, nongenuine behavior tends to be planned, manipulative, and indirect or circuitous. It is a key characteristic of the nongenuine child that he is indirect in his behavior. He frequently does things, not because he wants to do them, not because the activity in and of itself has personal value to him, but because he hopes to gain an extrinsic reward such as money or applause. And the less genuine he becomes, the more frequently his behavior depends upon these extrinsic rewards.

Three types of extrinsic rewards lead the nongenuine child toward self-alienating modes of behavior. Weiss sums up the range of choices the child has available to him—or has made for him—as follows: "If one is not loved for what one is, one can at least be safe—safe perhaps by being very good and perfect and being loved for it, or by being very strong and being admired or feared for it, or by learning not to feel, not to want, not to care."[31]

CONFORMING PATTERNS AND ALIENATION   Many a child finds acceptance by conforming. He wishes to be loved and accepted, and he interprets absence of hostility as evidence that his goals are achieved. Blandness, emotional flatness, and vicarious experiencing tend to be adopted because these seldom evoke strongly negative or hostile reactions. He is self-alienated because he is directed so much by his concepts of what others will say and think. He is often hesitant, even avoiding, in his movements, and rather than being in control he appears to be programmed or controlled by his environment. He learns to disapprove of his own impulses as he sees them in others; eventually he learns to deny their existence in himself. A near total lack of risk-taking characterizes the individual who reaches an extreme in this direction. He does what is expected of him. He is good.

PERFORMING PATTERNS AND ALIENATION   Another sort of child finds acceptance through more active behavior. He tends to interpret applause or laughter, or simply the absence of forcible restraint, as signifying acceptance and love. No more than his conforming counterpart has he developed a true sense of self. Those significant to him may have been ineffective in limiting his expression or may have tended to reinforce certain of his outgoing impulses. Perhaps to serve their own needs, others may have stressed his athletic ability, musical talent, sense of humor, looks, or some other attribute. Thus, through commitment to the goals of others, or through

[31] Frederick A. Weiss, "Self-alienation: dynamics and therapy," *American Journal of Psychoanalysis, 21:* 207–218 (1961).

indifference on the part of the adults about him, who seem not to care what he does, he has sought attention or achievement as a substitute for being loved and accepted as he is. He may appear free; he does what brings the applause of his peers; yet, really, he is as self-alienated as is the more conforming nongenuine child. He is bound and absorbed, and may be devoured, by his need for attention.

Neither the conforming nor the performing nongenuine person exhibits responsibility. The one avoids the necessity of the decision, the other responds to the roar of the crowd. Neither does what his *true* self would wish because neither knows what that might be.

WITHDRAWAL PATTERNS AND ALIENATION   The child who is being molded by those about him has a third way of defending himself. He can withdraw from the game, dimly aware that if he does not play he cannot lose, and those "others" who choose to mold him cannot win. He "turns off" or "tunes out" the attempts to change him; his defenses all are mustered in favor of desensitization. Dreaming a world more attractive than the one he meets, he thwarts the demands of others, at the cost of thwarting himself also.

The nongenuine child does not achieve his original goal—to be loved for himself. Frequently he misses his substitute goal—to be what others want him to be, or to avoid failure. Perhaps no substitute goal could be fully satisfying because of his unrealized need to be himself and to be loved for himself.

THE DEVELOPMENT OF ALIENATION

How does alienation develop? How do we convey to a child that his present self somehow lacks a quality that it would please us to see developed? Or how do we convey the idea that a given quality of his would be best eliminated or minimized?

There are harmful, dangerous, and unacceptable impulses in children that need to be resisted. No case is made here for allowing children to be destructive or harmful to one another or to adults; it is not on this level that our present concern lies. Our concern, rather, is that adults almost daily deny children thousands of harmless self-expressive acts.

In the area of sex-role identification, for example, Dad can hold the baby and feed him his bottle while Mother makes lunch, but Junior cannot play with dolls, showing the same healthy expressions of tenderness, without being told, "That's for girls. Boys don't do that." When he falls and skins his knee and cries, he is told, "Big boys don't cry." Or when he offers to help by mowing the lawn, his parents say: "When you're bigger. You're not big enough yet."

Upon the little girl we exert different but equally insidious pressures. "Don't soil your dress now. Be a little lady. We'll leave in a half hour and I want you to stay clean while I get ready." Mother has forgotten that a half hour is a lifetime to a three-year-old and that the mud in the back yard is of an irresistibly delightful consistency. And even if she scrubs her daughter clean again and wordlessly changes the dress, the message gets through: "You don't please me. Good girls don't do that."

Selective reinforcement in the area of sex-role identification produces not a genuine self but a set of expectations. Feshbach and Roe[32] found that six- and seven-year-old boys were reluctant to describe themselves as afraid. Gallagher[33] described gifted boys as more secure in their self-concepts, less sensitive and positive than gifted girls. The girls were described as better in arriving at solutions, more anxious and inhibited. Vroegh[34] asked teachers to rate *preschool* children. Those boys who were rated as masculine tended to be extroverted, whereas girls rated as most feminine were introverted. Wright[35] found that girls were more influenced by reinforcement than were boys.

No known physiological factors can account for some of these sex differences. Except for those that can be attributed to the faster maturation rate of girls, they result from internalization of adult expectations. The child is to some degree alienated from his true self whenever he must forfeit a natural inclination in favor of an assigned role.

And how is that assigned role conveyed? Often it is discussed smilingly. Adults suggest to boys that they hide their feelings: "Do you want the other children to think you're a crybaby?" Girls are told subtly and directly that adults would like it better if they sat quietly with folded hands, "like a little lady"—and the adult smiles. Charitable tones and smilingly benign faces convince the child: surely anyone who would not conform to such requests would be truly ungrateful and rather represensible.

THOUGHT CONTROLS AND ALIENATION   Even more repressive than the controls applied to behavior are the controls applied to thoughts. The child verbalizes (and what child hasn't?), "I get so mad at him, I just hate him!" And the response: "Your very own brother! The idea! You should be ashamed of yourself!"—or, perhaps worse, "Now, you don't really mean that."

In our concern to stifle "bad" thoughts we overlook the harm inherent in denying an honest and strong feeling. Children can, and should, be helped to verbalize more adequately. Surely a child may acceptably say,

[32] Norma D. Feshbach and Kiki Roe, "Empathy in six- and seven-year-olds," *Child Development, 39:* 133–145 (1968).

[33] James J. Gallagher, "Sex differences in expressive thought of gifted children in the classroom," *Personnel and Guidance Journal, 45:* 248–253 (1966).

[34] Karen Vroegh, "Masculinity and femininity in the preschool years," *Child Development, 39:* 1253–1257 (1968).

[35] Derek Wright, "Social reinforcement and maze learning in children," *Child Development, 39:* 177–183 (1968).

"It makes me so angry when he does that," but denying the feeling exists is one of the easiest roads to self-alienation and self-denial. After all, the child's feelings are part of him, and denying these feelings *is* self-denial.

Our middle-class morality, it would seem, militates against strong feelings—often *any* sort of strong feelings. Sophistication, evidenced by the absence of expressed emotion, is considered the acceptable mode of behavior. Blandness, of all the unlikely traits, is one of the most reinforced.

There is nothing wrong with an adult who experiences deep depression, ecstatic elation, paralyzing fear, or pure delight, if the stimuli are appropriate. To deny a child these feelings is to teach him that nothing is important.

The counselor is dedicated to freeing the thoughts of children, helping them understand their strong feelings and learning to cope with them. Children need, not denial, but facilitation of their genuineness. The teacher, too, is a critical participant in the facilitative process. As Moustakas says: "Life comes from life and the teacher is the living agent in the school. As a living agent, the teacher must not abdicate the human dimensions which he can communicate to the child: respect for his individuality, recognition of his particular interests, needs and directions, encouragement of his growth in identity. The human talents, the human resources of the teacher are the teacher's primary value in the educative process."[36]

Both counselor and teacher can well follow the Gestalt therapeutic concept, offered by Perls,[37] to live more in the NOW with the child, and less in the past and future. This is taken to mean valuing the child as he is, and the opportunity existing in the present moment as it is. Stein[38] makes it clear that children need person-oriented approval. Children need to be reinforced and approved for being real. Cottingham[39] asknowledges this challenge for counselors; certainly it applies to teachers as well.

FOUR TYPES OF GUIDANCE NEEDS

The guidance needs of children fall into at least four categories:

1. *Remedial needs*, arising from the child's patterns of living over time.

[36] Clark Moustakas, "Alienation, education, and existential life" (Paper presented at NDEA Counseling and Guidance Institute, Cedar Falls, Iowa, June 1965), p. 6.

[37] Frederick S. Perls, "Four lectures," *Gestalt Therapy Now*, Joen Fagan and I. L. Shepherd, eds. (Palo Alto: Science and Behavior Books, 1970), pp. 14–38.

[38] Aletha H. Stein, "The influence of social reinforcement on the achievement behavior of fourth grade boys and girls," *Child Development, 40:* 727–736, (1969).

[39] Harold F. Cottingham, "The challenge of authentic behavior," *Personnel and Guidance Journal, 45:* 328–336 (1966).

2. *Immediate needs*, arising from recent events that generate urgent interests, concerns, or problems.

3. *Exploratory needs*, arising either out of the moment or over time, which are not urgent but suggest pursuit at leisure.

4. *Developmental needs*, arising as the child enters various stages of growth—needs that may suggest remediation, immediate action, or exploration.

Each of these four categories is discussed in this section. The way each need is experienced by the child, and the way in which significant others react, affects both the child's self-concept and his genuineness.

CHILDREN'S REMEDIAL NEEDS

In remedial circumstances children often require help to alter negative self-images that affect school performance and interpersonal relationships. Lengthy and frequent contacts are often necessary to leap the hurdles to positive self-attitudes and successful attempts with other persons or activities.

Jimmy is an out-and-out bully who demands money from other children, threatening to beat them, yet he verges on tears when his school work is poorly done. Disciplinary actions may be needed; but beyond that, here is a child who seems to be crying out for help in relating to other children in positive ways.

Susie sits, pained by her own shyness, hoping no one will notice her, putting all but her entire fist in her mouth, and lowering her eyes whenever another's meet them. There is a nonverbal expression of eagerness to be involved in the classroom, a fleeting, vicarious smile when an amusing thing is said or an especially good response is given. Everyone in her environment, even those who have helped her become so painfully shy, has attempted to push and prod her into volunteering answers, saying hello to others, and sharing her special interests. Though her approach is quite different, her problem is the same as Jimmy's: both want others to confer a degree of acceptance. Both do things that are most unlikely to advance the ends desired.

Bart, by contrast, has basically good relations with his agemates. His father is a strong-willed, minimally educated, self-made man who laughs loudly, is a bit of a practical joker, and has limited tolerance for bookishness. Bart, an athletic leader and to some small degree an underachiever, is a nuisance in the classroom. He feels strongly the sense of acceptance and identification so vital to children, yet in his intolerance of education as a route to effective living he creates a problem.

Each of these children has a remedial need—one that may be shared by hundreds of other children in the school setting. The teacher has responsibility for each of these children, but the elementary school counselor cannot give intensive attention to each. Remediation efforts in the guidance program focus upon those children who have adopted self-defeating life styles that are remediable (accessible to remediation attempts), rather than upon those who have adopted self-enhancing life styles that inconvenience others.

Bart's behavior may be more of a classroom problem than that of Jimmy or Susie, and aspects of his behavior may need correcting and may therefore be considered remedial. Nonetheless, his behavior is basically self-enhancing in that he achieves the recognition that he wishes, affection and admiration are his, and he is successful in modeling after his father, a very important figure in his life.

In terms of guidance priorities, Bart must rank much lower than Jimmy, Susie, or anyone else whose behavior clearly misses objectives such as acceptance and affection that the child seeks.

Remedial guidance, then, guidance with the objective of change of behavior, should be devoted to children whose behavior defeats itself rather than to children whose behavior is a frustration to others, teachers and counselors included.

CHILDREN'S IMMEDIATE NEEDS

The immediate circumstances in the lives of children tend to evoke immediate needs, however temporary, for guidance and counseling. Many of these needs are brief and superficial, yet they afford an opportunity to show the child that an understanding person is accessible to him.

Johnny's best friend may have moved away yesterday. If he is understood, if his grief is neither maximized nor minimized, if he is helped to verbalize or express through play his sense of loss, frustration, and anguish, he may well say later to a chum who is highly angered over a home conflict, "Why don't you see the counselor? He helped me when I felt bad."

Often no action needs to be or can be taken when these immediate concerns arise. The death of a loved one, the loss of a new puppy, the anguish over a failure of some sort—perhaps when the child is not chosen for a Little League team—when these immediate concerns confront the child, often no action can be taken.

When the child meets such difficulties, as most do, the counselor and occasionally the teacher can provide understanding and a permissive atmosphere in which grief or anguish may be expressed. Many parents are well equipped to help a child express rather than deny his strong feelings; even so, the event or knowledge of it may occur to the child while he is in school. Far too many adults, however, are ill-equipped to accept strong expressions of emotion, and tend to suppress them—thus the especial need for guidance-oriented teachers and counselors.

A classic experience of immediate concern to millions of children is the loss of place in the home to a new baby, a situation that few children face without some anxiety. For most children the long-run values of learning to share and to relate to a broader world far outweigh the effects of anxiety. Many a child, however, who has seemed to weather the storm beautifully has expressed hostility symbolically through expression in play activities; such cathartic experiences (literally purging) can help him maintain a stable, progressing relationship to his environment.

Guidance contact that relates to immediate matters need not be problem-oriented. For every child who is disconsolate over a difficulty there may be two who want to share their excitement over a recent event, a planned visit by grandmother, or the winning of a scouting honor or badge. For every child who is upset over competing with a new baby in the home there may be two who exult: "We have a new baby at our house!" In a few days or weeks the same child, after either initial reaction, may express to some degree the opposite emotion.

Life is not an either-or proposition; ambivalent feelings (feelings that are both positive and negative toward a person, object, or event) are more common than recognized. A child may be happy that he has a new brother yet fearful of the competition, glad teeth will be straightened but concerned about the dentist's office, excited about summer camp but anxious about leaving home.

An important benefit of guidance contacts may be the simple knowledge that feelings of conflict and ambivalence are perfectly normal when the objective is both new and desired or feared and desired. Assistance through guidance at such times may be vital in showing the child that the school cares for him.

CHILDREN'S EXPLORATORY NEEDS

As an interested, participating individual, the child may encounter aspects of his immediate world that lead him to seek the guidance of adults. He needs time to explore his interests, discuss social relationships, or perhaps clarify his attitudes toward school or home life. Often when this occurs no difficulty is involved. The child is looking for a person with whom to share his thoughts; he is learning to "bounce his ideas off" someone else. He is discovering that "I don't know what I think until I hear what I have to say." The casual observer might remark, "He just wants to talk," minimizing the value of this "just talking." When the child's need to develop relationships with adult figures is overlooked, the result may be that no one responds to these overtures.

The guidance-oriented person, however, sees importance in the child's attempts to establish communication. He is willing to spend some time viewing a picture a child has drawn or listening to the child as he relates a personal anecdote, as well as dealing with him when he is upset or unhappy. He knows that communication lines established in this way are important links in the willingness of the child to communicate with others or specifically with adults.

CHILDREN'S DEVELOPMENTAL NEEDS

Certain tasks tend to appear at different points on the road toward adulthood that demand the child's attention. If these tasks are satisfactorily mastered, the road remains relatively free of obstacles and detours. Further, the mastering of these tasks is a prerequisite to the satisfactory handling of future related tasks. The guidance-oriented counselor or teacher is aware of the developmental tasks that present themselves and is alert to the need to help children to understand and cope with them.

Havighurst[40] has identified nine tasks that seem essential to growth in middle childhood:

Developmental Tasks of Middle Childhood

Learning physical skills necessary for ordinary games
Building wholesome attitudes toward oneself as a growing organism
Learning to get along with agemates
Learning an appropriate sex role
Developing fundamental skills in reading, writing, and arithmetic
Developing concepts necessary for everyday living
Developing conscience, morality, and a scale of values
Developing a responsibility for an independent self
Developing attitudes toward social groups and institutions

Each of these tasks, if successfully completed by the child, tends to improve the prospects for successful completion of the next task in the series. Each, in turn, tends to depend upon successful completion of tasks that arise earlier in childhood or infancy. Thus, a sequence of inter-dependent steps are involved in the growth toward maturity. These steps are finely graduated and not discrete entities; for example, a child does not either learn or not learn to get along with agemates so much as he achieves a certain degree of success, which might be plotted on a continuum from highly successful to highly unsuccessful. The need for guidance, then, is often actually a matter of degree, rather than need or no need.

Further evidence of the interdependence of related steps in the developmental sequence is given by Kagan and Moss, who conclude that ". . . many of the behaviors exhibited by the child during the period 6 to 10 years of age, and a few during the age period 3 to 6, were moderately good

---

[40] Robert Havighurst, *Human Development and Education* (New York: McKay, 1952), pp. 15–28.

predictors of theoretically related behaviors during early adulthood."[41] These writers found that certain aspects of the adult style of living, including withdrawal from stressful situations, ease of anger arousal, involvement in matters of intellect, anxiety in social interaction, and several other aspects, tended to relate to preadolescent behaviors. This is not to say that spontaneous remission and regression do not or cannot occur. On the contrary, it merely suggests that in most adults patterns of behavior may be carried over from childhood because no need for change is perceived or because no alternative pattern is readily available.

A somewhat different way of looking at the development of the child has been offered by Erikson,[42] who has conceptualized eight stages. During the first year of life, the child develops the *sense of trust*; during roughly the period from age one to three he develops a *sense of autonomy*; the *sense of initiative* tends to emerge around ages four to five; during the elementary school years the child develops a *sense of duty and accomplishment*; later, in sequence, he develops *a sense of identity*, *a sense of intimacy*, *a parental sense*, and *a sense of integrity*. Erikson sees these stages not as exclusive, but as preeminent at the varying age levels.

Still another way of viewing development is offered by Hill and Luckey, who list the following essential guidance learnings that humans need to acquire either as children, as adolescents, or as adults:

> The child must mature in his understanding of himself. . . .
> The child must mature in his sense of responsibility for himself. . . .
> The child must mature in his understanding of the world of education and the world of work. . . .
> The child must mature in the ability to make decisions. . . .
> The child must mature in the ability to solve his own problems. . . .
> The child must mature in his understanding of human behavior, especially as regards one's relations with others. . . .
> The child must mature in his ability to adjust to the demands of life, especially as regards his relations with other people. . . .
> The child must mature in his sense of values, in the achievement of high ideals. . . .[43]

Whether the developmental tasks, developmental stages, or essential guidance learnings are given particular attention, evidently certain developmental matters should be anticipated by those who work with the child. The number of adults who fail to adequately achieve a given developmental task or learning emphasizes the need for a readily available source of assistance in childhood. If the elementary school counselor and

[41] Jerome Kagan and Howard A. Moss, *Birth to Maturity* (New York: Wiley, 1962), p. 266.

[42] Erik Erikson, *Childhood and Society* (New York: Norton, 1963).

[43] George E. Hill and Eleanore B. Luckey, *Guidance for Children in Elementary Schools* (New York: Appleton-Century-Crofts, 1969), pp. 11–18.

guidance-oriented teacher can help children confront or anticipate these difficulties more adequately, he has made a successful guidance contribution in the school setting.

PRIORITIES

Hill and Luckey state: "Whether we like it or not the child who comes to school is a complex human being who carries with him the consequences of his past experiences, his own unique conception of himself, his own needs, his own strengths and weaknesses, his own aspirations and dreams. Thus he must be dealt with as if the school were responsible for *him*, not just for some part of him."[44] Children must be dealt with as whole persons, and all children from time to time have needs that deserve personalized attention. In this situation, every teacher and counselor must make certain choices, must set his own priorities. He will be limited by some of the demands of the school situation: if he concentrates on the children who evidence remedial needs, he may be working with the group that he may least affect, while overlooking children whose needs he might help meet before they require remediation.

Both the counselor and teacher should make themselves available so that a variety of children may seek assistance, while they also devote some time to children who need remedial help. For the counselor, seeing ten children twice a week for forty minutes, jotting down and reading the barest of notes, reflecting only momentarily upon the events of the interview, readying materials beforehand and straightening the room afterward, could tie up much more than half of his time. The boy who needs an immediate moment as a result of a playground incident, the girl who wants to share a picture, and the unexpressed developmental concern of a gangling sixth-grade girl would receive short shrift in such a situation. The counselor, also, does not have unlimited energy to devote to children with remedial difficulties.

Perhaps a more serious problem in such a situation is that the counselor may become "typed" in ways that radically limit his effectiveness, permanently prejudicing children into believing that all counselors serve certain specific functions. (This seems to have already been done in many secondary schools, where the counselor is "the one who helps you decide on a college.") Counseling programs in elementary schools offer unique opportunities to recast the role of the counselor more broadly.

To avoid limiting his accessibility or becoming "typed," the counselor should limit remedial contacts over an extended period to less than one-fourth of his time. This would tend to free him for exploratory, developmental, and immediate counseling contacts and for consulting activities.

[44] *Ibid.,* p. 10.

The teacher, too, must consider priorities. Unlike the counselor, he must work with all those to whom he is assigned as teacher; nonetheless, the special moments and lengthier time blocks he may devote to individual and personalized attention tend to express his priorities. He needs to be alert to immediate concerns; he needs to reach out toward children for whom long-term problems are ever-present; yet, he must also consider periodically whether there are children for whom educational or other life problems are creating difficult pressures. He may be able to identify and encounter some concerns before they balloon out of proportion and require a more remedial approach.

Alert teachers and counselors can contribute much by discovering and coping with the needs of children in their care.

SUMMARY

The child is not generally an innocent bystander in the development of his own concerns. While others act upon him to encourage or suppress his genuineness and to guide his self-concept, his own perceptions and his own behaviors also create considerable input. A variety of remedial, immediate, exploratory, and developmental needs derive from his own perceptions and actions as well as from the presses applied by others. Efforts in counseling and guidance are directed at meeting a variety of these needs of children, with special emphasis on the enhancement of the self-concept and the encouragement of genuineness.

REFERENCES

Allen, S. A., P. S. Spear, and J. Johnson. "Experimenter role effects on children's task performance and perception," *Child Development, 40:* 1–9 (1969).

Anderson, C. M. "The self-image: a theory of the dynamics of behavior," *Mental Hygiene, 36:* 227–244 (1952).

Barrett, R. L. "Changes in accuracy of self-estimates," *Personnel and Guidance Journal, 47:* 353–357 (1968).

Blain, M. J., and M. Ramirez III. "Increasing sociometric rank, meaningfulness, and discriminability of children's names through reinforcement and interaction," *Child Development, 39:* 949–955 (1968).

Carpenter, T. R., and T. V. Busse. "Development of self concept in Negro and white welfare children," *Child Development, 40:* 935–939 (1969).

Combs, A. W., ed. *Perceiving, Behaving, Becoming.* Washington, D.C.: Association for Supervision and Curriculum Development, 1962.

Cottingham, H. F. "The challenge of authentic behavior," *Personnel and Guidance Journal, 45:* 328–336 (1966).

Cronbach, L. *Educational Psychology*. New York: Harcourt, 1963.

Dember, W. N., and R. W. Earl. "Analysis of exploratory, manipulatory, and curiosity behaviors," *Psychological Review, 64:* 91–96 (1957).

Erikson, E. H. *Childhood and Society*. New York: Norton, 1963.

Fagan, J., and I. L. Shepherd, eds., *Gestalt Therapy Now*. Palo Alto: Science and Behavior Books, 1970.

Feshbach, N. D., and K. Roe. "Empathy in six- and seven-year-olds," *Child Development, 39:* 133–145 (1968).

Gallagher, J. J. "Sex differences in expressive thought of gifted children in the classroom," *Personnel and Guidance Journal, 45:* 248–253 (1966).

Gillham, I. "Self concept and reading," *Reading Teacher, 21:* 270–273 (1967).

Hamachek, D. C. *The Self in Growth, Teaching, and Learning*. Englewood Cliffs, N.J.: Prentice-Hall, 1965.

Havighurst, R. *Human Development and Education*. New York: McKay, 1952.

Hawk, T. L. "Self-concepts of the socially disadvantaged," *Elementary School Journal, 67:* 196–206 (1967).

Hill, G. E., and E. B. Luckey. *Guidance for Children in Elementary Schools*. New York: Appleton-Century-Crofts, 1969.

Jersild, A. T. *In Search of Self*. New York: Bureau of Publications, Columbia University, 1952.

Kagan, J., and H. A. Moss. *Birth to Maturity*. New York: Wiley, 1962.

Klausmeier, H. J., and W. Goodwin. *Learning and Human Abilities*. New York: Harper & Row, 1961. Pp. 423–461.

Lecky, P. *Self-Consistency: A Theory of Personality*. New York: Island Press, 1945.

Ludwig, D. J., and M. L. Maehr. "Changes in self concept and stated behavioral preferences," *Child Development, 38:* 453–467 (1967).

Maslow, A. H. "A theory of human motivation," *Psychological Review, 50:* 370–396 (1943).

Masters, J. C. "Social comparison, self-reinforcement, and the value of a reinforcer," *Child Development, 40:* 1027–1038 (1969).

Meeks, A. R. *Guidance in Elementary Education*. New York: Ronald, 1968.

Moustakas, C. *Creativity and Conformity*. New York: Van Nostrand-Reinhold Company, 1967.

———. "Alienation, education, and existential life." Paper presented at NDEA Counseling and Guidance Institute, Cedar Falls, Iowa, June 1965.

Munson, H. L. *Elementary School Guidance: Concepts, Dimensions, and Practice*. Boston, Allyn and Bacon, 1970.

O'Shea, A. J. "Peer relationships and male academic achievement: a review and suggested clarification," *Personnel and Guidance Journal, 47:* 417–423 (1969).

Stein, A. H. "The influence of social reinforcement on the achievement behavior of fourth-grade boys and girls," *Child Development, 40:* 727–736 (1969).

Vroegh, K. "Masculinity and femininity in the preschool years," *Child Development, 39:* 1253–1257 (1968).

Weiss, F. A. "Self-alienation: dynamics and theory," *American Journal of Psychoanalysis, 21:* 207–218 (1961).

Williams, R. L., and S. Cole. "Self concept and school adjustment," *Personnel and Guidance Journal, 46:* 478–481 (1968).

Wright, D. "Social reinforcement and maze learning in children," *Child Development, 39:* 177–183 (1968).

ARTICLES IN BOOKS OF READINGS

Dinkmeyer, D. C. *Guidance and Counseling in the Elementary School: Readings in Theory and Practice.* New York: Holt, Rinehart and Winston, Inc., 1968. Readings beginning on pages 99, 167.

Koplitz, E. D. *Guidance in the Elementary School: Theory, Research, and Practice.* Dubuque, Iowa: William C. Brown Company, Publishers, 1968. Readings beginning on pages 196, 199.

Mills, G. D. *Elementary School Guidance and Counseling.* New York: Random House, Inc., 1971. Readings beginning on pages 247, 257.

Peters, H. J., A. C. Riccio, and J. J. Quaranta, *Guidance in the Elementary School: A Book of Readings.* New York: Macmillan, 1963. Readings beginning on pages 25, 271.

Part Two

Determining the Need

4

Self-Selection, Observation, and Informal Procedures

There was a boy that all agreed
Had shut within him the rare seed
of learning. We could understand,
But none of us could lift a hand.

EDWIN ARLINGTON ROBINSON:
"Flammonde"

This chapter and the next will help the teacher and counselor to (1) determine who has need for guidance and counseling, and (2) define the areas in which the needs occur in individual children. The discussion, though extensive, is not exhaustive, and other sources (including but not exclusively those in the bibliography) should be consulted for further information and broader coverage.

SELF-SELECTION

Self-selection in guidance and counseling is based upon a very simple principle: *the child is often the best judge as to whether or not he needs assistance.* The commitment of the counselor to work with the self-selected child is based on a second simple principle: *the child most likely to benefit from a helping relationship is the child who is aware of his need.* Thus, when we want to determine who needs guidance and counseling we must not overlook the obvious: *let us ask the child.*

Self-selection, as the term is used here, goes beyond self-referral. Self-selection includes any and all methods by which a child conveys that he would like to discuss his interests, concerns, or problems with the counselor or teacher. Self-referral is the more formalized process by which a child asks for help.

Why does this matter merit special consideration? While self-selection is the common mode of operation for secondary school students and adults, the adults in the life of the child tend to make such decisions for him—to assume this responsibility. In 1959 Peters[1] suggested that elementary school children differed from secondary school children in three ways that might require others to make the referral decision: they are more dependent, they do not come to counseling ready to work on a concern, and they may not see as such the behaviors that adults view as indicating potential problems.

Since 1959, as elementary school guidance has been implemented in a great many schools, it has become more generally accepted for counselors and teachers to involve children in counseling and guidance via self-selection. Nonetheless, in many schools self-selection is avoided, either because its implementation is not understood or because counselor case loads preclude giving children much freedom to seek counseling on their own.

Biasco[2] has described a self-selection process much like the one below, which may readily be implemented by school counselors.

A method of self-referral often used is that of placing outside the counselor's office a mail box, a pad of paper, and a pencil so that children can request appointments for counseling. The counselor checks his mailbox frequently, sees the teacher to whom the child is assigned, and arranges the appointment at a time convenient for both teacher and child. One teacher in training as a counselor has posted a calendar in her room, on which a child can sign up for a conference before class in the morning or afternoon. Other children are requested to wait outside the room or on the playground until the five-minute warning bell sounds.

Much less formalized are the contacts in which a child slips his hand into the counselor's and chatters merrily or walks silently along the corridor or across the playground. The perceptive counselor at a suitable moment may state: "I think you're telling me that you'd like to come to my office and talk some time." If his perceptions are accurate, the counselor has become accessible beyond the setting up of a mail box.

Though a sign on the door is sufficient to make some children feel welcome, it is not enough to do so for others. Especially with younger

[1] Herman J. Peters, "Differential factors between elementary and secondary school counseling," *School Counselor, 1:* 3–11 (1959).

[2] Frank Biasco, "Encouraging self referrals in the elementary school," *School Counselor, 16:* 99–102 (1968).

children, the counselor increases his accessibility by being introduced or introducing himself before the classroom; by discussing his task in the school as a person to whom a child can go to talk about his interests, concerns, or problems; and by scheduling with the teacher opportunities whereby groups of five or six children, perhaps reading groups, can come to his office for brief visits. They can then become acquainted with the location, learn about the self-referral process, ask their questions, and sense in a deeper way the true degree of interest expressed in them as individuals by the counselor.

The teacher who would be accessible in similar ways must earnestly show himself willing to put aside other work, to ignore the clock for the specified period, and to become a better listener than teachers usually let themselves be.

Although the allotting of time is in itself important, success in maintaining accessibility is governed by the following principle: *accessibility to children is primarily an affective matter—it must be felt.*

VALIDITY OF SELF-SELECTION

Does self-selection do what it is intended to do? Can and do elementary children refer themselves? Do children perceived as needing assistance seek it? Does self-selection effectively supplement the more traditional referral practices current in most schools?

It is vital to consider whether self-selection is in fact a valid means of selecting students to receive help.

In the *Report of the 1965–66 Elementary Pilot Guidance Program,*[3] a program conducted in fifteen Indiana schools with National Defense Education Act funds, the five counselors who relied most on self-referrals reported that 85, 82, 60, 57, and 50 percent of their contacts, respectively, came from the children themselves. In another school none of the children were self-referred; however, the data from the first group of schools lends weight to the statement that children can and do refer themselves—and in their very first exposure to counseling.

Whether children perceived as needing counseling seek assistance is not so easy to answer in objective terms. In some classrooms every child shows an eagerness to talk with the counselor. Teachers frequently state their delight and surprise that the children whom they expected to see resist referral asked to talk to the counselor. But responsible adults, seeing a child in need, need not themselves stand idly by waiting for him to refer himself. It is certainly easier to work with a child needing counseling who refers himself, but encouragement can be given for self-referral by teachers

[3] Rolla F. Pruett, *Report of the 1965–66 Elementary Pilot Guidance Program,* Bulletin No. 253 (Indianapolis: Indiana State Department of Public Instruction, 1967).

and others—thus guaranteeing that the child who needs counseling gets assistance.

Several studies demonstrate that self-referral to some extent serves particular children. Esper[4] found that junior high school girls referred themselves more than did boys, and that those who marked more problems on a checklist more often referred themselves. Brough[5] found that children preferred a voluntary approach to counseling over a nonvoluntary one and that girls felt somewhat freer than boys to take advantage of the service. Tseng and Thompson[6] determined that children of higher socioeconomic level sought counseling more than did their lower-level counterparts. Finally, Pratte and Cole[7] noted that volunteers emerged from counseling with more positive perceptions of the experience than did nonvolunteers.

SUPPLEMENTING SELF-SELECTION

Depending somewhat on the counselor-pupil load, self-selection may supplement teacher referral, or teacher referral may supplement self-selection. Certainly for the greatest effect a combination of approaches should be used.

It seems especially desirable for the child to be referred when he is unaware of the service, when he has taken no action but he conveys the message that he may wish to receive help, or when he is genuinely unaware of a problem. In the latter event it is much more profitable to reserve referral for those children who might be expected to accept and understand the problem rather than to use up considerable time with children who are convinced no problem exists.

A variety of approaches may be used to involve the child in counseling—any of which should acknowledge his right to use or not to use the service. The teacher might suggest that the child refer himself. He might introduce the child to the counselor and ask whether he would be willing to talk with the counselor about the matter of concern. He might request that the counselor involve the child in a brief intake interview, acknowledging the concern and determining the willingness of the child to talk about it. He should *not* appear with the child at the door of the counselor's office

---

[4] George Esper, "Characteristics of junior high school students who seek counseling," *Personnel and Guidance Journal, 42:* 468–472 (1964).

[5] James R. Brough, "A comparison of self-referred counselees and non-counseled junior high school students," *Personnel and Guidance Journal, 47:* 329–332 (1968).

[6] Michael Tseng and Donald L. Thompson, "Differences between adolescents who seek counseling and those who do not," *Personnel and Guidance Journal, 47:* 333–336 (1968).

[7] Harold E. Pratte and Charles Cole, "Sources of referral and perception of the counselor," *Personnel and Guidance Journal, 44:* 292–294 (1965).

and say, "I don't want this child in my class until he straightens out! Do something with him!"

Self-selection is seen here as an appropriate supplement, even a prior commitment of the counselor, to traditional referral practices in the elementary school. It may be possible to enlarge the range of self-selected children by offering many opportunities for children to seek the counselor's services. A counselor may utilize (1) a mail box outside his office, (2) informal contacts with children in the halls and on the playground, (3) visits by small groups to the office, during which the self-referral process is described, (4) visits to the classroom, during which the counselor explains his functions and discusses self-referral, and (5) a variety of standardized and informal techniques that provide opportunities for the child to indicate his desire to discuss his concerns, interests, or problems.

Where such a broad-based self-selection program has been developed, the incidence of self-referrals by children who would be referred by the teacher is high. This program, supplemented by efforts of the counselor to educate teachers and others to "good referrals" and to the encouragement of self-selection, should fairly well assure that self-selection accomplishes the objectives set for it. The effective supplementing of self-selection depends in part on observation by teachers and others—a process that we shall now examine.

OBSERVATION

Peters, Shertzer and Van Hoose state: "Observation is a major part of living and learning about ourselves, others, and the world in which we live. To observe is a basic technique of science. Observation is also the foundational technique in guidance work. Every other technique and tool used in guidance work is an extension of our basic ability to observe."[8] Hutson notes: "In the service of . . . guidance, observation of behavior always has played and apparently always will play a major role. Teachers from time immemorial have observed the activity and the conduct of their pupils. To a certain extent they have commonly observed without understanding what they saw."[9]

Observation remains a frontier in elementary school guidance, since its potentiality for helping children has scarcely been tapped. Although observation is foundational to effective guidance, many incidents like the

[8] Herman J. Peters, Bruce Shertzer, and William Van Hoose, *Guidance in Elementary Schools* (Skokie, Ill.: Rand McNally, 1965), p. 87.

[9] Percival W. Hutson, *The Guidance Function in Education* (New York: Appleton-Century-Crofts, 1968), p. 378.

following escape the attention of the teacher or counselor, who may see them but not "let them in."

Susie put her head down when a boy in the class told about taking a trip with his family.

Archie hesitated at the doorway for several moments this morning —he used to come into the room just bubbling.

Alice tried to mention her new baby brother, but it happened during social studies and we didn't have time to listen.

Tommy seemed to be aching for trouble this morning, then he was absent this afternoon; maybe his dad is back and drunk again.

Teachers and counselors can ill afford not to take full advantage of observation of the child. As Willey points out: "From an objective, impersonal, reliable, and valid point of view tests are preferable to observation in gathering information about the child; yet their very objectivity and impersonal characteristics are their greatest weakness in studying the child as a dynamic human being. Although somewhat subjective, the method of direct observation of the child in real life action will give meaning to the data collected by formalized tests. Data from both sources are essential for complete understanding of the child."[10]

WHY OBSERVE? HOW?

Why is observation important? Hill and Luckey[11] suggest two reasons: (1) the adults who live with and work with children need to know them, and (2) children need to know and understand themselves. In addition, observation and subsequent discussion may contribute to the guidance of children by (1) pointing up the needs for child guidance; (2) pointing up directions for guidance and counseling to take: the place, time, activity, persons present, and apparent cause of a difficulty may well provide the major clues to developing a solution; (3) providing evidence of growth over time in all children; (4) pointing up the success or failure of techniques in use with particular children; (5) bringing teachers and counselors into meaningful communication with one another in the interests of children.

Teachers and counselors are engaged continually in the process of making informal observations. Thorndike and Hagen[12] urge that at least

[10] Roy DeVerl Willey, *Guidance in Elementary Education* (New York: Harper & Row, 1960), pp. 64–65.

[11] George E. Hill and Eleanore B. Luckey, *Guidance for Children in Elementary Schools* (New York: Appleton-Century-Crofts, 1969).

[12] Robert L. Thorndike and Elizabeth Hagen, *Measurement and Evaluation in Psychology and Education* (New York: Wiley, 1961).

some of these observations be made on an organized, directed, and systematic basis. These writers suggest that a particular behavior be selected for observation (aggressiveness, for example); that the behavior be defined and specified (e.g., hitting, kicking, name-calling); that, where possible, observers be trained in practice sessions so that categorization of behaviors is agreed upon (videotapes could be reviewed for the training of observational acuity); that observations be quantified (counting the occurrence of aggressive acts as defined) and the circumstances noted; and that procedures be developed for recording of observations (e.g., tally sheets, charts or graphs, and coding procedures).

Organizing for observations can help overcome several of the limitations observed by Thorndike and Hagen.[13] The whole undertaking must be realistic in terms of numbers of children to be observed and amount of time to be spent in observation. Observers can be fitted into the setting if they include teachers and familiar counselors, and if the task can be made specific, the observers can include children themselves. Subjectivity and bias cannot be factored out entirely but can be reduced by attempts at recording observations objectively, at devising a program of scheduled observations, and at specifying the behaviors to be observed. The limitation inherent in selecting meaningful behaviors for observation can, in part, be overcome by careful categorization of specific behaviors.

Advantages inherent in observational procedures include the following: they involve a record of actual behavior, as against behavior set up and tested at a particular point in time; they are especially useful with young children, who may be more active than verbal in presenting their concerns; and they may be conducted in natural settings, including the classroom, the playground, and the home.

SPECIFIC OBSERVATIONAL PRACTICES

Soar sees in observation the potentiality for a breakthrough that will permit effective teaching to become a science. He notes: ". . . a teacher who knows an observation system—who has a feedback loop established—teaches differently than one who does not. It seems likely that the major advances of the future are likely to come from . . . the use of systematic observation as a research measure and as a source of feedback."[14] Teachers have unique opportunities for limited systematic observations that may help them in their work as well as helping the child in his need.

The anecdotal record and more specific techniques such as diary description and time and event sampling can be useful in the accurate recording of observations. Wright, in the *Handbook of Research Methods*

[13] *Ibid.*
[14] Robert S. Soar, "Research finding from systematic observation," *Journal of Research and Development in Education, 4:* 116–121 (1970).

in Child Development,[15] gives an informative summary of observational techniques. Several techniques that may help optimize the use of observation are described below.

THE ANECDOTAL RECORD   The anecdotal record, although often biased in its selection of incidents to report, is nonetheless a useful tool. Anecdotal records are prepared when there is a valid purpose—for example, that of clarifying the child's degree of social adjustment or the kinds of situations in which the child shows interest—and when the behavior to be observed is sufficiently specified so that observations may be made.

Anecdotal records that integrate both observations and interpretations are considered undesirable, since they do not allow the reader his own interpretation. For this reason it is considered appropriate for an anecdote to be reported in at least two, often three, separate parts. The observation is first objectively reported, excluding all evaluative terms; then the interpretation is given; and, where appropriate, recommendations follow. Care is taken to include such identifying information as the place, time, activity, persons present, apparent cause, and the words and behavior of the child observed.

SAM—ANECDOTAL RECORD

OBSERVATION   Nine fifteen, Mr. Aid's fifth grade classroom. All present. Sam raised his hand several times and I called on him three times today in social studies during our discussion of the Suez Canal. The first time he asked: "Are there lots of sunk ships still in the canal?" The second time he said: "It used to be that ships had to go about five thousand miles extra around before they had the canal." The third time he said: "My brother's ship used to go through the canal lots and lots." I said after the third comment, "You really seem interested in our discussion of the Suez Canal today, and pleased that your brother has been through it." He smiled and nodded.

INTERPRETATION   Sam seemed to be trying especially hard to make his comments relevant to the topic this morning. He was interested but willing to let me call on other children, and when he did comment, his comments contributed. Our talk yesterday seems to have helped.

RECOMMENDATION   Sam needs the attention of the group. I plan to make every effort to incorporate his comments and compliment him on their relevance, where appropriate. Since our conference showed immediate results, perhaps a few moments alone with him now and then will be helpful. It's been hard for him to figure out what frustrates me and the class

[15] Herbert F. Wright, "Observational Child Study," in Paul H. Mussen, ed., *Handbook of Research Methods in Child Development* (New York: Wiley, 1960).

members about his irrelevancies. Perhaps talking about that will continue to help.

DIARY DESCRIPTIONS Diary descriptions may be general in character or may focus on a particular behavior. The former involves day-to-day notations about a given child's general attitude and behavior, the latter, a day-to-day record of specific behaviors. The two examples that follow should illustrate the differences.

TERRY—DIARY DESCRIPTION—GENERAL

Feb. 21   Terry participated actively in art class and in social studies, but she sat almost motionless during arithmetic and spelling.

Feb. 23   Terry played actively but alone on the playground during recess.

Feb. 24   Terry coughed a lot today. She leaned forward and listened and worked at her arithmetic and spelling for several minutes each.

Feb. 25   Terry was absent today. Her brother came by for her arithmetic and spelling book.

TONY—DIARY DESCRIPTION—ARGUMENTATIVE BEHAVIOR

April 3   Tony interrupted Sue today to correct her pronunciation of "Mediranean." He laughed and pointed when Joel was called out trying to steal second base. Joel's comment: "You couldn't do any better," was followed by an endless "Yes I can."—"No you can't." Then Tony got a hit and "stole" second on an error. At the end of the day the boys were still arguing and glaring at one another.

April 4   No arguments today.

April 5   Tony walked in saying, "That looks dumb," referring to the mural in process by one of the science committees. He interrupted to help with the pronunciation of words four times in reading. He criticized extensively on the playground. He fussed about our staying in at noon: "A little shower won't hurt us. Nobody'll melt. Can't those of us who want to go out?" He was told no and then muttered for a long time. I talked to him at recess in the afternoon, but he just argued throughout and I feel I got nowhere.

April 6   No arguments today.

April 7   It would take hours to write out my observations today. From the time he walked in until he left today Tony was in one continually changing argument. Since fussing and discussing have accomplished nothing I called Tony's mother and told her that starting Monday I plan to use, and get the class to use, an ignoring technique on argumentative statements and an attention-giving technique on more reasonable aspects of Tony's participation. His mother said she would try the same thing since the problem is worse at home.

April 10   The class agreed to cooperate by trying not to respond to Tony's argumentative comments. Tony criticized, interrupted, and otherwise attempted to undermine the resolve at least fifty times (by actual tally). I broke the resolve once, but the children did better.

April 11   Tony dominated discussion, and received lots of positive reinforcement. He seems to have decided to play another game, but this is one that I seem able to tolerate and that the children enjoy.

April 12   Tony went back to being argumentative today, but his innumerable attempts seemed to be less forceful and of shorter duration.

TIME AND EVENT SAMPLING   In an attempt to further objectify observations, time and event sampling involves periodic observations at preset intervals, whereas event sampling occurs every time a particular behavior is observed. Behaviors that are constant may be subjected to time-sampling scrutiny, whereas less frequent behaviors may be observed through event sampling.

Both procedures benefit from (1) careful definition of the behavior to be observed (e.g., aggressiveness, cooperation, anger, talkativeness, social interaction, oral habits, and the like), and (2) careful definition and analysis of the situation of the occurrence. Time sampling benefits from (3) careful control of times during which the behavior is observed.

JOSEPH—TIME SAMPLING (SOCIAL INTERACTION DURING SOCIAL STUDIES COMMITTEE SCHEDULE)

October 18
   11:10   Looked at book during discussion.
   11:15   Lifted lid of desk up, rested it on head while looking in.
   11:20   Stared at floor near feet.
   11:25   Did not look up when chairman mentioned his name.
October 19
   11:10   Looked at floor near feet.
   11:15   Asked Susie a question in whisper. She smiled and whispered back.
   11:20   Looked at chairman as he talked.
   11:25   Stared at book on desk.
October 20
   11:10   Susie showed him something in magazine. He sat closer to her.
   11:15   Watched Susie as she talked in group.

11:20 Susie (prearranged) had asked to borrow his red marking pen. At this time he was watching her use it.

11:25 Began a small drawing and crumpled it.

SARA—EVENT SAMPLING (OBSERVATIONS RELATING TO ANGER)

May 3

10:05 Became very angry when the boys lined up first for recess.

11:10 Raised hand in social studies while others were talking. When called on later, she said, "Never mind." She slouched in her chair and pouted.

12:00 Tried to shove to head of line of girls. Ethel pushed her back. She whispered, "Damn you, Ethel," and went back and sat down.

May 4

8:10 Slammed the classroom door and went to the restroom. I tried to talk with her when she returned. "Never mind," she said.

8:28 Broke her pencil point in arithmetic, threw it on the floor and sat with her head in her hands.

9:04 Interrupted report to ask, "May I go to the restroom?" I told her, "I'd prefer you to hear this report first, but you *may* leave." She sat back down and pouted and didn't leave until recess at 10:05.

9:15 Asked her if she needed to use the restroom. She turned away from me and said, "Never mind."

Wright describes Specimen Description as another procedure that may be of use: "This method begins with the scheduled and continuous observing and narrative recording of a behavior sequence under chosen conditions of time and life setting. . . . [T]he observer in the field is deliberately unselective in the sense that he aims to make a faithful recording of "everything" as it comes in the behavior and situation of the child."[16] This, of course, necessitates the presence of an observer who is not engaged in classroom activity, perhaps the counselor, school psychologist, or counselor aide, whereas several of the other techniques may be handled by one individual.

INFORMAL ASSESSMENT PROCEDURES

OBJECTIVES

Informal procedures and observation alike enhance adult understanding of children, yield developmental data, and help in the selection of

[16] *Ibid.*, pp. 83–84.

children for counseling or referral. Informal procedures also provide a direct and valuable basis of discussion in counseling with individual children.

Searching questions, however, must be asked about the use of informal procedures. Do we have the child's and his parents' consent to gather the information planned? Is the child aware of the data-gathering activity? If he is not, is the collection truly in his interests? Is privacy being invaded? Is the information elicited representative of the child's true feelings and thoughts, or is he giving what he thinks he should, what will shock us, or what will put us "off the track?" What will be done with the data? Will the material collected remain in the permanent record, or will it be pruned by the teacher or counselor in the interests of the maturing child? Use of such instruments with children demands awareness of these questions.

While the clinical psychologist needs to use devices to categorize, diagnose, and prescribe treatment, the elementary school counselor or teacher may be satisfied with informal instruments that provide bases for communication with children. His purpose is to obtain a clearer picture of the child and the group, not to engage in psychodiagnosis.

In the appropriate chapter much more will be said on the matter of referral. Let us note here that a counselor or teacher should permit himself the luxury of feeling a deep concern for an individual child, sensing the need to refer him to a psychologist or psychiatrist for assistance, without obliging himself to diagnose the problem first. His observations and information should be included in the referral material, but his application of psychodiagnostic terminology should generally be avoided.

Thus, when he uses informal procedures, the counselor or teacher is attempting to observe and know the child more deeply. He may find these procedures useful, interesting, and a valuable basis for discussion with the child, but he should not overrate their clinical value.

CHILD-COMPLETED INFORMAL PROCEDURES

Following the assumption of projective instruments, that people tend to read qualities of their own into amorphous situations, it may be assumed that many informal procedures generally elicit similar self-giving responses. Thorndike and Hagen state: "Psychologists have long recognized that the perceiving of even quite definite stimuli—an accident, a scene staged before a class, the content of a picture—is dependent upon the individual perceiver. He sees what he is set to see. The report reflects his readiness and predisposition."[17]

Children can be understood more adequately, and insight into specific concerns often may be obtained, through a variety of informal pro-

[17] Thorndike and Hagen, *op. cit.,* p. 422.

cedures: the autobiography, the diary, sentence completion, story telling and completion, wishes of children, the questionnaire, sociometrics, guess-who devices, work samples including drawings, and self-concept, inter-personal closeness, and other measures.

THE AUTOBIOGRAPHY Willey notes that "The autobiography has always been a useful diagnostic and therapeutic tool in psychiatry"[18] and goes on to discuss its usefulness in elementary school guidance. Shertzer and Peters[19] distinguish between an autobiography and a biographical inventory by noting that the autobiography is less specific in its requirements. The autobiography, in fact, may be either somewhat structured or totally unstructured.

In encouraging children to greater breadth and depth in the writing of the autobiography, it may be helpful to read to them several examples of brief autobiographies complete with emotionally oriented and personally significant materials. After discussion by the children, some of the key points of discussion could be written on a blackboard or dittoed. The children could then consider the key events in their lives for a few days. Later, with all stimulus materials removed, they would begin to write their autobiographies.

Here is a sample of the beginning of an autobiography which could be read to an upper level elementary school class.

AUTOBIOGRAPHY OF AN ORPHAN

You know who your parents are. If you are lucky, they held you when you were a baby, they changed your diapers, they picked you up when you cried, they took you to the doctor when you were sick, and you knew someone cared.

Maybe my mother cared. Maybe she was poor, or died in an accident, or didn't have a husband, and maybe it broke her heart to leave me on the steps of a church when I was only a few weeks old, but I'll never know.

My adopted mother tells me she felt *I* was the one who needed her most when she first saw me when I was about a year old. She hadn't intended to adopt a baby. Hers were almost grown. She did adopt me, though.

The most glorious thing in my life was, and I guess is, to have a mother, a father, two older brothers, a name, and a birthday. No one knows exactly when I was born, but Mom and Dad gave me a birthday.

You had to take the day when you were born, but my folks looked at the calendar, took the doctor's guess as to how old I was, found a spot

[18] Willey, *op. cit.,* p. 74.
[19] Bruce Shertzer and Herman J. Peters, *Guidance: Techniques for Individual Appraisal and Development* (New York: Macmillan, 1965).

between holidays and other family birthdays and they picked out May Third. What a day!

One approach would be to have children take turns using a tape recorder and "talk" their autobiography, then jot down notes on replay and begin to draft the actual document.

THE DIARY   Willey[20] tells of a class that kept diaries over a period of time, providing much information that could be of great value to a teacher or counselor. The general procedure suggested for the autobiography could be advantageously followed here: providing samples, discussing appropriate and valuable entries, and then starting. A sample might be the following:

DIARY ENTRIES FOR WEEK OF OCTOBER 20

10–20   We spent a quiet Sunday at home. No one dropped in, and the weather was dreary so we stayed inside. I thought and thought about something to write tonight and I finally decided that I'd just say that it's hard to write when you don't do anything.

10–21   We were discussing geography at school and I remember drifting off in my thoughts as currents became currants and currant pie became a ship and I began to sail to some of the tropical islands. It's funny how I can sometimes know all that's going on and still have my own thoughts. Miss Jackson called on me and I knew the answer, then I went right back to my thoughts.

10–22   Sometimes I'm just mean to other kids. I don't want to be, but I just am. S—— showed her buck teeth and I wanted to say something worse than I did. I called her Bucky. I could see the tears in her eyes and I just got worse and called her it more. Afterwards I wished she had called me something, then maybe we could make friends.

10–23   . . . .

SENTENCE COMPLETION   Formal instruments such as the Rotter Incomplete Sentences Blank and the Rhode-Hildreth Sentence Completion Blank have been commercially prepared, and detailed scoring keys have been developed in those instruments for clinical purposes. However, a brief homemade sentence completion form may yield valuable insight into children's thinking; if used as an interview procedure, it offers a way of getting into contact with children. In the sample that follows, material in parentheses was dictated by a child as part of an interview. Counselor comments are in brackets.

[20] Willey, *op. cit.*

SENTENCE COMPLETION

1. I wish . . . (I could do better school work).
2. My sister . . . (is a pest—always getting into my things).
3. I would like to . . . (get out of school quick).
4. I like . . . (to have good friends).
5. My mother . . . (is nice but she always talks about my school work and says you can do better. And I can't.)
6. Boys my age . . . (think I can't do things). [Can't do things like . . .] (Like play baseball and football and do school work.)
7. When I grow up . . . (I'd like to be a race driver because I watch the 500 and they go so fast). [Do you think you'll get to do that?] (No, probably just work at some job in a factory. Same thing all day.) [You wouldn't like that.] (No!)

A long discussion followed at this point between Charles and the counselor. They resolved to devote part of the counseling time to looking for some jobs that a boy who "don't do good school work" could do. The remainder of the sentence completion was saved for a future meeting.

STORY TELLING AND STORY COMPLETION   Story telling, writing, dictating, and recording may be used in innumerable ways. Magazine pictures of a confrontation, a child crying, a child engrossed in school work or an athletic activity, and the like, may create a stimulus; or perhaps none may be needed. Stories with emotional themes such as fear, anger, love, prejudice, happiness, despair, loneliness, and success may provide much insight into children's outlook and at the same time give them an outlet for their feelings.

Any emphasis on grades, spelling, or correct expression will surely inhibit the production of many children. "This is a time you can write (or tell) the story just the way you feel it should be. We can think about corrections *if* you want to put your story on the bulletin board. Otherwise you won't have to concern yourself about that."

Following are two examples of story completion themes, which may be handled orally or in writing.

MY LUCKY DAY

I was kicking leaves as I walked down the street one pretty October day. The leaves were red, gold, and orange and brown and they made a crackling sound as I kicked them or stepped on them.

As I turned the corner at Fourth and Main there was an especially big pile that someone had swept together. I didn't want to scatter the pile, but I did walk through it and I felt something more solid than leaves move as I touched it. It felt like it just might be a tiny animal, so I fished into the leaves and picked it up.

I had found a thick wallet. It had a good deal of money in it—about eighty-five dollars. The cards in it all showed it belonged to Jerome Jones of 18 West Mulberry. (You complete the story.)

THE GLASS IN THE PICTURE

Mrs. Thompson had been called out of the room to take a long distance telephone call. Tim got playful with Sam after his work was completed and tossed his baseball to him. Sam threw back a perfect strike, but Tim hit his elbow on the desk and the ball went past him.

Crash! A family picture which Mrs. Thompson kept on her desk fell to the floor. Tim rushed over and looked. The glass was broken, and it looked like the picture was cut.

"Boy, Mrs. Thompson will sure be mad at you, Tim," said Sam.

"If you don't tell her she'll never know who did it," said Tim.

Tim glared at the rest of the class, "None of you better tell either. Just leave it there. Nobody knows what happened, see!"

The class was quiet for a moment and footsteps could be heard coming down the hall. It sounded like Mrs. Thompson. (You complete the story.)

WISHES OF CHILDREN   "The needs of children are frequently expressed through their wishes," Willey notes,[21] and he suggests that these wishes may be discovered through questionnaires, observation, informal discussion, written compositions, and creative art work. Cottingham notes that a guidance-oriented individual can easily devise his own items and group them into categories appropriate for the grade level. Items from a New Castle, Indiana, check list of wishes that Cottingham reprinted are shown here as examples (Figure 4–1).[22]

QUESTIONNAIRES   Tremendous varieties of information can be elicited by professionally constructed and teacher- or counselor-prepared questionnaires. Attitudes may be assessed, interests ascertained, and patterns of real and ideal behaviors may be polled. Questionnaires may also be useful in conveying interest in the child. While the reliability and validity of responses may be questioned, and intensity of feelings, concerns, or interests often cannot be accurately ascertained, nonetheless the statements involved may be extremely useful as a basis for communication with a child.

One guidance class, planning to observe third through fifth grade children and interview them in an inner-city setting, helped to construct

[21] *Ibid.*, p. 77.
[22] From Harold F. Cottingham, *Guidance in Elementary Schools* (Bloomington, Ill.: McKnight, 1956), pp. 50–51.

<u>My Wishing Star</u>

Star light, star bright,
First star I see tonight
I wish I may, I wish I might
Have the wish I wish tonight.

Wishes about Home

4. I wish my family noticed when I did things right.
6. I wish I could help to plan things.
13. I wish I did not have so much to do.

Wishes about School

5. I wish my classmates liked me.
6. I wish I were not afraid to speak up in class.
7. I wish I knew how to study.

Wishes about Myself

2. I wish I could do more things without having people tell me what to do.
3. I wish I did not worry about things.
6. I wish I were not afraid of being criticized.

Wishes about Play

1. I wish I had someone to play with after school.
3. I wish I played games so well that children would want me on their side.
4. I wish my friends wanted to play the games I want to play.

Wishes about People

3. I wish people did not hurt my feelings.
4. I wish people did not tease me.
5. I wish people liked me.

FIGURE 4–1 *Check List of Wishes*

the accompanying questionnaire (Figure 4–2) and found it useful. Those interviewers who seemed to gain the most from it departed from the questions, discussed answers to particular questions, and felt no need to complete the entire document. Thus it became a vehicle for communication and exploration.

SOCIOMETRICS AND RELATED DEVICES   Barr states: "Social growth has been accepted as a responsibility of the educational pattern. As a part

PERSONAL DATA INTERVIEW SCHEDULE

ALL INFORMATION IS TO BE FILLED IN BY INTERVIEWER

Father's Occupation_____

Mother's Occupation_____

Number of Brothers_____ How many older?_____ How many younger?_____

Number of Sisters_____ How many older?_____ How many younger?_____

Are there any other people living in your home?_____

Do you have your own room?_____

AT THIS POINT IT SHOULD BE EXPLAINED THAT THE REST OF THE QUESTIONS ARE TO BE ANSWERED BY THE STUDENTS FINISHING THE STATEMENTS. THE INTERVIEWER IS TO RECORD ANSWERS. CIRCLE CHOICES.

My spending money comes from_____

My hobby is_____

I like to do this because_____

My favorite way of spending after school time is_____

_____

On my last vacation I_____

At home I have to_____

I (like) (don't like) this because_____

One thing I sometimes worry about is_____

When I have done something wrong I usually_____

_____

The best thing about a brother or sister is_____

I (would) (would not) rather be an only child because_____

_____

If I got a low grade on a test my parents would_____

BECAUSE_____

Some things my family does all together are_____

_____

FIGURE 4–2 *Personal Data Interview Schedule*

When I grow up my parents would like for me to be a_____._____

_____

I think my parents (do) (do not) expect too much of me because_____

_____

I like to discuss my troubles with_____BECAUSE_____

_____

I'm sure my friends generally think my ideas are (good) (not good) because_____

_____

Talking to people I don't know is (easy) (hard) for me because_____

_____

My best friends are (boys) (girls) because_____

I (am) (am not) friendly with my classmates because_____

_____

I have (many) (few) friends because_____

_____

If a new boy or girl sat next to me in class I would_____

_____

I prefer to play with (other children) (toys) (pets) because_____

_____

If I could be anyone or anything in the world I would like to be_____

_____BECAUSE_____

I (could) (could not) be like that person or thing because_____

_____

I (like) (don't like) being the age I am because_____

_____

I like best to play (with a large group of children) (with a small group of children) (by myself) because_____

_____

The best way I know to have fun is_____

I (wish) (don't wish) I played an instrument because_____

_____

I (wish) (don't wish) I had a sister or brother my age because_____

_____

FIGURE 4-2 (Continued)

I (wish) (don't wish) my parents could spend more time with me because_____

_____

If I had $100 to do with as I please I would_____

_____

My favorite subject is_____BECAUSE_____

_____

I (do) (don't) get bored during class time because_____

_____

Books that have a lot of pictures are_____

_____

I (do) (don't) like to play outside during recess because_____

_____

I'm (glad) (sorry) I have to go to school because_____

_____

In school my teacher is_____

I (do) (don't) study and work for good grades because_____

_____

If I were the only one who saw somebody cheat on a test, I would_____

_____

BECAUSE_____

Tests make me feel_____

The worst thing about school is_____

_____

The best book I have ever read is_____

I liked it because_____

I like_____

What bothers me most is_____

I hate_____

I (like) (dislike) being a (boy) (girl) because_____

_____

When people tell me I am wrong and I know I'm right I_____

_____

FIGURE 4–2 (Continued)

ASK THE CHILD TO READ THE FOLLOWING ITEM ALOUD AND THEN CHECK THE ANSWER HE
PREFERS. COMMENT ON READING BELOW THE QUESTION.

I WOULD RATHER:

    A. Have people on the street notice me because   A._____
        I am good looking.

    B. Have people on the street notice me because   B._____
        I am nicely dressed.

    C. Not have people notice me at all.   C._____

COMMENTS:

ANY OTHER ITEM MAY BE PLACED ON BACK OF THIS SHEET

FIGURE 4–2 (Continued)

of that social growth people are continually exhibiting preferences for some individual and not for others. Sociometry has recognized this fact and has provided means for helping teachers better understand interpersonal relationships."[23]

Generally a sociometric device asks questions such as the following:

Which three members of your class would you like to have sit beside you?

Which three members of your class would you like to be with on a committee?

Which three members of your class would you like to invite to a small party at your own home?

[23] John A. Barr, *The Elementary Teacher and Guidance* (New York: Holt, Rinehart and Winston, Inc., 1958), p. 144.

Chosen

Chooser	Ada	Betty	Charlene	Donna	...	Al	Bruce	Carl	Dick
1. Ada		X	X	X	...				
2. Betty	X				...				X
3. Charlene	X				...			X	
4. Donna		X			...	X			
1. Al			X	X	...				
2. Bruce					...	X			X
3. Carl				X	...	X			
4. Dick					...	X	X		
Total	2	2	2	3		4	2	0	2

FIGURE 4–3   *Top, A Sociometric Chart; Bottom, The Resulting Sociogram*

Moreno,[24] who developed this procedure, has shown how to chart and diagram the results of such questions.

As the sample sociometric chart and sociogram (Figure 4–3) demonstrates, usually some children are chosen frequently and others perhaps not at all. Al was chosen by Donna, Bruce, Carl, and Dick, thus becoming a *star* in sociometric terminology in relation to this group. Carl, having received no choices, may be considered an *isolate*.

To facilitate diagramming the choices, the most chosen students, Donna and Al, were placed near the center. Also, since boys and girls in the elementary school more often choose from among same-sex members of their class, there tends to be an advantage in grouping boys on one side of the page and girls on the other side.

[24] J. L. Moreno, *Who Shall Survive?* (New York: Beacon House, 1934).

The value of the sociogram is that it reflects the general cohesiveness within the classroom and points up cliques, mutual choices, stars, isolates, and near isolates. It is highly advantageous that sociometric data be acted upon—for example, in selecting or changing seating patterns in the classroom—rather than being collected merely for the information of the counselor or teacher.

Barr[25] points out that asking children to make friendship choices is not requesting something new, since children make such choices in the regular course of their activities. He also contends that teachers and others are influenced by the way children get along with adults and may make errors in judgment about the way they get along with each other. This supplemental information can be useful to counselor and teacher alike. For example, a child may be interested in moving into a clique that is closed to him. If this closure is made apparent through a sociogram, relevant discussions may be held with the child, the group, or both.

It is tempting to ask negative questions: Which three members of your class would you prefer *not* to work with, sit by, go to a movie with, and so on. Certainly such information is relevant. If such questions are made optional, they are less likely to draw the criticism of parents that negative ideas are being planted. For example, the question might be stated as: If there are any persons in your classroom you would prefer not to work with (or whatever), please list their names here. Wherever practicable, however, requests for negative selections should be restricted to research projects.

A device closely related to sociometrics is the *social distance scale*. Here each student is asked to rate everyone else in his class on a scale consisting usually of three or more points that are descriptive in nature. This device has the advantage of demonstrating small increments in group cohesiveness and in individual acceptance within the group. At the same time it seems advantageous to limit its use generally to answering research questions.

In the sample social distance scale shown here (Figure 4–4) it is apparent that Gage feels very positive toward Wayne, somewhat positive toward Tom, rather neutral toward the three girls whose names are shown, and somewhat negative toward Bob. A second administration of this device in a classroom that had become more generally cohesive might yield generally more positive ratings throughout the class.

Johnston, Peters, and Evraiff present a six-point Social Distance Scale as follows:

1. My very, very best friends.
2. My other friends.
3. Not friends, but okay.

[25] Barr, *op. cit.*

MY CLASSMATES

Directions: 1. Draw a line all the way across the page through your name.	2. Make a check (√) or x (X) by the name of every person in the class to show how you feel about them.				
	1 My <u>best</u> friends	2 Good friends	3 Not friends but OK	4 Don't know them	5 Others in the room
Tom A.		X			
Susie B.			X		
Wayne C.	X				
Alice D.			X		
Sherry E.			X		
~~Gage F.~~					
Bob G.					X
. . .					

FIGURE 4–4   *Social Distance Scale*

4. Don't know them.
5. Don't care for them.
6. Dislike them.[26]

For their purposes they suggest each individual become anonymous by rating himself with a number four (4); in this way, although all children are rated, no child's personal ratings are evident.

Social distance scales are unwieldy to summarize, and they fail to clarify the cliques within a classroom, yet in certain research they may have distinct advantages in showing children's gain or loss of social acceptance within groups.

GUESS-WHO TESTS   Instruments containing a number of questions beginning "Guess who . . ." have come to be known as guess-who tests or devices. They provide another way of examining social acceptance within classroom groups. They have the advantage of specifying peer perceptions, so that more information is obtained about the individual child who is negatively perceived, but they are extremely difficult to summarize.

Johnston, Peters, and Evraiff criticize the guess-who device, perhaps overrating the observational powers of the teacher (or counselor):

[26] Edgar J. Johnston, Mildred Peters, and William Evraiff, *The Role of the Teacher in Guidance* (Englewood Cliffs, N.J.: Prentice-Hall, 1959), p. 173.

Although this type of instrument will reveal the highly chosen and the rejected, it will not reveal any more than the sociometric and the data are harder to process. The qualities that are brought out in the items can be observed in the behavior of the children anyway, and the level of generality does not tell us specifically what the group members really do, and how they relate to one another on a sub-group level.[27]

Despite such criticisms, which cannot be ignored, there may be valid uses for guess-who devices. For example, a counselor might find highly meaningful the reporting of results to individual children who are interested. But obviously such devices must be used sensitively, with caution and understanding.

Some items that might be included in a guess-who device are:

1. Guess who is the happiest girl in the room. She always has a smile and seems to like everyone.
2. Guess who is the "gloomy Gus" around the classroom. He never seems happy and is often grouchy.
3. Guess who is the best student among the girls in the class. She often seems able to come up with an answer when no one else can.
4. Guess who is the best sport among the boys. He may not always win, but that doesn't "get him down."
5. Guess who is the girl who is a pest. She never seems to stop talking and is always bothering someone.

Johnson, Stefflre, and Edelfelt[28] present a guess-who device in the form of a casting technique for an imaginary class play. On the basis of descriptive statements somewhat like the above, children are asked to cast the parts of a well-liked boy and girl, a mean person, someone to whom no one pays attention, a know-it-all, and so on. They then are asked to cast themselves in a part, indicate what part the teacher would select for them, and tell what part other children would pick them to play.

As these same writers state: "The analysis of this information obviously needs to be tempered with caution, and the material is best used in conjunction with data gathered by other means."[29]

WORK AND ACTIVITY SAMPLES In the consideration of informal procedures that may suggest guidance needs in the child, the obvious should not be overlooked. Through his compositions, drawings, written assignments, musical participation, physical activity, and the like, the child is telling us much about himself. Alertness to his work and activity may point

27 *Ibid.*, p. 174.
28 Walter F. Johnson, Buford B. Stefflre, and Roy A. Edelfelt, *Pupil Personnel and Guidance Services* (New York: McGraw-Hill, 1961), p. 277.
29 *Ibid.*

up needs for guidance and counseling or for medical assistance (such as glasses or physical examination), and on the other hand may show signs of progress and development.

Willey[30] suggests that cumbersome productions by the child (such as flower arrangements, woodwork or metalwork products) be photographed, dated, and the photographs filed along with dated compositions, drawings, arithmetic papers, and the like, since grade-to-grade comparisons of these items may be very valuable in demonstrating progress made by individual children.

SELF-CONCEPT, INTERPERSONAL CLOSENESS, AND OTHER MEASURES Some formal scales dealing with self-concept have been developed, but for the teacher or counselor who wants a brief measure that provides a point of departure for discussion with the child or an insight into feelings generally present in a classroom, informal, homemade devices may meet these needs.

Figure 4–5 is an example of an individually administered device of this type, extending the mirror technique used by many counselors. Figure 4–6 represents another kind of device that may be used to determine how a child sees himself.

The concept of interpersonal closeness needs to be examined. We need to know not only how the group responds to the child, but how the child feels he is accepted by the group. Such measures have not been extensively developed. To assess general reactions and provide a basis for discussion with children, the interpersonal closeness scale shown in Figure 4–7 may be useful.

The interpersonal closeness scale may, of course, be expanded to include mother, father, neighborhood children, other relatives, grandparents, and so on.

Other measures of great variety may be constructed and used to obtain rough indices of children's attitudes, understandings, knowledges, fears, hopes. Such measures, though lacking in statistical sophistication, may be well justified by their use to facilitate adult-child communication.

ADULT-COMPLETED INFORMAL PROCEDURES

Much can be gained through informal assessment procedures completed by adults. Along with interviews and observational reports, a whole host of devices may be used by teachers and counselors to assess development within individual children and within groups. We shall consider here

---

[30] *Op. cit.,* pp. 114–116.

[31] Adapted from F. P. Kilpatrick and H. Cantril, "Self-anchoring scaling, a measure of individuals' unique reality worlds," *Journal of Individual Psychology, 16:* 158–173 (1960).

SELF-CONCEPT INVENTORY

1. Pretend (imagine) you are out-of-doors and lots of other girls and boys your age are in an active game.
   What do you do?

   Do you have a good time?

   Do you know how to play the game?

   Do other children want you to play?

   Do you like what you do when others are playing?

2. Pretend (imagine) you have to be with many boys and girls you don't know.
   What do you do?

   Do you have a good time?

   Do you make friends?

   Do the other children like you?

   Do you like what you do when you have to be with other boys and girls you don't know?

3. Pretend (imagine) you have to clean up a big yard or a big house.
   Do you get it done?

   Do you like doing it?

   Do you like what you do when you have a big job like that?

4. Pretend (imagine) you are in a school room and you have many hard things to do.
   Do you get them done?

   Do you like doing them?

   Do you like what you got done?

FIGURE 4–5 *Self-concept Inventory*

5. Pretend (imagine) you are asked to tell a story in front of your class. What do you do?

   Do you have a good time?

   Do you know what to say?

   Do you like what you say?

   Do other people like what you say?

6. Pretend (imagine) you see a little boy or girl all alone and crying. What do you do?

   Do you know how to help?

   Do you like what you do when you see a little child crying?

7. Pretend (imagine) you are sent to the store and you lost the money on the way. What do you do?

   What do your parents do?

   Do you like what you did after you lost the money?

8. Pretend (imagine) there is a mirror in front of you. Look at yourself in that mirror and tell me what you see.

   How do you like what you see?

   How do other people like what they see?

   If you could change anything about your looks or yourself in general, what would you change? Why?

FIGURE 4–5   (Continued)

the structured interview and such devices as rating scales and the semantic differential.

INTERVIEWS   Both structured and unstructured interviews may be used to gather data and obtain a level of interpersonal interaction with both parent and child. The former uses as the focus for the discussion a group of questions prepared in advance. The latter may be characterized by a freewheeling discussion that varies according to the presses and interests of the moment, although there may be a central focus.

Name _____ Grade _____ School _____

SELF-DESCRIPTION

Circle the words on each line which describe you best or circle the "?" if you
are undecided.

IN SCHOOL:

I am a leader	?	I am a follower
I am a hard worker	?	I am lazy
I am fast finishing things	?	I am slow
I am nervous	?	I am calm
I am likeable	?	I am not likeable
I am interested	?	I am bored
I am happy	?	I am gloomy
I am noisy	?	I am quiet
I am easily discouraged	?	I keep at the work
I have enough friends	?	I don't have enough friends

AT HOME:

I am hard-working	?	I am lazy
I am happy	?	I am gloomy
I am sociable	?	I am alone
I am quick-tempered	?	I am slow to anger
I am often upset	?	I am calm
I am helpful	?	I am not helpful

WITH OTHER CHILDREN:

I am unhappy	?	I am happy
I am easily upset	?	I am calm
I am bored	?	I am interested
I am a follower	?	I am a leader
I am well-liked	?	I am not well-liked
I am shy	?	I am bold

In general, I am a person who is _____

I would like to be a person who is _____

Circle the jobs you would really like when you are grown up. Draw a line through
the jobs you would not like when you are grown up.

> Nurse, doctor, policeman, carpenter, teacher, mechanic, engineer,
> pilot, telephone lineman, secretary, warehouseman, factory worker
> on assembly line, truck driver, bookkeeper, sales clerk in a store,
> manager of a store, construction laborer, janitor, farmer.

Name some other jobs you would like or things you would like to do _____

_____

Name some other jobs you would not like or things you would not like to do _____

FIGURE 4–6 *Self-description*

The teacher or counselor may find that interviews relating to the
child in general, his health, his activities, and his interests are beneficial in
conveying the school's interest and may provide much information that is
useful in understanding the child.

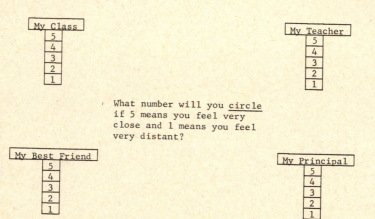

FIGURE 4–7 *Interpersonal Closeness Scale*

EXAMPLE OF A STRUCTURED INTERVIEW
WITH A CHILD

Counselor: Hi! Are you Paul Thomas?

Child: Yes.

Co: And you're in Miss Jacob's room. (Pause) You must be wondering why I called you in to my office.

Ch: Uh huh.

Co: Well, we are trying to get to know you and all of the children who are new to the school this year since we are interested in you and want to know if there is any way in which we can help you. (Pause) If it's okay with you, then, I'd like to ask you some questions.

Ch: That's okay.

Co: I'll ask you this again later, but I wonder if there's any way we can help you that you can think of now—are there questions about the school or the town which you'd like to ask?

Ch: (Pause) I can't think of any.

Co: That's all right, but if you do think of any, I'd like to try to help. (Pause) Well, one of the first things I'd like to know about is: What are the things that interest you? (Pause) Do you have any hobbies or interests or any school subjects you especially like?

Ch: You mean like my model cars?

Co: Yes. I would be interested in hearing about those.

Ch: Well, I've got this whole collection of models. Except for a little help I made 'em all myself. I got some real old cars even before 1900. . . .

From hobbies, the interview moved ahead to touch on family relationships, school attitudes, and the child's health. This boy, who had had no initial questions, when again invited to raise them asked a lot about recreational programs he had heard of after school and some of the school rules. The expression of interest in him, and his feeling that someone really wanted to listen to him, seemed to make it much easier for him to talk.

EXAMPLE OF AN UNSTRUCTURED INTERVIEW WITH A CHILD'S MOTHER

Teacher: Thank you for coming in to see me so early in the school year. Sometime during the year I'm going to be trying to have a visit with at least one parent of every child—that's why I asked you to come. I want some time when we just can chat about Sue and when I can get to know you and learn about Sue.

Mother: Oh, so there's nothing wrong, huh. Well, I had hoped not, but I know my kids are no angels, so I was ready for most anything.

Tea: Sue, then, sometimes disappoints you.

Mo: Well, I mean, she isn't perfect, but I think she's a good kid. I just don't expect her to be an angel. I think that would be hard on her.

Tea: You want her to do the right thing, but you understand when she doesn't.

Mo: Well, I want to understand, but of course I fly off the handle sometimes. She seems like such a baby sometimes. I tell her she's a baby and, you know, the other kids never just hung around and whined the way she does. It was worse last year when she was just starting to school, but honestly sometimes I think she'll never learn to do for herself. I would think a child would be ashamed to have her mother dress her in second grade, but she can be such a baby.

Tea: You find her very babyish and that kind of bothers you.

Mo: Well sometimes I think it's that I have no patience with her. I want things done right, and when she doesn't do them, I just take over.

Tea: Your lack of patience may make her dependent on you.

Mo: Yeah! (Pause.)

Tea: I wonder if you don't kind of appreciate someone to do things for and if she doesn't kind of appreciate the help.

Mo: Goodness. It doesn't sound very healthy, but, you know, I think you may be right. My husband used to say I was trying to keep her a baby, maybe now I'm just nagging her into it.

Tea: It seems to you it might be that way. . . .

This unstructured interview ranged through may topics, but the theme of the discussion throughout was this dependency matter, and Mrs. M. left with a resolve to reinforce self-sufficiency where she had previously and impatiently reinforced dependency.

Departing now from the highly informative, flexible structure of the interview, let us consider some more structured procedures that may also prove very valuable.

ADULT-COMPLETED DEVICES   Devices of various sorts that convey information about the child may be completed by any adult familiar with him, though most often the teacher is the adult involved. As examples of such devices we shall consider the rating scale and the semantic differential.

The rating scale is used in an attempt to quantify and make objective the kinds of information that might be obtained through interview procedures. As Thorndike and Hagen[32] indicate, a rater may be unwilling to take the trouble to do a conscientious job of rating others, or he may identify with the person being rated so that he is unwilling to give a rating that might hurt him; on the other hand the rater may find accurate rating impossible owing to lack of opportunity for observation, ambiguity of the quality being rated, lack of a uniform standard of reference, or rater bias.

Persons interested in developing or using rating scales should familiarize themselves—beyond the coverage here—with the problems inherent in such devices and the means of reducing them. The Thorndike and Hagen text[33] is one of many sources which deals helpfully with these matters.

Following are examples of two different types of rating scales.

Acceptance of Authority[34]

Circle One				
Defiant	Critical of Authority	Usually Obedient	Respectful and Compliant	Resigned, Never Challenges

Any trait that can be sorted into statements such as those above may be incorporated into such a rating scale, or a numerical rating may be used.

[32] Thorndike and Hagen, *op. cit.,* pp. 355–364.

[33] *Ibid.,* pp. 355–378.

[34] Ralph Garry, *Guidance Techniques for Elementary Teachers* (Columbus, Ohio: Merrill, 1963), p. 301.

Numerical Rating Scale

Circle number representing rating	Possesses none of the trait		Possesses an average amount of the trait			Possesses a maximum amount of the trait	
Honesty	0	1	2	3	4	5	6
Cheerfulness	0	1	2	3	4	5	6
Cooperation	0	1	2	3	4	5	6
. . .							

Phillips[35] found that teacher nominations of children exhibiting problem behaviors yielded five factors. Those factors are converted into a global teacher rating scale of seven factors (Figure 4–8, next page).

The semantic differential is a versatile device used to ascertain individuals' responses on various continua to a variety of conditions. Here it is adapted as a rating scale that asks teachers to respond to individual children.

Semantic Differential

Class List	Happy				Sad	Bright				Dull	Strong				Weak
Jim A.	::	::	::	::	::	::	::	::	::	::	::	::	::	::	::
Tom B.	::	::	::	::	::	::	::	::	::	::	::	::	::	::	::
Susie C.	::	::				::	::				::	::			
. . .	::					::					::				

A wide range of additional devices may, of course, be used to sample behaviors, interests, and concerns as seen through the eyes of the adults in the life of the child. The development of such related observational procedures is really limited only by the concern and imagination of the person wishing to understand children.

SUMMARY

In the process of determining children's needs for counseling and guidance, self-selection, observation, and informal procedures may each prove useful. Children, even those who are very young, are quite willing to volunteer for counseling, and they participate readily in guidance-oriented activities. Many advantages accrue from self-selection, not the least of which is that many children who would be referred voluntarily seek counseling.

[35] Beeman N. Phillips, "Problem behavior in the elementary school," *Child Development, 39:* 895–903 (1968).

Teacher Ratings of Children with Problems

Focus here is on locating children who may need special help.

| List names of children in your class. | In the space to the left of the name of the child <u>place the letter</u> beside the description below that fits best. <u>Circle the letter if it fits very well.</u> |

_____ 1 _____

_____ 2 _____

A   aggressive, impertinent, defiant, impudent, rude, cruel, bullying, <u>fights easily, resentful</u>

_____ 3 _____

B   withdrawn, inattentive, disinterested, lazy, uses laziness to gain attention

_____ 4 _____

_____ 5 _____

C   unsocial and withdrawn, sad, apathetic, fearful, unhappy, depressed, sensitive, shy

_____ 6 _____

_____ 7 _____

D   overcritical of others, tattles, exhibits righteousness or snobbishness, shows jealousy or hatred

_____ 8 _____

E   restless, disorderly, compulsive talker, attracts attention by being a nuisance, interrupts

_____ 9 _____

F   Other--please describe on back

_____ 10 _____

G   NONE of these characterizations fits

_____ 11 _____

_____ 12 _____

_____ 13 _____

_____ 14 _____

FIGURE 4–8   *Global Teacher Rating Scale*

Observation is important in determining the child's need for assistance, in helping to point directions for that assistance, and in assessing continuous progress and growth in children over periods of time. Informal procedures, which include autobiographies, sentence-completion devices, questionnaires, sociometric measures, and the like, are also useful in indicating which children may be experiencing pressures that call for counseling and guidance.

Self-selection, observation, and the variety of informal procedures may each contribute to determining children's needs for individual counseling. The use of these procedures must be loving and careful, supplemented by other data, and tempered with awareness of the implications of confidentiality and invasion of privacy. When the result is better communication with children, parents, and teachers, the expenditure of time and effort may be considered worthwhile.

REFERENCES

Barclay, J. R. "Sociometry: rationale and technique for affecting behavior change in the elementary school," *Personnel and Guidance Journal, 44:* 1067–1076 (1966).

Barr, J. A. *The Elementary Teacher and Guidance.* New York: Holt, Rinehart and Winston, Inc., 1958.

Biasco, F. "Encouraging self-referrals in the elementary school," *School Counselor, 16:* 99–102 (1968).

Boyd, G. A. "Sentence and story completions offer serviceable information," *Personnel and Guidance Journal, 37:* 504–508 (1959).

Brough, J. R. "A comparison of self-referred counselees and non-counseled junior high school students," *Personnel and Guidance Journal, 47:* 329–332 (1968).

Brown, B. B. "Experimentalism in teaching practice," *Journal of Research and Development in Education, 1:* 14–22 (1970).

Cottingham, H. F. *Guidance in Elementary Schools.* Bloomington, Ill.: McKnight, 1956.

Esper, G. "Characteristics of junior high school students who seek counseling," *Personnel and Guidance Journal, 42:* 468–472 (1964).

Feldhusen, J. F., J. E. Thurston, and J. J. Benning. "Sentence completion responses and classroom social behavior," *Personnel and Guidance Journal, 45:* 165–170 (1966).

Gage, N. L. *Handbook of Research on Teaching.* Skokie, Ill.: Rand McNally, 1963.

Garry, R. *Guidance Techniques for Elementary Teachers.* Columbus, Ohio: Merrill, 1963.

Guinouard, D. E., and J. F. Rychlak. "Personality correlates of sociometric popularity in elementary school children," *Personnel and Guidance Journal, 40:* 438–442 (1962).

Hill, G. E., and E. B. Luckey. *Guidance for Children in Elementary Schools.* New York: Appleton-Century-Crofts, 1969.

Hutson, P. W. *The Guidance Function in Education.* New York: Appleton-Century-Crofts, 1968.

Johnson, W. F., B. Stefflre, and R. A. Edelfelt. *Pupil Personnel and Guidance Services*. New York: McGraw-Hill, 1961.

Johnston, E. G., M. Peters, and W. Evraiff. *The Role of the Teacher in Guidance*. Englewood Cliffs, N.J.: Prentice-Hall, 1959.

Kilpatrick, F. P., and H. Cantril. "Self-anchoring scaling, a measure of individuals' unique reality worlds," *Journal of Individual Psychology, 16:* 158–173 (1960).

Kowitz, G. T., and N. G. Kowitz. "Elementary school attendance as an index of guidance needs," *Personnel and Guidance Journal, 44:* 944–949 (1966).

Long, B. H., E. H. Henderson, and R. C. Zeller. "Self-ratings on the semantic differential: content versus response set." *Child Development, 39:* 647–656 (1968).

Martin, H. F. "Counseling and guidance techniques with young children," *School Counselor, 10:* 178–182 (1963).

McKinney, F. "The sentence completion blank in assessing student self-actualization," *Personnel and Guidance Journal, 45:* 709–713 (1969).

Moreno, J. L. *Who Shall Survive?* New York: Beacon House, 1934.

Muro, J. J. *The Counselor's Work in the Elementary School*. Scranton, Pa.: International Textbook, 1970.

Peters, H. J. "Differential factors between elementary and secondary school counseling," *School Counselor, 1:* 3–11 (1959).

———, B. Shertzer, and W. Van Hoose. *Guidance in Elementary Schools*. Skokie, Ill.: Rand McNally, 1965.

Phillips, B. N. "Problem behavior in the elementary school," *Child Development, 39:* 895–903 (1968).

Pratte, H. E., and C. Cole. "Source of referral and perception of the counselor," *Personnel and Guidance Journal, 44:* 292–294 (1965).

Pruett, R. F. *Report of the 1965–66 Elementary Pilot Guidance Program*. Bulletin 253. Indianapolis: Indiana State Department of Public Instruction, 1967.

Shertzer, B., and H. J. Peters. *Guidance Techniques for Appraisal and Development*. New York: Macmillan, 1965.

Soar, R. S. "Research finding from systematic observation," *Journal of Research and Development in Education, 4:* 116–121 (1970).

Thorndike, R. L., and E. Hagen. *Measurement and Evaluation in Psychology and Education*. New York: Wiley, 1961.

Tseng, M., and D. L. Thompson. "Differences between adolescents who seek counseling and those who do not," *Personnel and Guidance Journal, 47:* 333–336 (1968).

Weinstein, L. "The mother-child schema, anxiety, and academic achievement in elementary school boys," *Child Development, 39:* 257–264 (1968).

Willey, R. DeV. *Guidance in Elementary Education*. New York: Harper & Row, 1960.

Wright, H. F. "Observational Child Study," in Paul H. Mussen, ed., *Handbook of Research Methods in Child Development*. New York: Wiley, 1960.

ARTICLES IN BOOKS OF READINGS

Dinkmeyer, D. C. *Guidance and Counseling in the Elementary School: Readings in Theory and Practice.* New York: Holt, Rinehart and Winston, Inc., 1968. Readings beginning on pages 180 and 185.

Peters, H. J., A. C. Riccio, and J. J. Quaranta. *Guidance in the Elementary School: A Book of Readings.* New York: Macmillan, 1963. Readings beginning on pages 59, 83, 112.

5

Testing and Appraisal

The man Flammonde appraised the youth,
And told a few of us the truth;
And thereby, for a little gold,
A flowered future was unrolled.
Edwin Arlington Robinson: "Flammonde"

Testing is often a matter both of interest and of assigned responsibility to teachers and counselors. Those who know a given child personally can supplement their understanding of him through observation, informal data collection, standardized testing, and examination of the cumulative record. While other procedures are no substitute for personal involvement, they can provide important data, adding in valuable ways to one's global impressions of the child. Both counselor and teacher may find that testing and appraisal are worthwhile when they are organized so as to support educational, counseling, and consulting efforts.

With its tangible, demonstrable products, testing may tempt the counselor into investing great blocks of time in test preparation, administration, and scoring, and in building impressive charts and tables. On the other hand the burden of test administration, the uncertainty of the benefits, and the incongruence of children's performances with expectations may tempt teachers to recommend the discarding of the testing program. More desirable than either extreme is a middle position—gleaning from tests what they may offer, yet avoiding the temptation to build an empire based on testing. There are both values to be gained and cautions to be observed in testing and appraisal.

This chapter considers the purposes of testing and appraisal; criticisms of testing; responsibilities for testing and appraisal; ability tests, readiness tests, achievement tests, and personality measures; a minimal testing program; the use and communication of test results; the cumulative record; the report card; and the guidance point of view.

PURPOSES OF TESTING AND APPRAISAL

Lyman[1] tells us that on any given school day more than one million standardized tests are likely to be administered in American schools, most of them tests of intelligence, aptitude, and achievement. The stated purposes in general are: (1) to help the teacher plan work that is as effective as possible with groups of children, (2) to help the teacher individualize instruction, (3) to measure individual and group gains, (4) to select children for special programs or special assistance, (5) to verify hypotheses, and (6) to enhance self-understanding in children.

TESTING FOR CURRICULAR PLANNING

Tests can be of great assistance in curricular planning if they are selected consistent with curricular purposes. A teacher who observes, for example, that an individual or a given group scored very low in arithmetic problem-solving can incorporate that information in curricular planning. A counselor who observes that map-reading skill is apparently quite well developed schoolwide can discuss this with teachers, and it can be taken into account as plans for the year unfold in the classrooms. The utilization of such information depends, of course, on the timing of achievement testing. Fall testing makes such utilization possible.

Both this purpose and that of testing for individualization of instruction may be relevant to what Cronbach[2] calls *classification decisions*. Bauernfeind[3] indicates that such classification may involve, for example, placement of elementary school children in reading groups or in foreign language study groups.

TESTING FOR INDIVIDUALIZING INSTRUCTON

Besides aiding in curricular planning, test data may also contribute to planning for individualized instruction. Certainly both kinds of planning should go hand in hand, although in practice it seems that they seldom do.

---

[1] Howard B. Lyman, *Intelligence, Aptitude, and Achievement Testing* (Guidance Monograph Series, Boston: Houghton Mifflin, 1968).

[2] Lee J. Cronbach, *Essentials of Psychological Testing* (New York: Harper & Row, 1960).

[3] Robert H. Bauernfeind, *School Testing Programs* (Guidance Monograph Series, Boston: Houghton Mifflin, 1968).

Group test results inevitably point up individual differences in children—an outcome that in itself should justify the time required. Testing may point up rather specifically the kinds of items that are correctly or incorrectly answered by the child who scores low in a given skill; a standardized achievement test, used for its diagnostic value, can do this with especial comprehensiveness and efficiency. Either through hand scoring of the answer sheets of selected individuals, or through scoring supplemental teacher-made tests, the test user may become aware that Jimmy has failed to respond correctly to the questions calling for subtraction with borrowing. While this may not justify the conclusion that the child's problem has been precisely diagnosed, it does indicate that a possible problem area has been identified.

Test administration manuals generally contain some information on item analysis, which may be used as suggested above; or, for assurance that the teacher-made test is comprehensive, the manual may be consulted and several items of each type may be included in the teacher's own diagnostic survey.

TESTING FOR GROUP AND INDIVIDUAL GAINS

Teachers and counselors need reinforcement if their attempts are successful and information if they are not. Standardized testing can clarify the gains made by children through the instructional program. This purpose cannot be effectively achieved either with the standard spring-to-spring or the recommended fall-to-fall achievement testing programs, which do not account for gains or losses over a summer period during which 30 percent of the children read extensively and another 30 percent assiduously avoid all contact with books.

Perhaps, for those teachers who are most interested in exploring such results, it would be sufficient to supplement the recommended fall testing periodically by spring testing, or perhaps one or two grade levels could be designated for retesting in spring so that every teacher could examine the gain he helped create over a period of time.

Any testing program—especially if conducted in spring—presents increased dangers of creating wasteful, competitive, threatening situations for teachers and children. There are dangers that test data about children, and inferentially about teachers, may be misused. Therefore, whoever organizes and develops the testing program should know and clarify its purposes, and he should cleave to these stated purposes.

Cronbach[4] classifies testing for group and individual gains as *evaluation of treatments*. Basically, he says, whether our purpose affects a group or an individual, we are asking whether our program is bringing about the results desired.

[4] Cronbach, *op. cit.*

TESTING FOR SELECTION

More often than they care to imagine, the teacher and counselor are engaged in selecting students for given purposes. Cronbach[5] indicates that *selection decisions* may be improved through the use of test scores. Tests may help to answer such questions as: Who will be referred to the reading clinic? Whom will the counselor see? Should John Jackson come to first grade or wait another year? Who should be recommended for individual special education testing?

Certainly the making of the best decisions in this yes/no area of selection/nonselection frequently demands the considered judgment of the professional teacher or counselor *and* objective data.

VERIFICATION OF SCIENTIFIC HYPOTHESES THROUGH TESTING

Cronbach[6] points out that scientific hypotheses may be verified through test scores. In other words, we need to see whether our hunches are correct. Members of the education profession do too little on-the-job research. Daily they formulate concerns that could be answered by research ("I wonder what would happen if . . ."), and daily they develop predictive hypotheses ("My hunch is that if I do that, the result will be . . .").

Effective research *can* be done by teachers and counselors, either for their own edification or for publication, and certainly tests can be used to demonstrate outcomes.

ENHANCING SELF-UNDERSTANDING THROUGH TESTING

Bauernfeind[7] notes that test scores may be used to enhance a child's self-understanding. This point is discussed further in the section on using and communicating test results; suffice it to say here that self-understanding through testing is not beyond the elementary school child.

Let us now consider some criticisms that have been made of the uses of testing.

CRITICISMS OF TESTING

A recent wave of criticism should alert counselors and teachers to an appropriate concern that testing be used in defensible and reasonable

[5] *Op. cit.*
[6] *Op. cit.*
[7] Bauernfeind, *op. cit.*

ways. As a tool, Black[8] indicates, mass testing may be used to do good or harm. This is certainly the case. The uses of testing must be consistent with valid purposes, and personal privacy and individual need must be considered.

Speaking of testing criticisms in general, Linden and Linden state: "When traced to their source, the bulk of those charges viewed to be valid may be attributed to the misuse of tests by uninformed and ill-prepared test consumers."[9] Counselors and teachers must be wary of misuses of testing and appraisal.

Barclay, after reviewing several articles, summarized the issues that have been raised regarding testing:

1. That counseling practice and the use of testing is a Communist-inspired plot to subvert and pervert the morals of American youth.
2. That testing is being misused by many so-called professionals and some individuals who are far from being professional.
3. That some tests are personally obnoxious to certain segments of the population and contain items which actually inform children of antisocial or law-breaking conduct.
4. That the prediction from some of these tests is nearly null for individuals.
5. That there is widespread "invasion" of personal rights through the use of certain types of tests and the dissemination of these test results.[10]

Barclay has analyzed these criticisms and, while discounting the hysterical and irrelevant elements in several sources, admits that poor judgment has indeed been used in some testing programs. "But the fact that some abuses of testing have taken place cannot alone imply that all testing methodology is wrong or that the counseling use of tests is a Communist plot."[11] Further, he indicates, counselors do need better training and better attitudes toward tests and testing theory; some counselors need to resist their inclinations to utilize devices that pry into personal experiences, and all need to consider children as normal until it is imperative to remove the child from the school setting for his good and the good of others.

Testing, it is clear, is a resource that can be used well or poorly. The counselor or teacher who contemplates the use of testing would do well to examine its purposes and the potential criticisms that may arise. These considerations, together with an examination of the instruments themselves, should lead to appropriate and desirable uses of testing.

[8] Hillel Black, *They Shall Not Pass* (New York: Morrow, 1963).
[9] James D. Linden and Kathryn W. Linden, *Tests on Trial* (Guidance Monograph Series, Boston: Houghton Mifflin, 1968), p. 2.
[10] James R. Barclay, *Controversial Issues in Testing* (Guidance Monograph Series, Boston: Houghton Mifflin, 1968), p. 5.
[11] *Ibid.,* p. 9.

RESPONSIBILITIES FOR TESTING AND APPRAISAL

The list below seems to represent an appropriate division of labor for the teacher, the building counselor, and the principal in conducting the testing program in the elementary school, though certainly individual schools may logically deviate from this pattern.

Teacher Responsibilities

1. Participating in test selection.
2. Administering group tests.
3. Scoring group tests (unless scoring service is used).
4. Making intelligent use of test results (grouping, individual instruction, curricular planning).
5. Referring children for further testing.

Counselor Responsibilities

1. Participating in test selection.
2. In-service training of teachers in administering tests and using test results in cooperation with the principal.
3. Ordering and maintaining schoolwide testing materials.
4. Administering *appropriate* measures and tests on a limited individual and small-group basis as a supplement to counseling.
5. Referring children for psychological examination and evaluation.

Principal Responsibilities

1. Supervising the testing program.
2. Providing clerical assistance for the recording of test data.
3. If possible, providing funds for assistance in scoring or scoring service.
4. When a scoring service is used, preparing test materials as necessary.
5. Aiding in or conducting the in-service program related to testing.

Occasionally a counselor complains that his assignment includes repetitive administration of achievement or intelligence tests to every class in a school building. The teachers in turn get an extended break, and for weeks little or no counseling or consulting goes on. Arguments that teachers do not like to test, are not accurate in keeping to test times, help children so that they themselves will appear in a good light, and the like, are made to support the "need" for counselor administration of tests. These arguments indicate, rather, the need for the education of teachers in test administration and for the clarification by the school principal of the uses to be made of results. Teachers who understand the values of testing and the uses made of results, teachers who understand the purposes of group-to-group comparisons, may not eagerly approach the task of test administration, but they will tend to keep to time limits and follow instructions.

The teacher—the logical administrator of the group testing program—should receive facilitative support and assistance from both the building counselor and the principal, who should be willing and helpful participants.

GROUP TESTS OF GENERAL ABILITY

Having considered the purposes of testing, criticisms of testing, and responsibilities in the testing program, let us now examine the tests themselves.

Johnny is functioning very poorly in school work and tends to be just below average on achievement tests, yet in recitation he sometimes shows excellent insight and an ability to generalize and synthesize. Is he more capable than his work indicates?

Sue does well in school but seems to be under pressure from home. She works very hard and seems to feel a great need to excel. Is more being expected of Sue than reason would dictate?

Frank is an attractive, mannerly boy who is a below-average student. He comes from a "good home," yet his work seems to be accepted there. Is he a good-looking boy of modest ability who is being accepted as he is, or is he a capable child who needs more motivation?

Situations such as the above may call for individual testing on such devices as the Wechsler Intelligence Scale for Children (WISC) or the Stanford-Binet. However, for the large number of children for whom we need simply some verification of their present level of functioning, rough indices obtainable through group testing may provide useful insights.

Among others, the following tests of general ability may be helpful in answering some questions of abilities within groups and, more tentatively, within individuals. They are listed alphabetically, together with comments by Buros reviewers.[12]

> *California Short-Form Test of Mental Maturity* (CTMM). K–1.5, 1–3, 3–4, 4–6, 6–7, 7–9+. Four scores plus language total, nonlanguage total, total. Hand scoring all levels, machine scoring grades 4 and over,

[12] O. K. Buros, *The Sixth Mental Measurement Yearbook* (Highland Park, N.J.: Gryphon Press, 1965).

10–12 pages. 39–47 minutes. Buros reviewer cited CTMM as most useful K–3 and commends using a variety of tests throughout the school life of pupils. Also available in longer form, testing time approximately 90 minutes.

Cooperative School and College Ability Tests (SCAT). Grades 4–6, 6–8+. Verbal, quantitative, total scores. Hand and machine scoring available. Buros reviewer cited these tests as models of planning, development, standardization, and validation, recommended usage from grades 5 up, and reacted favorably to the absence of IQ labels.

Culture Fair Intelligence Test (IPAT). Ages 4–8, 8–13+. Basically hand scored. Buros reviewer criticized the lack of research on the instrument while endorsing the potential usefulness of this device with culturally deprived segments of our population.

Henmon-Nelson Tests of Mental Ability. Grades 3–6, 6–9+. Hand or machine scored, 30 minutes. Buros reviewer saw this test as appealing because of its brevity and because it is more an index of intellectual skills and less a function of schooling.

Kuhlman-Anderson Intelligence Tests. K, 1, 2, 3–4, 4–5, 5–7, 7–9+. Hand scoring all levels, machine scoring grade 4 and above, 45–60 minutes. Buros reviewers found little to criticize and were complimentary about the wealth of valuable material in the general and technical manuals.

Lorge-Thorndike Intelligence Tests. Grades 1, 2–3, 4–6, 7–9+. Nonverbal, verbal scores, 35–85 minutes. Buros reviewers found this test among the best group intelligence tests available, well designed, easily administered and scored, and well normed.

READING READINESS TESTS

Jill stands out as a very shy child in her kindergarten class. On occasion she participates quite effectively in individual activities, but she shies away from group interactions and only minimally meets group norms for independent functioning. Is she ready for reading tasks but shy?

Timmy is an active child who seems to have great difficulty in carrying out tasks of any complexity. His verbal skills are limited, but he is capable of some leadership behavior and seems to want to be an effective group member. Does he need another year in kindergarten for socialization purposes before he contends with the small-muscle activities related to reading and writing?

Among the tests of general ability previously considered, some may be of use in assaying readiness; however, the following three tests (listed alphabetically) may be especially useful in placing children in terms of readiness or in making recommendations for individual testing.

> *Gates Reading Readiness Tests.* Grade one. Five scores, 50 minutes. Despite its years in operation without revision, the Buros reviewer regarded this untimed test as somewhat useful when accompanied by relevant supporting data.

> *Lee-Clark Reading Readiness Test.* K–1. Four scores, 20 minutes. The Buros reviewer found this to be a superior brief screening test as a rough measure for initial grouping.

> *Metropolitan Readiness Tests.* K–1. Three or four scores, 65–75 minutes. Buros reviewers pointed up deficiencies, but took note of the high level of workmanship and indicated that the MRT are among the superior reading tests now available.

ACHIEVEMENT TESTS

Susie moved into the school district at the beginning of this school year and seems ill-at-ease in the classroom. No records have been received as yet. Does Susie have some achievement strengths that might be capitalized upon? Does she have areas of weakness that might readily be counterbalanced?

Tom, Sammy, Adrian, Vicky, and Ken were in a special summer school program. Are there new-found strengths that may be utilized as bases for further growth? This whole group of children differs from other groups. Where are they in achievement? What special needs do they have?

If the school is to enhance the strengths and combat the academic weaknesses of the children in attendance, knowledge of these strengths and weaknesses must be obtained. Classwide and individual or small-group planning may be made more effective if early achievement testing is meaningfully utilized.

Six achievement testing batteries are briefly described in the following alphabetical presentation. Only direct examination and comparison, however, can reveal whether any one of these batteries is consistent with the curricular objectives of a given school system.

> *California Achievement Tests.* Grades 1–2, 2.5–4.5, 4–6, 7–9+. Eleven scores. A variety of scoring methods, 110–190 minutes. A Buros reviewer indicated that these tests are useful, implied that subsections may be too short, but recommended them in terms of total reading, arithmetic, and language scores.

Iowa Tests of Basic Skills. Grades 3–9 in multilevel edition. Fifteen scores. A variety of scoring methods including MRC, 315 minutes. Buros reviewers considered the ITBS a significant improvement in achievement testing, among the best available, and deserving of thoughtful consideration in any elementary school testing program.

Metropolitan Achievement Tests. Grades 1.5, 2, 3–4, 5–6, 7–9+. From 4–14 scores, depending on level. A variety of scoring methods including MRC, from 115 to 277 minutes. Flexibility, scope, format, and the interpretation manual have been commended by Buros reviewers, but newer curriculum revisions may be insufficiently reflected.

Science Research Associates Achievement Series. Grades 1–2, 2–4, 4–6, 6–9. From 7–11 scores. Hand and IBM scoring, 340–445 minutes. A Buros reviewer found much to criticize in this series, owing mainly to the large standard error of measurement.

Sequential Tests of Educational Progress. Grades 4–6, 7–9+. Seven scores. A variety of scoring methods. 600 minutes approximate total. A Buros reviewer indicated these tests are an important battery for assessing general aspects of educational development, noted that STEP diverges from the usual achievement test that bears a close relation to curriculum, and cautioned against adaptation without awareness of this divergence.

Stanford Achievement Tests. Grades 1.5–2.5, 2.5–3.9, 4–5.5, 5.5–6.9, 7–9. Four to six subtests. A variety of scoring including MRC, 150–290 minutes. A Buros reviewer commends the Stanford Achievement Tests if the desire of the school is to ascertain content knowledge and skill development and if the tests are found to be compatible with the school's instructional objectives.

PERSONALITY MEASURES

Tony, in fourth grade, sucks his thumb. Adrian seems to live in a world of fantasy at school. Gerry looks worried all of the time. Do these children need the assistance of the counselor or referral to nonschool, noncounselor resources?

At and beyond the secondary school level a multitude of effective paper-and-pencil tests are available for assessing a variety of personality factors, but no such effective measures have been prepared for use with elementary school children. This is not to say that there are no instruments; in fact there are many. Reviewers, however, tend to be so critical that one infers that general use of personality measures is not indicated in the elementary schools. Sensitive and careful observation by teachers and counselors apparently remains far more effective than paper-and-pencil measures as a basis for counseling referral.

With individual children, however, the counselor or teacher may be able to gain some insights and to select some areas for discussion through direct examination of individual personality measures. The Mooney Problem Check Lists, for example, available for grades 7–9, 9–12, and up, present lists of common problems; the student indicates those that concern him and states whether he would like to discuss his problems with someone. No scores are derived, but the individual items are examined by the counselor so that he and the student may have a basis for communication. Perhaps this is the personality measurement model that may be most helpful to the counselor and child in the elementary school. The child is not categorized or compared, nor is the intensity of his concern assessed, but he is given an opportunity to express his concerns and to indicate his interest in receiving assistance.

The children who were mentioned at the beginning of this section—Tony, Adrian, and Gerry—may profitably be discussed by the teacher and counselor and, if concern for them is great, in turn by the counselor and school psychologist or other appropriate referral resource. Teacher observation may be sufficient to generate or allay concerns. The counselor may either observe or make direct contact. Paper-and-pencil devices may further support the judgment that referral is or is not needed, but no single score or combination of scores on paper-and-pencil devices is likely to be as valuable as the observations of concerned professionals.

Not only are personality measurement devices designed for elementary school children of limited value, but they are subject to indiscriminate, unwise, or inappropriate use. Nonetheless, if they are used as a basis for communication with a child, if they are used cautiously when concern about a child is clearly present, or if they are used (perhaps anonymously) to assess the nature of children's concerns in general, personality measures may contribute significantly.

A MINIMAL TESTING PROGRAM

It is tempting to state that a minimal testing program should include only what will be used. Too many test profiles, their messages unacted on, do nothing but gather dust for twenty years until they are discarded. Too much money is spent to fill central office files with summary data sheets that never afterward see the light of day. Too many repetitive tests are administered to answer questions about groups of children and too little use is made of data to benefit individuals. The answer, however, is not in removing testing from the school program; it is in putting data to better use.

If test data are gathered only at the point when real utilization is planned, they have no cumulative, developmental message. Two fifth graders having a similar grade equivalent may have reached that level in very different ways. John, a child from an advantaged home where books abound, has good examples about him, but whereas he scored a grade equivalent of 4.8 in early third grade, he achieved a grade equivalent of only 5.7 in early fifth grade. Ted, on the other hand, who in previous years was at or below grade level, early this year scored 5.9 in fifth grade.

Some data must be accumulated in order to provide a developmental picture of each child and to locate children who cannot function well in the educational setting; thus a minimal testing program is in order in the elementary school.[13] Such a program would collect some data across all students and other data on individuals or small groups. Psychometrists, psychologists, reading specialists, teachers, and counselors are involved in the selection and administration of tests designed to meet idiographic (individual) needs. Money not spent on repetitive use of gross achievement and mental ability measures may well be used to buy devices for individual use. Data collected through these devices provide deeper insight into the individual child's world. As an example, the following program shows some devices that might be used with all children.

A SAMPLE MINIMAL PROGRAM, GRADES K–8, SCHOOL A

Grade	Type of Test
K (spring)	Reading readiness
1 (spring)	Mental ability
3 (fall)	Achievement battery
4 (winter)	Mental ability—repeat of grade 1 test
5 (fall)	Achievement battery—repeat of grade 3 battery
7 (fall)	Achievement battery—repeat of grade 3 battery

Note that the same tests, if available, are suggested for subsequent testings. This is much to be preferred in terms of both testing philosophy and expenditure. It makes much better sense to compare data at differing age/grade levels against the same normative populations than against different ones.

EXPANDING THE MINIMAL PROGRAM

Obviously not every testing program has to be minimal. Expansions of the minimal program ought to be related to the additional use of test results. School B, within the same district as school A, has been

[13] Richard C. Nelson and David H. Frey, "The elementary school counselor and testing," *Elementary School Guidance and Counseling*, 4: 59–63 (1969).

pursuing a study of testing's use and relevance. Teachers in school B make frequent use of achievement data in early program planning; they confer with children and parents early and late in the school year concerning skill development; and they see clear advantages in the following program:

EXPANDED PROGRAM, GRADES K–6, SCHOOL B

Grade	Type of Test
K (spring)	Reading readiness
1 (spring)	Mental ability
3 (fall)	Achievement battery
(spring)	Achievement—same battery, second form
4 (fall)	Achievement—same battery, first form
(spring)	Mental ability—repeat of grade 1 test
5 (fall)	Achievement—same battery, second form
(spring)	Achievement—same battery, first form
6 (fall)	Achievement—same battery, second form

Note that grades 3 and 5 are involved in the special within-year comparative testing program. Parents and children discuss test results early in the school year, and follow-up discussions occur late in the same year. Child and parent alike are urged to compare for progress within the child's scores rather than against other children. Parents are given considerable aid in finding the best ways to support the child's effort to improve his performance.

Thus, we see that a minimal testing program for a given school must be relevant to the staff's competence in using testing and to the uses planned. The counselor, the school administrator, a teacher, or an outside consultant may contribute to the program's effectiveness by leading other staff members in exploring the potential benefits. Gaining the most from either a minimal or an expanded testing program depends on periodic reexamination of the program and the uses to which testing is being put.

USING AND COMMUNICATING TEST RESULTS

Teachers use testing to help them plan and individualize instruction, to measure gains, to select children for special programs, and to help children develop self-understanding. As they examine test results for a great many students, they use them in ways that confirm existing information—often in such a cursory manner that teachers are virtually unaware that confirmation has occurred.

For example, Mr. Jackson scans the September achievement test results for his fifth grade and finds Al's total grade equivalent to be 6.2, corresponding reasonably to the 118 IQ score recorded the previous spring; Sandy's total is 5.1, which relates reasonably to her 102 IQ score; Frank's total is 4.2, which relates to his IQ score of 89. All of these figures, like many others, are quickly dismissed from his thoughts. None especially engages him until he sees Peggy's total grade equivalent of 4.1 and her recorded IQ of 112, and Jeff's total of 5.7 and his recorded IQ of 91.

"I had thought of Peggy as rather dull; maybe I'd better look for hidden potential. I hadn't recalled her IQ was that high."

"Jeff is definitely brighter than that score of 91 indicates. I wonder what went wrong that he scored so poorly here."

Confirmation may come so easily that Mr. Jackson is unaware it has occurred, but when reports are discrepant with observations or with other testing information his attention is readily alerted. This is as it should be. Since realistic expectations should be set for children, it is vital that discrepant information be given closer examination, and that, where necessary, further testing information be obtained.

AN ILLUSTRATION OF TEST-RESULTS COMMUNICATION

A few years ago the writer used the procedures discussed below to convey test results to children in a sixth grade class and their parents. The experience proved to be highly motivational for the class members and was enthusiastically received by parents. These procedures, therefore, are described here to illustrate the use of test results.

Step I. A test of basic skills was administered in early September.

Step II. Since immediate results were desired, the answer sheets were hand scored.

Step III. A profile was prepared for duplication, a straight line showing the norm for the subtests for the total population (6.0) and a dashed line showing the results for the total class.

Step IV. On this duplicated profile an individual profile was superimposed, showing an individual's results.

Step V. A brief individual interview was held with each child and subsequently with his parent(s), stressing the child's personal highs and lows rather than grade equivalents per se. Target areas of emphasis were selected in cooperation with the child and later discussed with his parent(s). Each was told in strong terms that the yardstick of growth was to be the child himself. The child's work in any area in which he gained a year or more by the end of the school year, unless he was already significantly above the 6.0 grade equivalent, was to be considered successful.

Step VI. Throughout the year the child was encouraged to use study time to strengthen himself in target areas in which his skills needed improvement, without neglecting areas in which he was already strong. Files of self-checking exercises and work sheets were made available for this purpose, work and sets of pages in appropriate workbooks and texts were called to his or her attention. An individual folder that included his personal profile was provided, where he could place his corrected study-skills work. In order to maintain the stress on self-comparison, children were encouraged not to show their work or discuss it with other children, except to get assistance.

Step VII. Occasional individual reviews were held with individuals desiring them, the folder and profile being consulted to see if reorientation of the target emphasis was needed.

Step VIII. Retesting and scoring was completed in May.

Step IX. Follow-up interviews accompanied the showing of new profiles to the children and their parents.

It was not possible to select a comparable control group, since the experience was conducted in a laboratory school, one classroom per grade. Neighboring school settings were so entirely different in their regimen that they could not be used. Lacking a control population, this piece of research remained incomplete. Nonetheless there *was* growth beyond reasonable expectations, the whole experience was clearly inspirational and motivational to the children, parents were highly accepting of the relevance of self-comparative growth, and children and parents made good use of home and in-school study time. Probably the most desirable outcome was that several children who tended to give up because they could not compete were encouraged by the self-comparison element and made substantial strides. One boy, the poorest in achievement in the pretest, became quite emotional with enthusiasm over the growth he could see in many of the skill areas on his profile.

THE CUMULATIVE RECORD, THE REPORT CARD, AND THE GUIDANCE POINT OF VIEW

THE CUMULATIVE RECORD

The cumulative record is a compendium of information about a given child. Since its nature and variety are well known to educators, samples need not be presented here. Rather, we shall consider its purpose, the responsibility for maintaining it, and the ways of handling it.

Shertzer and Peters[14] suggest that information should be collected and maintained in the cumulative record in the following eight areas:

[14] Bruce Shertzer and Herman J. Peters, *Guidance: Techniques for Individual Appraisal and Development* (New York: Macmillan, 1965), p. 300.

1. Identifying or census data
2. Physical health information
3. Home and family information
4. Educational development data
5. Academic test data
6. Vocational interests information
7. Key experiential data
8. Pupil self-concept data

Not all of these items are as pertinent to the elementary as to the secondary school record, but they suggest the topical areas to be considered as a cumulative record is built or critiqued. In selecting items to be included, the primary criterion should be: is this piece of information needed? Teachers spend too many hours filling in blanks merely because they appear on the cumulative record.

The value of a cumulative record should be its presentation of a longitudinal picture of the child, clarifying his strengths, his disabilities, and ways of working with him so as to create a maximal learning situation. Teacher comments designed to stress these aspects are much to be preferred over the usual comments, e.g., needs to try harder, an average student, a hard worker, slow, cooperative.

If the cumulative record is to present an adequate longitudinal picture of the child, responsibility for its maintenance cannot be vested entirely in one person. The child himself, his parent, the school nurse, the teacher, the counselor, and the administrator are among the persons who can provide valuable information.

A summer kindergarten call-out may be used to gather initial health and identifying information about children. Beyond this, the primarily clerical aspects should be handled by the school secretarial staff at the direction of the school administrator. The teacher should spend his time in recording meaningful comments and appropriate individual observations. The counselor should restrict his involvement to the handling of items that his contact with the child or teacher shows to be relevant. Other personnel should prepare appropriate material to be recorded by the school secretarial staff or should make entries themselves. If school assistance is limited, items that are deemed essential to the record of every child should be recorded by the teacher rather than by the counselor or administrator, if only because the task is much less formidable when shared than when concentrated in the hands of one individual.

It is likely then, that several persons—among them the principal, the school secretary, teachers, and the counselor—will make entries and have access to cumulative records. Current legal judgments increase the likelihood, also, that any given school record may be reviewed by parents or become a matter of court record. Thus, while effective security must be maintained, those who have information about the child must exercise judgment as to what will appear in the folder. The privacy, confidentiality, and integrity of the child and his home life must not be invaded, nor personal information become public.

Because of the need for security, cumulative folders should probably be kept in a central location that may be locked. This would tend to prevent the teacher or counselor from interrupting each other. There would appear to be a clear need in at least a few cases for a supplemental confidential file, handled separately, and to which, for example, the principal alone permits access.

Nelson[15] has suggested that the counselor keep three kinds of records. First, periodic reports are written on selected counselees; these do not divulge confidential material but are intended to guide the teacher's hand. They may be given to the teacher(s) and a copy placed in the cumulative folder for the benefit of future teachers. Second, confidential reports are kept in the confidential file referred to above. Third, abbreviated case notes, perhaps recorded on file cards in the counselor's own shorthand, supplement the counselor's memory by reminding him of topics confronted and behavioral changes under consideration. The data on these cards become the basis for the completion of the reports described above. While these latter points go beyond discussion of the cumulative record, they help answer the question: What should be done with information that is too personal or too petty for recording in the cumulative folder? The teacher, too, may find a supplemental folder useful in communicating with the child and his parents—a folder that conveys information about the child's strengths and weaknesses, and that contains material evidence of his attempts to maintain strengths and correct weaknesses. This folder may help the child, his parents, and the teacher alike to focus on individual growth.

A task that may be allocated to the counselor, especially if he is employed during part of the summer, or to someone else who may be expected to exercise discretion, is that of pruning the cumulative folders belonging to students in the departing grade. The fourth or fifth graders heading into a middle school, the sixth graders heading into a junior high school, or the eighth graders heading into a four-year high school need no miscellaneous trailer of irrelevant items from their past. A kindergarten bed-wetting problem, arithmetic papers from second grade, absence notes from a third-grade bout with a cold, and the like, are often "incompetent, irrelevant, and immaterial" at such a point and may be removed.

The counselor or teacher who can spend some quiet time poring

[15] Richard C. Nelson, "Record keeping in elementary school guidance," *Elementary School Guidance and Counseling, 3:* 126–130 (1968).

over records may contribute much through summarizing the developmental picture of the child and discarding the great bulk of paperwork that tends to accumulate, especially in the records of children about whom there has been concern. Because it can be used more readily, a summary that discusses the general developmental pattern, the kinds of problems, if any, that have occurred, what has been done to alleviate those problems, what approaches have seemed to work, and what strengths and interests may be capitalized upon, may be more valuable than great masses of data.

It would be well for pruning and summarizing of this kind to occur each year, for the teacher to pass on a sparse, descriptive, relevant, and current summary of information designed to help the next teacher, the counselor, and others in their understanding of the child. If this cannot be effectively managed, then at least when the record leaves the school setting it should be pruned of trivia and of material no longer pertinent.

The cumulative record as a kind of personal history of the child can be of inestimable value if maintained efficiently. It can also be a millstone around the necks of professional persons who may be required to spend endless hours in basically clerical pursuits. The school administrator should consider it an important leadership challenge to see that, on the one hand, essential information is obtained and recorded periodically to be indeed cumulative, and that, on the other hand, these tasks are handled efficiently, making appropriate use of the time of professional personnel.

THE REPORT CARD

Report-card marks customarily appear on the cumulative record, but in a great variety of forms. Reporting is done in some places through percentages, in some through letters to parents, in some through such rubrics as superior, satisfactory, unsatisfactory, and in most places through the familiar A, B, C, D, E, F or some similar pattern. In some situations an ability factor is built in, in others an effort factor. The discussion that follows is not framed either to support or criticize any particular procedure, but to raise some questions involving the guidance implications.

IS TOO MUCH TIME SPENT COLLECTING DATA FOR REPORT CARDS IN THE ELEMENTARY SCHOOLS?   Not uncommonly an elementary school teacher must assign report-card marks to every child in eight or more subject areas—e.g., arithmetic computation, arithmetic reasoning, reading comprehension, language arts, spelling, handwriting, social studies (or geography and history), science, health, art, music, physical education; also, certain other assessments are often required—e.g., work habits, cooperation, deportment. If a conscientious teacher were to set a minimum of six recorded grades for each of eight or more subject areas before assigning a grade, and if each graded exercise consumed an average of thirty minutes over a six-week grading period, 1440 minutes would have been consumed in data collection alone. Add to that the time the teacher spends preparing and grading some of these devices, and the time class members spend in exchanging and grading papers, and perhaps only half of the in-class time remains for clearly instructional activities. Time for sharing, story telling, passing and collecting materials, recess, lunch, lining up, handling behavior problems, school holidays, and study time must also be subtracted.

Do we gather data too early in the process?   Harold Taylor at an American Personnel and Guidance Association convention likened our penchant for evaluating to pulling up seeds to check how they are growing. With the report card always waiting in the wings, teachers can seldom permit children to savor a newly gained skill or concept very long before the inevitable requirement of evaluation puts it to the test. Where evaluation is continuous, knowledge is bound to be fragmentary.

The "aha!" of recognition comes at different points to different children. It must happen millions of times each year that a child gains the insight to cope with a given problem just before the teacher says: "That's all the time I can allow for that activity, Johnny. Besides it's time to get ready for music." A grade of 40 percent is recorded in the grade book and averaged with the 80 and 100 that follow. "He's slow to catch on, Mrs. Stephens. He usually gets the idea, though," explains to the mother the C on the report card. Johnny labels himself as slow, uses that as an excuse because he doesn't like arithmetic or language arts so much any more, and a pattern begins to develop.

Do we hold up a yardstick that is irrelevant to most children?   The concept of individual differences is mouthed constantly by educators, but children in the same classroom are too often fitted with the same size educational shoes. The constant pressure of grading and the meticulous avoidance of unfairness (resulting in an insistence that all be measured against the same criteria) militate against truly individual growth standards. Thus, the quick child often is not challenged and the slow child often is overburdened.

Do we create failures?   It seems that many children in our schools are punished for being who they are. The work set before them is not relevant to their level of mastery; the yardstick by which they are measured is not their own progress. Year after year we teach children who are very able to compete in the outside world that they are failures. Perhaps schools have helped to create some of the problems of the numerous people on relief, because as children they were infused with a sense of failure by unrelenting F's, U's, 64's, and notes that never ceased to say: "Needs improvement."

Willey[16] points out that the most able students often are the most discontent over grades. Taking this together with a concern to avoid damaging the self-concepts of less able children, it would be well for guidance-oriented educators to press for careful consideration of the entire grade reporting system. Perhaps it would be enough to suspend formal letter-grade progress reporting until basic skills are well in hand. Allowing time for children to cope with skill development is essential to educational progress.

THE GUIDANCE POINT OF VIEW

Educators who are aware of the guidance needs of children must encourage responsible action within the world of education. Through street classes, free universities, and many protest marches our more mature youth declare the irrelevance of much of our existing educational structure. That younger children do not similarly mobilize indicates only their dependence on adults, not that they experience education very differently. Teachers and counselors who are alert to the needs of children will act as change agents, encouraging modification of the existing milieu for a great many children. Some of the criticisms involving the misuse of testing, the unwise utilization of the cumulative record, and especially the destructive potential in the report-card system have been heard for many years. The fact that these systems survive in many places unchanged is no argument in their favor.

Those who espouse the guidance point of view will see to it that children are measured more often against their own previous achievement patterns, that ways are found to reduce the emphasis on evaluation and increase the time allotted to learning, that the warmth and genuineness of those who deal with children are reinforced and encouraged, that children are treated more often with respect and with awareness of their rights as human beings, and that data collected about children are used to serve their interests rather than being held as stereotypical evidence against them.

Information in itself is neither good nor bad, but it may be used in positive or negative ways. Data collection and utilization must be changed primarily in the direction of better utilization—a task calling for cooperation among teacher, counselor, and administrator.

Children's self-concepts may be positively developed through school experiences; testing may point the way toward greater growth; cumulative records may be used to clarify previous growth patterns; and reporting methods may be designed to improve the parent's understanding of the child. Guidance-oriented teachers and counselors can do much within their own settings to see that these goals are achieved.

[16] Roy DeVerl Willey, *Guidance in Elementary Education* (New York: Harper & Row, 1960).

SUMMARY

As counselors and teachers seek to determine which children will be given guidance and counseling, they depend partly on testing and appraisal. In curricular matters, in individualizing instruction, in assessing group and individual gain, in selection, in verifying scientific hypotheses, and in enhancing self-understanding, testing and related procedures play an important part. Criticisms of testing seem to arise more from misuse of testing than from any inherent defects in most tests. Responsibilities for testing should be parceled out among those who gain from it: e.g., teachers, counselors, and administrators.

A number of useful devices are available for ability, readiness, and achievement testing, but effective personality measures suitable for group usage seem largely to be unavailable, though several may be useful with individuals or for experimental or research purposes. Minimal testing should provide for a cumulative picture of progress by the individual child, and this testing should be supplemented primarily where use of results is planned.

The format and process for communicating test results vary with purpose, but it is clear that children and parents may be effectively involved in the process. The cumulative record and the report card tend to have more negative implications than are desirable; the counselor and the guidance-minded teacher might well examine the implications for guidance of these devices in their schools. Testing and assessment are tools subject to misuse, overuse, or underuse; they have, however, much potential for alerting school personnel to children's needs.

REFERENCES

Adams, J. F. "Using the pictorial norm curve in test interpretation," *Personnel and Guidance Journal, 41:* 812–813 (1963).

Baker, R. L., and R. P. Doyle. "Teacher knowledge of pupil data and marking practices at the elementary school level," *Personnel and Guidance Journal, 37:* 644–647 (1959).

Barclay, J. R. "Sociometry: rationale and technique for effecting behavior change in the elementary school," *Personnel and Guidance Journal, 44:* 1067–1076 (1966).

———. *Controversial Issues in Testing.* Guidance Monograph Series, Boston: Houghton Mifflin, 1968.

Bauernfeind, R. H. "Can tests facilitate the learning process?" in Don C. Dinkmeyer, ed., *Guidance and Counseling in the Elementary School: Readings in Theory and Practice.* New York: Holt, Rinehart and Winston, Inc., 1968. Pp. 143–148.

————. *School Testing Programs.* Guidance Monograph Series, Boston: Houghton Mifflin, 1968.

Black, H. *They Shall Not Pass.* New York: Morrow, 1963.

Buros, O. K., ed. *The Sixth Mental Measures Yearbook.* Highland Park, N.J.: Gryphon Press, 1965. (Fifth, Fourth, Third Yearbooks, 1959, 1953, 1949.)

————. *Tests in Print.* Highland Park, N.J.: Gryphon Press, 1961.

Cronbach, L. J. *Essentials of Psychological Testing.* New York: Harper & Row, 1960.

Davis, D. A. "Effect of group guidance and individual counseling on citizenship behavior," *Personnel and Guidance Journal, 48:* 142–145 (1959).

DeBotteri, L. "Primary school correlates of secondary school achievement," *Personnel and Guidance Journal, 47:* 675–678 (1969).

Dinkmeyer, D. C. "Test utilization for guidance purposes," *Guidance and Counseling in the Elementary School: Readings in Theory and Practice.* New York: Holt, Rinehart and Winston, Inc., 1968. Pp. 138–143.

Downie, N. M. *Types of Test Scores.* Guidance Monograph Series, Boston: Houghton Mifflin, 1968.

Findley, W. G. "The complete testing program," *Theory into Practice, 2:* 192–198 (1963).

Ganter, G., and N. Polansky. "Predicting a child's accessibility to individual treatment from diagnostic groups," *Journal of Social Work, 9:* 56–63 (1964).

Guinouard, D. E., and J. F. Rychlak. "Personality correlates of sociometric popularity in elementary school children," *Personnel and Guidance Journal, 40:* 438–442 (1962).

Jacobs, R. E. "A comparison of tests: The Primary Mental Abilities, The Pintner Mental Abilities: The California Test of Mental Abilities," *The School Counselor, 8:* 12–18 (1960).

Leonard, G. E. "Utilizing test results in the elementary classroom," *The School Counselor, 12:* 3–5 (1964).

Lessinger, L. M., and R. A. Martinson. "The use of the California Psychological Inventory with gifted pupils," *Personnel and Guidance Journal, 39:* 572–575 (1961).

Linden, J. D., and K. W. Linden. *Tests on Trial.* Guidance Monograph Series, Boston: Houghton Mifflin, 1968.

Lister, J. L., and D. H. McKenzie. "A framework for the improvement of test interpretation in counseling," *Personnel and Guidance Journal, 45:* 61–66 (1966).

————, and M. M. Ohlsen. "The improvement of self understanding through test interpretation," *Personnel and Guidance Journal, 43:* 804–810 (1965).

Lyman, H. B. *Intelligence, Aptitude, and Achievement Testing.* Guidance Monograph Series. Boston: Houghton Mifflin, 1968.

McCauley, J. G. "Guidance in practice: reporting results of the standardized testing program to parents," *Personnel and Guidance Journal, 41:* 56–57 (1962).

Nelson, R. C. "Record keeping in elementary school counseling and guidance," *Elementary School Guidance and Counseling, 3:* 126–130 (1968).

————, and D. H. Frey. "The elementary school counselor and testing," *Elementary School Guidance and Counseling, 4:* 59–63 (1969).

Prescott, G. A. "Standardized testing in the elementary school guidance program," in James J. Muro, *The Counselor's Work in the Elementary School.* Scranton, Pa.: International Textbook, 1970. Chapter 8.

Ricks, J. H. "On telling parents about test results," *Test Service Bulletin.* The Psychological Corporation, 1959.

Shertzer, B., and H. J. Peters. *Guidance: Techniques for Individual Appraisal and Development.* New York: Macmillan, 1965.

Tennyson, W. W., D. H. Blocher, and R. H. Johnson. "Student personnel records: a vital tool but a concern of the public," *Personnel and Guidance Journal, 42:* 888–893 (1964).

Tiegland, J., and B. J. Bosdell. "Problems discussed by underachievers in different treatment groups," *School Counselor, 12:* 222–227 (1965).

Walker, J. L. "Four methods of interpreting test scores compared," *Personnel and Guidance Journal, 44:* 402–404 (1965).

Willey, R. DeV. *Guidance in Elementary Education.* New York: Harper & Row, 1960.

Wilson, A. R., and L. D. Stier. "Instability of sub-scores on forms of SRA Primary Mental Abilities Tests: significance for guidance," *Personnel and Guidance Journal, 40:* 708–711 (1962).

ARTICLES IN BOOKS OF READINGS

Dinkmeyer, D. C. *Guidance and Counseling in the Elementary School: Readings in Theory and Practice.* New York: Holt, Rinehart and Winston, Inc., 1968. Readings beginning on pages 138, 143, 149, 158, 161.

Peters, H. J., A. C. Riccio, and J. J. Quaranta. *Guidance in the Elementary School: A Book of Readings.* New York: Macmillan, 1963. Readings beginning on pages 70, 76, 112, 321, 326.

Saltzman, G. A., and H. J. Peters. *Pupil Personnel Services: Selected Readings.* Itasca, Ill.: F. E. Peacock, 1967. Readings beginning on pages 284, 288, 312, 318, 329.

Part Three

Counseling

6

A General Examination

Oh, the comfort—the inexpressible comfort of feeling safe
* with a person,*
Having neither to weigh thoughts,
Nor measure words—but pouring them
All right out—just as they are—
Chaff and grain together
Certain that a faithful hand will
Take and sift them—
Keep what is worth keeping
And with the breath of kindness
Blow the rest away.

DINAH MARIA MULOCK CRAIK: "Friendship"

In their struggle for selfhood, acceptance, affection, and recognition, children and adults alike seek the help of others. All responsible human beings can improve in their alertness to their own needs and to the needs of others. All can learn to relate more effectively, to communicate more adequately, and to listen more understandingly to others. All who are involved in the life of a child—the teacher especially, and even the children about him—have input and therefore responsibility for their relationship to "the other." All are involved. All contribute, often unaware, often negatively, to the lives of others.

    The counselor has a special responsibility in this area, but he has no corner on understanding. Much that is said of the counselor here and in the next two chapters is also the concern of the teacher and others.

Effective counseling takes time, skill, and experience, but those who lack these may, nonetheless, learn through reading about counseling much that can help them interact and communicate more adequately.

As a counselor works with children, he eventually develops a personal style of counseling expressing his philosophy, his understanding and knowledge of the process of counseling, and his unique personality. The education of the counselor should permit and encourage the development of this personal style; at the same time it should clarify one or more styles of counseling. Too much leadership, or not enough, are equally likely to make things difficult for him. As Swensen puts it:

> The student is usually faced with one of two situations. Either he studies in a school with a teacher who follows one point of view and one general approach, in which case the student learns little of other approaches and gains the impression, implicitly or explicitly, that other points of view are inferior and less efficacious; or else he is taught a variety of systems which are presented with little attempt to relate them to one another, and he is faced with the necessity of developing some sort of system of his own.[1]

Thus, the writer on counseling faces the dilemma of bypassing his own orientation to preserve objectivity or of biasing the reader by presenting a point of view. Taking the rationale that counseling itself is a subjective experience and that exploring the topic with total objectivity is an unnecessary suppression of individuality, the present writer reviews a number of positions that have relevance for elementary school counseling, then briefly states his position as *a point of departure* for readers.

This chapter first gives some further definitions of counseling, goes on to discuss the counseling relationship, content and process in counseling, the implications of several viewpoints for elementary school counseling (psychoanalysis, transactional analysis, reality therapy, Adlerian theory, behavior therapy, self theory, gestalt therapy, and existentialism), and finally offers a brief statement of position.

COUNSELING: FURTHER DEFINITIONS

Earlier (Chapter 1) we noted: *Counseling is both a process and a relationship designed to provide the child with an opportunity to explore his feelings, thoughts, and actions and to learn to meet the challenges in his environment. In the elementary school, counseling is primarily preventive and developmental, secondarily remedial.*

---

[1] Clifford H. Swensen, Jr., *An Approach to Case Conceptualization* (Guidance Monograph Series, Boston: Houghton Mifflin, 1968), p. 182.

Stefflre and Matheny[2] indicate that the client's understanding of himself and of his life space is essential in effective counseling in order that he may make informed choices in areas where choice is available.

According to Dinkmeyer:

> Developmental counseling provides the child with an opportunity to explore his feeling, his attitudes, convictions. The counselor starts with the problems that the child perceives and helps him to solve them. The counselor in this situation provides a relationship that accepts, understands, and does not judge. It provides the counselee with constant clarification of his basic perception of life. This relationship enables the counselee to become increasingly self-directed so that the goal is one of enabling him to deal with both the developmental tasks and the general problems of living. This type of developmental counseling suggests that counselors would not only be problem-oriented, but would be concerned about all students in the school population.[3]

If counseling for all students is to be implemented in the school as Dinkmeyer suggests, the counselor must be accessible. Dependence solely on teacher referral would tend to limit the counselor's effective outreach; thus, self-referrals should be an integral part of the elementary school counseling program. (This point is elaborated in Chapter 4.)

Focus on strengths is another matter of importance. Peters states:

> The focus of developmental counseling is the strengths of the individual—educational, vocational, and social-personal—as opposed to the weaknesses. In a culture which emphasizes concern for wrongdoing and violations of mores, the counselor must pinpoint one's strengths and potential. This does not mean that the counselor minimizes, overlooks, or excuses the frailties of the human. . . . By focusing on a student's strengths, weakness can be kept in perspective and a more satisfactory solution of the troublesome concerns which could become major problems, can be more readily achieved.[4]

Both focusing on strengths and encouraging self-referral are viewed here as integrally related to preventive counseling. Boy put it this way:

> The school counselor has a potentially powerful contribution to make to mankind if he moves toward a professional rationale in which a preventive concept of counseling is the functional core of his existence. The school counselor is in a uniquely strategic position because he

---

[2] Buford Stefflre and Kenneth B. Matheny, *The Function of Counseling Theory* (Guidance Monograph Series, Boston: Houghton Mifflin, 1968), p. 8.

[3] Don Dinkmeyer, "Developmental counseling in the elementary school," *Personnel and Guidance Journal, 45:* 266 (1966).

[4] Herman J. Peters, "Developmental Counseling," *Clearing House, 41:* 111 (1966).

deals with clientele during the formative stages of their development. He deals with human problems as they begin to emerge. It is far more humane and logical for a school counseling program to be involved during the formative years of a person's development rather than standing aside and watching the seeds of personal disintegration being sown.[5]

Effective self-referral opportunities for counseling, if offered early, can make it unnecesary for a child to get worse in order to get attention.

Counseling is oriented toward emphasizing the strengths of the individual, helping him function effectively within his life space, and helping him clarify his alternatives and anticipate their consequences. Strategically, counseling is anticipatory in nature, dealing with the child's emerging concerns.

According to Dinkmeyer, the central purposes of counseling are to help the child:

1. To know and understand himself, his assets and liabilities, and through this self-understanding to develop a better understanding of the relationships among his own abilities, interests, achievements, and opportunities.
2. To develop self-acceptance, a sense of personal worth, a belief in one's competence, a trust in oneself, and self-confidence; and to develop an accompanying trust and acceptance of others.
3. To develop methods of solving the developmental tasks of life with a resultant realistic approach to the tasks of life as met in the areas of work and interpersonal relations.
4. To develop increased self-direction, and problem-solving and decision-making abilities.
5. To develop responsibility for his choices and actions; to be aware that his behavior is goal-oriented, and to consider the consequences when making a decision.
6. To modify faulty concepts and convictions so that he may develop wholesome attitudes and concepts of self and others.[6]

THE RELATIONSHIP IN COUNSELING

Though proponents of different schools of thought view the counseling relationship differently, all consider it deserving of thought and attention. The counselor's central question concerning relationship is: What effect do I have upon this interaction?

[5] Angelo V. Boy, "A rationale for school counseling," *Guidance, 4:* 112 (1966).

[6] Don Dinkmeyer, "Counseling theory and practice in the elementary school," *Elementary School Guidance and Counseling, 1:* 198–199 (1967).

Rogers noted in 1942:

> The counseling relationship is one in which warmth of acceptance and absence of any coercion or personal pressure on the part of the counselor permits the maximum expression of feelings, attitudes, and problems by the counselee. . . . In this unique experience of complete emotional freedom within a well-defined framework, the client is free to recognize and understand his impulses and patterns, positive and negative, as in no other relationship.
>
> This therapeutic relationship is distinct from, and incompatible with, most of the authoritative relationships of everyday life.[7]

An important element is the counselee's prior expectation of the counseling experience. In a 1951 publication, Rogers[8] indicated that the counselee may variously expect a shielding and protecting parental figure, a probing psychic surgeon, an advice-giver (either so that the advice may be taken or proven wrong), a harmful labeler, an extension of the authority figure by whom he was referred, or an individual who will help him solve his own concerns. Clearly, the individual who anticipates a kind of counselor he fears will enter into a counseling relationship much more apprehensively than the individual who anticipates solving his own concerns with the assistance of another kind of counselor. As Stefflre and Matheny state:

> . . . the client brings to the counseling interview a history of interaction with other people. On the basis of that history he has built an implicit theory of how he should behave and how others will behave toward him. On one hand, he wants to make this theory work so that life can go on in the familiar way, but, on the other, he realizes that it has not provided all of the satisfaction and fulfillment that he would have liked in the past and, therefore, he would like to change. In counseling he plays a game of wanting to change and wanting to stay the same.[9]

These same authors state that the client or counselee is, therefore, not a free agent in any sense, and point out that both he and the counselor enter with some clear expectations into the counseling relationship.[10] The counselee has his expectation of counseling and the maintenance of his self-concept to deal with, and the counselor has his theoretical position.

Borrenson[11] asked counselors to diagnose counselees as being concerned primarily about vocational, educational, or emotional matters and to

[7] Carl R. Rogers, *Counseling and Psychotherapy* (Boston: Houghton Mifflin, 1942), pp. 113–114.

[8] Carl R. Rogers, *Client-Centered Therapy* (Boston: Houghton Mifflin, 1951), pp. 66–67.

[9] Stefflre and Matheny, *op. cit.*, p. 14.

[10] *Ibid.*, p. 19.

[11] Ann M. Borrenson, "Counselor influence on diagnostic classification of client problems," *Journal of Counseling Psychology, 14:* 252–258 (1965).

indicate whether the major conflict resulted from lack of information about self or the environment, motivational difficulty, conflict with significant others, or lack of skill. Individual counselors emphasized different concerns across counselees, considering them, for example, as primarily affective or primarily resulting from lack of information. This suggests that counselor philosophy has much to do with perception of counselee problems.

Throughout his recent writing Rogers has stressed congruence in the counselor, unconditional positive regard for the counselee, and empathic understanding as critical in developing an effective helping relationship. He has raised the following ten questions:

How Can I Create a Helping Relationship?

1. Can I be in some way which will be perceived by the other person as trustworthy, as dependable or consistent in some deep sense?
2. Can I be expressive enough as a person that what I am will be communicated unambiguously?
3. Can I let myself experience positive attitudes toward this other person—attitudes of warmth, caring, liking, interest, respect?
4. Can I be strong enough as a person to be separate from the other? Can I be a sturdy respecter of my own feeling, my own needs, as well as his? Can I own, and if need be, express my own feelings as something belonging to me separate from his feelings?
5. Am I secure enough to permit him his separateness? Can I permit him to be what he is—honest or deceitful, infantile or adult, despairing or over-confident? Can I give him the freedom to be? Or do I feel that he should follow my advice, or remain somewhat dependent on me, or mold himself after me?
6. Can I let myself enter fully into the world of his feelings and personal meanings and see these as he does? Can I step into his private world so completely that I lose all desire to evaluate or judge it? Can I enter it so sensitively that I can move about in it freely, without tramping on meanings which are precious to him?
7. Can I receive him as he is? Can I communicate this attitude? Or can I only receive him conditionally, acceptant of some aspects of his feelings and silently or openly disapproving of other aspects?
8. Can I act with sufficient sensitivity in the relationship that my behavior will not be perceived as a threat?
9. Can I free him from the threat of external evaluation?
10. Can I meet this other individual as a person who is in the process of *becoming*, or will I be bound by his past and by my past?[12]

Although the relationship assumes vital importance in counseling, and although its quality is crucial, it is not the whole of counseling. Counseling may also profitably be viewed in terms of content and process.

---

[12] Abstracted from Carl R. Rogers, "The characteristics of a helping relationship," *Personnel and Guidance Journal, 37:* 6–16 (1958).

CONTENT AND PROCESS IN COUNSELING

Effective counseling involves content that includes (1) events, (2) feelings, (3) nonverbal communication, and (4) the process of counseling itself.

The content of counseling inescapably involves *events*. The counselee tells of his experiences in trying to enter the closed group he wishes to have include him; he discusses his attempts at behavior modification; or he reports on the circumstances that were present when he was so thoroughly embarrassed. Events and facts are important in counseling, and the skillful counselor assists the counselee in reporting them so as to gain maximal understanding of them.

Inescapably also effective counseling considers the *feelings* of the individual. Events are made more meaningful as the individual perceives in a true light his affective response to them. The counselee speaks of his anger, frustration, anxiety, hope, enthusiasm, love, hate; all feelings are received, incorporated, and encountered with honesty and sensitivity. The counselor helps the individual examine his true feelings and encourages him to look beyond the facts to the affective domain.

Nonverbal communication, although often overlooked, is clearly part of the content of counseling. Sandy or the counselor looks bored as the long story is told or the long explanation given; Timmy looks away as the subject of his younger brother enters the discussion; a smile of acknowledgement passes over Susie's face as the counselor notes that despite her irritation, she seems rather to enjoy the teasing by the boys. The counselor who is effective and alert to nonverbal behavior incorporates these messages as if they were words and encourages their expression in the counseling interview.

The *process* of counseling itself can clearly become an important part of its content. The counselor may find advantage in figuratively stepping back and analyzing what seems to be going on.

"You seem to be trying to tell me that accidents just happen when you are around—that you are not at fault, but you get blamed."

"I feel that you're working hard to make me get angry at you so you can shut me out."

"It seems to me I'm asking a lot of questions trying to find something you'd really like to talk about. I'm giving you the idea that all I want you to do is answer questions—and that's not really it at all."

The effective counselor incorporates this confrontative aspect of counseling because it clarifies, both in his and the counselee's behavior, elements that may be either blocking or promoting the development of effective counseling.

PROCESS AND PRODUCT

In later sections, dealing with the implications of differing viewpoints of counseling for elementary school guidance, a central question of counseling philosophy is raised: Is the process or the product the more important? Counseling may focus more on (1) the processes involved and the learning that thereby emerges, or (2) the product of counseling, the outcome to be achieved. No viewpoint ignores either process or product, but the question of balance is an important one.

When a counseling position is concentrated primarily upon process, the learnings involved in the affective and cognitive exploration of a concern or problem are considered a product in themselves. The counselor who concentrates on process does not consider outcome to be the epitome of counseling effectiveness; indeed, the counselor considers his work successful if, in exploring a concern or problem, the counselee comes to alter a damaging self-concept and learns to live more meaningfully with the problem. This counselor considers that the processes involved in understanding, in coping, and in exploring outcomes involve important learnings in and of themselves.

When a counseling system is concentrated upon product, the learnings involved in the affective and cognitive exploration of a concern or problem are viewed as means to an end. The counselor who concentrates on product considers outcome as the epitome of counseling effectiveness; he views his work as successful if a solution for the concern or problem emerges from the discussion. He expects that the product, solution, or outcome in itself will provide a meaningful learning experience for the counselee as a basis upon which future problems might be encountered and solved.

The counseling relationship, content, and process are useful concepts in examining counseling viewpoints. The sections that follow discuss briefly several such viewpoints and their implications for work with children in the elementary school. Relevant references are cited for deeper exploration of each.

PSYCHOANALYSIS

As a result of his contact with a wide range of people, most of them adults and most in great need of psychological understanding and assistance, Sigmund Freud developed the concepts fundamental to psychoanalytic counseling. Freud was an explorer in the realms of human emotions who had few landmarks before him. If his system of counseling has been subjected to much criticism and to many alterations by his followers, if it offers only limited direction for the elementary school counselor, nonetheless Freud deserves great credit for conceptualizing the mental and emotional processes he observed and for developing procedures for the treatment of disturbed persons.

PSYCHOANALYTIC CONSTRUCTS

Three of Freud's observations have overriding importance and have been incorporated into many personality theories: (1) early childhood experiences are highly important for adult behavior; (2) sex is a key determinant of behavior; and (3) unconscious determinants are present and important in the behavior of all individuals.

Freud viewed man as natively selfish, impulsive, and irrational. Ford and Urban,[13] in categorizing theories of the nature of man as either pilot or robot, have put Freud's philosophy in the robot group. Man may appear to be self-directing, but in fact his behavior results from unconscious determinants.

Freud used the term *id* to designate this basic and selfish aspect of man. He used the term *ego* to connote the reality-oriented process whereby the individual learns that his impulsive actions often fail to satisfy him and that he must take the external world into account. He used the term *super-ego* to designate the internalized voice of the individual's parents and significant others—his conscience—which limits his behavior so that he avoids certain misdeeds and escapes the painful consequences.

In Freud's view of neurosis, as Stefflre and Matheny[14] indicate, the neurotic is a person who develops a very severe superego that imposes guilt upon the ego in order to limit or censure impulses arising from the id. Repression and inhibition occur in vital areas of human experience, and anxiety is often observed as an external symptom, since the individual is fearful that his guarded impulses will erupt into consciousness.

The goals of psychoanalysis tend to involve the moderation of the demands of the superego, and the reduction of conflicts between the id, ego, and the superego through personality reconstruction.

Freud used hypnosis, dream analysis, projective devices, stream of consciousness, association, recall, transference, and interpretation in his processes of counseling. The analyst tends to stress listening in the early phases of counseling and interpreting in later stages; he is highly active in structuring the processes engaged in, and he attends to content in counseling above and beyond either the relationship or the process. Often seated behind the client, the analyst tries to maintain an objective relationship to a maximum extent and to let his own personality enter only in minimal ways. Diagnosis, prognosis, and history taking are important aspects of therapy.

[13] Donald H. Ford and Hugh B. Urban, *Systems of Psychotherapy* (New York: Wiley, 1963), pp. 595–599.

[14] Stefflre and Matheny, *op. cit.,* p. 25.

IMPLICATIONS FOR ELEMENTARY SCHOOL COUNSELING

Although the depth and interpretive nature of psychoanalysis go beyond the training and responsibilities of the elementary school counselor, and although generally the children who continue to function in the elementary school do not require such treatment, nonetheless, psychoanalytic theory offers some concepts relevant to elementary school counseling. First, the counselor needs to be aware that human beings are often motivated by impulses of which they are not fully conscious. Second, he needs to recognize the significance of child-rearing practices and of early influences on personality. Third, he can use the interview as a process through which to explore the feelings of anxiety that affect the child. Fourth, the counselor can learn from the psychoanalytic position to adopt a nonmoralizing attitude with the child. Psychoanalytic theory should also make the counselor aware of the possible depths of human problems, aware of his own limitations in dealing with them, and alert to the needs of children for referral.

On the other side of the coin, at least two implications from psychoanalytic counseling do not seem to belong in a current view of elementary school counseling. First, too much emphasis can be placed upon the deterministic nature of early experiences in the life of the child, thus making it seem that one need not accept responsibility because early events cannot be altered. Also, in the same vein, too much emphasis can be placed upon examining causation, when in fact many normal children can be helped to go on in new directions without such exploration.

Psychoanalysis particularly deserves historical attention by the elementary school counselor as one of the several precursors to the development of today's theories of counseling. Useful in such exploration are a number of sources directly relevant[15,16,17,18] as well as a number that help one compare psychoanalysis to other systems.[19,20,21,22,23]

[15] Anna Freud, *The Psychoanalytic Treatment of Children* (New York: International Universities, 1946).

[16] Sigmund Freud, *New Introductory Lectures on Psychoanalysis, Standard Edition* (London: Hogarth, 1964; first published in 1933).

[17] Philip S. Holzman, *Psychoanalysis and Psychopathology* (New York: McGraw-Hill, 1970).

[18] Melanie Klein, *The Psychoanalysis of Children* (London: Hogarth, 1963).

[19] Ford and Urban, *op. cit.,* chaps. 5 and 6.

[20] C. H. Patterson, *Theories of Counseling and Psychotherapy* (New York: Harper & Row, 1966), chaps. 12 and 14.

[21] Donald H. Blocher, *Developmental Counseling* (New York: Ronald, 1966).

[22] Paul T. King, "Psychoanalytic Adaptations," in Buford Stefflre, ed., *Theories of Counseling* (New York: McGraw-Hill, 1965), chap. 3.

[23] Bruce Shertzer and Shelley C. Stone, *Fundamentals of Counseling* (Boston: Houghton Mifflin, 1968), chap. 10.

TRANSACTIONAL ANALYSIS

Eric Berne and Thomas A. Harris have developed the concepts fundamental to transactional analysis. This system divides the personality of the individual into three parts that roughly parallel those of psychoanalysis (superego = Parent, ego = Adult, and id = Child); however, there are clear differences between the psychoanalytic emphasis on causation and the transactional emphasis on analysis of immediate behavior.

TRANSACTIONAL CONSTRUCTS

The transaction-analyst considers that each individual carries within him a set of memories, or recorded tapes—error-filled, but representing his best understanding of what he heard when he was a little child. Parts of these tapes echo such words as: do, don't, never, always, mustn't, should, can't, bad, good. These tapes are subject to ready recall as the *Parent* (capital P to discriminate from parent as mother or father) voice within the individual responds to situations, especially to new or stressful ones. The *Child* within is the feeling portion of the individual. The Child learns that he is "not OK," owing partly to his parents' larger size and partly to their predictive ability, which he does not share. ["It will be sunny tomorrow." "Santa Claus (or daddy) will be here soon." "If you eat all that you'll get sick."] To a great extent, however, he feels he is "not OK" because of messages indicating he is incapable or wrong. ["Don't" "You can't do the dishes." "When you're bigger."] The *Adult* is viewed as the logical, computing, information-seeking and information-giving portion of the individual —a portion that transaction-analysts believe is little developed in most individuals.

The goals of counseling for the individual include, first, the examination and updating of Parent tapes; second, the freeing of the Child from his "not OK" feelings, thus reducing his need for rebellious or compliant actions; third, the enhancement of the Adult, who then "comes on" straight and rational. A fourth objective is to develop awareness and improve transactions where necessary.

Every communication, whether verbal or nonverbal, to which any response is made is considered a transaction, which may be analyzed to determine which part of the individual is sending the message. For example, consider the following exchanges:

HUSBAND		WIFE		
"Why don't we	P	P	"That's a great	*or* "I'd like to, but I
go out for dinner	A⇄A		idea. I really am	haven't saved much
tonight, you look	C	C	worn out. Thank	this week. Can we
tired."			you for noticing."	afford it?"

In either of these exchanges a *complementary transaction* occurs; lines do not cross, the husband speaks with an Adult voice (asks for an Adult response at the same time) and gets an Adult response. Whenever the lines run parallel or do not cross, a complementary transaction has occurred. When the husband responds, another transaction has occurred. Suppose the message suggests a negative:

WIFE				HUSBAND
"I haven't saved much	P		P	"There you go again making
this week. Can we afford	A ————→		A	me feel my job is no good and I
it?"	C		C	don't earn enough money."

Here a *crossed transaction* occurs; lines cross, the wife speaks with an Adult voice (presuming the tone is not nagging or babyish) and the Child in her husband responds.

Positional analysis by transaction-analysts involves the examination of the individual's life style, to which it is assumed that one of four positions is basic.

1. *I'm not OK, you're OK.*

This is the position into which all children are born and which their early awareness tends to reinforce. "I can't do for myself. I'm in a world of giants. I can't choose when I want to play or sleep. Mommy and Daddy make the rain and sunshine, I can't. I try to think about things but I can't. I'm not OK." Every child needs to learn that he is OK. If his early inadequacies are reinforced by feelings that he is bad and unworthy, he may never move from this Child position.

2. *I'm OK, you're not OK.*

This is the parents' position as children see it. "I am strong and powerful. You are weak and powerless. I run things here. I can do as I please. I'm OK, but you're not." Every child needs to learn that others are OK. If he is surrounded by models who are strong, powerful, and prejudiced, or weak, vacillating, and inept, he may either model or usurp this Parent position.

3. *I'm not OK, you're not OK.*

When the child feels little confidence in himself or in the adults about him, he adopts a position that borrows from both positions above. The child sees weaknesses in himself and vacillation and ineptness in those about him. He speaks most often from his Child in such a way that he calls out the Child in others.

4. *I'm OK, you're OK.*

When the child learns that he is capable and that others are also able, he adopts this position. When two people who take this position are together, there is little Parenting and little is heard from the rebellious or compliant Child. There is valuing (updated Parent), there is feeling and there may be playfulness (free Child), and there is considerable straight communication (Adult-Adult).

Transactional analysis is a system that examines relationships and places rather equal emphasis on content and process. It works by examining the process of communication, bringing it to awareness, and examining its contents.

IMPLICATIONS FOR ELEMENTARY SCHOOL COUNSELING

Helping individuals to analyze the messages they send, to anticipate the effects of their messages, and to develop more effective messages, is a very appropriate goal in counseling. Whether the communication involves child and child, child and teacher, parent and child, teacher and parent, or a variety of others including siblings, other relatives, or neighbors, the counselor who understands what kinds of messages are being sent and received can help bring about more effective communication.

Children can understand the need for updating the Parent voice within, getting rid of Not OK Child feelings, and "coming on Adult." Harris[24] suggests the formation of parent groups that parallel children's groups to avoid jeopardizing communication. Otherwise the child who learns to use group jargon, such as "You're Parenting me," may begin confronting his mother and father with statements they can hardly help misunderstanding.

Every child needs to learn that he is OK. The counselor can afford to spend considerable time and energy in helping to convey that message to children—either through individual or group counseling, through teacher or parent consulting, or through classroom involvement. One of the remaining pieces of business for the transaction-analyst is that of clarifying some additional effective techniques, which can supplement those of (1) confronting a child with the opinion that he is Parenting or (2) exhibiting the rebellious or compliant Not OK Child and illustrating ways of communicating that are different. Nonetheless, transactional analysis as it exists provides a means for examining human interaction in a new light; it is oriented to the present, acknowledges the past, and plans for the future.

[24] Thomas A. Harris, *I'm OK, You're OK* (New York: Harper & Row, 1967).

Transactional analysis is a learning-oriented view that relies heavily on improved communication patterns. Harris[25] and Berne[26,27] provide the primary sources for examination of this viewpoint.

REALITY THERAPY

William Glasser has developed the basic concepts involved in reality therapy. This system relates to transactional analysis in that both are NOW-oriented, both capitalized upon reality (the Adult) within the individual, and both are logical and learning-oriented. Both systems are concerned with examining values and helping the individual to achieve his goals—in transactional analysis through examining individual transactions, in reality therapy through exploration of the individual's value system and the degree to which his behavior is consistent with his stated values.

REALITY THERAPY CONSTRUCTS

The reality therapist considers that every human being has three basic psychological needs: to love, to be loved, and to feel worthwhile. The child and the adult alike, through their behavior patterns, are attempting to meet their needs in the best ways they can, whether their behavior may be described as outgoing, acting-out, shy, or withdrawn. While the individual child or adult experiences needs, he also holds values that tend to remain unexamined and that may well be inconsistent with "irresponsible" aspects of his behavior.

Counseling is directed at examining values and behavior, ascertaining the degree to which the behavior examplifies the values held, and determining whether or not it meets the needs of the individual. Emphasis is placed on *what* the child is doing rather than *why*, and a goal of counseling is helping the child to develop better ways to fulfill his needs responsibly, without depriving others of fulfillment of their needs. Reality therapy may be characterized as content-oriented, with process secondary to content.

The value system of the counselor is not imposed upon the child; rather, emphasis is placed on examining the child's set of values. Further, the decision to change behavior is the child's decision—based on his belief that it will help him to meet his needs more satisfactorily and his conviction that it is consistent with his own values.

Besides taking part in examining the child's values, behavior, and

---

25 *Ibid.*

26 Eric Berne, *Transactional Analysis in Psychotherapy* (New York: Grove, 1961).

27 Eric Berne, *Games People Play* (New York: Grove, 1964).

possible behavior changes, the counselor contributes in several other ways. He helps the child examine the things he does well, so that he may capitalize upon his strengths. He encourages the child to make a plan for achieving any desired change in his behavior, and he praises the child for any progress toward his goal. He cares enough to reject behavior that will not help the child meet his needs. He confronts matters directly and openly with the child, discouraging the child's dependence upon excuses. He makes suggestions and enumerates alternatives that he believes will help the child live better within his environment, but he leaves the choice with the child. He is concerned with the present aspects of the child's behavior and so he limits discussion of long-past events.

In sum, the counselor offers an honest and human relationship in which a special kind of teaching or training occurs, which involves an analysis of the inconsistencies among the child's goals, values, and behaviors, and in which the child makes the decisions for or against behavior change. The child is seen as a responsible human being whose youth does not excuse him from acting in ways that are consistent with his own values.

IMPLICATIONS FOR ELEMENTARY SCHOOL COUNSELING

Helping children to examine the inconsistencies between the ways in which they act and the values and needs they own is very appropriate in elementary school counseling. Children are now-oriented and can readily tune in on the ways in which their behaviors may be self-defeating. Most children are capable of acting responsibly in relation to their own values, but they may remain unaware of their value system as well as their strengths unless helped to examine these matters.

Many children can advantageously become more conscious of their needs for love, for loving, and for worthwhileness and can be helped to become aware of their strivings to meet these needs. Explorations of their behaviors and the way in which they achieve or miss their goals are important as prerequisites to change. Not every child who has a concern needs to change his behavior; for those who do, however, the reality counseling approach has the advantage of being direct and straightforward, and, since it considers values as well as behavior, it is not superficial.

Reality therapy is a learning-oriented view that depends upon examination of values and behavior by the child and his counselor. Glasser[28,29] has provided the primary references for this viewpoint, while Muro[30] has interpreted it for the elementary school counselor.

[28] William Glasser, *Reality Therapy* (New York: Harper & Row, 1965).
[29] William Glasser, *Schools without Failure* (New York: Harper & Row, 1969).
[30] James J. Muro, *The Counselor's Work in the Elementary School* (Scranton, Pa.: International Textbook, 1970), chap. 4.

ADLERIAN THEORY

Rudolf Dreikurs (Alfred Adler's interpreter in the United States) and Don Dinkmeyer are most often cited as supporting the Adlerian theoretical position and applying it directly to counseling with children and consulting with teachers and parents. This position and reality therapy are related in that they conceptualize human beings in similar ways, they both acknowledge the discrepancy between ultimate goals and present behavior, and they both suggest confrontative counseling styles.

ADLERIAN CONSTRUCTS

Adlerian theory and practice emphasize the holistic nature of behavior, which is seen as goal-directed and purposive. The goal may be subjective, unconscious, or dimly perceived, but it tends to draw the individual. Significance and self-esteem are ultimate motivators; lacking these rewards, the individual compensates by substituting other goals (attention, revenge, power, or getting others to serve him by appearing inadequate). Behavior, then, has social, purposive meaning in terms of the reactions the individual expects will follow (the individual may come to feel that he has a special place in the group as a result of his being disruptive and creating upset).

Experiencing a sense of belonging and a unique place in his world are basic needs of the individual; fear and anxiety result when the individual does not experience belonging and acceptance. The individual may best be understood by viewing both his phenomenological field and his personal style of life. Ultimately he does what is useful to achieve his purposes as he perceives them. The Adlerian system stresses content somewhat more than process, and it gives the relationship some stress also.

Counseling is viewed as a learning process in which the individual explores, critiques, and, where necessary, alters his assumptions about the world, himself, and his relationships. Four phases of counseling are identified in the Adlerian system. Primary in the early stages of counseling is the *relationship* phase, characterized by trust and respect-building, listening, understanding, and exploring the private logic of the individual. The *investigation* phase involves exploration of the current life situation, the here-and-now, the purposes, and the person's characteristic reasoning processes. During this phase also the family constellation, its dynamics, and recollections of early childhood are explored. The *insight* phase involves the offering of tentative hypotheses that may reveal to the individual his goals. The counselee is asked if he knows why he is doing what he is doing; he is asked if he would like to know why; and he is then offered a mirroring of his behavior in tentative terms: "Could it be . . . ," "I have the impression. . . ." The object here is to develop insight and to find where the individual wants to change. The *reorientation* phase involves the discarding of mistaken concepts, beliefs, and resultant behaviors, and the development of new conceptual and behavioral patterns. Encouragement in the direction of positive self-concept building is an important aspect of the reorientation phase.

The style of the counselor-counselee interaction tends to be direct, straightforward, and confrontative. The child or adult is faced with his inadequate logic, his maladaptive behavior, and the ultimate consequences of maintaining his present relationship to his environment.

IMPLICATIONS FOR ELEMENTARY SCHOOL COUNSELING

Counseling involving Adlerian concepts has relevance in elementary school counseling because it assumes that most children are strong enough to be faced directly with the meaning and the consequences of their behavior, and because it assumes that perceptions about mistaken goals and their relationships to values held will lead to changes in behavior. The child has purposes; he ultimately wants both a sense of belonging and a unique place in his world; he does what achieves his purposes; and he can change both his purposes and his behavior in order to achieve his ultimate goals. The Adlerian counselor is willing to engage in straight talk with the child on all these counts.

The child needs to be seen as a part of a family *and* as an individual. He can benefit by being treated warmly and logically. He also needs to be offered the respect that assumes he can permit his style of life to be exposed and examined. These matters are treated in Adlerian counseling. Potential problems that may be overcome by sensitive application of Adlerian procedures include: an assumption of omniscience on the part of the counselor ("I know about you, and I will tell you about you."); an assumption that counselor insight into the problem must exist and must precede insight on the part of the child; an assumption that all concerns involve family constellations and past recollections; and an assumption that the individual needs to be examined and explained rather than encountered on his own terms.

Adlerian theory is a learning-oriented view that depends upon exploration of life style, purposes, and behavior by the child and his counselor. Dreikurs,[31] Dreikurs and Sonstegard,[32] Dinkmeyer and Dreikurs,[33] and Dinkmeyer[34,35] have provided current references for this viewpoint.

[31] Rudolf Dreikurs, *Fundamentals of Adlerian Psychology* (Chicago: Alfred Adler Institute, 1950).

[32] Rudolf Dreikurs and Manford Sonstegard, *The Teleoanalytic Approach to Group Counseling* (Chicago: Alfred Adler Institute, 1967).

[33] Don Dinkmeyer and Rudolf Dreikurs, *Encouraging Children to Learn: the Encouragement Process* (Englewood Cliffs, N.J.: Prentice-Hall, 1963).

[34] Don Dinkmeyer, "Conceptual foundations of counseling: Adlerian theory and practice," *School Counselor, 11:* 174–178 (1964).

[35] Don Dinkmeyer, "Contributions of teleoanalytic theory and techniques to school counseling," *Personnel and Guidance Journal, 46:* 898–902 (1968).

BEHAVIOR THERAPY

Early behaviorists interested in exploring learning processes, and present-day behaviorists interested in applying behaviorism in counseling, have contributed directly or indirectly to behavior therapy. Ebbinghaus, Thorndike, Pavlov, and Watson as early contributors explored memory reinforcement, conditioning, and extinction. Dollard and Miller, Wolpe, and Krumboltz, among others, have systematically applied the concepts that these men derived to the processes of counseling. Behavior therapy is related to reality therapy and Adlerian theory in that each deals with examining and altering behavior. They differ in that reality therapy and Adlerian theory explore the value system of the individual, whereas behavior therapy deals primarily with immediate behavior.

BEHAVIOR THERAPY CONSTRUCTS

Behavior is viewed by the behavioral counselor as lawful, learned, and determined by situational factors. Neuroses are considered to be unadaptive anxiety reactions that have become conditioned. The goals of behavioral counseling are essentially learning goals that the counselor casts in observable behavior terms after he hears the child (the counselee) state his problem; thus counseling stresses content in the behavioral system.

Two basic avenues may be taken in supporting behavioral change: reinforcement and extinction.

1. *Reinforcement follows immediately* after desired behavior is exhibited—for example, the shy child is rewarded immediately after he makes a contribution in a small group.

2. *Reinforcement may be verbal*—he may be praised—*or non-verbal*—he may be given a pat on the back.

3. *Reinforcement may be intrinsic*—the child experiences success in the activity—*or extrinsic*—he may be given points, candy, or a grade as a reward.

4. *Reinforcement may follow a pattern of successive approximations*—the shy child may be asked to imagine he is talking before successively larger groups; he may then be encouraged to talk with, then before, successively larger numbers of children, starting from one; and he may be encouraged gradually to increase the quantity of his verbalization.

5. *Extinction depends on absence of reinforcement*—no fuss is made when the acting-out child interrupts a comment; rather he is ignored.

6. *Extinction relates to the schedule of past reinforcement.* That is, behavior that has always been reinforced is extinguished *more*

quickly than behavior that has been intermittently reinforced. (For example, if a child always succeeded in getting his way when he argued, this behavior would more readily be extinguished than if he had occasionally succeeded, since the child expects he eventually will prevail again.)

7. *Extinction depends on identification and elimination of reinforcing stimuli*, where possible—classmates are encouraged to stop responding when the argumentative behavior appears.

8. *Extinction may be met with an increase in response rate*, followed by rage, after which adaptation may occur.

Krumboltz[36] has enumerated four general approaches, each incorporating reinforcement and extinction, that may be used when the counselor has determined what behavior(s) of the child need attention. These include: *operant learning*, in which selected behaviors are reinforced, and in which special attention is given to the timing of reinforcements; *imitative learning*, incorporating the use of behavioral models through audio and video tape recordings, programmed instruction, and autobiographies; *cognitive learning*, including verbal instructions, counselor-client contracts, and role playing; and *emotional learning*, involving pairing of anxiety-producing stimuli with those that are pleasantly associated.

Sulzer, Mayer, and Cody[37] have brought together several procedures useful in coping with behavioral-learning problems. *Time out* involves removal of the child from the setting; *satiation* is the enforced repetition of an act to make it less attractive (the child is required to follow his mother about when he starts to do so); *modeling* may involve demonstration of an act by an older child or a child who has status in the eyes of the counselee; *reinforcing incompatible behaviors* occurs when a child is reinforced for one act (coming home on time) while an incompatible activity that appears later (lateness) is ignored; and *stimulus change* suggests separation of two children who constantly bicker or tease.

In summarizing behavioral approaches in counseling, we may say that the child is offered a direct approach related to the problem he presents to the counselor. Greater emphasis is placed on content and outcomes than upon affective needs or the relationship developing between the counselee and counselor. Outcomes are regularly examined to determine whether the observed behavior has changed in the desired direction. Testing or other procedures are freely used in order to clarify the problem or to determine if objectives are being achieved.

[36] John D. Krumboltz, ed., *Revolution in Counseling* (Boston: Houghton Mifflin, 1966), pp. 13–20.

[37] Beth Sulzer, G. Roy Mayer, and John J. Cody, "Assisting teachers with managing classroom behavioral problems," *Elementary School Guidance and Counseling, 3:* 43–48 (1968).

IMPLICATIONS FOR ELEMENTARY SCHOOL COUNSELING

The elementary school counselor, facing a child who truly desires to change his behavior, may well draw upon behavioral counseling procedures. It is highly relevant that time be spent with some children in specifying desired behavioral changes, in planning for those changes, and in checking upon outcomes. As behaviorists suggest, behavior is learned—new behavior can also be learned.

Behavioral approaches are specific, providing means for checking upon progress in counseling, and so they move the art of counseling toward a science. Further, behaviorists have demonstrated ways in which environmental limitations can be counteracted. The child who experiences gain through a behavioral contract may gain in the larger matters of self-confidence and self-concept.

When warmth emanates from the counselor, when he takes the time to insure that his relationship with the child is secure, when the selection of behaviors for change is truly agreed upon by the child, and when the child understands and accepts the reinforcement procedures, many of the stated objections to behavioral counseling evaporate. The counselor who uses these approaches mechanically reinforces the criticisms that behavioral counseling is not sufficiently humane, that it does not involve the child in his own existence, that it is manipulative and produces alienation, and that it imposes counselor values upon the child. Set in the context of a significant human relationship, experienced as a process characterized by caring and understanding, behavioral counseling procedures may, however, be expected to meet the needs of a great many children.

Behavioral approaches in counseling seem destined for further development and expansion in the elementary school. Counselors need to be well informed so that they may incorporate behavioral approaches in their own work and may help teachers in working with children who desire behavioral change. Works by Hull,[38] Dollard and Miller,[39] Wolpe,[40] Krumboltz and Hosford,[41] Ullman and Krasner,[42] and those already cited by

[38] C. L. Hull, *A Behavior System* (New Haven: Yale University Press, 1952).

[39] J. Dollard and N. E. Miller, *Personality and Psychotherapy: An Analysis in Terms of Learning, Thinking, and Culture* (New York: McGraw-Hill, 1950).

[40] Joseph Wolpe, *Psychotherapy by Reciprocal Inhibition* (Stanford, Calif.: Stanford University Press, 1958).

[41] John D. Krumboltz and Raymond E. Hosford, "Behavioral counseling in the elementary school," *Elementary School Guidance and Counseling, 1:* 27–40 (1967).

[42] Leonard P. Ullmann and Leonard Krasner, *Case Studies in Behavior Modification* (New York: Holt, Rinehart and Winston, Inc., 1965).

Krumboltz[43] and by Sulzer *et al.*,[44] provide information relevant to behaviorism. In addition, sources already cited[45,46,47,48] provide comparisons of behavioral counseling to other systems.

SELF THEORY

Originally termed nondirective counseling, later referred to as client-centered counseling, self theory as applied to counseling was developed primarily by Carl Rogers. Self theory is phenomenologically based; it is not concerned with causation or with producing behavioral change. Rather it emphasizes the individual as an experiencing organism and stresses present interaction and affect (feeling) as opposed to content.

SELF-THEORY CONSTRUCTS

Self theory is dynamic and changing. Gendlin[49] suggests that the Rogerian position has shifted from an early emphasis upon avoidance of direction, toward emphasis upon facilitative counselor attitudes; from an early emphasis upon technique, toward spontaneity and genuineness on the part of the counselor in the interview; and from an early emphasis upon insight, toward affect, moment-to-moment experiencing, and full participation by both the counselor and the child.

Self theory accepts man as basically rational, forward-moving, realistic, and socialized. Hate, anger, and other strong negative emotions exist, but as responses to frustrated needs for love, belonging, and security. Man is seen as being basically cooperative, constructive, trustworthy, and self-regulating, seeking independence, autonomy, and self-actualization.

Self-concept and perceptual field are fundamental constructs in self theory. The self-perceptions admitted to awareness are crucial in defining the individual's self-concept. The perceptual or phenomenal field *is* reality for the individual. Behavior is designed to maintain and enhance the individual and his self-concept and to satisfy his needs as he experiences and perceives them. Adjustment exists when the individual is able to admit into the self all of the sensory and affective experiences he encounters; maladjustment exists when experiences are denied. Thus, healthy psycho-

---

[43] Krumboltz, ed., *Revolution in Counseling, op. cit.*

[44] Sulzer *et al., op. cit.*

[45] Ford and Urban, *op. cit.*, chap. 8.

[46] Patterson, *op. cit.*, chaps. 7, 8, and 9.

[47] Stefflre, *op. cit.*, chap. 4.

[48] Shertzer and Stone, *op. cit.*, chap. 9.

[49] Eugene T. Gendlin, "Client-centered developments and work with schizophrenics," *Journal of Counseling Psychology, 9:* 205–212 (1962).

logical adjustment depends primarily on the capability of the individual to handle threat.

The goals of self theory are oriented toward self-actualization and maximum self-realization by the individual. The counselor seeks to assist the individual to determine his personal valuing processes and to behave in ways congruent with those processes.

The counselor enters fully into a partnership with the child (or adult), being, in every way he can be, a congruent and genuine person. Respect, acceptance, and understanding are communicated to the child, along with a faith in him and a faith in the constructive value of his being helped to find his own way. Emphasis upon techniques such as reflection has largely given way to stress on the relationship; nonetheless these techniques remain useful tools of the counseling process as developed in self theory. Self theorists of today attend to the relationship and the process of counseling more than to the content of the interview. Whereas the early nondirectivists strove for a clinically objective relationship, current thinking stresses an affective, warm relationship in which the child experiences unconditional positive regard from the counselor.

The self-theory approach, as compared to those previously discussed, is less specific, requiring the counselor himself to engage in a present-oriented interaction with the child as a person—not as a problem. The warmth, reality, genuineness, and openness of the counselor are the major facilitators in producing warmth, reality, genuineness, and openness in the child. This system, as compared to those previously considered, requires and offers less in the way of procedures, yet may well demand more of the counselor himself.

Counseling sessions are focused on the child's perceptions of himself and of the world about him; during these sessions the counselor strives to increase the child's awareness of his feeling about himself and others. The counselor also strives to respond in ways that clarify his expectation that the child will actively express his own thoughts and feelings, and he attempts to respond in ways that clarify the meaning of the child's statements and behaviors.

Although procedures are indeed deemphasized in current writings based on self theory, nonetheless transcriptions of counseling sessions tend to exhibit at least five characteristic response patterns that facilitate the moment-to-moment experiencing of counselors espousing self theory. These responses are more extensively explored in the next chapter. Briefly stated, they are: *simple acceptance* ("Yes." "Uh huh." "I see"); *reflection*, the mirroring of a statement or an action with a verbalization ("He really makes you angry." "Your eyes are downcast—saying you are embarrassed." "You really smashed the clay"); *clarification*, in which an unclear statement is explored ("I wonder if you're telling me that your Dad just doesn't live up to your expectations." "When you say she's always 'on your frame,' I take it to mean she's always nagging at you"); *summarization*, the combining of a number of statements into one synthesized whole ("So when we take all those times when you got in trouble together it seems to you that your parents and teachers have just expected too much of you." "It comes through loud and clear that no one notices you when you try to do the right thing so you wonder why you should bother"); and *confrontation*, the direct encountering by the counselor of such matters as a child's unwarranted generalization, a game a child is playing, or a self-defeating behavior ("I don't really think everything will change if you have a big party for everyone; I don't think they can be bought." "So I keep coming up with suggestions as you request and you just knock them all down; I guess you really like things the way they are too much to change them." "You keeping turning Sue off and won't hear her—maybe that's part of the problem you have with keeping friends").

With heavy emphasis on the relationship, counseling based on self theory places almost no stress on testing, diagnosis, or other procedures lest these procedures foster dependency or cast the counselor in the role of expert rather than co-worker in the process of counseling. Relationship, minimal lead and clarification, rather than the counselor's collecting and use of information, are characteristic of self-theory counseling; thus the child experiences the interview as a situation in which responsibility resides with him for goal setting and for movement toward his own goals.

IMPLICATIONS FOR ELEMENTARY SCHOOL COUNSELING

The elementary school counselor may readily identify with some of the assumptions and procedures of self-theory counseling. Since he functions in a setting with children who meet the broad criterion of normalcy, it should be relatively easy for him to exhibit faith in the human striving toward self-realization children exhibit and to accept the varying pace they set. Since he is aware of children's needs to reach out, to form relationships, and to test themselves in new settings, he may well consider the relationship a very significant variable in counseling. Since he is constantly alerted to the struggle by children to develop, enhance, or maintain their self-perceptions, he doubtless expects to deal in this realm with children. Since the process of counseling is a slice of life, he should be sensitive to the relationship of the counseling process to the child's total life style.

The demands of the self-theory system upon the counselor *to be* rather than *to do* are great, and the counselor may not be adequate to the task. The importance of the self of the counselor, his warmth, his ability to develop with the child a relationship that has meaning, his ability to elicit feelings and facilitate growth in the child, and his skill in encouraging the child to assume responsibility for himself are at once the strengths and drawbacks of the system. Other factors, such as the information needed, institutional goals for the child, and the neutrality assumed by many counselors oriented to self theory, may also present problems if the counselor is unwilling to incorporate procedures from other systems of counseling. These problems do not exist for the counselor who is a whole person and who is determined not to let his own traditionalism limit his effectiveness in working with the children who present themselves to him.

Self theory as a counseling system is basically an intensive person-person encounter, which suggests that the counselor in the elementary school draw out the genuineness, warmth, and directness in the child primarily by exhibiting those traits in himself. Even the counselor who can do this will find that many children may benefit from other specific and efficient approaches. The counselor must supplement relatedness, no matter how effective that may be in itself for the self-deprecating, disheartened, self-alienated, or grieving child. A great many children, however, want only to be heard, and many others can find solutions, take action on their own, and be sustained by the confidence they gain from the minimal help given by the counselor.

Self theory or client-centered approaches characterize a great many current and developing elementary school counseling programs. Counselors need to be informed and updated regarding these approaches so that they may effectively enter the affective world of the child. Works by Rogers,[50,51,52] Rogers and Dymond,[53] Axline,[54,55] Snygg and Combs,[56] Boy and Pine,[57] and Arbuckle[58] explore this system directly, while sources already cited[59,60,61,62] compare self theory counseling to other systems.

[50] Rogers, *Counseling and Psychotherapy, op. cit.*

[51] Rogers, *Client-Centered Therapy, op. cit.*

[52] Carl R. Rogers, *On Becoming a Person* (Boston: Houghton Mifflin, 1961).

[53] Carl R. Rogers and Rosalind Dymond, *Psychotherapy and Personality Change* (Chicago: University of Chicago Press, 1954).

[54] Virginia M. Axline, *Play Therapy* (Boston: Houghton Mifflin, 1947).

[55] Virginia M. Axline, *Dibs: In Search of Self* (Boston: Houghton Mifflin, 1964).

[56] Donald Snygg and A. W. Combs, *Individual Behavior* (New York: Harper & Row, 1949).

[57] Angelo V. Boy and Gerald J. Pine, *Client-centered Counseling in the Secondary School* (Boston: Houghton Mifflin, 1963).

[58] Dugald S. Arbuckle, *Counseling Philosophy, Theory, and Practice* (Boston: Allyn and Bacon, 1965).

[59] Ford and Urban, *op. cit.*, chap. 11.

[60] Patterson, *op. cit.*, chaps. 15 and 18.

[61] Stefflre, *op. cit.*, chap. 2.

[62] Shertzer and Stone, *op. cit.*, chap. 10.

GESTALT THERAPY

Early explorations into gestalt psychology were made by Werthei-
mer, Koehler, and Koffka; however, the application of Gestalt psychology
as a system of counseling results primarily from work by Perls. Gestalt
therapy, like counseling based on self theory, is phenomenologically based
—that is, it emphasizes experiencing in the present and deemphasizes causation from the past. Stress is placed on understanding the individual as he
is, rather than how he came to be that way.

GESTALT THERAPY CONSTRUCTS

Only the NOW exists, and in the Gestalt view the emphasis is on
how the present is, not why, nor how it can be better tomorrow. The focus
in counseling is to stay with the feelings and thoughts of the present, to
explore those feelings, sensations, perceptions, and fantasies, to take responsibility for them and to own them, and thus to focus on the process
and the present relationship.

Actuality is valued in Gestalt therapy. In a temporal sense this
means the present is valued over the past or future; in remembering, or
in anticipating, one tends to negate and cover up a present experience
rather than accepting it. In the same way in a spatial sense the present is
valued over the absent; and in a substantial sense action is valued over
symbolism of any kind, including verbalization. Awareness, acceptance of
experience, wholeness, and responsibility are also valued. The concept of
responsibility is important to Gestalt therapy because it contradicts the
common perception that we and what happens to us are solely the products
of accident and circumstance.

The Gestaltist asserts that the individual who fails to act in the
present creates more unfinished business for the future. He considers that
the individual is where he wants to be, is doing what he wants to do—
even when it appears to be tragic. He accepts the paradoxical idea that
change occurs when one ceases to yield to the "should's" and becomes
what he is, not when he tries to be what he is not.

Perls suggests:

Now there are two ways of learning. In the first, you get information;
you get someone to tell you what your dreams mean, what concepts
will be useful, what the world is like. Then you feed into the com-
puter and play the fitting game. Does this concept fit in with these
other concepts? However, the best way of learning is not the computation of information. Learning is discovering, uncovering what is there.
When we discover, we are uncovering our own ability, in order to find
our own potential, to see what is going on, to discover how we can

enlarge our lives, to find means at our disposal that will let us cope with a difficult situation. And all this, I maintain, is taking place in the here and now.[63]

Some of the rules of Gestalt therapy, briefly stated, are: *Live now*; be alert when leaving the now and always go back to the now of present interaction and hidden fantasies. *Live here*; deal with those who are present and whatever is present. *Make speech patterns direct*; for example, avoid use of the word "it," change nouns into verbs, change "if" and "but" to "and," change "can't" to "I don't want to," change "I feel guilty" to "I resent." *Don't gossip about absent persons*; bring the absent one into a present encounter by having the speaker play both roles. *Take action*; stop imagining and thinking, rather act, express, taste, and see. *Accept no should or ought from other persons, past or present. Take full responsibility for actions, feelings, and thoughts. Ask "why" to mean "for what purpose," not "what is the cause."* Each of these rules is designed to facilitate present and responsible living.

IMPLICATIONS FOR ELEMENTARY SCHOOL COUNSELING

The stress placed upon present functioning and the responsibility of the individual in Gestalt therapy seems very appropriate in elementary school counseling. Children are highly accustomed to having responsibility for their actions assumed by parents, siblings, and teachers, among others; thus they readily yield responsibility and may actively blame others. Much can be taken from the Gestalt position and applied in individual and small-group counseling with normal children in the elementary school, increasing their self-awareness and self-reliance. The encouragement of present-oriented and responsibility-oriented verbal styles seems highly appropriate with children, as does the encountering in role play of an absent person, taking both roles, speaking directly, and taking action.

Before the Gestalt therapy system can be considered fully applicable in elementary school counseling it needs some direct adaptation for that purpose. Nonetheless, the "Four Lectures" of Perls,[64] the collection of readings by Fagan and Shepherd,[65] and the work by Perls, Hefferline, and Goodman,[66] present a number of Gestalt concepts that have relevance for elementary school counseling.

[63] Frederick Perls, "Four Lectures," in Joen Fagan and Irma Lee Shepherd, eds., *Gestalt Therapy Now* (Palo Alto: Science and Behavior Books, 1970), p. 18.

[64] *Ibid.*, pp. 14–38.

[65] Joen Fagan and Irma Lee Shepherd, eds., *Gestalt Therapy Now* (Palo Alto, Calif.: Science and Behavior Books, 1970).

[66] Frederick Perls, Ralph Hefferline, and Paul Goodman, *Gestalt Therapy* (New York: Dell, 1951).

EXISTENTIALISM

Kierkegaard, Tillich, Heidegger, Sartre, May, and Frankl are among the historical names that may be cited in an examination of existential counseling, or *Daseinanalyse*. Since existential philosophy is highly individual and is an aggregate composed of writings in the fields of theology, psychology, psychiatry, and philosophy, the present source can only begin to suggest the position of existentialism as applied to counseling.

EXISTENTIAL CONSTRUCTS

The existentialist views man as being and becoming, a complex organism in relation to the universe. He belongs in a world of natural and constructed things, yet he alone can reflect, make decisions, choose his destiny, and create his own meaning. Man is free. He is what he makes of himself—his own pilot. External influences may limit him, but they do not determine him.

Being and *nonbeing* are contrasting states that are fundamental to existentialism. The healthy individual is open to reality, is aware of himself, and truly exists. The state of nonbeing results from total conformity, resulting in loss of uniqueness and individuality.

Beck's summarization of thirteen propositions as a Credo for Counselors embodies the existential view of the nature of man, basic existential personality constructs, and the goals of existential counseling:

1. Every man, not mentally incompetent, is responsible for his acts.
2. Man can do little to change most of the physical universe, the given, but he can predict it and make his life happier by facing reality.
3. Each man must aid others and try to understand their feelings, for mankind is left alone in an uncaring world.
4. Man creates his own nature. This is an individual choice.
5. Man should act toward others as he would want them to act toward him.
6. Decisions should be made only by the criterion, "What is the effect on humankind?" Man must be treated with dignity; his status as a past-and-future-experiencing being, the only creature so endowed, makes this mandatory.
7. Determinism applies to physical laws; choice is a fact of human existence within the framework of the given surroundings.
8. Man counsels because no man can meet all problems alone.
9. Choices must be made by the counselee, for the counselor cannot claim omniscience.
10. The end of counseling is enabling fellow creatures better to bear the buffets of life, better to seek happiness and individual fulfillment.
11. Man must operate as if he is alone in the universe with his

fellows; it is futile to argue about supernatural creation; there is no proof.

12. Man's suffering can be relieved by suggestions from those who have traveled the road before, or a road like it.

13. It would be an act of cruelty not to try to benefit others; they are involved with us in life.[67]

Awareness, genuineness, commitment, experiencing, and meaning are among the goals of existentialism. Being, as opposed to nonbeing, is sought, as are participation, sensitivity, and encounter. The individual's *Eigenwelt*, his "own world" of a sense of self-identity, is examined and expanded to the end that he sees his capacity to rise above his past, to transcend himself.

May[68] considers existentialism more an attitude or an approach to human beings than a school of counseling or a set of techniques. Thus, he would emphasize the heightened values of moment-to-moment experiencing regardless of the kind of counseling relationship that emerges. If, as May suggests, existentialism contributes an attitude rather than techniques as such, the counselor is left free to include a wide variety of techniques; indeed, this is the case. The counselee is not a subject, but an "existential partner," and the relationship is an encounter in which no prescribed set of procedures is predestined to occur.

Recent literature in self theory[69] has established a clear relationship to existential thought, while the existential point of view has also characterized some psychoanalytic approaches.[70,71] Perhaps Frankl's Logotherapy[72,73] is the approach that most uniquely develops existentialism as a counseling philosophy in its own right, yet it would also appear to leave open a wide range of counseling procedures.

One special contribution by Frankl is his concept of *paradoxical intention,* a technique in which the individual intends and deliberately executes the behavior he wishes to eliminate. Intending, Frankl asserts, removes

---

[67] Carlton Beck, *Philosophical Foundations of Guidance* (Englewood Cliffs, N.J.: Prentice-Hall, 1963). Reprinted by permission.

[68] Rollo May, "Dangers in the relation of existentialism to psychotherapy," *Review of Existential Psychology and Psychiatry, 3:* 5–10 (1963).

[69] Carl R. Rogers, "Two divergent trends," in Rollo May, ed., *Existential Psychology* (New York: Random House, 1961), pp. 85–93.

[70] Ludwig Binswanger, "Existential Analysis and Psychotherapy," in Frieda Fromm-Reichmann and J. L. Moreno, eds., *Progress in Psychotherapy* (New York: Grune and Stratton, 1956), pp. 144–148.

[71] Rollo May, "Existential Bases of Psychotherapy," in Rollo May, ed., *Existential Psychology* (New York: Random House, 1961), pp. 75–84.

[72] Viktor Frankl, *Man's Search for Meaning* (New York: Washington Square Press, 1963).

[73] Viktor Frankl, *The Doctor and the Soul* (New York: Knopf, 1955).

the fear response that previously has created additional anxiety and maintained a vicious circle. Fear of perspiring before others is met with the intention to perspire: "I only sweated out a quart before, but now I'm going to pour out ten quarts."[74]

Generally speaking, however, Frankl's approach is intended much more to deal with the meaning of the individual's own life, his values and goals, his freedom and responsibility, about which discussion centers in this rather direct approach.

The process of counseling and the relationship between counselor and counselee are given high priority over product and procedures, since moment-to-moment experiencing supersedes other matters in existential counseling.

IMPLICATIONS FOR ELEMENTARY SCHOOL COUNSELING

The elementary school counselor may well identify with the present-valuing attitude in counseling that is characteristic of existentialism. Such a counselor is involved with children in their search for meaning and in their development of responsibility, acknowledging that these traits do not suddenly emerge with adulthood. He enters fully into the counseling relationship, concerned that the moments of encounter become as meaningful as he and the child can make them. He seeks by entering into a genuine relationship to aid the child to be his own most genuine self. He expects that his being in ways that reveal both himself and his perceptions of the child will demonstrate his belief in the child's strength and worth. His hope is that the spiraling process by which self-alienation develops in many children will be slowed or reversed and that the idealism present in children will be enhanced.

The elementary school counselor, in exploring the sources already cited, original sources,[75,76,77] and comparative sources,[78,79,80] may well find that the existential attitude has much relevance for his counseling. If he becomes existentially involved with others in his life he will *be* self-aware and will help others to *be* and *become* aware, present-oriented, and genuine. As Arbuckle suggests: "Man basically *is* free, and any man can come to learn and to grow and to become the free person he is. This is the

[74] Frankl, *Man's Search for Meaning*, p. 196.

[75] Paul Tillich, *The Courage To Be* (New Haven: Yale University Press, 1952).

[76] Jean-Paul Sartre, *Existential Psychoanalysis* (Chicago: Regnery, 1953).

[77] Rollo May, *Existential Psychology* (New York: Random House, 1961).

[78] Patterson, *op. cit.*, chaps. 19 and 20.

[79] Ford and Urban, *op. cit.*, chap. 12.

[80] Shertzer and Stone, *op. cit.*, chap. 10.

purpose of counseling—to help the individual to loosen himself from his deterministic shackles, and to come to realize and to see what he always had—choice and freedom."[81]

A BRIEF STATEMENT OF POSITION

In the present book, adult and child are viewed as both free and determined. Freedom depends in part on the intelligence, vision, and strength of the individual; and in most human beings there are overlays of limiting past events—so many that the freedom of the self may be denied and its genuineness subverted. Although the sense of freedom is limited, the reality of freedom is greater than experienced by most persons.

Adult and child are viewed here as striving toward personal meaning and self-realization in their lives; their actions tend to be purposive, supporting these major goals or other substitute goals. Meaning and personal significance, though not always achieved, act as motivating forces in the lives of all. Adult and child encounter problems and obstacles in experiencing a positive sense of self. At such times, in the view of others, they may cope with their needs inadequately and be referred for assistance, or they may seek the help of a counselor on their own.

What is the position of the elementary school counselor when the child appears before him? The view taken in this book is that there is no single right position. Children may need to explore their feelings, they may need insight into their ways of coping with reality, they may be lacking in the cognitive area and need information, or they may need skills that they do not possess and that they can learn.

Early influences and traumatic experiences in the life of the child may limit him in his present functioning. However, for the child who can function within the school setting, and for the counselor who is employed by the elementary school, the emphasis on ferreting out basic causation seems generally unnecessary, often inappropriate or impossible, and, when indicated, better left to those with greater experience in such matters. Although we must acknowledge that early influences and unconscious motivations exist, nonetheless not all causation is based in infancy or early childhood, and most children continue to function adequately without spending long hours on matters of causation. Some exploration of causation may be beneficial in certain cases, however; the child who is helped to explore may find, for example, that his immediate experiencing of anxiety is related to a recent act of his, or a series of actions over time, that cause him great guilt or deep concern.

[81] Dugald S. Arbuckle, "Existentialism in counseling: the humanist view," *Personnel and Guidance Journal, 43:* 562 (1965).

Present-centeredness, exploring now, making choices now, making decisions now, seem highly appropriate as objectives for many children in counseling. The individual or group counseling setting, when now-oriented, becomes a slice of life in which the child may learn how he is perceived and received and may explore and express his perceptions and feelings about himself, the counselor, and others. The counseling interview can be a nondetermined, exploratory experience focused upon the needs the child perceives in himself, the ways in which he functions in order to meet those needs, and his evaluation of the effectiveness of his ways of meeting his needs. The child discovers that the responsibility for these ways and for their success or failure is ultimately his own, however many others he may find accountable in the process.

At the same time, every act and word of the child results from a message sent from his brain to his body members. Decisions and choices are made, *then* acted upon. Thus, present-centeredness carries an element of planning for the future that is also relevant. If, in counseling, the child can decide to state a point or take an action and then carry the decision out, he may also plan for time that will exist outside the counseling situation. Adult interactions with children often are oriented too much to causation and past events or too much to a distant future. The immediate present and the near-immediate future deserve much more attention in the counseling process than they generally receive.

The counselor can serve the child by helping him see the sorts of messages he sends, the guidelines and limitations he places upon himself, the degree to which he acknowledges his own, genuine, present-oriented feelings, and the extent to which he permits himself to be a rational and responsible human being. In transactional analysis terms, the counselor may clarify the source of the child's transactions from the Parent-Adult-Child frame of reference, and he may encourage the updating of the Parent, the freeing of the Child from Not-OK feelings, and the developing of the Adult in the individual. The counselor can help the child to find positive qualities in himself and others and help him to develop a concept of self and of others as worthwhile ("I'm OK, you're OK").

The counselor can help the child examine his value structure, explore his behaviors, and understand his goals. He may help the child clarify the extent to which his values, goals, and behavior are compatible or incompatible. Where appropriate, he can encourage the child to examine and to restructure either his behaviors, goals, or values, since he must ultimately be responsible for himself.

The process of counseling involves *listening,* to ascertain how the child sees himself, his world, and his problems; *exploring,* to examine the present moment, to deepen the understandings of both participants, to check on the child's and the counselor's assumptions, and to clarify how and where the counselor and child are with one another; *confronting,* to test the relationship by facing up to unexplored or self-defeating perceptions and actions; and, ultimately, *planning*, to functionalize the discussion in action that takes place both inside and outside the counseling setting and that promotes growth and progress.

In terms of counseling style, straightness and directness are valued over subtlety and inference, and assertions are valued over questions. Exploration of affect and cognition are both valued. Since few opportunities outside counseling are given the child to explore his affect, his doing so in counseling is particularly important.

When the child seeks to change his behavior or agrees that behavior change is necessary, the counselor should be ready to participate meaningfully in meeting his needs. He should be prepared to explore and to define with the child the specific behaviors to be eliminated, so that success in this venture may be evaluated. He should also be prepared to explore the matter with the relevant adults in the life of the child, so that all can be helpful in reinforcing his attempts to alter his behavior.

In the present book the view is taken that choice and freedom are constants. At every turn the individual chooses his words, his gestures, his attitudes, and his actions. He makes many of his choices at a reflex-habitual level, but most can be brought to conscious awareness, and then other choices can be made. Even when the only freedom available is to choose with what attitude he will do what he must do, that choice remains. Most situations are not that desperate; generally the individual has much opportunity for producing change in himself and in the environment.

Meaning can derive in grand ways; perhaps for the child, however, it derives most frequently from a sense that moment-to-moment choices and actions have been basically effective, and that the opportunity to continue to take effective action remains. The child who has meaning in his life can say: "I make good choices. I care about myself. I care about others. Others care about me. I will be able to handle the tasks that lie ahead."

Elementary school counselors must be about the business of making their own free and effective choices, of encouraging free and effective choices in children, of bringing to awareness enhancing and self-defeating concepts and behaviors, of helping children to believe in themselves—to believe that they do make a difference and that they can be genuine, caring, and responsible human beings. They must work to help children in ways that promote self-help, since ultimately self-help is the child's best resource. Further, they must convey belief in the child's capabilities; even while helping, they must let the child see that they believe in his ability to help himself.

Counseling can be directed toward the exploration of causation; it can be concentrated upon helping the child understand how his messages are received; it can be focused on examining discrepancies between values and behaviors; it can be a search for and a confronting of self-defeating behavior patterns; it can be focused on behavior change; it can be directed toward the development of self-realization; it can be oriented toward helping the child see his responsibility for himself; or it can be a search to discover meaning in the child's life. It can be any one or more of these and be effective.

Above and beyond all else, however, counseling is two or more people in touch with one another, concerned together about matters that each agrees are important. It is a human encounter. It can be a monologue or a dialogue that reinforces loneliness and self-alienation—there is no greater aloneness than being in another's presence and not being in touch; but it does not have to be this way. The child and the counselor must accept that all they really have are these moments together, moments that can become a genuine encounter, a caring experience. Whether the road taken is behavioral, existential, or any other, it is a road that is likely to be new to the child and well traveled by the counselor. If the experience is a mechanical repetition by the counselor of other experiences, it will not achieve all it can. Thus, the counselor and the child have a mutual responsibility, regardless of the direction taken, to make their moments together meaningful.

Perhaps the attitude conveyed in the thoughts of an individual counselor can help to create this meaningfulness: "Where are you, child, and where am I with you? Can we reach each other? Can we search and find living, breathing, genuine human beings? Can we listen and talk with each other and find that we can make a difference to each other? Can we be who we are and become who we can become—together?"

SUMMARY

It is important that the individual counselor develop a personal style of counseling consistent with his philosophy and his own personality. In order to form his position, he must deal with several considerations. He must decide how important he considers the relationship to be and how he will go about creating a helping relationship that is compatible with his philosophy. He must consider both content and process in counseling and determine whether he will emphasize one or the other or attempt to keep both always in focus.

Among the many positions he might take are several of which he ought to be aware. Psychoanalytic counseling puts the emphasis on causality, stresses unconscious determinants of behavior, and points up the formative nature of early experiences. Transactional analysis examines the processes of communication and the life style (life position) of the individual in order to understand the messages he sends. Reality therapy concentrates on examining values and behaviors and confronting the discrepancies. Adlerian theory considers the purposes of the child's actions, his mistaken goals, and his self-defeating behaviors, and it confronts these concerns.

Behavior therapists note that since behavior is learned, new learning may be substituted; thus, counseling emphasis is upon determining desired changes and planning the reinforcement of new behaviors. Self theory places primary emphasis on the relationship as a vehicle for self-discovery; its proponents believe that counselees need the freedom to explore their own needs and concerns and that an accepting relationship will make possible any necessary attitudinal and behavioral development. Emphasis in Gestalt therapy is upon present functioning and the responsibility of the individual in the present. Existentialists stress the search for meaning in life and in the moment; a genuine relationship with emphasis on process is sought in counseling. Each of these positions offers something of value to the elementary school counselor.

Ultimately the counselor constructs his own position, whether aware or unaware; it is his responsibility to become as effective as he can be by drawing upon views that fit him and his concept of the needs of children. The range of directions he can take is enormous—which should be seen not as a problem but as an opportunity, since it permits personal freedom and allows the expression of many personalities through counseling. Freedom and responsibility, both with the child in general and in the moment, present the counselor with continuous challenges.

REFERENCES

Arbuckle, D. S. *Counseling Philosophy, Theory, and Practice*. Boston: Allyn and Bacon, 1965.

———. "Existentialism in counseling: the humanist view," *Personnel and Guidance Journal, 43:* 558–567 (1965).

Axline, V. M. *Play Therapy*. Boston: Houghton Mifflin, 1947.

———. *Dibs: In Search of Self*. Boston: Houghton Mifflin, 1964.

Beck, C. *Philosophical Foundations of Guidance*. Englewood Cliffs, N.J.: Prentice-Hall, 1963.

Berne, E. *Transactional Analysis in Psychotherapy*. New York: Grove, 1961.

———. *Games People Play*. New York: Grove, 1964.

Binswanger, L. "Existential analysis and psychotherapy," in Frieda Fromm-Reichmann and J. L. Moreno, eds., *Progress in Psychotherapy*. New York: Grune & Stratton, 1956.

Blocher, D. H. *Developmental Counseling*. New York: Ronald, 1966.

Borrenson, A. M. "Counselor influence on diagnostic classification of client problems," *Journal of Counseling Psychology, 14:* 252–258 (1965).

Boy, A. "A rationale for school counseling," *Guidance,* 4: 111–117 (1966).

———— and G. J. Pine. *Client-Centered Counseling in the Secondary School.* Boston: Houghton Mifflin, 1963.

Brammer, L. M., and E. L. Shostrom. *Therapeutic Psychology.* Englewood Cliffs, N.J.: Prentice-Hall, 1968.

Dinkmeyer, D. "Developmental counseling in the elementary school," *Personnel and Guidance Journal,* 45: 262–266 (1966).

————. "Counseling theory and practice in the elementary school," *Elementary School Guidance and Counseling,* 1: 196–207 (1967).

————. "Conceptual foundations of counseling: Adlerian theory and practice," *School Counselor,* 11: 174–178 (1964).

————. "Contributions of teleoanalytic theory and techniques to school counseling," *Personnel and Guidance Journal,* 46: 898–902 (1968).

———— and Rudolf Dreikurs. *Encouraging Children to Learn: the Encouragement Process.* Englewood Cliffs, N.J.: Prentice-Hall, 1963.

Dollard, J., and N. E. Miller. *Personality and Psychotherapy: An Analysis in Terms of Learning, Thinking, and Culture.* New York: McGraw-Hill, 1950.

Dreikurs, R. *Fundamentals of Adlerian Psychology.* Chicago: Alfred Adler Institute, 1950.

———— and Manford Sonstegard. *The Teleoanalytic Approach to Group Counseling.* Chicago: Alfred Adler Institute, 1967.

Fagan, J., and I. L. Shepherd, eds. *Gestalt Therapy Now.* Palo Alto, Calif.: Science and Behavior Books, 1970.

Ford, D. H., and H. B. Urban. *Systems of Psychotherapy.* New York: Wiley, 1963.

Frankl, V. *The Doctor and the Soul.* New York: Knopf, 1955.

————. *Man's Search for Meaning.* New York: Washington Square Press, 1963.

Gendlin, E. T. "Client-centered developments and work with schizophrenics," *Journal of Counseling Psychology,* 9: 205–212 (1962).

Glasser, W. *Reality Therapy: A New Approach to Psychiatry.* New York: Harper & Row, 1965.

————. *Schools without Failure.* New York: Harper & Row, 1969.

Gronert, R. R. "Combining a behavioral approach with reality therapy," *Elementary School Guidance and Counseling,* 5: 104–112 (1970).

Harris, T. A. *I'm OK, You're OK.* New York: Harper & Row, 1967.

Hull, C. L. *A Behavior System.* New Haven: Yale University Press, 1952.

Johnson, E. L. "Existentialism, self theory and the existential self," *Personnel and Guidance Journal,* 46: 53–58 (1967).

King, P. T. "Psychoanalytic adaptations," in Buford Stefflre, ed., *Theories of Counseling.* New York: McGraw-Hill, 1965. Chapter 3.

Krumboltz, J. D., ed. *Revolution in Counseling.* Boston: Houghton Mifflin, 1966.

———— and R. E. Hosford. "Behavioral counseling in the elementary school," *Elementary School Guidance and Counseling,* 1: 27–40 (1967).

May, R. *Existential Psychology*. New York: Random House, Inc., 1961.

————. "Dangers in the relation of existentialism to psychotherapy," *Review of Existential Psychology and Psychiatry, 3:* 5–10 (1963).

Muro, J. J. *The Counselor's Work in the Elementary School*. Scranton, Pa.: International Textbook, 1970.

Nelson, R. C. "The Emerging Role of the Elementary School Counselor: The Counseling Role." Paper read at American Personnel and Guidance Association Convention, Dallas, 1967.

Parker, C. A. *Counseling Theories and Counselor Education*. Boston: Houghton Mifflin, 1968.

Patterson, C. H. *Theories of Counseling and Psychotherapy*. New York: Harper & Row, 1966.

————. *The Counselor in the School*. New York: McGraw-Hill, 1967.

Perls, F. "Four lectures," in Joen Fagan and Irma Lee Shepherd, eds., *Gestalt Therapy Now*. Palo Alto: Science and Behavior Books, 1970. Chapter 2.

————, R. Hefferline, and P. Goodman. *Gestalt Therapy*. New York: Dell, 1951.

Peters, H. J. "Developmental counseling," *Clearing House, 41:* 111–117 (1966).

Rogers, C. R. *Counseling and Psychotherapy*. Boston: Houghton Mifflin, 1942.

————. *Client-Centered Therapy*. Boston: Houghton Mifflin, 1951.

————. "The Characteristics of a Helping Relationship," *Personnel and Guidance Journal, 37:* 6–16 (1958).

————. *On Becoming a Person*. Boston: Houghton Mifflin, 1961.

————. "Two divergent trends," in Rollo May, ed., *Existential Psychology*. New York: Random House, 1961. Pp. 85–93.

———— and R. Dymond. *Psychotherapy and Personality Change*. Chicago: University of Chicago Press, 1954.

Sartre, J.-P. *Existential Psychoanalysis*. Chicago: Regnery, 1953.

Shertzer, B., and S. C. Stone. *Fundamentals of Counseling*. Boston: Houghton Mifflin, 1968.

Snygg, D., and A. W. Combs. *Individual Behavior*. New York: Harper & Row, 1949.

Stefflre, B. B. *Theories of Counseling*. New York: McGraw-Hill, 1965.

———— and K. B. Matheny. *The Function of Counseling Theory*. Guidance Monograph Series, Boston: Houghton Mifflin, 1968.

Sulzer, B., G. R. Mayer, and J. J. Cody. "Assisting teachers with managing classroom behavioral problems," *Elementary School Guidance and Counseling, 3:* 40–48 (1968).

Swensen, C. H., Jr. *An Approach to Case Conceptualization*. Guidance Monograph Series, Boston: Houghton Mifflin, 1968.

Tillich, P. *The Courage to Be*. New Haven: Yale University Press, 1952.

Ullmann, L. P., and L. Krasner. *Case Studies in Behavior Modification*. New York: Holt, Rinehart and Winston, Inc., 1965.

van Kaam, A. "Counseling from the Viewpoint of Existential Psychology," *Harvard Educational Review, 32:* 403–415 (1962).

Walker, D. E., and H. C. Peiffer, Jr. "The Goals of Counseling," *Journal of Counseling Psychology, 4:* 204–209 (1957).

Wolpe, J. *Psychotherapy by Reciprocal Inhibition.* Stanford, Calif.: Stanford University Press, 1958.

ARTICLES IN BOOKS OF READINGS

Dinkmeyer, D. C. *Guidance and Counseling in the Elementary School: Readings in Theory and Practice.* New York: Holt, Rinehart and Winston, Inc., 1968. Readings beginning on pages 220, 228, 235, 244, 250, 260.

Koplitz, E. D. *Guidance in the Elementary School: Theory, Research, and Practice.* Dubuque, Iowa: William C. Brown, Publishers, 1968. Reading beginning on page 222.

Mills, G. D. *Elementary School Guidance and Counseling.* New York: Random House, Inc., 1971. Readings beginning on pages 15, 25.

Peters, H. J., A. C. Riccio, and J. J. Quaranta. *Guidance in the Elementary School: A Book of Readings.* New York: Macmillan, 1963. Reading beginning on page 149.

Peters, H. J., and M. J. Bathory. *School Counseling: Perspectives and Procedures.* Itasca, Ill.: F. E. Peacock, 1968. Readings beginning on pages 84, 105, 125, 364, 372, 396.

7

Child Counseling

Perhaps there is more understanding and beauty in life when the sunlight is softened by the pattern of shadows. Perhaps there is more depth in a relationship that has weathered some storms. Experience that never disappoints or saddens or stirs up feelings is a bland experience with little challenge or variation in color. Perhaps when we experience confidence and faith and hope . . . this builds up within us a feeling of inner strength, courage, and security.

We are all personalities that grow and develop as a result of all our experiences, relationships, thoughts, and emotions. We are the sum total of all the parts that go into the making of a life.

VIRGINIA AXLINE: *Dibs: In Search of Self*

When Jack goes into the counseling office, a bit afraid, he expects this adult, the counselor, to perform as other adults do. He wants to maintain his maladaptive behavior and have others change. He may pay lip service to his desire for change, but he believes that if only Bill would stop poking him, and Frank would ask him to play, things would be better. If Jack is to be given the help he needs, he needs to meet beyond that door an alive, genuine, warm, human individual who will not be too distracted to help, who will encourage him to see his own responsibilities, and who will make every effort to keep the moments they have together special, unique, and meaningful.

Will he meet a perceptive individual who is able to understand him, support him, believe in him, care about him, and challenge him? Or will the needs, the techniques, or the weaknesses of the counselor prevent the progress the child could tolerate at this time?

This chapter develops further the position presented briefly in the previous one. The approach emphasizes a self-theory-existential view, which expands to include the planning and examination of values that are characteristic of behavioral and reality therapy approaches. The first objective here is to set forth a style of counseling that may be used as a point of departure for the individual counselor. The second objective is to examine communication techniques, so that the teacher or counselor may look at his own processes of communication and revise or add to them as he sees appropriate. The view is taken here that the most effective counseling occurs when multidimensional approaches are used in a flexible manner.

Topics to be dealt with include relationship and technique, an existential attitude, phases in counseling, understanding responses, affective responses, process and confrontative responses, the use of questions, behavioral approaches, and three cautions in child counseling.

RELATIONSHIP AND TECHNIQUE

Stefflre and Matheny[1] note that self theory has developed in the direction of acknowledging the importance of the relationship and of counseling attitudes while deemphasizing technique; the same deemphasis of technique is characteristic of existentialism in counseling. Since the present book supports those two approaches, and since much of this chapter is centered around examination of technique, an explanation is in order.

Everyday person-to-person communication is generally quite successful in warding off concerns of children, and for that matter of adults; but most human beings experience periods in their lives when their approaches to their personal problems are not sufficiently effective. Often, before seeking or being referred for counseling, children have presented their problems to several adults and have received very logical suggestions. However, problem solving frequently involves giving up familiar approaches, and even those children who seek assistance may be hesitant to change.

The counselor, therefore, needs a wide repertoire of response patterns—a multiplicity of approaches from which he can select his own personalized approach to counseling. As Blocher[2] indicates, the counselor will tend to respond in one of three ways: (1) he may use a response mode

---

[1] Buford B. Stefflre and Kenneth Matheny, *The Function of Counseling Theory* (Guidance Monograph Series, Boston: Houghton Mifflin, 1968), pp. 27–28.

[2] Donald H. Blocher, "Counselor education: facilitating the development of a helping person," in Clyde A. Parker, ed., *Counseling Theories and Counselor Education* (Boston: Houghton Mifflin, 1968), pp. 138–142.

that may be termed *immediate-intuitive*, relying on approaches that he has found successful in his previous experience and that are sufficiently habitual to be at a rather low level of conscious awareness; (2) he may use a *cognitive-theoretical* response mode, emulating rather rudimentary concepts of how a counselor might best perform; or (3) he may use an *empirical-pragmatic* response mode, based on results that he believes to be predictable—"When I behave in certain ways, counselees tend to talk more about important personal issues." In other words, habits and perceptions enter heavily into the response processes used by the counselor.

While the highly effective, highly experienced counselor may successfully emphasize the relationship almost to the exclusion of technique, a prerequisite may be that a wide range of responses is truly available to him at a low level of consciousness. Perhaps, before he can wisely put aside technique considerations, the counselor needs a rich developmental experience that helps him to be reflective, to confront, to tolerate silence, to provide clarification. It seems likely that the genuineness of the counselor will emerge more adequately when the overlay of habitual responses *and* the discomfort with newer approaches are both removed.

Another point concerns the quickness of thought enjoyed by any intelligent adult. The protestation, "I couldn't think of a thing to say," may often be translated as, "I blocked because I couldn't decide which of the available alternatives would be most facilitative."

For example, when a child makes an emotional statement: "I hate my brother," a rush of competing thoughts assail the beginning counselor:

"Oh, I wish he hadn't said that—but I'm a counselor now and I shouldn't deny him his thoughts."
"Oh, he doesn't really mean that—does he?"
"He's making me uncomfortable with all that anger."
"Boy, he really gets angry at his brother."
"What makes him say that?"
"I wonder why he feels that way."
"What kind of parents must this kid have?"
"I wish he'd talk about his drawing—it'd be more pleasant."
"What did I learn in my practicum that I can apply here?"
"He needs to know that I'm with him—not that I agree, but understand."

At such moments the counselor must contend with two overriding considerations—one that involves the relationship: "I must help this child know my interest and concern," and one that relates to technique: "How may I best convey my interest and concern?"

Here the position is taken that the relationship is preeminent: the counselor can make many small technical blunders that only convey his humanity and even earn him appreciation for his imperfections, but technical competence without attention to the relationship is not likely to produce any great good.

Subsequent sections of this chapter will discuss the enhancement of the relationship through effective communication processes. It should be noted, however, that Rogers[3] posits the necessary and sufficient conditions for a therapeutic relationship without specific reference to technique. These conditions are: (1) that the counselee and counselor are in *contact* with each other—willing and able both to talk about the same matters and to understand each other; (2) that the counselee is in a state of *incongruence*, experiencing anxiety or vulnerability; (3) that the counselor is *congruent* in the relationship—his feelings and his verbalizations are together; (4) that the counselor experiences *unconditional positive regard* toward the counselee—he does not imply: "I will like you if . . ."; (5) that the counselor experiences *empathic understanding* of the counselee's internal frame of reference—he "feels with" the counselee; and (6) that the counselee at least minimally *perceives the counselor's unconditional positive regard and his empathic understanding*.

Throughout the subsequent discussion of technique, one should remain aware of its purpose: to improve relationship conditions.

AN EXISTENTIAL ATTITUDE

The existentially oriented counseling relationship embodies counselor attitudes toward the counselee that are relevant to the moment and significant to the experience underway. The counselor implies to the counselee: "I am with you. Our being together is important. Let us make it meaningful since it is where we are right now, at this moment. What you are saying is important to me. You are heard; what you say goes on the record. I believe in your reality, your nowness. But if you are different when next we meet, I'll be able to accept that, for I see you as having potential in many directions.

"Your thoughts and your feelings are important to me, but I am here, too; and if you cannot make these moments be significant, I shall try to help. I sense your struggle—your wanting to protect yourself and your need to grow. I will give you the chance to examine your strengths, your problems, your concerns, your feelings, and your needs. And you shall know I am with you."

As Moustakas puts it, the counselor conveys to the child by his words and his actions: "These are your feelings. These are your ways. You

[3] Carl R. Rogers, "The necessary and sufficient conditions of therapeutic personality change," *Journal of Consulting Psychology, 21*, 95–103 (1957).

have a right to cherish them because they belong to you. I hold your pe-
culiarities, your loves and your hates, your mannerisms and your habits
in esteem and honor as I do all aspects of your self."[4] Schoettelkotte has
said it another way:

> You *are* an OTHER—more than I have ever known you to be before.
> I like you. I am in communion with you. I can no longer hurt you or
> try to be better than you. You have become important to me. You
> have inherent dignity and uniqueness. I stand before you in reverence,
> wonder, awe. I am deeply concerned about you, concerned about those
> things and persons and situations that are important to you. I am
> concerned because I see and hear and feel your concern as it is NOW.
> Your concern may not be the same tomorrow or next month or next
> year. I shall try to remain open to you, keeping in touch, allowing my
> conceptions of you to change as you change.
>
> I will work in the present moment and respond to the present need
> in whatever way I can for it is only in this moment that I can grow,
> become, live . . . REALLY LIVE![5]

Such attitudes, conveyed without a false sense of mysticism and
experienced by children in genuine ways that are felt to be honest, down
to earth, and human, are the cloth of which existential encounter is made.

In an article that deals with a concern clearly relevant to existentialism in counseling, Leona Tyler[6] has questioned the concept of personality reconstruction as an objective in counseling and has suggested that
minimum change through counseling is more appropriate for many individuals. Surely, for most children counseling that produces maximum
change is *not* the best counseling; significant moments that unleash the
child's strengths, on the other hand, may produce the minimum change
needed in this moment.

Perhaps it is useful to think of the emotional balance of the normal
child as an ever-changing spiral. While most of the time it describes a
circle, a few events accumulating in one direction send it on an upward
or downward course. A real human encounter in which the child feels
heard, understood, and valued acts to reflect the downward spiral upward
or to sustain upward movement.

Through this kind of moment-to-moment experiencing and through
the counselor's determination to be as genuine and as effective as he can
be, counseling relationships may develop a quality far beyond those from

---

[4] Clark A. Moustakas, *Psychotherapy with Children* (New York: Harper &
Row, 1959), p. 5.

[5] Alice M. Schoettelkotte, "Counseling the other," *School Counselor, 17:*
259 (1970).

[6] Leona E. Tyler, "Minimum change therapy," *Personnel and Guidance
Journal, 38:* 475–479 (1960).

which, until now, our standards for success and failure in child counseling have had to be derived.

PHASES IN COUNSELING

Each single interview tends to develop a structure that has certain common elements, and within each interview series additional common elements tend to occur. The initiating of a counseling relationship, the structuring or clarification of the process that occurs in early phases of counseling, the closing of a single interview or a total relationship, and the orientation around listening that may develop into focusing, may be viewed as phases in counseling. The more the counselor treats these phases as predictable, the more he will tend to bring them about—often to the detriment of the counseling relationship. On the other hand, an appreciation for the process and its phases may help the counselor meet differing demands more adequately and help him understand the relationship.

INITIATING COUNSELING

It used to be that attention was devoted in the first moments of counseling to the "building of rapport," until Wall[7] called rapport an outmoded concept, criticizing the illusion that it was a doorway through which the counselor and counselee must pass.

In the name of rapport a period of small talk was indulged in and the concern of moment was deferred until an atmosphere of friendliness characterized the situation. This concept may be criticized on three bases: (1) the artificiality of rapport-constructing procedures, (2) the unnecessary delay in getting to the concern of the child, and (3) the treatment of the relationship as any other relationship in which certain rituals must be observed.

The precise way of initiating counseling cannot be prescribed, yet certain guidelines may be of assistance. *Attention can be given directly to the purpose of the child's self-referral:*

"I'm wondering what brought you here to see me."
"I'd like to know how I might help you."

Attention can be given to the immediate response of the counselee—then to the topic of the counselee's choice.

---

[7] Bartholomew D. Wall, "Rapport: an outmoded concept," *Mental Hygiene,* *3:* 340–342 (1958).

"You seem a bit worried and tense."

"I see that you're curious about my office and some of the books and pictures."

Attention can be given to the need of the referred child to understand why he is being seen by the counselor.

"I called you in because Miss Thomas is a bit worried about you—you suddenly seem so sad."

"Mr. Jackson wanted me to see you because you don't seem to be studying. He thought our getting together might help you; but I'd like this time to be especially ours rather than his. So I guess I'd like to know if that is something you'd like to talk about with me."

"You checked on this questionnaire where it says: 'I'd like to talk with someone about my interests, concerns, or problems.' I thought I'd call you in to give you a chance to talk about this."

Basically, honesty and directness are called for here as well as in other aspects of the relationship, including structuring.

PROVIDING STRUCTURE

The counselor has an obligation to help the child understand his expectations of the counseling process and the activity he sees as appropriate for himself as counselor. Some of the most irrelevant remarks, the most demanding actions, and the most personal inquiries made by the child are related to his struggle to understand the process of counseling, the counselor's expectations of him, and the parameters of the situation. Often in disbelief of the freedom of the situation the child asks in many subtle ways whether the freedom is truly available.

Brammer and Shostrom[8] point out that structuring, in actuality, is a continuous process, but that "formal structuring" may necessarily come early with some counselees and may need clarification at later points in the relationship.

In structuring the situation the counselor has an excellent opportunity to convey or reaffirm his concept of his role. He should view his discussion of structure as a kind of contract, which should be altered only after careful consideration and with the accord of the counselee. Here are some examples of structuring:

(1) This is a situation which you can use as you may wish. We can use the time to get to know one another or you may talk about any interest, concern, or problem that you wish.

[8] L. M. Brammer and E. L. Shostrom, *Therapeutic Psychology* (Englewood Cliffs, N.J.: Prentice-Hall, 1968), p. 211.

(2) What I'd like to do here is have us talk together—perhaps to help you to pick out something you do that bothers you, some behavior you think you'd like to change, and see if we can help you to make a change that suits you.

(3) (Response to a nonverbal request for structure) Right now you seem to me to be asking me what I expect of you. You don't want to waste our time together, but you're not sure how to take advantage of it. [Yeah!] I guess what I'd like you to do is just go on talking like you have been about some of these worries you seem to have—to see if there's something you want to do about them.

(4) (Changing the structure) We've been talking for a long time about you and your brother, and though it worries you that you don't get along, you don't seem to be doing anything about it. I'm wondering if you'd like to change gears. Instead of our just talking about whatever you want, I'm wondering if you think it's important that we do some planning to help with that.

(5) (Changing the structure) We've been going on here planning how you are going to try to get your homework done so that you'll do better in school. But I'm getting the feeling that we're talking about that because you think that's what I want. I'm wondering if it wouldn't be better for us to stop planning so busily and just talk about whatever you want—whatever you are thinking about or worrying about.

The variations on such themes are almost innumerable, depending somewhat on the orientation of the counselor. Selected brief comments setting forth the counselor's expectations for his own behavior can do much to enhance the relationship by making its possibilities clearer to the counselee. Especially if the relationship is unique and different from that previously experienced by the child, there may be some need for periodic clarification of the structure.

CLOSING AN INTERVIEW OR RELATIONSHIP

Many children are perfectly capable of deciding when a counseling interview or relationship may come to a close, while others need to have the topic raised by the counselor. In managing the closing, the counselor should strive for brevity and straightforwardness. On the other hand, enough development should occur so that the child, forgetting the words spoken, has in retrospect a feeling that the counselor has accepted him and views him as worthy of his time and attention.

CLOSING AN INTERVIEW A child's need to feel that closing implies no rejection is often met if he can anticipate the end of the interview. Since his sense of timing may be inadequate to provide this anticipation, a comment by the counselor is often helpful:

"We have about five minutes left now. As you were saying. . . ."

[Then:] "Our time is up for today. I think we've gotten started on some things you may want to talk about more, so if you like I can see you on Thursday at this same time. Perhaps we can talk more at that time about the problem you've raised about fighting."

[Or:] "It seems like we've hardly begun and it's time for you to go to music. I'd really like to talk with you again if you think you would like to come back."

Like other aspects of an interview, the matter of closing is a matter of maintaining or developing a relationship rather than solely a matter of technique. This is also true of terminating the process of counseling.

TERMINATING A COUNSELING RELATIONSHIP   Below, three samples of closing comments illustrate counselee closing, counselor closing when the process seems to have been completed, and counselor closing when little progress seems to be occurring. Each leaves the door open to further contact to be initiated by the child.

(1) TIM: I guess I don't need to come to see you anymore.

COUNSELOR: Things are OK now and you don't need for us to talk anymore.

TIM: Yeah. I'll put a note in your mailbox if I need to talk. But I guess it's time for other kids to have a turn.

(2) COUNSELOR: It seems to me we're kind of through here. You wanted to make friends with some of the kids in your class, and now you seem to have done it.

ALICE: Yes. That's right.

COUNSELOR: I'm wondering if you think we need to continue to keep our regular time on Thursdays or if you think you can handle things from here.

ALICE: Oh, I can handle things now.

COUNSELOR: But if anytime you need to talk, you know, you can put a note in my mailbox. And if you want to let me know how things are going anytime, I'd be interested to know.

(3) COUNSELOR: It kinda seems like you came to see me out of curiosity and now we don't seem to be getting anywhere.

FRANK: That's right. Nowhere.

COUNSELOR: Maybe what we ought to do is stop meeting on a regular schedule like this and, if later you had something you wanted to talk about, you could put a note in my mailbox and I'd really be glad to talk with you about it.

FRANK: Yeah. Let's do that. Sometime I may need help.

COUNSELOR: Right now you don't need any, but you might later.

FRANK: That's right.

CHILDREN'S TERMINAL COMMENTS   Adults and adolescents are more sophisticated than children in handling those awkward moments when they can't think of anything to say. Apparently counselors find it easier to cope with, "I can't think of any more to say," than the child's, "That's all." The counselor who thinks of such a comment as clearly terminal may be closing an interview because of a brief momentary lapse in the discussion that the child caps with a comment that the counselor misreads.

Sometimes, of course, children are interested in terminating an interview when they make such statements. The counselor may, however, find it useful first to reflect a temporary void: "You've finished with that topic and you're not sure what to talk about just now." After a brief pause the child may continue discussion on either the same or a new topic. If, however, he actually wishes to terminate, he is likely to be capable of handling this. Many a child in such a situation has given further nonverbal clues or has made comments like the following:

Well, it's time for music.
Our class is supposed to see a movie now about. . . .
Can I go back to class?
Was there anything more?
Do we get together next Wednesday?

The point here is that terminal comments by children should neither be leaped upon as a way to help a child out the door, nor be ignored.

LISTENING AND FOCUSING PHASES

Deep listening is crucial in all phases of counseling, but especially so in the earliest contacts. Inexperienced counselors too often zero in on the first stated concerns of the counselee, either to plan behavior change, to explore the affective components, or to examine the history behind it. While the matter first mentioned may be the one of greatest consequence, often it is a tentative feeler by the child, who is seeking to examine the situation: Are you interested in me? Will you take time with me? You don't really care about my troubles, do you?

Counselor behavior that zeroes in on the first mentioned concern may be taken to mean that the counselor wants to rush through to apply the right balm, then stand up and ask for the next customer because of the long waiting line. This is hardly conducive to development of a relationship that will deal with the child's more crucial concerns.

Thus, the counselee needs to experience deep reflective listening, especially as he first encounters the counselor.

At a later time, specific to the counseling relationship, there is need for focus and often for planning. When Tammy has returned a few times, after miscellaneous excursions into other areas, to the competitive relationship she has with her older sister, perhaps it is time to focus:

Tammy, you seem to be telling me that if your relationship with Julie didn't bother you so much, that lots of other worries might go away. [Pause. Nod.] I wonder if it would be a good idea to work on that—on talking and planning, if we can, so that you can feel better about this.

The matter of focus may be contracted, as with Tammy, or it may just emerge with the full agreement of the counselor. The point is that focus often is required before a particular child may be helped—and the topic may often come to light through deep listening on the part of the counselor. The level of emotionality surrounding a given topic, or the frequency with which the topic emerges, may help the counselor ascertain whether or not it should be the focus of counseling.

Alertness to the phases of counseling is important to both the counselor and the child. The special needs in initiating counseling, in providing structure, in closing an interview or interview series, and in the listening and focusing phases of counseling require the counselor's attention.

Another way to look at the process of counseling is to examine counselor responses.

UNDERSTANDING RESPONSES

Understanding responses are those that *intend* to convey understanding. They answer the question: When I want to tell Alex that I hear him, I'm with him, I know what he is saying, what are my options?

NONVERBAL RESPONSES

When comfort characterizes a relationship, whether that of counseling or not, silence may do as much to convey understanding as any other response available. A nod, a smile, or some other facial expression consistent with the atmosphere of the moment, a movement in one's chair, a gentle touch in a moment of anguish are all ways in which human beings communicate understanding to one another. Often the nonverbal avenue is most adequate, most convincing, and most genuine.

VERBAL RESPONSES

Among the verbal responses used primarily to convey understanding are simple acceptance, reflection, summarization, and clarification.

SIMPLE ACCEPTANCE   *Yes. I see. Mmhm.* These are examples of acceptance responses, saying in effect: *I understand you. It's safe. Go on.*

REFLECTION   As Brammer and Shostrom put it, reflection is "the attempt by the counselor to express in *fresh* words the essential *attitudes* (not so much the content) expressed by the client."[9] The "mirroring" that is characteristic of reflection gives the child a chance to evaluate his own attitudes and to examine the accuracy with which he is conveying his feelings and his conceptions. This response pattern has another advantage in being readily available to the counselor; that is, of the many thoughts that enter his mind as he hears a statement, one that occurs with great frequency is a kind of *reiteration* of what he is being told. Further, skillful and nonrepetitious reflection clearly conveys to the child the degree to which he is understood. Several examples of reflection follow.

(1) BETSY: If she'd just leave me alone instead of bothering me all the time!

COUNSELOR: Things would be a lot better if she just wouldn't bother you so much.

(2) KENT: My mother just thinks I ought to be studying all the time I'm home, and my dad wants me outside. He tells her he doesn't want me to be a sissy.

COUNSELOR: So she pulls one way and he pulls another and you are in the middle.

(3) SUE: I just don't think I can do things. Sometimes I try and they work out, but I don't expect them to.

COUNSELOR: Sometimes you're surprised, but mostly you don't feel you can do things.

(4) EDDIE: Just when I think she trusts me something goes wrong and she treats me like a baby again.

COUNSELOR: Something happens and there you are—a baby again —and it bothers you.

Because of its relevance and because of its ready occurrence in the thoughts of many counselors, skillful reflection appears to be one of the most useful and valuable response patterns for conveying understanding. Its incorporation into a counselor's repertoire to the point where it "fits"

[9] *Ibid.*, p. 195.

and feels comfortable and genuine may often mean a great deal in the development of effective counseling relationships.

CLARIFICATION   When the child makes statements that are unclear in meaning or feeling, clarification is an available verbal response through which the counselor conveys his tentative understandings, thereby inviting further exploration.

(1) THAD: So I work and don't get much done, but then she fusses and that's OK because I deserve it.

COUNSELOR: You seem to be telling me that it's OK with you when she fusses if your work isn't done, but you wish she didn't or didn't have to.

(2) SALLY: They always want to know what we're talking about when we whisper about them, but we just don't tell them.

COUNSELOR: It seems like you kinda want them to ask, but it annoys you a bit, too.

SUMMARIZATION   The understanding response that may be used to tie together a number of details or a whole series of statements by the child is called summarization.

(1) MARK: This is how it happens. I just want to use one of his things or see a book of his for a minute and he just yells and fusses until Mom comes and she always asks him what's wrong and screams at me until I could just . . . just . . . smash him. But if I fuss at him she tells me I'm older and I should let him use my things and . . . boy, it's just not fair!

COUNSELOR: He can get away with things that you can't and it just doesn't seem fair to you even if you are older.

(2) COUNSELOR: You've just been telling me how your dad blamed you for losing some of his tools, earlier you were telling that your mother thought you lost some of her old spoons and pans, and then you also mentioned your sister thought you had her scissors and art paper. Seems like you get blamed for lots of things.

(3) COUNSELOR: So much has happened that you don't understand and it kind of feels like—well—why is this all happening to me!

Understanding responses come in many forms, both verbal and nonverbal. Since the child's basic concern about counseling may be that he be understood, the elementary school counselor would do well to incorporate understanding responses into his counseling repertoire.

AFFECTIVE RESPONSES

Cognitive statements are of great consequence in counseling. Often, however, until a child has examined the feeling behind his statements he may find it difficult to determine an appropriate objective; that is, he may be unaware of how important it is for him to develop new responses. While often the child knows the course he might best take, he may not understand the feelings that cause him difficulty in changing his behavior. Thus, examination of feelings is as important as the discussion of behavior.

Children often lack the verbal skills to describe their feelings. Many counselors therefore omit the affective orientation to counseling and concentrate upon cognitive matters. Instead, however, the counselor should help the child to examine his feelings and to develop the vocabulary needed for more adequate affective expression.

The relationship generally is least aided by counselor comments that are argumentative and that imply rejection of the child's negative feelings— hate, anger, and so on. "Oh, you don't really mean that," no matter how it is stated, often leads the child to catalogue his reasons at great length. He wants to prove to us that he *is* right. On the other hand, acceptance of his feelings: "He really makes you *so* angry," allows him to hear the intensity of his emotion reflected; he may then reconsider the rashness of his statement. His other alternatives, when his intense emotions are argued, are to reject the counselor or to reconsider his feelings quickly and line them up with counselor expectancies. Neither of these alternatives results in genuine communication.

Ambivalence often characterizes a child's attitudes toward the behavior he wishes to change. The counselor who can help the child to examine his feelings and his ambivalences, and to extract his feeling tone from his cognitive statements, is dealing in an area that often desperately needs consideration and that outside of counseling is seldom discussed. Several examples follow:

(1) GINGER: I plan to just really take hold this six weeks and start studying, but it'll be hard.

COUNSELOR: Even though it'll be hard it's something you want to do. Even though you're afraid some of your girlfriends may make fun of you, you want to try.

GINGER: Well, I guess I did say that, too, and I don't know if I can do it when they'll laugh.

COUNSELOR: You're not sure if you're strong enough or if it means enough if they laugh.

(2) WARREN: At recess today I was only fifth in the race of all the boys in my room.

COUNSELOR: You don't seem pleased with that.

WARREN: Yeah, but last year I was fatter and slower and I always finished one of the last.

COUNSELOR: So you really are pleased with the change.

(3) CATHY: If I start helping with the dishes and things, Mom will be glad about that.

COUNSELOR: Mom will be glad, but I don't get the feeling that you'll be so happy.

CATHY: No, the other kids don't help, and besides Mom just fusses like I don't do it right.

COUNSELOR: So you wonder what the point is if she doesn't tell you she's pleased.

CATHY: Yeah, but I want to do something so she doesn't only fuss.

COUNSELOR: You want her to appreciate you—to like what you do—but it seems hard to find the way.

Helping a child to understand and cope with his feelings as well as his logical thought patterns is a distinguishing feature of effective counseling. Since affective responses may not have been habitually available to the counselor before his training, it behooves him to enhance his attentiveness to affect and to enlarge his response repertoire so that he can help the child deal meaningfully with his feelings.

PROCESS AND CONFRONTATIVE RESPONSES

Counselor statements that examine the counseling process or are confrontative often reach into the interpretive realm. Process responses examine the interaction between the counselor and counselee; the counselor figuratively steps back to ask questions, such as: "What is Tommy trying to accomplish? What concept of himself is he trying to project?" When the answers are verbalized, a combination of process and confrontative responses may result.

Tommy was considered a model child—for good reason, since that was his objective. When the counselor found himself tuning Tommy out as he described at great length the family's sacrifices for Dad's new business venture, the small cut in his allowance, the offer he had made to loan or give his Dad his savings of over $100, he began to take a long look at the process developing between Tommy and himself. It sounded like a well-rehearsed story, one that Tommy's mother might have told over the telephone many times, and one that Tommy himself had gained much mileage through telling.

The counselor remarked: "The most important thing to you, Tommy, is that I know and everyone knows how hard you try to show that you're a good boy." He thought the point had been entirely missed, but in the next interview Tommy interrupted a story he was telling, which seemed directed toward further demonstrating his goodness, by saying: "Sometimes it's no fun to be good."

From that moment Tommy and the counselor began to develop a more effective relationship, Tommy seemed to become more his own person, and eventually he began to demonstrate clear insight by paraphrasing a counselor comment: "There I go again, trying to tell you how good I am."

Some other examples of process responses by counselors are:

(1) COUNSELOR: You seem to want me to get angry at you, maybe so then you can say, "He's just like everyone else."

(2) COUNSELOR: I'm wondering why you're working so hard to convince me that you and your father do lots and lots of things together.

(3) COUNSELOR: I seem to be trying to talk you into changing your behavior and I think I'd better stop. You have to decide whether you want to change things or not.

Confrontative responses are a type of process response in which the interaction is examined and challenge is thrown directly at the child. In certain selected situations this can be a most meaningful avenue of exploration. Some examples:

(1) COUNSELOR: What are you going to do about that?

(2) COUNSELOR: You *say* you want to work harder, but I get the feeling you just want me to *hear* that.

(3) COUNSELOR: You want her to like you, but you don't seem to want to see anything you can do about it. Maybe you really don't want her to like you.

Sometimes confrontative response can be used repeatedly with good effect, as in the following dialogue with Alice, who seemed thoroughly caught up in her need to figure out what others expected of her and then to do it.

ALICE: Mom thought I ought to go to summer school rather than camp this summer so I'd improve in my English grade.

COUNSELOR: She thought that would be important for you.

ALICE: Well, and I thought so, too. I had a C+. Anybody knows you have to do better than that.

COUNSELOR: C+ is just not good enough.

ALICE: Camp wouldn't have been much fun anyway.

COUNSELOR: You're trying to convince yourself that camp wouldn't have been much fun.

ALICE: Yeah! I like doing all those things but I've got to learn to be a lady.

COUNSELOR: Even now when you're ten years old you've got to worry about that.

(Dialogue continued in this vein for some time, as Alice continually deferred to the judgment of others.)

COUNSELOR: Seems like its—uh—hard for you to do anything because *you* want to.

ALICE: What do you mean?

COUNSELOR: You're so busy worrying how others—your mom, dad, sister, and teacher—will react that you can't even think about what you really want. You don't even know.

ALICE: Yeah. That's right. But what do they care what I want?

COUNSELOR: Maybe the question is what do *you* care what you want?

In this dialogue and the one that followed, Alice was readily demonstrating her willingness to subjugate herself in all ways to the will of others. The process of confrontation, gentle and yet direct as it was, began to encourage her to think somewhat more for herself and to be her own person. Eventually she could say: "There's plenty of time for me to be a lady. I'm going to have fun now."

Process and confrontative thoughts can lead to extremely meaningful moments in counseling. Many counselors are willing only to imply such responses, and the child concludes, often correctly, that the counselor is afraid to deal directly with these thoughts. Often the fear is communicated more effectively than the inference, and at that point the issue is closed.

Direct, honest confrontation, screened through a concern as to whether the child is strong enough to deal with it, is often the best route to genuine communication. Oftentimes the elementary school counselor thoroughly screens out process and confrontative responses in order to avoid hurting the child. He should, instead, welcome and examine his thoughts along these lines and become comfortable in stating his responses; otherwise he may be avoiding helping the child.

THE USE OF QUESTIONS

Since most counselors come from the ranks of teachers, there will doubtless always be counselors who are basically questioners (perhaps a potential source of difficulty in counselor recruitment from among teachers). This section will examine the heavy reliance on questions characteristic of many counselors. An effective teacher may be a skillful questioner; an effective counselor may seldom question. Certainly, however, the aspiring counselor can learn to rely somewhat upon noninterrogative responses.

THE MOST ADVANTAGEOUS TYPE OF QUESTION IS OPEN-ENDED   In counseling, as in teaching, the open-ended question is the best. There will always be a place in counseling for questions such as the following:

(1) Since you want to get better grades, would you tell me what you've tried up until now?
(2) What are some ways that you can think of that might help this situation with your sister?
(3) You started to mention your fight with Larry: would you tell me about that?
(4) What does it feel like to you when you say you get "bugged" —could you tell me about that?

It can be argued that any of the above might be altered into statements. The point, however, is that some use of open-ended questions is highly relevant.

DISADVANTAGES OF QUESTIONS

QUESTIONS TEND TO CONVEY TO THE CHILD A ROLE CONCEPT: THE COUNSELOR IS TO QUESTION; I AM TO ANSWER   Children often readily assume the role assigned in relations with adults. Questions that appear to the child to be patterned, after he states his initial concern, may be interpreted as telling him that the counselor expects to run this show with his questions. Often this is comfort-producing for the child, who then concludes: "When he has asked all his questions then he'll know how to solve my problem."

Even though the child may find such a situation familiar (my teachers and parents question me) and safe (this way I don't have to worry about what to say) it is not likely to produce the kind of involvement that helps the child feel that he is participating in the process of solving his own concerns.

YES-NO QUESTIONS ARE PARTICULARLY LIKELY TO REINFORCE A LOW LEVEL OF VERBALIZATION ON THE PART OF THE CHILD   Many a child is content to shift all the interaction responsibility to the counselor, even knowing that his concern is not being dealt with. Terry senses that the counselor is more comfortable in his Yes-No world and he does not care to confront the counselor with his problem. So while what he wanted to talk about is that he still is afraid of the dark and sometimes wets the bed rather than get up, he lets the counselor have his area of comfort in asking about hobbies, his relations with other children, his school work, whether his parents and his brothers and sisters do things together, and what he hopes to be when he grows up. Yes-No question patterns result in strong counselor leads that may bypass areas of genuine concern to the child.

QUESTIONS ORIENTED TO ELICIT FACTS SUGGEST THAT FEELINGS ARE NOT AS IMPORTANT   Many counselors are more comfortable in the realm of questions that elicit facts.

Adam is telling about a fight he just had. The counselor responds with fact-oriented questions:
What happened then?
This boy—was he older or younger?
Why do you suppose he picked on you?
What did you do to him that got things started?
You mean that this happened on the playground at recess?

Nowhere in this dialogue is time taken for Adam to feel that his hurt, his anger, and his guilt are of concern to the counselor.
The helping person who wishes to distinguish himself from the others who may hear this story will care at least at much about the feelings Adam has as the facts that are communicated. Facts and feelings alike are important. However, if Adam is to feel understood, he may well need to express the anger and hurt inside. Often the salient facts will emerge as the feelings are discussed.

QUESTIONS ORIENTED TO ELICIT FEELINGS SUGGEST A MINIMAL LEVEL OF UNDERSTANDING   Many counselors habitually use questions related to feelings: How did you feel about that? What were your feelings then? What do you mean you were mad? How did it feel when you were so angry? When such questions are asked, children may well feel they are not really understood.
"Well, don't you *know*?" is a frequent internal response.
A question asking how the child feels tells him that the counselor does not know. It would appear to be much more appropriate for the counselor to hypothesize about feelings than to question. Even if he makes an error of shading, calling a feeling fear when the child experiences it as anger, the child feels the counselor is trying to understand and is getting something of the message. Some alternatives to asking questions about feelings are:

You must have been very worried then.
I can tell you're still excited about that.
Your anger must have almost exploded then.

I can imagine you even shook then, and your hands were cold or very sweaty, and your stomach felt tight.

QUESTIONS THAT OPEN NEW TOPICS ARE OFTEN EXPERIENCED AS MANIPULATIVE BY THE CHILD   When a counselor suddenly introduces a new topic, particularly through a question, two effects ensue. The child feels that the topic under discussion was not worthwhile, and the child feels manipulated—he must talk about this new topic, whether it seems relevant or not to him, or risk possible rejection by the counselor. He generally accedes, feeling that the counselor is another manipulative adult who may say he has freedom, but then clearly sets the topic. Two examples follow:

(1) COUNSELOR: I'll bet you were glad that that bee missed you.
EDWARD: It wasn't a bee—it was a wasp.
COUNSELOR: I see.
EDWARD: I'm glad it wasn't a green hornet! (Pause)
COUNSELOR: Well—how do you feel about school?
(2) ELLEN: (Discussing brother) Him and me fights some of the time. Boy, we really do! (Pause)
COUNSELOR: How do you get along with other kids at school?

The sudden shift indicated in these and similar illustrations could have been handled in at least two other ways. One would be through a gradual transitional movement, the other through an explanation of the reason for the new topic's being introduced, which often does not require a question. For example:

(1) (Using transitional movement)
COUNSELOR: I'll bet you were glad that that bee missed you.
EDWARD: It wasn't a bee—it was a wasp.
COUNSELOR: I see.
EDWARD: I'm glad it wasn't a green hornet! (Pause)
COUNSELOR: You've kinda run out of something to say.
EDWARD: Yeah.
COUNSELOR: The bee story is over and now it's hard to find something to talk about.
EDWARD: Hm hm.
COUNSELOR: Would it help if I suggested something to talk about?
EDWARD: Yeah. Go ahead. Ask me something.
COUNSELOR: Well, if you'd like to talk about it, I'm wondering how you feel about school.

(2) (Stating reason for new topic)

ELLEN: (Discussing brother) Him and me fights some of the time. Boy, we really do! (Pause)

COUNSELOR: You know, that makes me wonder. You don't seem to get along with Billy very well, and I'm wondering how you get along with other kids in your neighborhood and at school.

The whole area of questions in counseling could occupy us for many more pages. Suffice it to say that the use of open-ended questions is highly appropriate, the more so the more clearly they are relevant to the topic under discussion. The counselor is well advised to develop his non-interrogative repertoire to the point where it is at least as natural to him as is questioning.

BEHAVIORAL APPROACHES

This book takes the position that behavioral approaches are useful to the counselor both in his direct contact with children and in his consultation with adults. Many of the techniques involved were discussed in the previous chapter, and further discussion occurs in Chapter 10. Behavioral counseling may be explored still further through the relevant references cited. The present section briefly expands the discussion of behavioral procedures in elementary school counseling.

When a child states a desire to change his behavior and the counselor feels that concentration upon that behavior is appropriate, a behavioral approach may be strongly indicated. As Krumboltz and Hosford pointed out: "A counselor's success is judged by the degree to which he can help pupils engage in appropriate types of behavior."[10] The sensitive application of behavioral approaches to matters that are clearly behavioral may do a great deal very quickly in giving support to the child, and may help him examine his behavior as an aspect of whatever concerns he may face.

The counselor generally starts out by specifying the behavior to be focused upon and by collecting base-rate data. That is, he moves beyond the generalized statement: "I don't have enough friends," to a determination of the kind and frequency of friendly acts that the child initiates and receives, and to a determination of the kind and frequency of friendly acts that the child would desire to initiate and receive if counseling were successful. He thus identifies the problem, specifies the general goal, and determines the ideal objective.

[10] John D. Krumboltz and Raymond E. Hosford, "Behavioral counseling in the elementary school," *Elementary School Guidance and Counseling, 1:* 28 (1967).

The counselor may then seek to identify operational objectives—behaviors that constitute reasonable and reachable intermediate objectives. Perhaps the child might be satisfied if within a week he could see some specific change in his own outreach and in the response made by others; this would let him know he was moving toward his ultimate objective—having more friendly relationships.

The next steps for the counselor would include working with the child to identify tasks that might be expected to produce some success, such as a compliment to another child, or an invitation to a child for the two to spend some time together. This would be followed by evaluation of the success of the performance and, if successful, a gradual increase in the difficulty of the task. Each step would be followed by feedback to the counselor so that successes could be reinforced and tasks could be adjusted. Upon the achievement of the child's initially stated goal, either counseling would be terminated or a new counseling objective could be agreed upon.

LEARNING PRINCIPLE: SUCCESSIVE APPROXIMATION

With a child who, for example, experiences great difficulty in getting up before a classroom to speak, the counselor uses a successive approximation technique. That is, he creates a role-play situation in which the child starts with a brief report and practices in the counselor's office getting out of his seat, coming to the front of the room, and saying a few words. The counselor's task is to give encouragement and reinforcement. Concurrently, as a result of consultation, the teacher gives the child small classroom tasks on committees and the like and provides brief response opportunities while reinforcing all improvement in verbal responses. The idea is to begin with low-stress conditions that gradually change until the child is participating fully.

LEARNING PRINCIPLE: ABSENCE OF REINFORCEMENT

Krumboltz and Hosford[11] suggest that negative behavior patterns are often reinforced by teacher action. Raising a commotion or disrupting the classroom activities may well be the unstated objectives of a child's behavior. These authors discuss the tantrum behavior of a given child in these terms, noting that when the teacher did not respond with a high level of attention, either by ignoring the child's behavior or by escorting him from the room, it was extinguished. Absence of reinforcement at the time of the tantrum and positive reinforcement at other appropriate times can be effective behavioral procedures applied by teachers. The counselor can be a helpful observer and a participant in planning, while offering the

[11] *Ibid.*, pp. 32–33.

child a special kind of individual attention that must not be experienced as a reward for misbehavior.

RELATED PROCEDURES

Other techniques are used in behavior therapy. Krumboltz and Hosford,[12] Krumboltz and Schroeder,[13] and Johnson,[14] among many others, mention systematic positive reinforcement. An example occurs when a child no longer receives a negative response; he is ignored when he clamors for a particular toy, but he is consistently rewarded when he asks politely for it. Krumboltz and Thoresen[15] and Bandura[16] have presented models of desired behavior through tape recordings. This procedure might be used with a child who is new to a school and has difficulty making friends: on a video-taped interview a counselee who has reinforcement value (an athletic-looking boy, an attractive girl) is shown discussing the same problem and role-playing some ways in which he might attack the problem. Role play and behavior contracts are discussed further by Kiersey.[17] For example, the child may be asked to plan a behavior (asking his mother to stop "bugging him" about his homework) and to act it out in a role-play situation, and at the same time he would be asked to contract to spend a specific number of minutes per day in executing his homework.

Wolpe[18] and Lazarus[19] explore systematic desensitization of anxieties. In this successive approximation process, the child is gradually moved through simulation to actual contact with anxiety-producing situations, which initially are weak and gradually become stronger. The child who is afraid of participating in class is moved gradually, first imagining his answering a question by the counselor alone, then imagining the presence of another child, and so on. Subsequently, in logical stages, he experiences

[12] *Ibid.*

[13] John D. Krumboltz and W. W. Schroeder, "Promoting career exploration through reinforcement," *Personnel and Guidance Journal, 44:* 19–26 (1965).

[14] C. J. Johnson, "The transfer effect of treatment group composition on pupils' classroom participation" (unpublished doctoral dissertation, Stanford University, 1964).

[15] John D. Krumboltz and C. E. Thoresen, "The effect of behavioral counseling in group and individual settings on information-seeking behavior," *Journal of Counseling Psychology, 11:* 324–333 (1964).

[16] Albert Bandura, "Psychotherapy as a learning process," *Psychological Bulletin, 58:* 143–159 (1961).

[17] D. W. Kiersey, "Transactional casework: a technology for inducing behavior change" (paper read at California Association of School Psychologists and Psychometrists, San Francisco, 1965).

[18] Joseph Wolpe, *The Practice of Behavior Therapy* (New York: Pergamon, 1969).

[19] A. A. Lazarus, "Group therapy of phobic disorders by systematic desensitization," *Journal of Abnormal and Social Psychology, 63:* 504–510 (1961).

actual participation. Reciprocal inhibition, Wolpe's[20] term, involves a related process. The child is introduced to a fear- or anxiety-provoking situation in the presence of something comforting, such as food or a loved one, and gradually the proximity to the negative stimulus is increased. The child might be brought into a large room and kept at a distance from a man with a beard (negative stimulus) while being held by his father (positive stimulus). Over time the closeness to the bearded man and the distance from his father are increased.

One last related process, paradoxical intention, is suggested by Frankl.[21] The child who is afraid of perspiring or stuttering embarrassingly counters this fear by deliberately intending to perspire profusely or to stutter extensively. As a consequence, the feared behavior no longer develops the same feeling in the child.

CAUTIONS   Behaviorist approaches have clear advantages with a great many children, yet some cautions should be observed. First, the child should rightly sense that his interests are being served, rather than those of, say, his teacher or parent. Second, the child should not experience a push toward conformity, whether or not he has designated the behavior to be changed. Third, the ambivalence that causes a child both to want and not to want to change his behavior must be given adequate consideration. Fourth, the counselor should take sufficient time to determine whether the self-concept of the child, guilt over some act that cannot be reversed, or some other concern, rather than a specific aspect of his behavior, is in need of attention. Fifth, the child must sense acceptance by the counselor whether or not he succeeds in achieving specific objectives.

The behavioral thrust, appropriately and sensitively used, may certainly increase the effectiveness of counseling with children whose behavior is of genuine concern to them. Many counselors of a self-theory or existential persuasion would avoid such approaches, expecting the child to use an effective relationship as a springboard to appropriate behavior change, but this attitude seems unnecessarily narrow. The counselor must be as ready to assist the child with behavioral concerns as with matters oriented around feelings or the self-concept.

THREE CAUTIONS IN CHILD COUNSELING

Several cautions regarding child counseling have been discussed in this chapter: for example, the counselor has been cautioned against

---

[20] Joseph Wolpe, *Psychotherapy by Reciprocal Inhibition* (Stanford, Calif.: Stanford University Press, 1958).

[21] Viktor Frankl, *Man's Search for Meaning* (New York: Washington Square Press, 1963).

stressing either relationship or technique exclusively, against taking terminal comments by the child to indicate more than a momentary pause, and against depending upon questions. Let us now explore three additional cautions concerning manipulation, dubiousness, and support.

MANIPULATION WITHOUT INVOLVEMENT

It is possible to make a good case for environmental manipulation; certainly where the child is helped to become aware of the reasons for changes, and where the changes are defensible in themselves, they may be supported. Too often, however, children are treated by adults as if they were objects.

Teachers summarily change children's seats, seldom sharing their intentions in warm, positive terms: "I hope that this will help you to get your work done since you and Wade won't be able to talk as easily." Counselors jump willy-nilly from topic to topic, regardless of the feeling the child may have about relevance, returning moments later to a matter that could better have been developed when first raised. Appointments are broken with a brief: "I won't be able to see you today. How would ten o'clock tomorrow be?" Conversation is manipulated so that the child can clearly infer the behavior expected of him, but without the honesty and directness that might make it more palatable.

The respect given to the child should, if anything, exceed that given to adults, since adults are better equipped to handle disrespect. Manipulative actions or words by the teacher or counselor may contribute to nongenuine behavior by children. Adults in helping relationships should be particularly alert to their tendency to manipulate the situation, the conversation, and the child without involving the child in the decision.

DUBIOUSNESS

A particular kind of manipulation apparent in many counseling episodes is the counselor's expression of dubiousness. Dubiousness is a form of confrontation that lacks the advantage of directness.

"You mean she never takes you *anywhere*?"

Clearly, the counselor is saying "I don't accept that," without having the courage to do so directly. In response, often the child feels obliged to reexamine and justify the facts, when what is really at issue is not so much the literal truth as the way the child perceives and feels about reality at the moment.

Three alternatives to dubiousness are (1) acceptance of the perception, (2) direct confrontation, or (3) a combination of the two. The former is often the most useful, since discussion is not as likely to bog down in the facts of the matter. In terms of the example above, the counselor's response could be either:

"It seems like she never takes you anywhere,"

or:

"I wonder if that isn't kind of an exaggeration when you say she never takes you anywhere,"

or the two in combination:

"I wonder if that isn't kind of an exaggeration, but it feels to you like she never takes you places."

Dubiousness is more likely to damage a relationship than to contribute to it in any constructive way.

SUPPORT

Support is most appropriate when the child needs it. It can then be direct and strong. When it is part of a habitual response pattern, support can inhibit future consideration of matters that are not consistent with the supported statements or behavior. Support, therefore, should be applied only after careful, critical consideration.

If the counselor gives support when the child has no particular need for it, his own needs for a positive response by the child may be motivating his statements. Support used in this way as a manipulative device may create dependency.

In the domain of counseling the long-run objective is self-sustenance. Therefore, reinforcing the attitude of the child seems far more relevant than an outside evaluation. For example:

"I can see you're really pleased with that picture."

"You're really glad you talked with your mother and worked that out."

A child's spontaneous enthusiasm about his actions or reactions should certainly be shared with him by the counselor. If, however, out of an evaluative set the counselor says, methodically, "That's good," either verbally or nonverbally, the child learns that certain verbalizations or behavioral reports are reinforced by the counselor while others are not. He may therefore feel guilty and hesitant about dealing with his slippages—reports of feelings or behaviors that do not square with the reinforced patterns. This does not necessarily help him in changing his behaviors; on the contrary, he may become less genuine in the sense that he shares less with the counselor because he feels his acceptance limited.

On the other hand, for a child facing a particularly difficult set of circumstances, especially if they will continue after counseling has ceased, some supportive statements might be appropriate and extremely valuable.

Marie, a fifth grader, is being raised in the shadow of her mother's prostitution; she is loved and protected, but faces a real moral crisis. At the close of the school year the counselor sums up a number of previous discussions and gives support for the future:

"You face a really hard choice every day—every single day. You want to choose differently than your mother, and you think you can—and so do I. You think it won't be easy for you—staying at home and wanting to be a good person in your own eyes. You may have real difficulty—and maybe you won't always succeed in being the kind of person you want to be. But you *are* a good person, and bright, and you won't always be at home. You can grow up to be the kind of person you want to. I really believe you can."

To reiterate, the value of support in counseling depends on whose need it serves. When needed by the child, it is of great importance. When needed by the counselor, it may deny the child an opportunity to grow in the direction of self-evaluation.

SUMMARY

This chapter takes the position that child counseling is a matter of both relationship and technique, and that an existential attitude—making the moments meaningful—is significant to child growth in counseling. The relationship can be understood and enhanced if the counselor is alert and sensitive to the phases of counseling: initiating, providing structure, closing, listening, and focusing. The effective counselor is a person who can provide understanding responses, who can deal in the affective realm, who can help the child look at the process of counseling, who can confront the child in meaningful ways, and who can help if behavioral approaches are indicated. He places reasonable limits on his use of questions, he tends to avoid manipulative behavior, he confronts directly instead of exhibiting dubiousness, and he limits his support-giving to situations in which the child has a need. He is aware of the nature of counseling and its potential with elementary school children, and he is determined that his experiences with the child will be both significant and genuine.

REFERENCES

Aspy, D. N. "Empathy-congruence-caring are not singular," *Personnel and Guidance Journal, 48:* 637–640 (1970).

Aubrey, R. F. "The legitimacy of elementary school counseling: some unresolved issues and conflicts," *Personnel and Guidance Journal, 46:* 355–359 (1967).

———. "Misapplication of therapy models to school counseling," *Personnel and Guidance Journal, 48:* 273–278 (1969).

Axline, V. *Dibs: In Search of Self.* Boston: Houghton Mifflin, 1964.

————. *Play Therapy*. Boston: Houghton Mifflin, 1947.

Bandura, A. "Psychotherapy as a learning process," *Psychological Bulletin, 58:* 143–159 (1961).

Batdorf, R. L., and W. P. McDougall. "Evaluating the effectiveness of a global elementary counseling program," *Elementary School Guidance and Counseling, 3:* 90–97 (1968).

Blocher, D. H. "Counselor education: facilitating the development of a helping person," in Clyde A. Parker, ed., *Counseling Theories and Counselor Education.* Boston: Houghton Mifflin, 1968.

————. "Developmental counseling: a rationale for counseling in the elementary school," *Elementary School Guidance and Counseling, 2:* 163–172 (1968).

Bordin, E. S. "Ambiguity as a therapeutic variable," *Journal of Consulting Psychology, 19:* 9–15 (1955).

Boy, A. V. "Educational and counseling goals," *Elementary School Guidance and Counseling, 3:* 83–89 (1968).

Brammer, L. M., and E. L. Shostrom. *Therapeutic Psychology.* Englewood Cliffs, N.J.: Prentice-Hall, 1968.

Broedel. J. W. "The use of questioning in counseling," *School Counselor, 10:* 12–15 (1962).

Combs, A. W. "Counseling as a learning process," *Journal of Counseling Psychology, 1:* 31–36 (1954).

Dinkmeyer, D. "Counseling theory and practice in the elementary school," *Elementary School Guidance and Counseling, 1:* 196–207 (1967).

Doverspike, J. E. "Counseling with younger children: four fundamentals," *Elementary School Guidance and Counseling, 5:* 53–58 (1970).

Fischer, C. T. "Rapport as mutual respect," *Personnel and Guidance Journal, 48:* 201–204 (1969).

Frankl, V. *Man's Search for Meaning.* New York: Washington Square Press, 1963.

Gladstein, G. A. "Is empathy important in counseling?" *Personnel and Guidance Journal, 48:* 823–827 (1970).

Hansen, J. C., and R. R. Stevic. *Elementary School Guidance.* Toronto: Macmillan, 1969.

Hawkins, S. "The content of elementary counseling interviews," *Elementary School Guidance and Counseling, 2:* 114–120 (1967).

Hillman, B. "The elementary school counseling process: an Adlerian model," *Elementary School Guidance and Counseling, 2:* 102–113 (1967).

Holmes, J. E. "Counselee listening—another dimension of the counseling process," *Counselor Education and Supervision, 3:* 153–157 (1964).

Johnson, C. J. "The transfer effect of treatment group composition on pupils' classroom participation." Unpublished doctoral dissertation, Stanford University, 1964.

Kennedy, D. A. "A behavioral approach to elementary school counseling," *Elementary School Guidance and Counseling, 1:* 118–125 (1967).

Kiersey, D. W. "Transactional casework: a technology for introducing behavior change." Paper read at California Association of School Psychologists and Psychometrists, San Francisco, 1965.

Krumboltz, J. D. *Revolution in Counseling: Implications of Behavioral Science.* Boston: Houghton Mifflin, 1966.

———— and R. E. Hosford. "Behavioral counseling in the elementary school," *Elementary School Guidance and Counseling, 1:* 27–40 (1967).

———— and W. W. Schroeder. "Promoting career exploration through reinforcement," *Personnel and Guidance Journal, 44:* 19–26 (1965).

———— and C. E. Thoresen. "The effect of behavioral counseling in group and individual settings on information-seeking behavior," *Journal of Counseling Psychology, 11:* 324–333 (1964).

Lazarus, A. A. "Group therapy of phobic disorders by systematic desensitization," *Journal of Abnormal and Social Psychology, 63:* 504–510 (1961).

Macguffie, R. A., G. Q. Jorgensen, and F. V. Janzen, "Need for approval and counseling outcomes," *Personnel and Guidance Journal, 48:* 653–656 (1970).

McGowan, J. F. "Developing a natural counseling style," *Education, 4:* 246–249 (1956).

Meeks, A. R. *Guidance in Elementary Education.* New York: Ronald, 1968.

Moustakas, C. A. *Psychotherapy with Children.* New York: Harper & Row, 1959.

————. "Authentic and inauthentic learning." Paper read at Purdue University Education Colloquium, Lafayette, Ind., 1966.

Nelson, R. C. "Counseling versus consulting," *Elementary School Guidance and Counseling, 1:* 146–151 (1967).

————. "The process response and the limited contract in counseling." Paper read at University of Northern Iowa, Cedar Falls, 1968.

————. "The emerging role of the elementary school counselor: the counseling role." Paper read at American Personnel and Guidance Association, Dallas, 1967.

————. "The preparation of elementary school counselors: a model," *Counselor Education and Supervision, 6:* 197–200 (1967).

Parker, C. A. *Counseling Theories and Counselor Education.* Boston: Houghton Mifflin, 1968.

Patterson, C. H. *The Counselor in the School,* New York: McGraw-Hill, 1967.

Peters, H. J., B. Shertzer, and W. Van Hoose. *Guidance in Elementary Schools.* Skokie, Ill.: Rand McNally, 1965.

———— and M. J. Bathory, eds. *School Counseling Perspectives and Procedures.* Itasca, Ill.: F. E. Peacock, 1968.

Rogers, C. R. "The necessary and sufficient conditions of therapeutic personality change," *Journal of Consulting Psychology, 21:* 95–103 (1957).

————. *Client-Centered Therapy.* Boston: Houghton Mifflin, 1951.

Schoettelkotte, Alice. "Counseling the other," *School Counselor, 17:* 257–259 (1970).

Slinger, G. E. "Utilizing specific behavioral goals in elementary school," *Elementary School Guidance and Counseling, 3:* 190–197 (1969).

Stefflre, B., and K. Matheny. *The Function of Counseling Theory.* Guidance Monograph Series, Boston: Houghton Mifflin, 1968.

Sundberg, N. D., and L. E. Tyler. *Clinical Psychology.* New York: Appleton-Century-Crofts, 1962.

Thompson, E. "A model for developmental counseling," *Elementary School Guidance and Counseling, 2:* 135–142 (1967).

Tindall, R. H., and F. P. Robinson, "The use of silence as a technique in counseling," *Journal of Clinical Psychology, 3:* 136–141 (1947).

Tyler, L. E. "Minimum change therapy," *Personnel and Guidance Journal, 38:* 475–479 (1960).

———. *The Work of the Counselor.* New York: Appleton-Century-Crofts, 1969.

Van Hoose, W. H. *Counseling in the Elementary School.* Itasca, Ill.: F. E. Peacock, 1968.

Wagner, R. F. "Short term counseling in the school setting: a diagnostic-therapeutic approach," *Journal of School Psychology, 1:* 42–50 (1963).

Wall, B. D. "Rapport: an outmoded concept," *Mental Hygiene, 3:* 340–342 (1958).

Warters, J. *Techniques of Counseling.* New York: McGraw-Hill, 1964.

Wolpe, J. *Psychotherapy by Reciprocal Inhibition.* Stanford, Calif.: Stanford University Press, 1958.

———. *The Practice of Behavior Therapy.* New York: Pergamon, 1969.

ARTICLES IN BOOKS OF READINGS

Dinkmeyer, D. C. *Guidance and Counseling in the Elementary School: Readings in Theory and Practice.* New York: Holt, Rinehart and Winston, Inc., 1968. Readings beginning on pages 26, 235, 244, 250, 260, 267.

Koplitz, E. D. *Guidance in the Elementary School: Theory, Research and Practice.* Dubuque, Iowa: William C. Brown Company, Publisher, 1968. Readings beginning on pages 222, 230.

Mills, G. D. *Elementary School Guidance and Counseling.* New York: Random House, Inc., 1971. Readings beginning on pages 125, 130, 137.

Peters, H. J., A. C. Riccio, and J. J. Quaranta. *Guidance in the Elementary School: A Book of Readings.* New York: Macmillan, 1963. Reading beginning on page 149.

Peters, H. J. and Michael J. Bathory. *School Counseling Perspectives and Procedures.* Itasca, Ill.: F. E. Peacock, 1968. Readings beginning on pages 29, 60, 84, 105, 118, 126, 143, 160, 167, 178, 200, 251, 364, 372, 396.

8

Play Media in Counseling

*Is not the most beautiful expression of child life . . . a playing child?
—a child wholly absorbed in his play?—a child that has fallen asleep
while so absorbed. . . . To the calm, keen vision of one who truly knows
human nature, the spontaneous play of the child discloses the future
of the man.*

F. W. FROEBEL: *The Education of Man*

Few children have had the experience of sitting down and discussing a
concern with an adult over an extended period of time; still fewer children
have found an adult willing to listen to their ideas and to be appreciative
of their individual stage of development and processes of thinking. The
recent increase in counseling services at the elementary school level has
pointed up many children's special needs to be listened to and to be active
as they consider a concern or problem. Many counselors find the inclusion
of play media in the counseling situation a valuable, facilitative resource
that helps to meet children's needs for activity and provides them a familiar
situation offering minimum pressure.

Play therapy in its traditional sense has been used for analytical and
therapeutic purposes; that is, play therapy situations have been structured
for children who have been asked to reveal themselves in this way. By
contrast, the primary intent in *counseling with play media* is to facilitate
spontaneous expression and communication by the child. Insights gained
by the counselor and therapeutic value experienced by the child are secondary benefits.

This book takes the position that play media may be advantageously used by children of all ages in the elementary school. Most of the examples included deal with the everyday concerns of normal children who have referred themselves for counseling. The counselors in these illustrations have media available in their offices that may be used by all elementary school children regardless of age. The rationale is that children do not suddenly cease being the energetic action-oriented individuals they are in their preschool years. When media are available in the counselor's office, when the suggestion is made that some young people like to have something to do with their hands while they talk, many children of primary and intermediate age readily accept the opportunity and use it advantageously.

While this chapter focuses on the utilization of play media in counseling, it is recognized that teachers often have even better opportunities than counselors to observe and to interact with children at play. Certainly both teachers and counselors need to be aware of the expressive and communicative advantages of play, both need to be alert to opportunities to help children to grow in their interactions with other children through play, both can gain in understanding children through observation of play, and both can provide opportunities through play that are creative —a welcome change from the more sedentary activities that fill much of the child's day. In general, teachers do not need to be convinced of the renewing, refreshing advantages of play activities—though in their rush to complete curricular tasks, they may provide inadequately for them. Counselors, on the other hand, do need to weigh rather seriously the matter of incorporation of play. Thus it is to them and to the special advantages of play media in counseling that this chapter is specifically addressed.

In exploring play media in elementary school counseling, this chapter considers the following topics: the role of play in the life of the child, philosophical considerations in using play media, advantages of play media, disadvantages of play media, structured and unstructured materials, use of play materials and counselor-counselee interaction, and limit setting.

THE ROLE OF PLAY IN THE LIFE OF THE CHILD

A lingering Puritan tradition in our society suggests that work is good, while play is frivolous, unnecessary, or bad. We seem unable to accept play activity as normal, wholesome, reconstructive, renewing, and valuable in its own right. Counselors who hold such views are hesitant to incorporate play media in counseling; they want to "get down to the real business of counseling." When counselors develop an appreciation for the significance and potentiality of play in and of itself, they may then cease to be inhibited in their use of play media. Therefore, we shall begin by considering the role of play in the life of the child.

Lowenfeld sees play as an expression of the child's relationship to the world.[1] Woltmann[2] sees play activities as providing opportunities for the child to conceptualize and to bring to awareness his experiences and his feelings about them, and to act out situations that trouble or confuse him. Erikson considers play by children as ". . . the infantile form of the human ability to deal with experience by creating model situations and to master reality by experiment and planning."[3]

The child develops his self-awareness and relatedness to the world through play, suggests Matterson: "Nature is on the side of our offspring and has equipped them with all the instincts and attributes necessary to develop their potential. They have curiosity, pertinacity, and tremendous energy. It is our job to see that these instincts are not inhibited by our living conditions to a degree which will stultify development."[4] Bender and Schilder[5] see play as the child's means for investigating and experimenting with nature and human relationships.

When such importance is ascribed to play activities, it would seem that attention must be paid to them in the process of counseling. Rather than asking the child to limit himself to the verbal medium with which adults are comfortable, adults should be attempting to reach out toward the child. As Nelson states: "Any activity that occupies so much of the child's time and through which he tests his abilities, interests, and skills so extensively in a role play sense must be considered grist for the counseling mill."[6]

Thus play is an integral part of the child's life, through which he strives to explore his capabilities and to find his place. Counseling with play media can facilitate the child's communication and expression while simultaneously helping the counselor to interact with him and to understand him.

[1] Margaret Lowenfeld, *Play in Childhood* (London: Gollancz, 1935).

[2] Adolf G. Woltmann, "Concepts of play therapy techniques," in Mary R. Haworth, ed., *Child Psychotherapy* (New York: Basic Books, 1964), p. 21. (The Haworth book is cited as a source in a number of footnotes throughout this chapter; consult the list of references at the end of the chapter for the original sources.)

[3] Eric Erikson, "Toys and reasons," in Mary R. Haworth, ed., *Child Psychotherapy* (New York: Basic Books, 1964), p. 10.

[4] E. M. Matterson, *Play and Playthings for the Preschool Child* (Baltimore: Penguin, 1967), p. 1.

[5] Lauretta Bender and P. Schilder, "Form as a principle in the play of children," *Journal of Genetic Psychology, 49:* 254–261 (1936).

[6] Richard C. Nelson, "Pros and cons of using play media in counseling," *Elementary School Guidance and Counseling, 2:* 144 (1967).

PHILOSOPHICAL CONSIDERATIONS IN USING PLAY MEDIA

A number of philosophical considerations already suggested favor the use of play media in counseling children.

1. Play is renewing, wholesome, reconstructive, and therefore relevant in counseling.
2. Through his play the child, whether in or out of counseling, expresses his relationship to the world.
3. The child uses play to experiment in human relationships; he may be helped to do this in counseling.
4. Play facilitates the child's communication and expression.
5. The adult more readily enters the child's world by relating to him while he plays.

Nelson expands the philosophical justifications:

The younger elementary school child is only beginning to emerge from the stage wherein all objects are toys, all the time is for play, and work is a construct developed through role playing (accent on the latter word). While he is being indoctrinated successfully into the concept that his work is school work, he remains a creature who, largely through play, develops his social relations, tests various roles and concepts, and works through his frustrations and concerns. In contrast with his older sibling who can and does *verbalize* frustrations, love, anger, and acceptance, the younger child *acts* these feelings. He crashes cars together, he hugs his Mom, he shoots the enemy, and he hands another child a toy. He tends less to talk about his feelings than to live them; he is an activist.[7]

Further:

Suitable materials can help the counselor create an environment that is less strange to the child, that does not demand verbalization to the exclusion of other modes of expression, that may facilitate both expression and communication, and that may aid in holding the interest of the child. Philosophically, one might observe that incorporating play into counseling is justified because it is so much a part of the child's world and because it is, in a broad sense, his employment.[8]

With a concerned adult present the child may explore varied avenues of play—trying on new behaviors, experimenting with ways of reaching out to people, tentatively experiencing how another person receives him in a

---

[7] Richard C. Nelson, "Elementary school counseling with unstructured play media," *Personnel and Guidance Journal, 45:* 24 (1966).

[8] Nelson, "Pros and cons of using play media in counseling," p. 145.

new role. The child may be helped to try out, in a secure place, new ways of relating to others.

Erikson[9] observes that "playing out" concerns is a natural and, when necessary, a healing experience; Woltmann[10] agrees, suggesting that play allows the child to "live out" inner feelings, vague perceptions, and conflicts.

The present book takes the position that the use of play media in counseling can be of great value in opening the door to the child's world, producing comfort for him, providing him tryout opportunities, and encouraging his expression and communication; this, however, should not be taken as an exhortation to all counselors to incorporate play media in counseling. What *is* recommended is that the counselor give play media an extensive tryout to see whether he may find them facilitative and valuable.

Nelson puts it into perspective in this way: "The use of play media should not be considered to represent a philosophy of counseling, but a facilitator to comfort, expression, and communication within counseling. It is not a substitute for a good counseling relationship, but a medium through which a good relationship may be clarified and extended. It is not a technique that can stand in isolation, but a part of a larger body of skills that may help the child and the counselor gain understanding."[11]

ADVANTAGES OF PLAY MEDIA

Beyond the philosophical considerations, the use of play media offers certain additional advantages. Moustakas describes some of them:

> In the playroom, the child eventually feels a sense of relatedness and harmony in all that he sees. He is at one with the environment. He feels the pure aspects of the setting, the absence of preconceived standards, expectations, and pressures, the lack of prejudice or bias. In the positive sense, he perceives the constant tenderness of feeling, the profound respect for him and the honoring of him. . . . There is a reverence for everything he says and does. A sense of tranquility is felt by the child. Although he may be disturbed and agitated, an atmosphere of peacefulness and quietude surrounds him and gradually enters into his private world of perception. Outside the playroom there is a busy, moving, goal-directed world, but in the playroom there is a constant sense of peace. Even when the child is actively at play and noisily expressing himself he recognizes the calm atmosphere.[12]

[9] Erikson, *op. cit.*, pp. 10–11.

[10] Woltmann, *op. cit.,* p. 22.

[11] Nelson, "Pros and cons of using play media in counseling," p. 145.

[12] Clark E. Moustakas, *Psychotherapy with Children* (New York: Harper & Row, 1959), pp. 7–8.

Nelson considers the reduction of pressure important:

> One possible advantage in utilizing play media is that it reduces pressure on the child and counselor. The time is being utilized, so the urge to "fill the unforgiving minute," to which Kipling refers, is less often felt by the counselor and counselee. Thus, instead of the counselor feeling a need to probe or the counselee feeling a need to fill an embarrassing silence, each may contemplate the object being constructed when the discussion wanes, and the object may become secondary when the discussion resumes.[13]

Playing through concerns, suggests Rexford,[14] should also help many acting-out children to perceive the world as a friendlier environment. Amster sees the child's play as observational material: "In his play, his behavior, ideas, feelings and expressions help our understanding of his problem and how he sees it."[15] She also contends that play gives the child an opportunity to share himself with the counselor. Woltmann[16] agrees, noting that interviews involving children's play may be regarded as projections of their inner lives, since personality is assumed to be dynamic. Woltmann also points out: "Play activities . . . can be seen as progressive and regressive trends. Progressive trends show the desire to go forward, to discover, and to take in the world. Regressive trends are . . . the compulsion to regress to and to replay traumatic events. . . . The child's primary job is to grow; his main tool, play, is therefore in the service of progressive trends."[17]

Experimental evidence in this area is rare; however, in a study that explored group counseling involving play media with underachieving black and white children, Moulin[18] found an increase in both nonlanguage and language functioning.

In sum, then, the use of play media in counseling has several advantages. The child experiences an environmental relatedness, a personal sense of freedom, a tranquility, and a reduced sense of pressure; his progressing capabilities are released and he perceives the world as friendly. At the same time, the counselor experiences the advantage of a participatory

---

[13] Nelson, "Play media and the elementary school counselor," p. 269.

[14] Eveoleen N. Rexford, "Antisocial young children and their families," in Mary R. Haworth, ed., *Child Psychotherapy* (New York: Basic Books, 1964), p. 62.

[15] Fanny Amster, "Differential uses of play in treatment of young children," in Mary R. Haworth, ed., *Child Psychotherapy* (New York: Basic Books, 1964), p. 19.

[16] Woltmann, *op. cit.,* p. 23.

[17] *Ibid.,* p. 26.

[18] Eugene K. Moulin, "The effects of client-centered group counseling using play media on the intelligence, achievement, and psycho-linguistic abilities of underachieving primary school children," *Elementary School Guidance and Counseling,* 5: 85–98 (1970).

opportunity in which the child may be himself and find ways in which to interact.

DISADVANTAGES OF PLAY MEDIA

There are many potential disadvantages to the use of play media in elementary school counseling. However, just as their advantages may be nullified by unwise use or overdependence, their disadvantages may be overcome by effective counselors. Some possible disadvantages are:

1. The child may be ready to deal with a concern but be distracted by an attractive array of materials.
2. The child may use play activities as an escape from classroom pursuits.
3. The counselor may be less alert to the verbal cues as he attends to uses of play materials.
4. The counselor may use play activities to disguise a lower level of counseling competence.
5. The use of play materials is likely to extend the duration of counseling.

Other criticisms also may be applied to the use of play media. The statement that follows was written prior to the somewhat more encouraging findings of Moulin,[19] but further evidence is needed before it can be discounted: "The most telling criticism of the utilization of materials in elementary school counseling is that while it has not been invalidated experimentally as an ineffective addition to the counseling situation, neither has it been established as an effective addition."[20]

Behaviorists such as Krumboltz and Hosford[21] indicate that counseling effectiveness is judged by behavior change, and they would, therefore, zero in on behaviors and help the child plan and execute changes; this would, in their views, circumvent the need for play media. One might object, however and suggest that behavior may be observed and planning for behavior change may occur as a result of the child's use of play media.

Counselors who see value in incorporating play media would do well to consider these disadvantages and criticisms, attempting in every way possible to conduct the process of counseling with play media so that the criticisms are not validated and reinforced.

[19] *Ibid.*
[20] Nelson, "Pros and cons of using play media in counseling," p. 145.
[21] John D. Krumboltz and Raymond E. Hosford, "Behavioral counseling in the elementary school," *Elementary School Guidance and Counseling, 1:* 28 (1967).

STRUCTURED AND UNSTRUCTURED MATERIALS

Ginott,[22] in devoting an entire chapter to toy selection from a psychotherapeutic frame of reference, offers some valuable guidelines that are appropriate for elementary school counselors. Materials that facilitate the establishment of contact with the child may include such things as dolls, puppets, noisemaking devices, rubber darts, and a typewriter; the very inclusion of such things suggests a kind of permissiveness that is readily conducive to the development of a counseling relationship. Materials such as water, paints, clay, chalk, marking pens, and paper tend to encourage cathartic expression. While no specific materials are recommended as contributing directly to insight development or reality testing, situations present themselves in which children may demonstrate and may be confronted with their habitual and self-defeating modes of behavior.

Gerry moved continuously to close out the counselor. She leaned over her drawing and maneuvered so the counselor was facing her back. Her verbalizations stopped.

COUNSELOR: You seem to be shutting me out. (Pause. No response.)

COUNSELOR: You kind of want me to get angry. (Pause. No response.)

COUNSELOR: Maybe that's what you do to people that gets them mad at you. (Pause. No response. Some bodily movements.)

COUNSELOR: You say you want people to like you but then you shut them out—like you're shutting me out. (At this point Gerry sat up, turned toward the counselor, and showed her picture.)

GERRY: I'm drawing a house.

Materials such as the marking pen and paper that Gerry used give the counselor a chance to see clearly the response and avoidance patterns that Gerry uses, often to her great disadvantage, in her communication with others.

Axline[23] offers a comprehensive listing of materials along with cautions that playthings should be simple in construction, easy to handle, and durably constructed.

Nelson offers some suggestions on the selection of play materials:

Those that may be readily adopted for use by the elementary school counselor are clay, paints, crayons, paper, pipe cleaners, building

[22] Haim G. Ginott, *Group Psychotherapy with Children* (New York: McGraw-Hill, 1961), chap. 5.

[23] Virginia M. Axline, *Play Therapy* (Boston: Houghton Mifflin, 1947), chap. 3.

materials, toy telephones, puppets, dolls, perhaps a dollhouse with furniture, a bounceback figure, rubber knives, cap gun, typewriter and finger paints; but no counselor should feel particularly handicapped if, due to the necessity of mobility, all the equipment must be carried in a small briefcase. Then, drawing materials, some construction materials, such as scissors, paper, pipe cleaners, and tooth picks, plus some soft hand puppets or small dolls may well suffice.[24]

Since the objectives of using play media are to produce a familiar situation and to encourage expression and communication, highly structured mechanical toys and games are not among the more useful materials. In addition they tend to be expensive and highly vulnerable to loss or damage. True, some of these materials may be expected to elicit some communication and expression, though mostly in areas prescribed by the manufacturer. It may be advantageous for a counselor to know whether a child feels a strong need to win, whether he is inclined to cheat, and how he handles losing, but gains in these areas may be offset by the loss of free expression by the child in creative, nonprescribed domains of play.

Woltmann[25] notes that the specific selection of materials is less important than providing for the child's need to structure material and to endow it with conceptual content. Moustakas[26] presumably states his preference for unstructured and simply structured materials by mentioning no more complex game or toy than checkers. Axline[27] objects to items as highly structured as checkers and mechanical toys because they get in the way of creative and expressive play. And Nelson observes: "Generally, the more flexible the materials used in the counseling office, the better; the more readily the imagination of the child can let this or that piece of equipment be what he needs it to be, the more desirable it is. Structured games, fancy dolls, models, and other such toys have limited adaptability, are limited in expressive and communicative possibilities, and should probably not be used."[28]

USE OF PLAY MATERIALS AND COUNSELOR-COUNSELEE INTERACTION

Techniques of child counseling, discussed in the previous chapter, will be related specifically here to the use of play media. After examining

[24] Nelson, "Elementary school counseling with unstructured play media," p. 26.

[25] Woltmann, *op. cit.,* p. 25.

[26] Moustakas, *op. cit.,* pp. 6–9.

[27] Axline, *op. cit.,* p. 56.

[28] Nelson, "Play media and the elementary school counselor," in Don Dinkmeyer, ed., *Guidance and Counseling in the Elementary School* (New York: Holt, Rinehart and Winston, Inc., 1968), p. 268.

the introduction of play materials into counseling, we shall consider several examples of counselor-counselee interaction.

INTRODUCING PLAY MATERIALS

Moustakas[29] recommends that we use play materials to help us enter the child's world. We may introduce them to the child by saying, for example, "Any of these materials are for you to use if you wish while we talk." For the older child, if his nonverbal behavior indicates he is unsure about entering into this activity, a second statement may help: "Lots of people find it helpful to do something with their hands while they talk." The counselor needs to stay in touch with the child by either verbal or nonverbal means. He may well *feel* in touch only when there is at least occasional verbal contact; thus, for himself he stresses "while we talk," and through his behavior he makes it clear that he offers play materials as a communication medium.

If the play behavior is meaningful, some verbal contact may well enhance its meaningfulness; if it is not meaningful, the child may divert his play behavior into channels of greater significance as he experiences the counselor's response.

The child should be left to select his own play materials instead of being given a situation that has been set up for him. The shy child who is given a playground scene with pipe cleaner figures, one of which is on the sidelines, can no longer assume that he has the full freedom to be in this setting. Such a "setup" may be useful to the diagnostician but it contributes little to the relationship in counseling. On the other hand, if the child has set up a similar scene it seems most appropriate for the counselor to wonder aloud what will happen next.

If the counselor adds or removes material that he believes is significant in counseling, he has an obligation to the relationship to convey his motives. Thus:

(a) I brought some Magic Markers today because you seemed to want your picture finished and you felt the crayons weren't fast enough.

(b) I didn't bring (or didn't set out) the checkers today because I felt I wasn't getting to know you. We both worked so hard at it we could hardly talk.

"In dealing with the child's play," Nelson recommends, "it . . . should be treated as if it were verbalized behavior, with the response made to the emotionalized content of the behavior or to the behavior itself rather than to any extension into the interpretive realm."[30] The counselor should be willing to reflect upon the activities observed, to confront and challenge

---

[29] Moustakas, *op. cit.*
[30] Nelson, "Elementary school counseling with play media," p. 25.

them, to elicit the affective overtones, to share with the child his concepts of the process in which they are engaged, and, in general, to relate to the child's play behaviors in ways that reflect his philosophy of dealing with verbal statements. Some counselors seem to regard play behavior as sacrosanct and beyond reach; thus they wait for verbal behavior to confirm what the play behavior has said. This seems both unnecessary and unwise.

The examples that follow illustrate ways in which the counselor may respond to play behavior.

EXAMPLES OF COUNSELOR-COUNSELEE INTERACTION

1. Sandy made clay figures for some time. Wordlessly she shared them with the counselor; there were long pauses; and as the counselor kept in touch verbally and visually, Sandy smiled and nodded. Here are some of the counselor's verbal observations made over a five- to eight-minute period.

> COUNSELOR: You're really working over that clay. (Smile)
> COUNSELOR: You're wondering what to make. (Nod)
> COUNSELOR: Now you know what you want to do. (Continues working)
> COUNSELOR: It's going to be an animal. (Smile)
> COUNSELOR: Such long legs. Maybe a cow or horse.
> SANDY: Horse. (Smile)
> COUNSELOR: You're pleased I thought it might be a horse. (Nod)
> COUNSELOR: But it didn't turn out right so you're starting over.
> COUNSELOR: You wanted it to, but it didn't. (Quizzical look) You were a little disappointed that he didn't look like you wanted him to. (Nod)
> COUNSELOR: Now it's going to be something else. (Smile)
> COUNSELOR: A person now. (Smile)
> COUNSELOR: A girl.
> COUNSELOR: And she turned out right.
> SANDY: Well, it's my aunt. She's only four years older than me. And she worries me. She's going around with some kids that my mother thinks would do *anything*.
> COUNSELOR: She worries you because your mother thinks she's with the wrong group.
> SANDY: Well, I know them too and I think Mom's right.

2. Ted suddenly and violently crushed a clay figure that he had previously called his brother.

> COUNSELOR: You're angry and so you smashed the clay figure.

Discussion. A lump of clay in seconds can be many things or it may still be Ted's brother. The response above, which attempts to respond faithfully to "the knowns" of the situation, still allows the child to convey that he did indeed smash his brother.

TED: Yeah. I was thinking about what he did yesterday to me.

It also allows for a change in the nature of the figure.

TED: Did I tell you what Mr. Gibbs did to embarrass me today? I wish he was this clay! (Pounds it again)

3. Bobby had played a scene with puppets in which he had asked to play in a game, had been rejected, and had broken up the game.

COUNSELOR: Seems to me that's just like what happens most every day.
BOBBY: Yeah! They don't let me in the game and I just ruin it.
COUNSELOR: I wonder if you'd like to try out some other ways with the puppets—some different ways of asking to get in the game—to see what happens.

Discussion. Since Bobby asks aggressively, expecting rejection, he gets it. The counselor offers to help him plan new behaviors.

4. Mary's eyes filled with tears after paint ran on her picture.

COUNSELOR: It bothers you to see your picture messed up like that.

Discussion. The emotional content of the moment is the key here. Many persons would rush in and say: "Don't cry, there's plenty more paper," thus in effect denying Mary her right to be upset. While wallowing in self-pity is not to be encouraged, it is important for Mary to learn to cope with her moments of frustration in ways that she can use when an adult is not at hand. Here is the ensuing discussion, in which Mary adapted to the event rather nicely.

MARY: Things just don't turn out right for me. I always mess things up or something happens.
COUNSELOR: It bothers you that lots of things turn out wrong.
MARY: Yeah. (Pause) Well (sigh), I guess I'd just better start over again.
COUNSELOR: Things happen that bother you, but you just give a sigh and start over.

MARY: Yeah. (Beginning on a new sheet of paper) That's the best way.

5. Joe, a bright, active sixth grader, illustrated the advantage of the availability of some play media. While the conversation ranged through some of Joe's worries about campus unrest and international problems, he fingered a large lump of clay. His manipulatory speed and his verbalization rate were highly correlated. When he was agitated and his speech flowed, his fingers fairly flew; when he was pensive and halting, his fingers moved slowly, with deliberation. While still considering some of the problems in the day's news, he began a more purposeful construction. It became clear he was molding a boat. He reached for pipe cleaners and made two stick figures and set them in the boat, continuing to deal with his concerns related to wars and threats of wars past and present. Fully ten minutes after his boat was begun and three minutes after he finished setting his figures in the boat, he stopped discussing his worldly concerns.

JOE: You know, another thing bothers me—and that's about my dad.

COUNSELOR: Something about your dad bothers you.

JOE: Well, he fusses and fusses with our neighbor, Mr. Jackson, to go fishing, but Mr. Jackson doesn't even like to fish. And here I'd like to go and he never asks me. He took me years ago and I got cold and wanted to come home. But that was at least three years ago.

Discussion. Apparently Joe had been dealing with two levels of concerns for some period of time. His constructing efforts, doubtless, helped him to sustain his level of personal concern and hold it in abeyance while he dealt with broader matters verbally.

In summary, the child may find it facilitative to experience a situation in which he has the freedom to choose or to reject media for expression and to utilize materials as he chooses. The counselor is attentive to the child's statements and his actions, treating these as he does verbalized statements—reflecting, summarizing, clarifying, confronting, and so on, and generally remaining in touch with the child as he engages in his chosen activity.

LIMIT SETTING

In the process of counseling involving play media the counselor will need to set some limits. Alexander discusses the need for limits in therapy in terms that are clearly applicable to elementary school counseling:

The child finds himself in a situation with a very minimum of limit from which he can branch out and discover his true feelings. The limits serve as a superstructure from which he can build rather than a fenced in enclosure from which he cannot escape. By struggling through the limits the therapist and child come closer to each other and the child gains security in knowing where he stands. The limits emerge from the requirements of the situation and are not arbitrarily imposed in terms of external values. This in itself is a learning experience. The child learns to appreciate realistic structure.[31]

Limits should be few, yet sensible to the child, protective of his and the counselor's safety and situation-determined. Axline[32] stresses these points, while reminding counselors that many times the activities of the child would bring on severe criticism if carried on outside of counseling; yet in a sense this is exactly what counseling is about.

Moustakas[33] suggests that a limit is a boundary of the counselor, and that a bond is formed when the child accepts the limit. When the limit is broken, it is a boundary held by the counselor alone, and no bond exists. This view makes the importance of reasonable limits patently obvious. If reasonable limits are present, a living and working through of the limit may be a basis for greater growth in the relationship.

Dorfmann[34] sees a limit against physical harm as being very important, since the child who hurts the counselor or another child experiences deep guilt and anxiety and has to contend with a fear of retribution and the withdrawal of the comfort of counseling.

Ginott's[35] six-point rationale for the setting of limits is adapted here.

1. Limits help the child to express his strong feelings symbolically. The counselor permits and encourages expression through socially acceptable channels including discussion, doll and puppet play, painting, and modeling.
2. Limits help the counselor maintain attitudes of acceptance, empathy, and positive regard for the child.
3. Sensible limits with regard to health and safety protect both the child and the counselor.
4. Limits strengthen the child's capacity to live in the real world if he can see them as reasonable and necessary. The child "learns

[31] Eugene D. Alexander, "School centered play-therapy program," *Personnel and Guidance Journal, 43:* 258 (1964).

[32] Axline, *op. cit.,* pp. 130–131.

[33] Moustakas, *op. cit.,* p. 13.

[34] Elaine Dorfmann, "Play therapy," in Carl R. Rogers, *Client-Centered Therapy* (Boston: Houghton Mifflin, 1951), pp. 257–258.

[35] Ginott, *op. cit.,* pp. 103–123.

that he may feel all of his feelings, but he may not act as he pleases."[36]

5. Some limits are set because of legal or ethical considerations or standards of social acceptability.

6. Some limits are set because the expense of replacing destroyed chairs or materials is excessive.

In the application of limits every effort is made to help the child to understand both his feelings and his actions and to maintain his self-respect. The following are illustrations of limit setting behavior by the counselor:

1. Ted moves to attack Bobo, the inflated bounce-back clown, with a screw driver.

COUNSELOR: You may punch Bobo, but not stab him.

2. Ted throws paints in the direction of the counselor.

COUNSELOR: Paints are for painting. I'm for talking with.

3. Mary paints a bit on the inside of a shell she has brought with her. She shows it silently to the counselor. Another dab of paint and she brings it closer to the counselor. A third dab and she brings the shell within a very small distance of the counselor's nose.

COUNSELOR: You'd like to just put that right on my nose. You can make a clay face and put it on the clay nose. (Should Mary press the issue, the counselor is prepared to grasp her wrists gently and firmly to enforce the limit.)

4. The counselor has announced several moments before that time would be up shortly. Butch resists.

COUNSELOR: Our time is up for today. (Rising)

BUTCH: Well, there's just one more plane and boat I want to draw.

COUNSELOR: I understand that you want to stay longer, but there's no more time. (Butch continues to draw) You many put the drawing in this drawer and finish it next week or take it with you.

BUTCH: OK. I'll take it with me, but I'll have to take these Magic Markers with me to finish.

COUNSELOR: You really want to do that, but the markers have to stay. (Butch begins to put them down and to place the drawing in the drawer)

BUTCH: You tell me I can do what I want to, but then you say, "No, no, no!"

---

[36] *Ibid.*, p. 105.

COUNSELOR: You're angry at me and you want me to change my mind.

BUTCH: You should let me take those things with me. You have plenty.

COUNSELOR: You would like that rule better.

BUTCH: Yeah. But I suppose after awhile there'd be nothing left to use here. (Skipping off) See you next week.

If the child learns from the application of limits that the world has stability, that the counselor has human rights, that the child himself is respected and supported, and that his strong negative feelings are accepted and channeled, the limit-setting process has been constructive and is likely to be productive.

SUMMARY

This chapter suggests that the utilization of play media is philosophically sound, since it is related meaningfully to the child's world and is a way in which he tries out new behaviors. The point is stressed that materials are utilized, not as a philosophy of counseling, but because they are potentially facilitative of the child's expression and communication. Flexible, unstructured materials that the child may utilize in a variety of ways are preferable to highly structured materials whose limits are set by the manufacturer. Counselors are urged to treat play behavior as if it were verbalized—reflecting, summarizing, confronting, and so on—yet remaining true to "the givens" of the situation rather than extending into the interpretive realm. Limits are considered important because they have growth-producing potential; through limits the child is helped to deal with reality, to understand his feelings and actions, and to maintain and enhance his self-respect.

REFERENCES

Alexander, E. D. "School-centered play therapy program," *Personnel and Guidance Journal, 43:* 256–261 (1964).

Allen, F. H. *Psychotherapy with Children.* New York: Norton, 1942.

Amster, F. "Differential uses of play in treatment of young children," *American Journal of Orthopsychiatry, 13:* 62–68 (1943).

Axline, V. M. *Dibs: In Search of Self.* Boston: Houghton Mifflin, 1964.

———. *Play Therapy.* Boston: Houghton Mifflin, 1947.

Baruch, D. W. *One Little Boy.* New York: Julian Press, Inc., 1952.

Bender, L., and P. Schilder. "Form as a principle in the play of children," *Journal of Genetic Psychology, 49:* 254–261 (1936).

Bills, R. E. "Nondirective play therapy with retarded readers," *Journal of Consulting Psychology, 14:* 140–149 (1950).

————. "Play therapy with well-adjusted retarded readers," *Journal of Consulting Psychology, 14:* 246–249 (1950).

Dahlem, G. G. "Clay therapy in elementary guidance," *Illinois Guidance and Counseling Association Newsletter,* 45–46, 1961.

Dorfmann, E. "Play therapy," in Carl R. Rogers, *Client-Centered Therapy.* Boston: Houghton Mifflin, 1951. Pp. 235–277.

Erikson, E. H. *Childhood and Society.* New York: W. W. Norton, 1950.

Ginott, H. G. *Group Psychotherapy with Children.* New York: Mc-Graw-Hill, 1961.

Glasser, W. *Reality Therapy: A New Approach to Psychiatry.* New York: Harper & Row, 1965.

Haworth, M. *Child Psychotherapy.* New York: Basic Books, 1964.

Krumboltz, J. D., and R. E. Hosford. "Behavioral counseling in the elementary school," *Elementary School Guidance and Counseling, 1:* 27–40 (1967).

Lambert, C. B. *Play: A Yardstick of Growth.* New York: Play School Association, 1948.

Lebo, D. "A formula for selecting toys for nondirective play therapy," *Journal of Genetic Psychology, 92:* 23–34 (1958).

Lowenfeld, M. *Play in Childhood.* London: Gollancz, 1935.

Matterson, E. M. *Play and Playthings for the Preschool Child.* Baltimore: Penguin Books, 1967.

Moulin, E. K. "The effects of client-centered group counseling using play media on the intelligence, achievement, and psycho-linguistic abilities of underachieving primary school children," *Elementary School Guidance and Counseling, 5:* 85–98 (1970).

Moustakas, C. E. *Psychotherapy with Children.* New York: Harper & Row, 1959.

————. *Children in Play Therapy.* New York: McGraw-Hill, 1953.

———— and H. D. Schalock, "An analysis of therapist-child interaction in play therapy," *Child Development, 26:* 142–157 (1955).

Muro, J. J. "Play media in counseling: a brief report of experience and some opinions," *Elementary School Guidance and Counseling, 3:* 104–110 (1968).

Murphy, G. W. "Play as a counselor's tool," *School Counselor, 2:* 53–58 (1960).

Nelson, R. C. "Elementary school counseling with unstructured play media," *Personnel and Guidance Journal, 45:* 24–27 (1966).

————. "Pros and cons of using play media in counseling," *Elementary School Guidance and Counseling, 2:* 143–147 (1967).

————. "Play media and the elementary school counselor," *Guidance and Counseling in the Elementary School: Readings in Theory and Practice.* New York: Holt, Rinehart and Winston, Inc., 1968. Pp. 267–270.

Rexford, E. N. "Antisocial young children and their families," in

Lucie Jessner and Eleanor Pavenstadt, eds., *Dynamic Psychopathology in Childhood*. New York: Grune & Stratton, 1959.

Sears, P. S., and V. S. Sherman. *In Pursuit of Self-Esteem*. Belmont, Calif.: Wadsworth, 1964.

Solomon, J. C. "Therapeutic uses of play," in H. H. Anderson and G. L. Anderson, eds., *An Introduction to Projective Techniques*. New York: Prentice-Hall, 1951. Pp. 639–661.

Woltmann, A. G. "Concepts of play therapy techniques," *American Journal of Orthopsychiatry*, *25:* 771–783 (1955).

Zeligs, R. "Children's new year's resolutions," *Childhood Education*, *40:* 244–246 (1964).

ARTICLES IN BOOKS OF READINGS

Dinkmeyer, D. C. *Guidance and Counseling in the Elementary School: Readings in Theory and Practice*. New York: Holt, Rinehart and Winston, Inc., 1968. Reading beginning on page 267.

Koplitz, E. D. *Guidance in the Elementary School: Theory, Research, and Practice*. Dubuque, Iowa: William C. Brown Company, Publisher, 1968. Reading beginning on page 230.

Mills, G. D. *Elementary School Guidance and Counseling*. New York: Random House, Inc., 1971. Readings beginning on pages 194, 200, 209.

Peters, H. J., A. C. Riccio, and J. J. Quaranta. *Guidance in the Elementary School: A Book of Readings*. New York: Macmillan, 1963. Readings beginning on pages 96 and 162.

9

Group Procedures with Children

If you don't know the kind of person I am
and I don't know the kind of person you are
a pattern that others made may prevail in the world
and following the wrong god home we may miss our star.
WILLIAM STAFFORD: "A Ritual to Read to Each Other"

Everywhere the individual child turns, he is expected to function as a member of a group. Much of his well-being and his sense of personal adequacy derives from the degree to which his groups reinforce him. The group is a powerful reinforcer for many, and for some a powerful force that withholds reinforcement. Groups help cause many problems of personal adjustment; on the other hand, they can contribute much to the alleviation of many personal problems.

Group procedures are highly potent. Like almost all procedures with a potential for good they also have a potential for misuse. With proper concern for the building of understanding of self and others and with appropriate referral and consultation resources in the wings, it seems eminently reasonable that the group process be turned to the advantage of professionals in education.

Taking the position that the power of the group many appropriately be turned to the advantage of teachers and counselors as they work with elementary school children, this chapter is devoted to a discussion of group procedures with children. It considers the following topics: a rationale for group procedures with children; problems and limitations of group procedures; group counseling; and group guidance. This discussion, hopefully, will motivate the reader to examine his interaction within groups and to consider how he might better function in a group setting, will alert him to techniques and approaches, and will develop his awareness of the limitations and possible dangers in utilizing group procedures.

RATIONALE FOR GROUP PROCEDURES WITH CHILDREN

Groups exist wherever children exist. Therefore, groups are real to children. The elementary school child may well see his problem or concern primarily in relation to his functioning with his peers. By the same token, group members understand the child primarily as a group member.

Elementary school children are at a growth stage during which learning to get along with agemates and developing a responsibility for an independent self are crucial matters.[1] Effective group procedures should help—must help—the individual child in both areas.

The timing is right in the elementary school. Kagan and Moss[2] have noted that such behaviors as ease of anger arousal, withdrawal from stressful situations, and social-interaction anxiety may be predicted from behavioral dispositions observed during early school years (ages 6 to 10 in particular). Bloom notes: "There is an increasing level of determination in the individual's characteristics with increasing age and this is reflected both in the increased predictability of the characteristics and in the decreased amount of change in measurement of the characteristics from one point in time to another."[3] If many children are to be given the preventive assistance they require, and if that assistance is to be relevant to their concerns, group procedures are indicated.

Dinkmeyer,[4] in giving a rationale for group counseling, indicates several factors that have relevance to group procedures in general. These are included in the list below.

1. Most problems of children are interpersonal or social. Group procedures provide direct experience in social interaction.
2. The characters and personalities of children are expressed in social situations. Group procedures provide children an opportunity to express themselves and to be understood by others.

[1] Robert Havighurst, *Human Development and Education* (New York: McKay, 1952), pp. 15–28.

[2] Jerome Kagan and Howard A. Moss, *Birth to Maturity* (New York: Wiley, 1962), p. 266.

[3] Benjamin S. Bloom, *Stability and Change in Human Characteristics* (New York: Wiley, 1964), p. 230.

[4] Don C. Dinkmeyer, *Guidance and Counseling in the Elementary School: Readings in Theory and Practice* (New York: Holt, Rinehart and Winston, Inc., 1968), pp. 272–273.

3. Children often need acceptance as they are before they can undertake any change. Group procedures provide children a sense of belonging regardless of their deficiencies.

4. Children need to develop social interests. In the group, children can show concern for others and can sense the concern of others for them.

5. Children need to sense a oneness with others. Group procedures provide children an opportunity to realize they are not alone, that others have similar problems.

6. Children need time to change. Within an accepting group, children may approach problems at their own speed.

7. Children express their needs and purposes through their behaviors. The group helps children to become aware of their needs and purposes and to examine the routes through which they attempt to satisfy them.

8. Many children need to change in their behaviors and attitudes. Group procedures give children opportunities to gain feedback regarding their behaviors or attitudes and to try out new behaviors.

9. Counselors need to understand children in a group context. Group procedures provide opportunities for counselors to observe children in social settings.

10. Counselors need to facilitate communication and understanding among children. Group procedures provide a vehicle through which they can mobilize assistance to individual children.

In setting forth their rationale, Nelson and Callao[5] indicate that the child may be helped in the group by receiving feedback after he tries new behaviors, may learn to function in a democratic, interactive environment, may experience with his peers that listening and being listened to are valued, and may find group experiences valuable in making the transition away from total dependence on adults. Through group procedures the influence of the counselor may be extended to a larger number of children, who become aware of the potential in counseling for alleviating their own concerns. Thus, through groups, individual counseling can be facilitated and supplemented.

PROBLEMS AND LIMITATIONS OF GROUP PROCEDURES

Group activity today is widespread and varied. Marathons (intensive group counseling experiences occurring in single extended sessions), T-groups, encounter groups, sensitivity groups, and process groups have been

---

[5] Richard C. Nelson and Maximo J. Callao, "Groups and accountability," *Elementary School Guidance and Counseling, 4:* 291–294 (1970).

conducted in great abundance. Some consider these terms interchangeable, relating to a variety of structured and unstructured group experiences; others see them as discrete entities with different shades of meaning. Other activities range from nude therapy groups and drug-stimulated groups to antidrug groups such as Alcoholics Anonymous; in fact an indeterminable variety of related conservative to ultraliberal group experiences can be had for the asking by adults.

Against this backdrop it is highly understandable that the term "group" itself generates deep enthusiasm in the minds of millions of people and anxiety in the minds of millions of others. Today's elementary school counselor or teacher cannot conduct a personalized group experience without evoking some of the same suspicions that emerge when adult group work is discussed. Perhaps this is the way it should be.

Goldman[6] has taken the counselor to task by criticizing his injudicious invasion of privacy with a captive audience. Though his remarks were directed primarily at secondary school and college level counselors, the elementary school counselor is equally subject to such temptations, and his audience is even more captive. Perhaps the first problem related to group procedures is: *How can the counselors serve children in groups, a highly potent process, without going beyond the bounds of ethics?*

Huckins[7] and Schmidt[8] have prepared extensive discussions on ethics, and the American Personnel and Guidance Association[9] has drafted a statement to cover such matters. The counselor must be alert to the possible harm to the well-being of a child and the possible liability that he, himself, may incur if he encourages the exposure before a group of material that is extremely potent and either personal in nature or revealing of family confidences. Some question of liability exists where those who do not have a legitimate interest become informed. As Huckins states: "Generally, truth, or a sincere belief in the truth of transmitted information, informing only those who have a legitimate interest, and the absence of malice are good defenses against charges of libel."[10] A strong case can be made, then, for appropriate selection of group members, for the encouragement of confidentiality regarding material discussed, and for counselor intervention to restrict highly volatile material to individual counseling.

A second problem in group procedures is that even the best counselor may be overwhelmed by the variables to which he might well

[6] Leo Goldman, ed., "Privilege or privacy: I," *Personnel and Guidance Journal, 48:* 88 (1969).

[7] Wesley C. Huckins, *Ethical and Legal Considerations in Guidance* (Guidance Monograph Series, Boston: Houghton Mifflin, 1968).

[8] Lyle D. Schmidt, "Some ethical, professional, and legal considerations for school counselors," *Personnel and Guidance Journal, 44:* 376–382 (1965).

[9] American Personnel and Guidance Association, "Ethical standards," *Personnel and Guidance Journal, 40:* 206–209 (1961).

[10] Huckins, *op. cit.,* pp. 55–56.

respond. *How can the counselor cope with the multiple variables that occur in group procedures?*

Of course, no ready answer can be given, or there would be no problem. The counselor must elect to respond to the verbal or nonverbal communication that he believes will create the optimum growth within the group. Skill in selection and in intervention must be developed through a combination of education and experience.

Several other limitations also affect group procedures:

1. It is unrealistic to expect group procedures to save counselor time. As Dye states: "Thorough study is likely to reveal that counseling in groups requires *more* rather than *less* counselor time"[11] in order to meet the differential objectives and needs of students.

2. Some concerns of students are too personal or revealing of family matters to be dealt with in groups.

3. Not all personal revelation is good for individuals, and guilt or other adverse reactions may follow the revealing of personal concerns.

4. Confidentiality is a real matter of concern with elementary school children, since they may not thoroughly understand its implications.

5. Not all counselors are trained in group procedures, and not all who are trained are comfortable or competent in their employment.

6. Scheduling, while it may be easier than in the secondary school counseling program, is often complex, and it certainly requires diplomacy and good counselor-teacher relationships.

None of these limitations need block the effectiveness of group procedures for a particular counselor; however, they are often cited by counselors as interferences to effective group work, and as such they are worthy of concern and attention. Group counseling and group guidance can be valuable tools of the counselor, and in some cases of the teacher, if awareness of their problems and limitations accompanies their considered use.

GROUP COUNSELING

COMPARISON WITH GROUP GUIDANCE AND GROUP PSYCHOTHERAPY

Group counseling is distinguishable from group guidance primarily in terms of focus of the experience and the numbers served. Focus in group

[11] H. Allan Dye, *Fundamental Group Procedures for School Counselors* (Guidance Monograph Series, Boston: Houghton Mifflin, 1968), p. 14.

guidance tends toward the general, and it serves larger numbers. Group counseling focuses on the individual and on group interaction and serves smaller numbers in a more intimate, personal environment. Group counseling is distinguishable from group psychotherapy in terms of the intensity of the problems considered and the setting in which the group experience occurs. Group psychotherapy tends to involve children with more severe levels of disturbance and is more likely to occur in an institutional or private, nonschool setting.

Mahler and Caldwell have stated two primary objectives common to group guidance, group counseling, and group psychotherapy that are equally appropriate for elementary and secondary school students: ". . . to help youth obtain a deeper understanding of themselves and better control over their lives."[12] In addition to the overlap in objectives, there is much overlap in the effective application of group guidance and group counseling on the one hand and group psychotherapy and group counseling on the other. When a teacher is dealing with a total class and the focus is on "friendship," that is group guidance; if, however, an individual child and his concern for friendships becomes the focus, group counseling may well emerge. When a psychotherapist works with five acting-out children using a Freudian model, that is group psychotherapy; if, however, the psychotherapist were to use a client-centered (self-theory) model, he might not function in any discernibly different way than would a client-centered school counselor. Thus, while theoretical distinctions can be made, the practical reality is that overlap does occur—and in abundance.

To reflect the reality of school practice, the ensuing discussion of group counseling assumes that the counselor will be the adult leader; the subsequent discussion of group guidance assumes that either the teacher or the counselor might function as leader. There are no references to group psychotherapy, which is in part a legal term and tends to be reserved to describe actions by psychologists and psychiatric personnel.

SELECTION OF GROUP MEMBERS

Elementary school counseling groups vary greatly in size and composition, owing often to counselor preference. Some counselors restrict groups to a single school grade, include members of only one sex, keep to a specified number, seek to include children who have similar concerns, and arrange groups on a self-referred basis as a result of classroom contact. Other counselors experience what they feel is success without observing any of these limitations.

In the selection of group counselees, counselor preference is probably a reasonable yardstick, provided the counselor attempts to become increasingly more flexible in order to meet children's needs. A beginning

[12] Clarence A. Mahler and Edson Caldwell, *Group Counseling in Secondary Schools* (Chicago: Science Research Associates, 1961), p. 24.

counselor who needs to experience success in group counseling might hope to find a small (four- or five-member) group of verbal fourth grade girls who are constantly vying for academic superiority, and who come through the route of self-referral. Perhaps the principal- or teacher-referred mixed group of eight passive- and active-aggressive sixth grade boys and girls should wait until the counselor feels he can cope with the variables involved.

Group counseling can be successful under a wide range of circumstances. Certain conditions, however, as reflected in Table 9–1, seem to be preferred by counselors and stressed by counselor educators.

Table 9–1   GROUP-MEMBER SELECTION AND COUNSELOR PREFERENCE

Counselor tends to prefer	*Counselor tends not to prefer*
Moderate size (4–7)	Small group (2–3)
	Large group (8–15)
Self-referred	Assigned to group
	Required to attend
Problem recognized	Problem unrecognized
	Coping with problem resisted
Some sharing of mutual problem	Same problem shared precisely
	No common ground
Narrow age range	Wide age range
All boys/girls	
Balanced group	Unbalanced group

Elementary school counselors seem to prefer working in groups with children in the upper grades, although it would appear that counseling experience with younger children might well be facilitative of reciprocal interaction, since this skill seems to develop gradually and becomes evident between the ages of nine and eleven.[13] In their review of literature on this topic, Mayer and Baker[14] suggest that if younger children are to be involved in group counseling, smaller numbers (below six) may be advisable.

PREPARATION OF GROUP MEMBERS

It is certainly possible to gather a group of children together and begin the process of counseling. Ohlsen,[15] however, has offered a more

[13] J. H. Flavell, *The Developmental Psychology of Jean Piaget* (New York: Van Nostrand-Reinhold, 1963).

[14] G. Roy Mayer and Paul Baker, "Group counseling with elementary school children: a look at group size," *Elementary School Guidance and Counseling, 1:* 140–145 (1967).

[15] Merle Ohlsen, *Guidance Services in the Modern School* (New York: Harcourt Brace Jovanovich, 1964), pp. 152–154.

sophisticated approach that is clearly appropriate for elementary school counseling groups.

Step 1. One or several classes are gathered for a discussion of group counseling, which is described as an opportunity for the individual to discuss his concerns, receive help from the counselor and the others in the group, and give help to others as they struggle with their concerns. The class members are encouraged to raise questions, and the counselor facilitates this process by such statements as: "Perhaps you wonder what the counselor does in the group." Through a combination of counselor statements and children's questions consideration is given to such matters as: who will be in the group; what will be expected of group members; how group members might help one another; whether group members can trust one another; and how often and long the group members will meet.

Step 2. By filling out a questionnaire or problem check list, or by simply writing his name and Yes or No on a piece of paper, the child indicates his interest in becoming part of a counseling group. Devices that make the raising of hands unnecessary are clearly to be preferred.

Step 3. The counselor meets individually with those interested in group participation, attempting to assess which of them might fit into the group in terms of the similarity of their interests, concerns, or problems and their readiness to be helped and to help others.

Step 4. Members are selected and the group begins to meet.

This procedure in itself may generate a great deal of interest in group counseling. Over a period of time the counselor should make every effort to include all who volunteer in some group or other, unless severity of personal problems suggests otherwise.

The topic of confidentiality needs to be carefully discussed with elementary school children, who are often unaware of all of the implications of material they might be inclined to repeat. Thus, the counselor has an important task before him in clarifying the concept of confidentiality: "What others say in here is just for us, we can't share it with other people who aren't in our group. It is confidential—it stays with us."

INTERACTION PROCESSES

Group counseling tends to demand active and alert participation by the counselor. He needs to achieve a fine balance between facilitating group movement and encouraging the group to develop in its own way. Using fewer words than he might in individual counseling, he finds it necessary to intervene in the interaction, to be facilitative and to reinforce facilitative behaviors that he hopes to see group members adopt, and to examine the process as it unfolds in the group.

Group and individual counseling differences derive partly from the numbers of children involved, and therefore the numbers of verbal and non-verbal behaviors, and partly from children's familiarity with group settings. A face-to-face meeting with an adult may present a new situation for which the child has limited behavioral norms, but a group situation is familiar. The child knows how to play, to talk, to feel his way, and to structure the situation so that it is similar to previous experiences. If he determines that the adult is functioning as an observer, his attention turns to fulfilling his expectations of himself in child-to-child interactions. The group counseling situation should be designed not merely to reiterate previous group experiences, but to present a new, freer environment in which the child can test out different behaviors and deal with concerns that he is unlikely to mention in other group settings. To allow this to occur, the counselor needs to blend a combination of behaviors appropriate to individual counseling with intervention, facilitation, and process examination, adding these to his repertoire of behaviors designed to produce and maintain rapport, to convey acceptance, to demonstrate permissiveness, to provide for feeling recognition through reflection, to convey respect for the child's ability to solve his own concerns, to allow for maximum lead by the child, to permit a concern to be worked through gradually over time, and to provide realistic and appropriate limits—in short, those behaviors suggested by Axline[16] in 1947.

In order to meet the special needs of group counseling, as Ohlsen[17] points out, the counselor must assist children to accept responsibility for developing and maintaining an environment within which help can be given; group-member acceptance of responsibility in turn increases group productivity. Group members must be assisted to help one another as well as to receive help; counselees must be assisted to interact dynamically with each other; and both those who wish to change and those who wish to influence change must feel a strong sense of group belonging.

INTERVENTION   To enhance the likelihood that group members will deal with topics relevant to group counseling, and to encourage expression of attitudes that show themselves nonverbally, intervention by the counselor may be needed.

A.   Ted has been carrying forth at great length on the topic of his scouting adventures. The group members respect his status and seem to be

[16] Virginia M. Axline, *Play Therapy* (Boston: Houghton Mifflin, 1947), chaps. 8–15.

[17] Merle M. Ohlsen, "Adapting principles of group dynamics for group counseling," *The School Counselor, 13:* 159–162 (1966).

reinforcing his story telling. The counselor intervenes as another adventure begins to unfold.

TED: Then, boy, I want to tell you about this guy at the camp who knows all about how to make canoes . . .

COUNSELOR: Ted, excuse me, but I need to stop you. I find I'm just not listening anymore because I hoped some other things would happen today.

TED: Oh, yeah. (Pause) But everyone *seemed* to be listening.

PAUL: Yeah, I thought it was interesting.

BARBARA: I want to know about the canoe guy.

COUNSELOR: You know, I think that's part of what bothers me. Everyone is so willing to listen to anyone else's story.

TED: You mean as long as we're just telling stories we aren't helping Roger or Barb or anyone.

ROGER: Uh huh.

COUNSELOR: It seems like maybe it's safer and easier.

TED: Yeah, but inside I get a little mad 'cause I know I'm doing all the talking and everyone wants me to, but that's not helping anyone.

COUNSELOR: So it makes you mad at yourself . . .

TED: . . . and the others, 'cause I know they want me to.

B. Marybeth has been talking about her reaction to her mother's favoring of her brother and the fact that she has to take care of him. Unnoticed by Marybeth and some other group members, Chuck has paled and seems to be agitated internally, though he is staring at the floor.

MARYBETH: . . . Then if I even scold him while I'm taking care of him I get yelled at. What do you do in a case like that? Honestly, it just makes me so mad. And yesterday, you know it was Sunday. Well . . .

COUNSELOR: Pardon me for interrupting, but Chuck seems to be bothered right now. I wonder, Chuck, if there's something you want to say.

CHUCK: It just all seems so dumb. (Pause)

COUNSELOR: Something seems dumb to you.

CHUCK: (Pause) Well, Marybeth just argues with anyone and she makes mountains out of nothing. She expects Eddie to be perfect.

MARYBETH: Well, you should have to put up with him.

COUNSELOR: You can't see Marybeth's problem. You think she's at fault.

CHUCK: No, I know Eddie and I wish he were my brother. I got a brother Eddie's age and he's flat on his back in a hospital. He's retarded and handicapped and when she talks about Eddie she just doesn't know how lucky she is.

COUNSELOR: It seems like a big problem to her but it's a small one to you.

In A above, the counselor accepted the need for a change of direction as primarily his; appropriately, he did not project his feelings onto other group members. In B above, the need for a change in direction was flagged by the behavior of a child.

Situations in which intervention might well occur appear often in group counseling. The counselor need not intervene at every opportunity, constantly interrupting the flow of discussion. It seems more likely that the majority of counselors will err in the direction of missing valid and important opportunities for intervention.

FACILITATION   Counselors take two kinds of facilitative actions in group counseling. Those of one kind, characterized by reflection, summarization, clarification, simple acceptance and similar actions directed toward an individual child, differ in no major way from the facilitative responses that occur in individual counseling. (See Chapter 7.) Those of the second kind are designed to elicit or reinforce facilitative behaviors on the part of the children themselves.

In the following illustration[18] the counselor had explained at the outset four ways in which members could help the group to be as effective as possible. These behavioral expectancies he hoped to reinforce in a summary at the end of the session, at which time he added two facilitative expectancies for the group's future consideration. The six expectancies are:

1. *Deep listening.* Members of the group are encouraged to listen through the comments being made to see if all the meaning and feeling seems to be expressed.

2. *Helping each other talk.* Members of the group are encouraged to help the person talking to continue to express himself in order to be sure that the meanings and feelings behind his comments are clear.

3. *Discussing problems and concerns.* Group members are encouraged to focus on matters of concern to them with which they believe the group can help.

4. *Discussing feelings.* Group members are encouraged to think through and discuss their feelings about the concerns for which they believe the group can provide insight, understanding, or assistance.

5. *Confronting.* Members of the group are encouraged to point out when they feel differently about the matter being discussed, when they feel the individual is not being entirely truthful or accepting responsibility, or when they feel that an obvious solution is being overlooked.

6. *Planning and reporting.* Group members are encouraged to test out in the group their ideas for solving their concerns, to formulate

[18] Based on Richard C. Nelson, "Organizing for groups," *Personnel and Guidance Journal, 50:* 25–28 (1971).

these into plans for action, and to report on the success or failure of their undertakings.

A. In October a fifth grade group was started; it is early November and Ann has begun to tell of her feelings toward herself and her new school situation.

ANN: I don't know what I did, but I must have done all the wrong things 'cause no one likes me, but in the other school I know kids liked me, so if someone can tell me what I did. . . . (Pause)

COUNSELOR: You need to know what you did, but it seems as though no one can help you.

TONY: Well, Ann, it wasn't that you did anything, but you still talk all the time about the other school and we're just tired of hearing that.

COUNSELOR: I can feel that you really want to help Ann, and. . . . (Interrupted)

JACKIE: I think we all do, but she always seemed like such a snob. Until just now I thought she didn't care about us and just wanted to go back. . . . (Pause)

COUNSELOR: But now. . . ? (Brief pause)

JACKIE: Now I see she wants to be friends and I think she can do it.

ANN: Well, I can *try* to stop talking about the other school if you think that'll help. But. . . . (Pause)

COUNSELOR: But you're not sure it will help.

ANN: No. But I'll try.

COUNSELOR: Gloria, you look like you understand Ann and wish you could help.

GLORIA: Yeah, well. . . . Well, everyone's telling Ann it's her fault and last year you said it was my fault when I came in fourth grade. But I still don't feel like. . . . Well, I don't know if it'll make any difference if Ann stops talking about her old school.

COUNSELOR: You're not really sure others accept you so you're not sure Ann will be accepted.

JACKIE: Yeah. . . . (Pause)

ANN: That's what I feel like too.

TONY: Well, uh. . . . (Pause) I guess we do kinda make it hard on anybody new.

JACKIE: But that's not all. We still make it hard for Steve and he's been in this school since kindergarten.

TONY: And Janice.

COUNSELOR: Seems like we know at least four people, Ann, Gloria, Steve, and Janice, who get . . . who aren't very well accepted. We seem to be willing to be honest with each other and to try to help Ann. Should we try to think through the group problem or Ann's problem?

B.   Later in the same session.

COUNSELOR: It's about four minutes until we have to stop. I suggested four behaviors we might try to work on and check at the end of the session today. How do you feel we did on deep listening, really discussing problems or concerns, helping each other talk, and discussing feelings?

ANN: Great. I think that I listened and others listened to me and I know we talked about a real problem, 'cause I was just about to go nuts trying to figure out what's wrong with me.

TONY: We helped each other talk by staying on the subject . . . most of the time.

COUNSELOR: Now I wonder if it was helpful to have those things in mind.

GLORIA: Yeah, well it was for me. I was gonna tell a lot of things about how things happened in fourth grade but that wouldn't have been helping Ann right then and that *was* last year.

JACKIE: And I know we discussed feelings 'cause I told everyone that I thought our class should be split up because we hurt people. But everyone helped me see that we can change that. I feel better now. I'm gonna tell my gang that I think Ann's a good kid—and Gloria—and tell 'em if they won't be friends . . . well, they oughta.

COUNSELOR: I feel like there's been lots of progress today. You've even already done the other two things I was going to suggest. Sometimes it's helpful if you *confront one another*, tell that other person how you see things, or ask what he's going to do about a problem. Gloria, you helped us on that by suggesting it wasn't all Ann's fault, but a group problem, and others helped here, too. The other is to *make a plan for action*. I heard Ann say she was going to try to stop mentioning the other school, and Gloria say she wanted to be friends with Ann, and Jackie plans to tell her gang to be friendly with both Ann and Gloria, and Tony said he was interested in helping Steve. It'll be good to hear how those plans turn out next week.

Any other comments you want to make before we close up shop for today?

All of the discussion relating to the six behaviors mentioned at the beginning and end of the session is designed to elicit or reinforce facilitative behaviors on the part of the group members. In addition, the counselor's first response (". . . it seems as though no one can help you") was designed to elicit group interaction on Ann's question, his second response ("I can feel you really want to help Ann") was intended to reinforce Tony's willingness to enter into the matter, his fifth response ("Gloria, you look like you understand . . .") facilitated the verbal expression of a nonverbal message, and part of his seventh response ("We seem to be willing to be honest with each other and to try to help Ann") reinforced both genuineness and helping behaviors. Effective group counseling with elementary school children can be enhanced by counselor attention to facilitative behaviors designed to shift some of the helping responsibility from the counselor to the group members.

PROCESS EXAMINATION It is helpful in both individual and group counseling, but especially in the latter, if attention is directed periodically to the counseling process itself. In doing this, the counselor can help the group examine the interaction and can state his opinions or elicit group-member opinions regarding the procedures that are successful or unsuccessful. Some examples follow:

A. In which the counselor states his concerns about the process.
COUNSELOR: I get the feeling that from the time we shut the door this afternoon there was a sort of agreement that everyone would just tell his own story and no one would really try to listen or help if there were a problem.

B. In which the counselor reinforces the process.
COUNSELOR: Before we close, I want to mention that I think we were a strong group today. We really listened particularly to George's concern, helped him see it a little differently, and maybe saw him differently, too.

C. In which the counselor elicits process examination.
COUNSELOR: I wonder what it seems to you we've been doing for the last ten minutes in talking with Ann.
GERRY: Well. . . . (Pause) We've been telling her that we understand why she gets so upset and cries a lot.
COUNSELOR: But I wonder why Ann doesn't seem to be hearing us.
BOB: Maybe because we haven't really listened to her. Everytime she tries to tell us and starts crying, somebody starts telling her they understand.

D. In which the counselor examines his own interaction.
COUNSELOR: Hey, just a minute. I see I've just been telling you that you need to try harder in Mr. Archer's physical education class. Maybe I haven't wanted to hear you fuss about him because he's my friend. But that's not fair to you.

Process examination complements, and is related to, intervention and facilitation. The counselor who can become comfortable and natural in applying these measures, together with other sensitive counseling procedures, offers much to his counselees.

LIMITS IN GROUP COUNSELING

To allow children to experience a sense of freedom within which they can deal with their personal issues and the issues between them, an environment involving very few limits is considered helpful. Largely speaking, limits should be imposed as the need arises, rather than being catalogued as the children enter the group; the latter conveys a sense of restrictiveness rather than freedom. Time limits, limits on the duration of counseling, if any, and limits relating to destructive or aggressive behavior are realistic and often are necessary to progress in group counseling.

Time limits are a part of the counselee's and counselor's real world. The statement: "We have forty minutes for our group today," is a recognition of the need for teacher-counselor cooperation and for the counselor to work with other children. Only in exceptional circumstances should this limit be violated—when a child is very upset, or the group is intensively working on a concern—and then for the briefest possible time. Time pressures often can be alleviated by a two- to five-minute signaling of the approaching end of the session and the suggestion that the group think about the problem at hand and discuss it in the coming session.

Limits to the duration of counseling are often advantageous. The counselor states his intent to select children who wish to meet for a particular number of sessions (5 to 10) or over a specified period of weeks (3 to 8) with a known frequency (once or twice each week). Since children are accustomed to school activities of year-long duration, such specification clarifies the actual plan and may accelerate the growth of the group. Those who seek further counseling or who are selected by the counselor may, of course, be invited to take part with another group or participate in individual counseling.

Limits on destructive behavior in the school setting are entirely appropriate. Since the counselor should be working within the broad range of the normal school population, children who cannot function within reasonably defined limits on destruction should be selected-out when counseling groups are formed, or restricted within the group, or excused from group participation. Destructive use of equipment, such as tearing or cutting dolls or doll clothes, throwing heavy items through windows, and the like, must be controlled. Ginott's phrasing: "Walls are not for painting,"[19] is useful here.

Limits on aggressive behavior are sometimes necessary for the benefit or protection of the other children, the child himself, or the counselor. The guilt that often follows a vicious, uncontrolled attack by a

[19] Haim G. Ginott, *Group Psychotherapy with Children* (New York: McGraw-Hill, 1961), p. 108.

child would appear to counterbalance any gain that might be derived from the experience.

Ginott[20] describes a four-step sequence in limit setting that may be of use to the counselor; it is paraphrased here, and an example follows:

1. The counselor gives recognition to the feelings or wishes of the child and helps him to verbalize them.
2. He clearly states the limit.
3. He indicates other ways in which the child's feeling or wish can be expressed.
4. He helps the child verbalize the feeling of resentment that often ensues.

A. Tony is shaking his fist at Gil for accusing him of lying.

COUNSELOR: You're really angry, Tony, and you'd like to hit Gil, but kids aren't for hitting.

TONY: Oh, that Gil, I could just. . . . (Sputters)

COUNSELOR: You could draw Gil's face or make it out of clay and show him how you feel.

(Tony silently leers at counselor, then reaches for the clay.)

TONY: Hm!

COUNSELOR: I understand. You're kinda mad at me now.

TONY: Yeah!

Limits should emerge as the need arises, should not unduly restrict the freedom of the children involved, should be delivered with understanding, and should be presented in such a way that children see alternative modes of behavior. If these criteria are met, then the process of limit setting offers children real opportunities to grow.

STIMULUS ACTIVITIES IN GROUP COUNSELING AND GUIDANCE

Stimulus activities enable children to come to a greater understanding of their classmates and allow the individual to present himself to his group in a clearer perspective. While some stimulus activities are highly controversial and would be most inappropriate for use in the elementary school setting, others could well be utilized either in group counseling or in group guidance settings. Some activities appropriate for children's groups have been adapted from other sources and are described below.

Positive feedback bombardment. A circle or several circles of less than ten children are formed. A volunteer goes in the center and,

[20] *Ibid.,* p. 107.

for one minute each, all other children in the group are asked to tell the center child what they like about him. After each child has been in the center, reactions and feelings are discussed.

Circle break-in. Circles of less than ten children are formed. A volunteer goes outside the circle and attempts to break in, within one minute, in whatever way he can. Each child has a turn. Brief discussion is held after each break-in attempt. Focus might be on how it felt to be an outsider, to be a group member, to see a friend being kept out, and on the variety of tactics used.

Secret pooling. Each child in the circle is asked to write a secret of his on a slip of paper without identifying himself. When all slips of paper have been shuffled, each child draws a slip, reads the secret aloud and tells how he thinks it must feel to be that person. Others are invited also to react to the secret or the way in which others have discussed it.

Animal identification. Each child in the circle either demonstrates the kind of animal he would like to be or tells the group about it. After each demonstration or telling, group members discuss the choice as to size, aggressiveness, solitariness, and so on.

Line crossing—1. Imaginary or real limits are set within a room, and a line bisects the space defined. Group members are told the line represents those who are exactly halfway between being leader and follower, and one end is designated as the leader, the other the follower end. Children are asked to place themselves where they belong in the group. Brief discussion is held as to the positions taken.

Line crossing—2. Procedures as above except the line represents the point halfway between happiness and unhappiness.

Line crossing—3. Procedures as above except the line represents the point halfway between making one's own decisions and having others make them.

Imaginary circle. A child in the group is given an imaginary circle (square); he does something with it in pantomime, then passes it to the next person.

Mail box. Each child writes a note to each other person in the group.

Mirror passing. Each child in sequence is handed a small mirror and tells what others see as they look at him. Discussion follows:

These examples of stimulus activities for elementary school group counseling and guidance may be creatively expanded by teachers or counselors. Such experiences ideally are brief, can readily be shared in group settings, and may be opened for discussion. They act as springboards for more intensive communication, they permit self-expression in a group environment, and they promote child-to-child understanding.

GROUP GUIDANCE

Group guidance may include a great range of activities focused upon self-understanding and understanding of others. These activities tend to be less personal or private in their orientation than occur in group counseling, but, nonetheless, involve children in ways that can help them in their perceptions of their personal interactions.

The potentialities of group guidance explorations are limited only by the teacher's or counselor's imagination and the materials available. We shall consider here a number of experiences that can be articulated in different ways and enlarged in scope: classroom mental health approaches, health-text exploration, exploration of human behavior, the discussion of emotions, career and life-space exploration, role play in group guidance, composition assignments in group guidance, and commercial audiovisual materials.

CLASSROOM MENTAL HEALTH APPROACHES

Ralph Ojemann,[21] a proponent of the use of stories and discussion for the development of personal mental health in children, has developed a series of graded materials for that purpose. As a story unfolds, questions and points for discussion are interspersed that realistically recognize the many alternative thoughts and behavior outcomes that might result as the characters interact. Some of these stories are too lengthy, and the discussion might wane if a teacher or counselor felt the need to "cover the outline" totally; however, if used flexibly, and if the leader becomes comfortable with his "own" questions based on those presented, these materials can indeed have values for children and result in meaningful discussions.

Another approach, developed by Random House, involves reading to the class certain children's books that have guidance themes. For example, *Horton Hatches the Egg* by Dr. Seuss develops the theme of responsibility. Teachers and counselors should be wary here and avoid setting unrealistic goals for children, lest they contribute to undue guilt feelings in those who cannot achieve to the level implied. However, with appropriate attention to realistic goals and alternative modes of behavior, these materials may have considerable value.

[21] Ralph H. Ojemann, *A Teaching Program in Human Behavior and Mental Health* (Cleveland: Educational Research Council of America, 1968).

HEALTH-TEXT EXPLORATIONS

Most health texts give some attention to matters of mental health that could be expanded into important guidance units. Because of the pressure upon the teacher to turn in grades, such units may be taught primarily for tests or grading and thus become stilted and textbookish. If this problem can be circumvented, however, such explorations can be meaningful.

One problem is exemplified in the Scott, Foresman cartoon series, "Not this—But this," presenting simplistic right-or-wrong alternatives. The teacher can effectively expand such issues by inviting a class discussion of, say, (1) all the ways in which a child could state the need for a dollar advance on an allowance; (2) the way the child feels who asks timidly, aggressively, or confidently; (3) the likely response to a given way of asking; and (4) the reasons residing within the other person, likely the parent, that prevent him from responding as desired. Expanding in this way, as well as using and going beyond the teacher's manual, the teacher can make the health text an important vehicle for developing a group guidance experience.

EXPLORATION OF HUMAN BEHAVIOR

A teacher or counselor, in cooperation with a classroom of children, can develop a unit or series of units on human behavior. Following traditional unit development procedures, the leader can solicit answers to such questions as:

> What behavior by people makes you curious—makes you ask why this or that happens?
> What behavior do you see that shows strong emotions, that frightens you or excites you?
> Do you think we learn all of our behavior, or is some of it born in us?
> Would it help, do you think, to discuss some of the behaviors we have identified?
> What are some ways we can find out about human behavior?
> How can this study help us understand our own behavior?

A flexible outline emerging from such questions can lead to a meaningful study project for a group of children, particularly if the accent is placed on discussion.

DISCUSSION OF EMOTIONS

Since it is helpful for children to learn to identify their own emotions, some direct consideration of emotions can be most appropriate. One Indiana counselor has built a very effective brief program around emotions and has combined this with art work. As a get-acquainted procedure that contributes to her developmental guidance program, she visits classrooms and focuses for an hour or so each on several emotions—for example, happiness, fear, sadness, and anger. Discussion questions such as the following provide the focus in the classroom:

> What makes people happy?
> How do you know people are happy?
> What has made you very happy?
> What did you feel like doing then?
> What did you do?
> Did you feel any different then?
> What are some different ways people act when they are really happy?
> Can you show through drawing a picture or telling a story how it feels to be *really* happy?

Such an experience in a classroom situation, handled by either a counselor or teacher, can help children understand their own feelings, help them appreciate the emotions of others, increase their acceptance of differences in ways of expressing emotions, and offer them a wider range of responses to their own feelings.

CAREER AND LIFE-SPACE EXPLORATION

Much can be done in classroom groups to expand the career and life-space horizons of children before they need to make career decisions. This is, perhaps, one of the ways in which teachers and counselors can work together most effectively in a truly developmental guidance activity. Since a chapter is devoted to this topic, it may be sufficient at this point to indicate that career and life-space exploration is an extremely important elementary school group guidance activity.

ROLE PLAY IN GROUP GUIDANCE

Many teachers and counselors make extensive use of role play in any group-guidance activity. This seems most appropriate, since it is a way of making graphic the problems children face. Although it may remain a part of other activities, it deserves some special attention here.

In role play a problem is posed, derived through spontaneous discussion or from other sources. It is important to stress the search for a range of possible approaches and outcomes rather than "the one workable approach."

TEACHER/COUNSELOR: Tom wants to get his younger brother to stop bothering his models while he's out playing. What are all the ways you can think of that he might try to solve the problem?

TERRY: He could talk with his brother and explain it. Jimmy is old enough to understand. Maybe he could help Jimmy get started on some of his own models.

SUE: Knowing Tom, I think he might want to yell and beat up on Jimmy. Anyway, that's what I sometimes do.

GERRY (sadly): In our family I'd have to talk it over with my mom. I couldn't just hit him or nothin'. Mom would probably say I ought to let him play, too.

JEFF: I think I'd just slug him. No! That probably wouldn't work. I was kiddin'. But why couldn't he let Jimmy in the games outside. Jimmy's OK, but Tom don't want him in our games. Maybe that's why he does it.

TEACHER/COUNSELOR: I think we've got lots of good ideas here. There seem to be a lot of things Tom could try. Let's see if we could role-play some of these to see how they might work.

At this point Tom is asked which of the ideas he would like to see tried out and whether he would like to take one of the parts. The roles are discussed, the emotions anticipated, the cast selected, the role play proceeds, and brief discussion follows. Alternative ways of trying to solve the problem are also portrayed. The search is for alternative behaviors that might work for other children as well as for Tom.

Caution must be observed in role playing to select concerns appropriate for the entire group to deal with and become informed about, and to select concerns of children who appear to be able to benefit from such group exposure. The teacher or counselor must be ready to intervene if the discussion begins to be harmful or to delve into inappropriate areas. At this point he might well offer to discuss the matter individually and offer an alternative suggestion for the group's attention.

COMPOSITION ASSIGNMENTS IN GROUP GUIDANCE

If the expression of ideas and concerns of children can be divorced from the inevitable process of evaluation, compositions can offer children legitimate means of expression. Such topics as the following, if suggested in a free spirit and if used in an understanding manner can provide children an outlet and can help the teacher or counselor gain insight into children's needs and problems.

My Ambitions	If I Could Be Anything
If I Had a Thousand Dollars	The Saddest Day
When I Grow Up	My Best Friend
My Most Awkward Moment	My Enemy
The Happiest Time	My Spare Time
The Day I Was Born	When I Am Old
When I'm Twenty-One	My Own Life
The Fright of My Life	

Such a list, which can be extended greatly, is both relevant to children and of value to counselors and teachers. The completed compositions, when used judiciously and with the permission of the children involved, may also offer much for classroom discussion.

COMMERCIAL AUDIOVISUAL MATERIALS

Motion pictures, filmstrip series, and the like have been prepared with a group-guidance focus. Many of these materials can be strongly criticized for moralizing to youngsters and portraying oversimplified solutions to real difficulties. Nonetheless, teachers and counselors can use them advantageously as focal points for discussions of reality.

One commercial filmstrip presents a boy who doesn't want to go on a classroom picnic at a lake because others will find out he doesn't know how to dive. Almost magically, a diving instructor appears and the situation works out nicely. Some of the questions that might be raised during and after the filmstrip presentation are:

What do you think will happen next on the filmstrip?
Is that the way you think it would happen for you?
What are some other things that might really happen here?
Does this story seem to be a little unreal?
Do things always work out so well?

Role play might be used to portray other ways in which the story might develop, and an objective consideration of consequences of other actions could expand the discussion effectively. It would be important for children to see reality in the presentation, to be alerted to alternative possibilities, and to examine possible consequences.

SUMMARY

The world in which the child lives presents him with group experiences almost continuously; therefore it is of great consequence to him that he learn to cope within groups. Group procedures conducted by a sensitive adult have the potential of helping children in gaining understanding *of* and *by* the others about them. Alert counselors and teachers will deal effectively with such problems and limitations as staying within ethical bounds, coping with multiple variables, restricting highly personal matters to individual counseling, and maintaining confidentiality. Group counseling can be facilitated by the use of appropriate criteria for selection of members, by the preparation of group members for the experience, by the development in the counselor of appropriate skills in group work, and by the wise application of group limits. Efforts in both group counseling and group guidance can be enhanced by appropriate and relevant stimulus activities.

Group-guidance activities can be conducted by both teachers and counselors in a variety of appropriate ways.

The significance of his peers for the developing elementary school child demands the best the school can offer in helping him both to maintain his individuality and to learn to participate effectively in groups. It seems inevitable that this development will need the kinds of assistance that the counselor and teacher can provide.

REFERENCES

American Personnel and Guidance Association, "Ethical standards," *Personnel and Guidance Journal, 40:* 206–209 (1961).

Anandam, K., M. Davis, and W. A. Poppen. "Feelings . . . to fear or to free," *Elementary School Guidance and Counseling, 5:* 181–189 (1971).

Axline, V. M. *Play Therapy.* Boston: Houghton Mifflin, 1947.

Bates, M. "Themes in group counseling with adolescents," *Personnel and Guidance Journal, 44:* 568–575 (1966).

Bedrosian, O., N. Sara, and J. Pearlman. "A pilot study to determine the effectiveness of guidance classes in developing self-understanding in elementary school children," *Elementary School Guidance and Counseling, 5:* 124–134 (1970).

Bennett, M. E. *Guidance and Counseling in Groups.* New York: McGraw-Hill, 1963.

Berk, P. "A group guidance club in the elementary school," *School Counselor, 14:* 173–178 (1967).

Berzon, B., and L. Solomon. "The self-directed therapeutic group: three studies," *Journal of Counseling Psychology, 13:* 491–497 (1966).

Bloom, B. S. *Stability and Change in Human Characteristics.* New York: Wiley, 1964.

Caplan, S. W. "The effect of group counseling on junior high school boys' concepts of themselves in school," *Journal of Counseling Psychology, 4:* 124–128 (1957).

Carlson, Jon. "Case analysis: Parent group consultation," *Elementary School Guidance and Counseling, 4:* 136–141 (1969).

Combs, C. F., B. Cohen, E. J. Gibrian, and A. M. Sniffen. "Group counseling: applying the technique," *School Counselor, 11:* 12–18 (1963).

Davis, D. A. "Effect of group guidance and individual counseling on citizenship behavior," *Personnel and Guidance Journal, 38:* 142–145 (1959).

Davis, R. G. "Group therapy and social acceptance in first grade," *Elementary School Journal, 49:* 219–223 (1968).

Derell, G. R. "A human relation class in the middle school," *School Counselor, 17:* 384–387 (1970).

Dimick, K. M., and V. E. Huff. *Child Counseling.* Dubuque, Iowa: William C. Brown Company, Publisher, 1970.

Dinkmeyer, D. C. *Guidance and Counseling in the Elementary School: Readings in Theory and Practice.* New York: Holt, Rinehart and Winston, Inc., 1968. Pp. 271–278.

———. "Developmental group counseling," *Elementary School Guidance and Counseling, 4:* 267–272 (1970).

Dreyfus, E. A., and E. Kremenliev. "Innovative group techniques: handle with care," *Personnel and Guidance Journal, 49:* 279–283 (1970).

Duncan, J. A., and G. M. Gazda. "Significant content of group counseling sessions with culturally deprived ninth grade students," *Personnel and Guidance Journal, 46:* 11–16 (1967).

Dye, H. A. *Fundamental Group Procedures for School Counselors.* Guidance Monograph Series, Boston: Houghton Mifflin, 1968.

Flavell, J. H. *The Developmental Psychology of Jean Piaget.* New York: Van Nostrand-Reinhold Company, 1963.

Foulkes, S. H. *Therapeutic Group Analysis.* New York: International Universities Press, 1964.

Frank, M. G., and J. Zilback. "Current trends in group psychotherapy with children," *International Journal of Group Psychotherapy, 18:* 447–460 (1968).

Gazda, G. M. *Innovations to Group Psychotherapy.* Springfield, Ill.: Charles C Thomas, 1968.

———, J. A. Duncan, and P. J. Sisson. "Professional issues in group work," *Personnel and Guidance Journal, 49:* 637–643 (1971).

Ginott, H. G. *Group Psychotherapy with Children.* New York: McGraw-Hill, 1961.

Glanz, E. C., and R. W. Hayes. *Groups in Guidance,* 2d ed. Boston: Allyn and Bacon, 1967.

Goldman, L. "Privilege or privacy: I," *Personnel and Guidance Journal, 48:* 88 (1969).

Gordon, M., and N. Liberman. "Group psychotherapy: being and becoming," *Personnel and Guidance Journal, 49:* 611–618 (1971).

Hansen, J. C., T. M. Niland, and L. P. Zani. "Model reinforcement in group counseling with elementary school children," *Personnel and Guidance Journal, 47:* 741–744 (1969).

Havighurst, R. *Human Development and Education.* New York: McKay, 1952.

Huckins, W. C. *Ethical and Legal Considerations in Guidance.* Guidance Monograph Series, Boston: Houghton Mifflin, 1968.

Kagan, J., and H. A. Moss. *Birth to Maturity.* New York: Wiley, 1962.

Kemp, C. G. *Perspectives on the Group Process.* Boston: Houghton Mifflin, 1970.

Kirby, J. H. "Group guidance," *Personnel and Guidance Journal, 49:* 593–598 (1971).

Laxer, R. M., J. J. Quarter, C. Isnor, and D. R. Kennedy. "Counseling small groups of behavior-problem students in junior high school," *Journal of Counseling Psychology, 14:* 454–457 (1967).

Mahler, C. A. *Group Counseling in the Schools.* Boston: Houghton Mifflin, 1969.

———. "Group counseling," *Personnel and Guidance Journal, 49:* 601–608 (1971).

————— and Edson Caldwell. *Group Counseling in Secondary Schools.* Chicago: Science Research Associates, 1961.

Mayer, G. R., and P. Baker. "Group counseling with elementary school children: a look at group size," *Elementary School Guidance and Counseling, 1:* 140–145 (1967).

Moulin, E. K. "The effects of client-centered group counseling using play media on the intelligence, achievement, and psycho-linguistic abilities of underachieving primary school children," *Elementary School Guidance and Counseling, 5:* 85–98 (1970).

Moustakas, C. "A human relations seminar at the Merrill-Palmer School," *Personnel and Guidance Journal, 37:* 342–349 (1959).

Nelson, R. C. "Organizing for groups," *Personnel and Guidance Journal, 50:* 25–28 (1971).

————— and M. Callao. "Groups and accountability," *Elementary School Guidance and Counseling, 4:* 291–294 (1970).

Ohlsen, M. M. *Group Counseling.* New York: Holt, Rinehart and Winston, Inc., 1970.

—————. "Adapting principles of group dynamics for group counseling," *School Counselor, 13:* 159–162 (1966).

—————. *Guidance Services in the Modern School.* New York: Harcourt, 1964.

Ojemann, R. H. *A Teaching Program in Human Behavior and Mental Health.* Cleveland: Educational Research Council of America, 1968.

Otto, H. A., and J. Mann. *Ways of Growth.* New York: Grossman, 1968.

Patzau, C. "An experiment in group guidance with the whole class," *Elementary School Guidance and Counseling, 5:* 205–212 (1971).

Rogers, C. R. *Freedom to Learn.* Columbus, Ohio: Merrill, 1969.

Schmidt, L. D. "Some ethical, professional and legal considerations for school counselors," *Personnel and Guidance Journal, 44:* 376–383 (1965).

Seeley, J. R. "The Forest Hill Village 'Human Relations Classes'," *Personnel and Guidance Journal, 37:* 424–434 (1959).

Shaw, M. C., and R. Wursten. "Research on group procedures in schools: a review of the literature," *Personnel and Guidance Journal, 44:* 27–34 (1965).

Tosi, D. J., C. Swanson, and P. McLean. "Group counseling with nonverbalizing elementary school children," *Elementary School Guidance and Counseling, 4:* 260–266 (1970).

Vriend, T. J. "High-performing inner-city adolescents assist low-performing peers in counseling groups," *Personnel and Guidance Journal, 47:* 897–904 (1969).

Warters, J. *Group Guidance.* New York: McGraw-Hill, 1960.

Werry, J. S., and J. P. Wollersheim. "Behavior therapy with children: a broad overview," *Journal of American Academy of Child Psychiatry, 6:* 346–370 (1967).

Winkler, R. C., J. J. Tiegland, P. F. Munger, and G. D. Kranzler. "The effects of selected counseling and remedial techniques on underachieving elementary school children," *Journal of Counseling Psychology*, *12:* 384–387 (1965).

Woal, S. T. "A project in group counseling in a junior high school," *Personnel and Guidance Journal*, *42:* 611–613 (1964).

Zimpfer, D. G. "Expressions of feelings in group counseling," *Personnel and Guidance Journal*, *45:* 703–708 (1967).

ARTICLES IN BOOKS OF READINGS

Dinkmeyer, D. C. *Guidance and Counseling in the Elementary School: Readings in Theory and Practice*. New York: Holt, Rinehart and Winston, Inc., 1968. Readings beginning on pages 185, 200, 208, 271, 278, 288, 295, 302.

Koplitz, E. D. *Guidance in the Elementary School: Theory, Research and Practice*. Dubuque, Iowa: William C. Brown Company, Publisher, 1968. Readings beginning on pages 165, 175.

Mills, G. D. *Elementary School Guidance and Counseling*. New York: Random House, Inc., 1971. Reading beginning on page 146.

Peters, H. J., A. C. Riccio, and J. J. Quaranta. *Guidance in the Elementary School: A Book of Readings*. New York: Macmillan, 1963. Readings beginning on pages 182, 229.

Part Four

Consultation and Coordination

10

Consultation with Parents, Teachers, and Others

For it is important that awake people be awake,
or a breaking line may discourage them back to sleep;
the signals we give—yes or no, or maybe—
should be clear: the darkness around us is deep.

WILLIAM STAFFORD: "A Ritual to Read to Each Other"

Margaret performs well in the fourth grade classroom, but she is quite morose. Other children seem to ignore her because of her quiet attitude. There is nothing spontaneous about her; every move she makes is deliberate and cautious. The teacher reports that her mother seemed to convey satisfaction in a conference, saying: "Margaret's just like I was when I was her age. I was always quiet and serious and the teachers seemed to like that. I *want* her to do what is expected of her."

Bob is a third grader who "bugs" the teacher with his level of activity. He finds it difficult to become involved with any activity for more than two minutes. He is a likeable, pleasant, active child of whom the teacher says: "I'm not sure he has a problem, but if he doesn't, I do!"

While individual counseling may be of great value to these children, especially to Margaret, consultation would seem vital in order to achieve the indicated changes in behavior or attitudes. With many children, consulting is an essential complement to counseling. While the elementary school child should not be viewed as an innocent bystander who has no input into his own circumstances, neither should he be seen as an independent agent upon whom outside forces have little effect. Because he is involved, he can benefit from counseling; because others are involved, he can benefit through consulting.

The necessity of combining these approaches for the survival of guidance services is demonstrated by the fate of an effective Indiana elementary school counseling program. Focused on individual counseling, this program did not adequately involve or help teachers, who in turn placed other items higher in a system of priorities. Thus the program lost financial support and, consequently, the opportunity to help children. Another reason for combining counseling and consulting efforts is given by Anderson,[1] whose research suggests that together they produce changes of a positive nature in counselees' self attitudes and attitudes toward peers.

McGehearty cautions against losing sight of the central objective: ". . . to help develop the individual so that he learns more effectively, is more self-actualized and more competent within the limits of his capacity to operate productively."[2] Certainly the elementary school counselor can more readily realize this objective if he uses both counseling and consulting activities.

One of the dangers in emphasizing consulting alone is that the child experiences the manipulation of factors in his environment without understanding the reasons for them. Certainly, the child can often be enlisted as an ally in his own behalf—for example, in his agreeing to a reinforcement procedure. This enlists another ally, the Hawthorne effect—the salutary effect often produced by the very fact that special interest is shown—and increases the chance for success. Peters, Shertzer, and Van Hoose[3] have noted that the child who is not involved in the solution of his own concerns may well be adversely affected. Self-alienation results in part from environmental manipulation centered on promoting conformity. Unless the child is individually helped to see what is valued in him beyond the changes that are sought, he is likely to experience environmental manipulation as a squeeze on his individuality.

There is no reason why a reinforcement schedule to be carried out by a parent, teacher, or counselor cannot be discussed in advance with the child. In fact, it seems most appropriate that the counselor combine the

---

[1] Ethel C. Anderson, "Counseling and consultation versus teacher consultation in the elementary school," *Elementary School Guidance and Counseling, 2:* 277–285 (1968).

[2] Loyce McGehearty, "The case for consultation," *Personnel and Guidance Journal, 47:* 258 (1968).

[3] Herman J. Peters, Bruce Shertzer, and William Van Hoose, *Guidance in Elementary Schools* (Skokie, Ill.: Rand McNally, 1965).

Adlerian approach, examining with a parent or teacher the purposes of a child's behavior; a behavioral approach designed to modify inappropriate behavior; and a client-centered approach, discussing with the child the concern for him and the interest in assisting him.

Given a suitable, sensitive approach, consulting that supplements counseling and at times moves independently of counseling can be helpful to the parent, teacher, or counselor, and subsequently to the child.

In this chapter, which explores the process of consulting in the elementary school guidance program, we shall first define consultation and then examine parent consulting—its rationale, discrepant parent and consultant expectations, parent-consulting responsibilities, and parent groups; teacher consulting—its rationale, teacher expectations, teacher-consulting responsibilities, and teacher groups; and counselor-principal and counselor-specialist consultation.

DEFINING CONSULTATION

Dinkmeyer sees consulting as "a process by which teachers, parents, principals, and other significant adults in the life of the child communicate about him. . . . Consultation involves coordinating and exchanging information. Joint planning and collaboration is emphasized in contrast to the superior-inferior relationships of some consultation situations. The purpose of the consultation is to consider all of the available data and formulate decisions about future procedures. Recommendations that ensue usually consider the uniqueness of the teacher as well as the individuality of the child."[4]

According to Faust, "The counselor, as a consultant, and the teacher focus on the child, class, or some other unit external to the teacher. It amounts to an exploration of data, information, ideas, all within a relatively safe, accepting environment."[5]

Consultation is an exchange between equals involving listening and discussing in the interest of a child. It has the potential for releasing the creativity of the parent or teacher and counselor for the benefit of that child. Each person's ideas have a sounding board, and the outcome tends to be a more considered plan than either could have expected to achieve alone. In an environment of mutual respect and mutual assistance, positive outcomes tend to occur.

[4] Don C. Dinkmeyer, *Guidance and Counseling in the Elementary School: Readings in Theory and Practice* (New York: Holt, Rinehart and Winston, Inc., 1968), pp. 106–107.
[5] Verne Faust, "The counselor as a consultant to teachers," *Elementary School Guidance and Counseling, 1:* 112–113 (1967).

PARENT CONSULTING

Given the opportunity, many parents seek help from counselors. The world creates pressures on parents, which are then visited upon their children. Many parents are frustrated, some are frightened, and most are eager to help their children grow into effective adults. The view of an independent observer can occasionally be helpful even to the most successful parent, and those who do not fall into that category may benefit more often from such assistance.

RATIONALE

The values inherent in home-school consultation are so obvious that they need not be discussed at length here. The fact that parents often seek help is sufficient justification in itself. McNassor tells us:

> American parents are among the most frustrated in the world in raising children. They become intimidated by the rapid changes in the educational tasks of the child. They are expected to produce a winner and feel guilty when the child isn't moving toward the winner's circle. The child and the parent grow farther and farther apart in today's world, knowing less and less about one another, each being less dependent on the other.[6]

McNassor's remedy is a professional friend of the family, which is what a great many parents seem to be seeking. Validation of actions and attitudes or a viable plan for changing either or both tends to be a central theme of parents' concerns. Hansen and Stevic[7] enumerate some parental concerns about the child:

1. The level of his educational progress.
2. The potential he possesses.
3. The degree of participation and cooperation he exhibits.
4. The status of his peer relationships.
5. Any special abilities (or disabilities) observed by educators.
6. The discrepancy between their expectations for him and his actual achievement.
7. The discrepancy between their values and those which appear to be espoused within the school.
8. Advice that may help them in problems of child rearing.

[6] Donald McNassor, "High priority roles for elementary school counselors," *Elementary School Guidance and Counseling, 2:* 87 (1967).

[7] James C. Hansen and Richard R. Stevic, *Elementary School Guidance* (New York: Macmillan, 1969), pp. 108–110.

There are some concerns that lead those in the school to seek consultation with parents. Van Hoose[8] notes that the child's dependency itself makes it difficult to help a child without giving appropriate consideration to his home environment. Much of the responsibility for change, when it is needed, must rest with the significant adults in the child's life. Hillman[9] notes that the child tends to change behavior in response to changes in the environment. McGehearty[10] sees the counselor as having a role in helping to produce decisions. Even though final decisions are generally made by the child and his parents, the counselor or teacher as consultant may be part of the process.

But it is not only in the realms in which behavior clearly needs to change that the school seeks the counsel of parents. Many times the opportunity for consultation should be organized so that the child can be better understood, so that the life he brings into the school can be effectively considered in coping with his needs, and so that the school is in effective communication with the home when no crisis is present. This is to say that the role of interpreting the school to the home is not crisis-oriented— that opportunities to understand the home, so that he can interpret it to the school, should be sought by the counselor under normal (noncrisis) conditions where possible.

DISCREPANT PARENT AND CONSULTANT EXPECTATIONS

Discrepancies often exist between consultant and parent expectations in consulting. Internally, the parent may be anticipating the kind of experience he had as a child in school. He may have had marvelous experiences and fully expect a warm and understanding reception; or he may have felt continuous tension and an overwhelming sense of adult authority, which perhaps he plans to resist in defiance of all that once troubled him.

The teacher or counselor, on the other hand, may expect a mature, cooperating, involved adult; or—perhaps more out of habit than design— he may expect an adult who will permit him to maintain a leadership-authority position.

A call from a parent may concern or perhaps disturb the teacher or counselor; likewise, a call from "the office" may send a message incongruent with the objectives sought.

[8] William H. Van Hoose, *Counseling in the Elementary School* (Itasca, Ill.: F. E. Peacock, 1968), p. 115.
[9] Bill Hillman, "The elementary school counseling process: an Adlerian model," *Elementary School Guidance and Counseling, 2:* 102–113 (1967).
[10] Loyce McGehearty, "Consultation and counseling," *Elementary School Guidance and Counseling, 3:* 155–163 (1969).

Parents or school personnel may both want clear and definitive answers and plans for modification of the environment. Kaczkowski[11] encourages the consultant to help parents see the therapeutic values of changed behavior on their part.

Parenthetically it seems well to note that any of the principals involved—the parent, teacher or counselor—may be inclined to believe that he has a simple solution to the problem that will inevitably change the situation for the better.

Suffice it to say, here, that although much harmony exists in parent-counselor-teacher consulting, there is the realistic possibility that prior conceptions and present irritations may make the conference unpleasant and unprofitable. Perhaps the teacher or counselor who is alert to discrepant expectations, who views consulting as a two-way process of communication, and who develops consulting opportunities at times other than when a crisis is present, can reduce the frequency of these unprofitable contacts.

PARENT CONSULTING RESPONSIBILITIES

ATTITUDINAL STANCE   Whose person is the counselor? Is he an advocate—the child's person? Does he defend against the injustices perpetrated upon the child? Is he a change agent—wishing to change the home, the school, or both? Is he a mediator—a person who stands between pairs of other individuals, attempting to increase communication between them? Or is he his own person, owing his major responsibility to himself, yet fully aware of the demands of his society, responsive to the dependency of the child, and conscious both of the concerns of the teacher and the efforts of the parents?

Ideally the counselor is, indeed, his own person. At the moment in time in which he stands he must take his stance. He can be an advocate; often the parent is involved with the child in a self-defeating vicious circle and strong confrontation may be relevant. He can be a mediator; often the encouragement for communication by those involved is appropriate and sufficient. He can be a change agent; many times the environment must undergo alteration if the interests of the child are to be served. More often, however, he needs to be a good listener; he needs to facilitate the decision-making process by providing the opportunity for consideration of the nature of the problem, the processes that have been utilized in attempts to solve it, and other avenues that may be considered.

Ideally, too, the counselor values the present moment especially and is fully conscious and aware of the individual with whom he is in communication. He feels respect, and his behavior shows that he treats

[11] Henry Kaczkowski, "The elementary school counselor as consultant," *Elementary School Guidance and Counseling, 1:* 103–111 (1967).

people as unique human beings, not objects—not, for example, as parents-in-general. Through his own behavior and his verbalization he attempts to encourage respect and person-behavior rather than object-behavior in the dealings of the parent with whom he is consulting.

Wolfe[12] asks the counselor not to play the role of an authority; while the balance of give and take does not have to be even, both must experience receiving. Lee[13] asks the counselor to be the teacher's extra eyes, ears, hands, and brain—to help him focus on the child differently. This stance seems most appropriate also to the teacher or counselor in his dealings with the parent.

Thus the person consulting has his stance defined by his own person, by the individual with whom he is consulting, and by the situation with which he is attempting to cope. He does not lose himself in an attempt to play a role; he finds meaning in the relationship with the parent or other individual with whom he is consulting; and he maintains awareness of the child whose problem or situation brought them together.

EXAMINING PURPOSES   The parent in consulting may wish to, or be encouraged to, understand his child's behavior. In such instances, Adlerian psychology can help the counselor or teacher in consulting by providing a view of behavior as purposive. Dinkmeyer notes: "Behavior is goal-directed. Each psychological movement has a goal and our behavior is directed by the dominant motive. These goals must be recognized as being subjective, creative, and frequently unconscious, or dimly perceived by the individual. The goal becomes the final cause or final explanation. Ideas for corrective action often follow upon awareness of the purpose of misbehavior."[14]

A useful way of looking at purposive behavior has been provided by Dreikurs,[15] who suggests four basic goals of misbehavior.

1. *Attention.* Attention-getting behavior may be the first step on a hierarchical ladder.
2. *Power.* A struggle for power may ensue if the attempt to get attention does not adequately accomplish the child's purposes.
3. *Revenge.* A revengeful pattern may emerge if the adult proves more powerful than the child.
4. *Dependency.* A yielding, dependent pattern that signals a feel-

[12] H. E. Wolfe, "Consultation: role, function, and process," *Mental Hygiene, 50:* 132–134 (1966).
[13] Murray Lee, "Is a guidance consultant needed in the elementary schools?" *Illinois Guidance and Personnel Association Newsletter,* Fall, 1963.
[14] Don Dinkmeyer, "Elementary school guidance and the classroom teacher," *Elementary School Guidance and Counseling, 1:* 19 (1967).
[15] Rudolf Dreikurs, *Psychology in the Classroom* (New York: Harper & Row, 1967).

ing of inadequacy may result if the child finds revenge unavailable to him, or if the struggle for power or attention is too anxiety-producing.

Dreikurs and Sonstegard[16] point out that an easy way to examine which of the goals is being served is for the adult to see how he responds to the misbehavior. Usually the response is in line with the intention. If the parent spends a good deal of the time nagging or attempting to stop behavior, the goal of attention, albeit negative, is being achieved; if the parent feels determined to stop the behavior exhibited at all costs, a power struggle is in evidence; if the behavior of the child motivates the parent toward retribution and strong punishment, the revenge cycle is present; and if the parent finds he is constantly reminding, doing things the child should be doing for himself, and thinking of the child as inadequate, dependency has become a mistaken goal.

Adlerian psychology also points out that the child tends to exhibit an overriding purpose to find a place of his own within the family. If he perceives that one of his siblings is "the smart one" and the other is "the good one," he may unconsciously seek a place as "the troublemaker" or "the shy one." Parent attitudes and comments may inadvertently reinforce the self-concept; for example, the mother tells a guest over the head of her clinging daughter, "You just can't get a word out of her. She's always like this. So shy! But I was kind of like her when I was little, too."

In subsequent sections we shall consider ways of breaking the vicious circles of ineffective parent-child interaction patterns. An important task of the counselor may be to help the parent see the unconscious or dimly perceived purposes that may motivate the child.

EXAMINING PROCESSES OF BEHAVIORAL CHANGE   While extensive attempts at eliciting behavioral change seem more generally appropriate in counselor-teacher than counselor-parent consulting, nonetheless the principles seem to have value for both interactions. There are two basic ways of supporting behavioral change—reinforcement and extinction. Knowingly or unknowingly, both parents and teachers are involved extensively in reinforcement-extinction attempts. The counselor who helps a parent to select behaviors to reinforce and others to ignore alerts him to his part in problems of communication, and provides him with other communication alternatives.

Sulzer, Mayer, and Cody caution that reinforcement and extinction attempts, though they provide alternatives, do not assure instant success—a reinforcement schedule needs to be maintained over time:

[16] Rudolf Dreikurs and Manford Sonstegard, *The Teleoanalytic Approach to Group Counseling* (Chicago: Alfred Adler Institute, 1967).

Mother and teacher may conclude too rapidly that their technique of ignoring the child is not effective, give up, and again reinforce the child. This situation sets up the occasion for intermittent reinforcement. Its effect, increased resistance to extinction, has already been noted. In the long run the behavior then may actually become strengthened. When a mother or teacher complains, "I've tried everything and nothing works," they have probably been trapped into this bind.[17]

The following example illustrates the use of behavioral procedures with an individual child. The behavioral procedures suggested are explored further in Chapter 7.

TED

Ted was a difficult child whose least endearing characteristic was that of pushing other children out of the way, not taking his turn, and insisting that he be first to line up for all occasions in school, while at home he abused his brothers and sisters similarly. Both the teacher and Ted's parents were encouraged to follow the same pattern in attempting behavioral modification. This illustration, however, is cast in terms of his home environment.

On any occasion in which Ted was observed yielding any advantage to his brother or sisters he was immediately reinforced. His mother and dad, if both were present, thanked him for letting Jim or Sue have a turn. Shortly thereafter he was given a slip of blue construction paper and was told, "If you have five or more of these at bedtime, you may choose the story that I'll read to you in bed tonight"—one of Ted's favorite activities. A schedule was worked out for sequencing many of the household activities. When, for example, Ted pushed ahead at the dinner table to have his plate served first, his request was silently ignored, and the dish was passed to another member of the family. No yielding was made to his demand to be served out of turn. Ted pleaded to be first on many occasions that were not on the schedule, resorting to cajoling and making extravagant promises, but the schedule was kept. It had been guessed that the stir he created around him when he demanded to be first was reinforcement to him; therefore every attempt was made to ignore him or make a minimal and neutral or positive response to him when he demanded to be first. After several crying outbursts, a broken plate, several spillings of food, and Ted's leaving the table to have a tantrum, his behavior began to change for the better. Eventually he began to help on giving out assignments and became very fair in seeing that they were carried out.

[17] Beth Sulzer, G. Roy Mayer, and John J. Cody, "Assisting teachers with managing classroom behavioral problems," *Elementary School Guidance and Counseling, 3:* 42 (1968).

A number of other procedures (also mentioned in Chapter 7) have been described by Sulzer *et al.*,[18] by Krumboltz and Hosford,[19] and by Frankl (specifically, paradoxical intention).[20]

Krumboltz[21] encourages the person consulting to conceptualize behavior problems as problems in learning that may be treated with reinforcement and extinction procedures. This conceptualization has the advantages that specific changes are sought, procedures are specific, outcomes sought are specific, and those involved in the child's environment are included in the treatment.

A variety of behavior modification approaches may be used in parent consulting, most of which may readily be used by the parent himself. Certain other procedures, described below, are basically intended to improve parent-child communication and are not specifically behavior-modification procedures.

IMPROVING PARENT-CHILD COMMUNICATION   Consulting in elementary school guidance can make a vital contribution by improving parent-child communication. In many homes in which there is conflict, children are shown, and therefore show, too little respect. They are heard too seldom, and their grammar is heard above their concerns; therefore they listen too seldom. Information from several sources can be utilized in improving parent-child communication.

Dorothy Baruch[22] prepared a pamphlet entitled: *How to Discipline Your Children*; the title notwithstanding, its contents are basically oriented around better communication in the home. Among other useful ideas, she suggests that misbehavior is most often the result of feelings of hurt, anger, or fear. Children need to have their feelings *and* behavior understood. Others can help the child to help himself by acknowledging his bad feelings, providing safe outlets for his bad feelings, and providing him acceptable action-pathways.

Ginott's *Between Parent and Child*[23] is based entirely on the premise that parent-child communication can be better. Some of his messages, which he expands with relevant examples, can well be incorporated

[18] *Ibid.*, pp. 40–48.

[19] John D. Krumboltz and Raymond E. Hosford, "Behavioral counseling in the elementary school," *Elementary School Guidance and Counseling, 1*: 27–40 (1967).

[20] Viktor Frankl, *Man's Search for Meaning* (New York: Washington Square Press, 1963), pp. 195–204.

[21] John D. Krumboltz, *Revolution in Counseling: Implications of Behavioral Science* (Boston: Houghton Mifflin, 1966).

[22] Dorothy Baruch, *How to Discipline Your Children* (New York: Public Affairs Committee, 1949).

[23] Haim G. Ginott, *Between Parent and Child* (New York: Macmillan, 1965).

in teacher-counselor-parent consulting. Examples: Children's idle questions often convey hidden meanings. Communication should be designed to preserve the child's and the parent's self-respect. Statements conveying understanding should precede statements of advice. Feelings are more important than facts. Children have ambivalent feelings; that is, they are attracted to and fear the same objects or events—kindergarten, for example. Praise should be specific ("You did that well") and appropriate; it is often guilt-producing when it is generalized ("You are a good boy"). Criticism should be devoted to pointing out what has to be done ("Here's the dust pan and brush"), omitting destructive negative generalizations ("You are clumsy"). Angry feelings of parents should be expressed ("I am very irritated") without attack on a child's personality or character. Self-defeating patterns of relating to children involve threats, bribes, promises, sarcasm, sermons, ridicule, and such anomalies as rudeness by the adult in the teaching of politeness. Responsibility and independence can be fostered in children.

The counselor might well have a number of copies of this source on his shelf for use with parent and teacher groups and for loan to members of both groups.

Another source of ideas relevant to parent-child (also teacher-child) communication is Dreikurs' *Children: the Challenge*.[24] More action-oriented than Ginott's book, Dreikurs' source has many ideas that the counselor or teacher may want to convey to the parent.

Perhaps the central idea Dreikurs presents is that children cannot be expected to function as effective citizens if they have grown up in a autocracy. Dreikurs offers the family council, not as a means of abdicating responsibility and handing power over to children, but as a means of sharing responsibility and reducing the power struggle present in many homes. Among his many other ideas the following are extracted:

1. Children need encouragement and tend to misbehave when they are discouraged. "You can do it"—NOT—"Let me do that for you."
2. Reward and punishment systems frequently set up patterns of authority, of vying for power and praise, and occasionally of retaliation and revenge.
3. Natural and logical consequences are often most effective in producing behavior change. A mother who chases after her son daily with his school lunch can change the pattern by deciding that he must be responsible.
4. Firmness without domination is often fruitful. A mother who stops a car and states, "I will not drive as long as there is misbe-

[24] Rudolf Dreikurs, *Children: the Challenge* (New York: Duell, Sloan, and Pearce-Meredith Press, 1964).

havior in the car," is stating her own intention, telling what she plans to do, and leaving the decision to stop fighting to the children.

5.   The desired outcome of mutual respect requires that parents show respect for the child. For example, children who trade things, even at some loss, should have the trade respected.

6.   Inducing respect for order and the rights of others is necessary. The child who is frequently late for dinner is being reinforced if mother waits dinner and clean-up for his arrival.

7.   Criticism should be eliminated and mistakes minimized, lest the attendant attention become the goal of the child.

8.   Training takes time. Parents need to be willing to give time to training for many of the functions of living.

9.   The tendency to give undue attention should be avoided, since it results in demands for more attention.

10.   Parents may effectively withdraw from many conflicts and watch them dissolve over time.

11.   Parents should allow children to settle their own differences whenever possible. "I am sure you two can work it out."

12.   The tendency to feel sorry for a disappointed or handicapped child should be resisted. Matter-of-fact responses based on understanding are much better than pitying responses, which may imply the child is too weak and helpless to meet life's challenges. "I can surely understand how disappointed you must feel about canceling the picnic. We'll try again tomorrow."

Dreikurs'[25] presentation of the family council suggests that it be a regular and fixed part of the routine with every member present. Everyone has a right to bring up a problem and to be heard, and all enter into the decision-making process. The course of action decided upon holds until the next meeting. The chairmanship is rotated so that no one member dominates and every member is consulted about the decisions made. Dreikurs suggests that parent suggestions be placed in the form of questions: "How do you think it would work if . . ." or "What would happen if. . . ." He further recommends that parents respond to suggestions in the way they would handle such suggestions from their adult friends. Such procedures are not inevitably effective, but are better suited in general to developing mutual responsibility and respect and are better preparation for democratic living than the autocratic alternative.

Smith and Smith[26] have prepared a kind of programed text for use with parents that could also be used as a basis for parent consulting. Their

[25] *Ibid.*, pp. 301–305.

[26] Judith M. Smith and Donald E. P. Smith, *Child Management: A Program for Parents* (Ann Arbor: Ann Arbor Publishers, 1966).

approach is focused on consistency in parent behavior and the establishing of a comfortable atmosphere in the home. The rather stilted presentation might be supplemented most effectively through parent group discussion.

Parent-child communication problems nourish conflict in many of the homes where it is present. The counselor or teacher who can help improve communication in the home is helping both parent and child. Conflicting demands of parents who expect too much in some areas and too little in others, patterns of verbalization and behavior that convey lack of respect and trust, and self-defeating styles of interaction are amenable to change. The counselor who contributes here is fulfilling a significant responsibility. Let us focus on one specific way in which this task may be carried out.

PARENT GROUPS

Groups involving parents can be focused on any of the printed sources described above. Parents working with a teacher or counselor may purchase or borrow the works suggested as focal points for discussion. The source must, of course, be within the reading comprehension of the parents involved. Certainly one should not overlook the potential effectiveness of the group in encouraging changes in parent behavior, in clarifying to each parent that he is not alone in facing child-rearing difficulties, and in making specific suggestions for environmental alteration. Many of the organizational and procedural points discussed in Chapter 9, "Group Procedures," are relevant to the conduct of group work with parents.

Parent groups organized around a variety of child-study approaches, including case study, also offer possible advantages. Although not as personally relevant, such procedures can readily lead to highly personalized discussion. A constructed composite child's case is presented, and questions are raised such as: What is Eddie trying to accomplish? What do you see as his problem? How do his parents "encourage" him in his behavior? What view does Eddie hold of himself? How close is this to how his parents seem to see him? Do you see any possible ways in which the vicious circle might be broken? What are all the ways in which parents might respond here? What effects would each have on the child? What are all the ways in which Eddie might respond here? What effects would each have on his parents? What verbal responses or behaviors might be expected to show Eddie the greatest respect and the most positive support? How would these responses be viewed by Eddie? How much does Eddie's situation and that of his parents have to say to you personally?

Discussion of a limited number of constructed cases for a specified period of time might help parents gain much insight, setting the stage for their presentations—already partly clarified—of their own concerns.

Shaw[27] attempted a research design involving developmental consulting with parents for whom no particular problem was present—as a preventative measure. Counselors especially trained in a brief workshop invited parents of first and seventh grade children to participate in small discussion groups focused on normal concerns of parents about their growing children. Face-to-face contacts with minority ethnic parents and letter contact with middle-class parents resulted in a highly satisfactory response, and groups of fifteen were formed. Discussion revolved around the children of these parents and ways in which they as parents could assist their children. Counselors were primed to deal with, but generally did not need to raise, age-graded topics for parents of first grade children, such as increasing independence, interest in learning to read, and changing play interests; and topics for parents of seventh grade children, such as physical and emotional changes during puberty, individual differences in growth patterns, and increasing demands for independence. The success of this experiment suggests that such a loosely structured approach would likely prove valuable to the counselor, the parents, and the children involved.

Another procedure with high potency, but also, perhaps, with high risk, is available in the family-group consultation model offered by Adlerians.[28] This involves a combination of individual and group contacts with all members of a family and suggests a confrontative, leader-dominated, somewhat manipulative set of procedures. The counselor sees individuals in a variety of settings designed to help him draw inferences from their behavior, which he then offers to the individuals involved. Focus is on ferreting out the purposes of the behavior, confronting all concerned with how they contribute to the pattern, and challenging them to change. In the hands of a sensitive, alert counselor and in selected situations some ramifications of this procedure seem highly appropriate. The counselor is cautioned, however, to gradually build toward the use of such procedures by testing his personal effectiveness in using them initially in what might be termed "friendly environments," and with families whose members are clearly willing for him to try something that, for him, is new and different.

Parent groups, whether oriented around books or free discussion, show much potential for improving parent-child relations and for placing the school in an appropriate consulting role with regard to child-rearing practices. While face-to-face contact may be necessary to involve lower socioeconomic parents whose cooperation is desired, the potential advantages on behalf of children seem most beneficial. Some successful programs,

---

[27] Merville C. Shaw, "The feasibility of parent group counseling in elementary schools," *Elementary School Guidance and Counseling, 4:* 43–53 (1969).

[28] Rudolf Dreikurs, R. Corsini, R. Lowe, and M. Sonstegard, *Adlerian Family Counseling* (Eugene, Ore.: University of Oregon Press, 1959).

such as that discussed by Carlson,[29] have utilized parents to contact other parents and have met in informal settings in homes over coffee. The counselor who perceives parent groups as having potential that he wishes to tap can find ways to realize this objective. Further ideas about parent consulting may also be derived from the discussion of teacher consulting that follows.

TEACHER CONSULTING

As suggested above, teacher and parent consulting have much in common. Both the parent and the teacher stand in an authority relationship to the child; both may perceive themselves as having a more central responsibility than getting to the child's special needs (teaching a substantial number of children, maintaining a household, fulfilling employment expectations); both may be unwitting contributors to the vicious circle surrounding a child who has an ineffective relationship to his environment; and both may benefit from the perspective of an outsider, a consultant, concerned for them and for the child and willing to hear them out and make a positive contribution.

The discussion that follows will cast the consulting responsibility in somewhat different terms, hopefully also expanding the concepts presented in the preceding section by adding new dimensions. The two sections are intended to be interdependent, rather than independent, and should be so viewed.

RATIONALE

Brison[30] suggests that the teacher and counselor combine their efforts for efficiency. Franken[31] sees the outcome as greater teacher awareness, while Dinkmeyer[32] more boldly looks for increased teacher competency. Certainly the counselor also may be expected to increase in competency as he gains information and ideas through consulting. Mindel[33] sees the teacher as feeling freer to reveal his inadequacies to the counselor

---

[29] Jon Carlson, "Case analysis: parent group consultation," *Elementary School Guidance and Counseling, 4:* 136–141 (1969).

[30] D. W. Brison, "The role of the elementary guidance counselor," *National Elementary Principal, 43:* 41–44 (1964).

[31] Mary W. Franken, "A consultant role in elementary school guidance: Helping teachers increase awareness of the behavior dynamics of children," *Elementary School Guidance and Counseling, 4:* 128–135 (1969).

[32] Dinkmeyer, *Guidance and Counseling in the Elementary School,* 1968.

[33] M. Toby Mindel, "The role of the guidance specialist in the in-service education of teachers," *Personnel and Guidance Journal, 45:* 692–696 (1967).

than to the school administrator; he suggests that the matter of total class management be an agenda item when counselors work with teachers.

Kaczkowski[34] sees a need for the counselor to help teachers and the principal examine the affective impact of instruction on children, and McGehearty[35] envisions the counsulting process as influential in removing the blocks to learning. Samler sees the objective for teachers as follows: "We do not want to make therapists out of teachers; we do want to make teachers whose relations with children are therapeutic."[36]

Nelson has presented some of the advantages specific to consulting as follows:

> 1. There is involvement of the persons who can most directly in-
> fluence the external environment of the child. These persons, whether
> parent or teacher or both, . . . as central participants in the develop-
> ment of the concern, need, or interest, . . . may . . . benefit by partici-
> pating in its discussion, and may often aid in the solution of the prob-
> lem.
> 2. The participants in the consulting situation receive a mutual benefit
> that results both from being heard and from the kind of brainstorming
> that may expand the horizons of each in providing aid to the child.
> 3. A larger number of children can be served through the indirect
> process of consulting. . . .
> 4. Counselors and teachers can take a dynamic part in their role as
> change agents through consulting. As a result of the conferences there
> develops an approach to the child that may be more united or comple-
> mentary in attempting to serve the needs exhibited by the child.[37]

In discussing the idea that consulting serves more children, Nelson comments: "No special advantage accrues to the children themselves who are merely checked off on a counselor-teacher consulting list. . . ."[38] One must beware, that is, of using consulting in a mere numbers game to account for more children. In fact, consulting and counseling revolving around the same child may consume more time than either by itself. On the other hand, the combination may result in much more effective action, and it may also "rub off" on the way the teacher or counselor copes with other students.

To summarize, teacher-consulting is a highly appropriate coun-selor activity that can benefit the teacher, the counselor, and the child.

[34] Kaczkowski, *loc. cit.*

[35] McGehearty, *Elementary School Guidance and Counseling,* 1969.

[36] Joseph Samler, "Basic approaches to mental health: an attempt at syn-thesis," *Personnel and Guidance Journal, 37:* 341 (1959).

[37] Richard C. Nelson, "Counseling versus consulting," *Elementary School Guidance and Counseling, 1:* 149–150 (1967).

[38] *Ibid.,* p. 150.

Clearly, many concerns related to specific children can best be met through some changes in classroom management, through some changes in teacher perceptions, or through some changes in teacher behavior. The effective counselor is, in part, the kind of person who can produce these changes through his consulting activities with a minimum of unnecessary friction.

DISCREPANT TEACHER AND COUNSELOR EXPECTATIONS

In consulting, counselors frequently find discrepancies between their expectations and those of parents. Parents may expect an authoritarian approach, may want clear and definitive answers, and may want to change their children without any change in their own behavior. Teachers may hold some of the same attitudes; thus, teachers and counselors may also have discrepant expectations.

While many teachers are quick to admit their own failings and their need for help, some find it extremely difficult to admit that they are not self-sufficient. Krumboltz and Hosford[39] suggest that when teachers seek help, often in their own eyes the diagnosis is already complete; they want action; and they judge the counselor by his effectiveness in producing behavior change in children. That they may expect this change without any contribution on their part is suggested by Kaczkowski,[40] who indicates that they may resist and resent suggestions that the teacher modify classroom procedures in order to produce behavior change. In the face of this, Dinkmeyer[41] underscores the need for counselors to aid teachers in examining the impact and consequences of instructional processes on children, and to help teachers understand the impact of their own behavior on the children they teach.

By and large, however, teacher and counselor purposes are much more harmonious than discrepant, and the counselor is more likely to be swamped with appropriate counseling and consulting requests than be mistrusted, ignored, or resisted. McClain and Boley point out: "Elementary school teachers frequently are the major source of influence outside the home. They care about their pupils, try to understand them, and are quick to appreciate help from a counselor whose training includes emphasis in the mental health aspects of classroom management."[42]

Let us now examine the help the counselor gives.

[39] Krumboltz and Hosford, *loc. cit.*

[40] Kaczkowski, *op. cit.*, pp. 104–105.

[41] Don C. Dinkmeyer, "The counselor as consultant: rationale and procedures," *Elementary School Guidance and Counseling, 2:* 187–194 (1962).

[42] A. D. McClain and Kaye J. Boley, "Counseling and consulting interrelationships," *Elementary School Guidance and Counseling, 3:* 33 (1968).

TEACHER CONSULTING RESPONSIBILITIES

In a great many ways the responsibilities of the elementary school counselor in consulting with teachers are the same as those in consulting with parents. Sometimes his actions will be those of an advocate on behalf of the child, less often he will need to be an advocate on behalf of the teacher; sometimes he will be a mediator between the teacher and child; sometimes he will be a change agent and his focus may be the teacher or the child; and continuously he will be a facilitative, effective listener.

The counselor in working with both parents and teachers may find it extremely useful to help them to consider purposes of children's behavior and to improve in modes of communication with children. Thus, in order to achieve maximum consulting effectiveness, the counselor is seen as needing a foundation in client-centered approaches, in situational analysis, and in behavioral techniques. These points have been extensively discussed earlier under the heading of parent consulting, so they are not further elaborated upon here.

Dinkmeyer[43] suggests that the counselor bears several responsibilities in teacher-consulting: as a specialist in human relationships, he is actively involved with teachers in a helping relationship; he collaborates, rather than providing ready answers; he develops an atmosphere of mutual trust and respect, since both he and the teacher share the same goals; and he aids in the development of self-understanding and decision-making. Dinkmeyer takes the counselor to task for listening to students and helping them think through problems to solutions while avoiding involvement in his relationships with parents and teachers and relying primarily on advising.

Van Hoose highlights the necessity for the counselor to take initiative in involving himself with teachers, saying: "The counselor cannot develop an effective guidance program without strong collaborative relationships with teachers and other members of the school staff. Thus, he should take the initiative in establishing these relationships and in developing free and open lines of communication between himself and other staff members. This requires that the counselor exhibit the same warmth and understanding that he has accepted as a necessary component of his work with students."[44]

Faust[45] places primary emphasis on teacher consulting and counseling and on group work with teachers. "Working with one teacher," he asserts, "can effectively free thirty children to learn."[46] Thus, teacher

[43] Dinkmeyer, *Guidance and Counseling in the Elementary School,* pp. 106–112.

[44] Van Hoose, *Counseling in the Elementary Schools,* pp. 117–118.

[45] Verne Faust, *The Counselor-Consultant in the Elementary Schools* (Boston: Houghton Mifflin, 1968).

[46] *Ibid.,* p. 118.

counseling and consulting may represent a way to reach many children by influencing learning climates.

An important component of the counselor's responsibilities in consulting is related to curriculum development. This is an area of consulting that the counselor may want to have written into his job description. He should make every attempt to influence the learning environment within the school in ways that make it a creative, varied, exciting, and warm place for children. Evraiff *et al.*[47] have suggested an even more direct involvement by recommending a counseling-learning team, consisting of a counselor and a learning specialist, jointly working with teachers and children, developing the strategies necessary to change the learning environment in order to help children learn. Dinkmeyer and Owens[48] have described a teacher-pupil planned project involving independent study and pupil-teacher conferences. Certainly such involvement and the evaluation of outcomes should be one of the motivational activities utilized by the elementary school counselor in his work with teachers. While the consultant in this report was a university faculty member, an in-building counselor can do the same kind of job in supporting teacher efforts and in helping teachers to find creative ways to involve children.

To summarize, the counselor has important consulting responsibilities involving teachers. Besides helping them to examine purposes of children's behavior, to plan behavioral approaches, and to develop better communication modes, he can make other significant contributions. Through active involvement and as a result of developing mutual trust, the counselor aids the teacher by means of individual and group approaches designed to contribute to the classroom learning atmosphere. Special attention is given in the next section to approaches involving teacher groups.

TEACHER GROUPS

A variety of groups can be developed by the counselor to work with teachers. He can arrange case conferences, guidance committees, classroom problems groups, in-service training experiences, child-study groups, and teacher-counseling groups.

CASE CONFERENCES Case conferences offer a direct potential for meeting needs of particular children. These groups draw together interested personnel for two basic objectives: (1) to pool information about a par-

[47] William Evraiff, Louis Falik, Annabelle Markoff, and Betty McShea, "The counseling-learning team: A model for elementary school guidance," *Elementary School Guidance and Counseling, 3:* 260–268 (1969).

[48] Don C. Dinkmeyer and Karen Owens, "Guidance and instruction: complementary for the educative process," *Elementary School Guidance and Counseling, 3:* 260–268 (1969).

ticular child and the problem he is observed to have, and (2) to plan approaches designed to meet his needs.

Essentially a teacher group, occasionally developed with no other personnel present, the case conference may include a wide range of persons. For example, to discuss the needs of an acting-out fourth grade boy named David, the following persons were brought together: his fourth grade teacher, his third grade teacher, the music teacher, the physical education teacher, the assistant principal, the nurse, and the counselor. Psychologists, social workers, speech teachers, or remedial reading specialists, for example, are other personnel who might be included for their special input with individual children.

In the case of David the counselor chaired the meeting; he read a testing report from the school psychologist; each of the persons involved told how he saw the child, and it was speculated that a tight lid on David's free expression at home was influencing the acting-out behavior in school. Outcomes included the following plans: a teacher conference with David's parents; a counseling contact with the child; a general freeing-up of the classroom environment, giving reinforcement only for responsible behavior; a reduction in the number of restrictions placed on David's behavior; a simultaneous resolve to enforce those fewer restrictions; and a plan to meet for follow-up purposes in two weeks.

This approach offered some major advantages: (1) all involved became aware of some of the background factors contributing to David's acting-out behavior, (2) a general awareness developed of the restrictive nature of many of the classroom expectations as David experienced them, (3) some plans emerged that could be put into practice by those working with him, (4) David's world at school began to take on a more predictable, unified, orderly, and sympathetic appearance, and (5) David and his parents became aware of the concern for him and the planning on his behalf.

There are two overall outcomes from this and similar case conferences. First, the needs of a specific child are clarified and planned for. Second, the staff in a most direct and appropriate way gains invaluable in-service training in individualizing instruction and providing guidance services to children.

GUIDANCE COMMITTEES   The guidance program needs involvement, the counselor needs input from teachers, and teachers need to know what is going on in guidance in the school. A schoolwide guidance committee or a number of committees with specific viable tasks can be a potent force for the guidance and counseling program. An open forum could be conducted through a guidance committee to provide dialogue on questions such as the following:

1. What should be the relative position of counseling and consulting in this school?

2. How much involvement should the counselor generate with parents?

3. How does confidentiality contribute to or detract from counselor effectiveness?

4. How can teachers be kept actively involved in guidance services so that the contributions of a counselor do not result in less help for children?

5. How can the teachers and the counselor work together so that each improves in his effectiveness?

6. To what extent (and how formally) should the counselor attempt to involve the staff in in-service activities in guidance?

7. How extensive should the career development program be in this school? How should it be developed? By whom?

8. How extensive should the testing program be in this school? Who should do what?

The counselor who believes that teachers are interested in the guidance of children does not fear the outcomes and is not hesitant to involve himself actively in such discussions. On the contrary, he finds this forum a natural place in which to raise his concerns about the learning climate or about his own status or involvement in the school, and in which to gain feedback from teachers about the impact of his efforts or about unmet needs that he should consider for the future.

CLASSROOM PROBLEMS GROUPS   Another kind of forum the counselor might wish to utilize is focused directly on classroom problems. The attention of a small group of teachers—those who wish to join in the discussion—is devoted to ways of making the learning environment more effective and exciting and at the same time improving classroom management. In an atmosphere of acceptance, support, and mutual concern, approaches to problems can be discussed and contended with.

This group may benefit greatly by the use of audio and videotapes for critical analysis and discussion. This relatively inexpensive equipment is readily available, and the failure to use it in helping teachers become more analytical and effective is inexcusable. Teachers feel so threatened by it, however, that a setting might well be limited to a trusted counselor, functioning as a consultant on human behavior problems, and a small number of accepting colleagues. This procedure might be initiated as a special service to new teachers, who often readily acknowledge their inadequacies and their needs for assistance.

IN-SERVICE TRAINING EXPERIENCES   The term in-service training conjures up so many negative images in the minds of many teachers that it should probably be avoided. If it leads teachers to picture vague, long, dull late-afternoon sessions of interminable droning by highly verbal consultants, lecturers, or colleagues, then the counselor should dispense with the term as well as such activities. Counselor-sponsored activities involving teacher groups should be

1. impact-filled;
2. interesting;
3. brief;
4. voluntary;
5. on released time or scheduled at the convenience of volunteers (the half hour before children enter the building may be one answer); and
6. focused—that is, each session should be related to a specific objective (such as informing upper-grade elementary school children about high-paying, nonprofessional jobs of which they should be aware, or interpreting the achievement test and using its results in curricular planning).

There is a need for the counselor to help expand teachers' guidance awareness, but there is no gain if the attitudes generated are negative. If he keeps the attitudes generated positive, the counselor can make a real contribution to teachers in such areas as mental health, early career development, the testing program, human development, children's needs, and guidance and curriculum. Van Hoose[49] further exhorts the counselor to include information and data that teachers can use in their daily efforts with children, and to provide specific suggestions rather than deal wholly in generalities.

CHILD STUDY GROUPS   Teachers and counselors alike can benefit by periodic attention to child study to accomplish two goals: (1) to develop insights into the purposes, problems, and possible approaches relating to the child being studied, and (2) to increase alertness to needs of children in general.

Meeks[50] has suggested that counselors involve teachers in child study groups focused on observing individual and group behavior, organizing data collected formally and informally, using sociometry to understand individual and group interaction, and utilizing test results to gain further insight for the purpose of helping children. Cottingham[51] accords with the need for study of children in faculty groups, suggesting that teach-

[49] Van Hoose, *op. cit.*, pp. 121–122.

[50] Anna R. Meeks, *Guidance in Elementary Education* (New York: Ronald, 1968), chap. 11.

[51] Harold F. Cottingham, *Guidance in Elementary Schools: Principles and Practices* (Bloomington, Ill.: McKnight, 1956), chap. 5.

ers give attention to children's physical growth and skills, social progress, intellectual growth and activity, and emotional development. Garry[52] calls for study designed to help teachers separate facts and value judgments from one another so that interpretations are not viewed as inherent in the facts.

Outcomes of child study groups should include better understanding by teachers of children, better use of such understandings, more effective processes of child study (such specific outcomes as better anecdote writing, more skill in child observation, and more comprehensive case studies), and more appropriate use by teachers of counseling and guidance services for children. Counselor-teacher planning for child study seems much more likely than counselor-imposed structure to yield these outcomes.

TEACHER COUNSELING GROUPS   The experienced counselor who is particularly effective in his adult relationships might wish to consider the development of teacher counseling groups. Faust[53] points out that when teachers or other individuals meet for a number of times within a setting in which they can deal with their personal feelings, they are likely to move away from consultation and toward counseling. At the same time, teachers may fear that their weaknesses will be exposed or that their self-images will be destroyed. Such fears may be expected to cause the building of resistance toward group counseling. Thus, while counseling in teacher groups has great potential for positive gains on behalf of both teachers and children, it also has the potential of scuttling the elementary school guidance program.

The formation of teacher counseling groups should follow, not precede, the development of teacher trust of the counselor. These groups should be entirely voluntary, and the maintenance of confidentiality should be carefully observed. Individuals who need deeper counseling should be steered away from the counseling group for the protection of all concerned.

Certainly focus should never be far from the question of how particular personal concerns and ways of interacting relate to teacher functioning with children. Faust[54] suggests making plain that the problems to be considered should be closely related to the effectiveness of teacher interaction with children. Marital problems and other concerns removed from direct effect upon children are withheld in the teacher counseling group, to be considered elsewhere individually or referred, or else they are dealt with mainly in terms of the behaviors that affect the teacher-child relationship.

[52] Ralph Garry, *Guidance Techniques for Elementary Teachers* (Columbus, Ohio: Merrill, 1963), pp. 20–27.
[53] Faust, *The Counselor-Consultant in the Elementary Schools*, pp. 119–121.
[54] *Ibid.*, p. 124.

The counselor who wishes to function more fully and genuinely as a participant, ready to exercise leadership in a limited way, may wish to center his group work around encounter tapes or the use of stimulus activities, perhaps for a beginning utilizing those suggested in Chapter 9.

In his dealings with teachers in groups, as in his work with children, the counselor is accepting, a good listener, ready to intervene so that important issues are dealt with, and courageous enough to confront others in the group when it seems appropriate. The degree of personal security that teacher group counseling requires suggests that it not be entered into lightly by the counselor; the degree to which counseling groups are under attack in the literature suggests that it will not be entered into lightly by teachers. With appropriate attention to reasonable cautions, teacher group counseling can be an important aspect of the counselor's role.

COUNSELOR-PRINCIPAL, COUNSELOR-SPECIALIST CONSULTATION

The principles of consultation already dealt with in this chapter do not differ substantially whether parents, teachers, administrators, or specialists are involved; thus the present section can be brief.

COUNSELOR-PRINCIPAL CONSULTATION

Van Hoose[55] reminds the counselor that the principal is responsible not only for the operation of the total school, but also for the work of the counselor himself. The counselor is obliged to keep the principal informed and should do so to maintain his cooperation and support. His approach to the principal should demonstrate an acceptance of that individual's professional dignity and his awareness that input is needed and valued from him.

Administrators often achieve an image of effectiveness through their perceptivity in seeing tasks and in delegating them so that they are carried out. The counselor who comes to his employment interview or to his professional assignment with the attitude: "Tell me what to do and I'll do it," often finds himself carrying out a myriad of functions that may have little or no guidance value. On the other hand, the counselor who has professional self-assurance is generally able to carve out his areas of functioning with little or no interference from the administrator, who perceives him as having commitments that are no less clearly defined than his own. Thus the consulting relationship with the school administrator begins in the first contact, and the shape of the counseling and guidance program may in some important ways be established at that time.

[55] Van Hoose, *op. cit.*, pp. 122–124.

Some areas of agreement that should be established in counselor-principal consultation are:

1. The extent to which the counselor and principal expect to inform one another and the extent to which each expects to be kept informed in matters involving counseling and discipline.
2. The processes of self-referral and teacher referral of children to the counselor, and counselor referral of children to other services.
3. The relative position of counseling and consulting in the school guidance program.
4. The extent of the counselor's involvement in record keeping and the testing program.
5. The extent to which the counselor engages in special services, such as parent counseling, parent group consultation, teacher counseling, and teacher group counseling or consultation.
6. The extent to which the counselor participates in the decision-making process involving curricular and related matters that affect classroom climate.

Like other such relationships, the counselor-principal consulting relationship requires that each accept the other and respect the other's competence. The counselor has an important responsibility to maintain contact with the principal and to obtain support for the activities he plans. The principal also has an important responsibility to show his interest and to provide support for the guidance program.

COUNSELOR-SPECIALIST CONSULTATION

In some school districts a great variety of personnel may be involved with children. Within the building there may be a remedial reading specialist, a nurse, and a speech and hearing consultant; within the district there may be school psychologists, school social workers or visiting teachers, psychometrists, curriculum consultants, subject-matter consultants, and an attendance officer; and within the community at large there may be a variety of resources, public and private, including family service and child welfare agencies and practicing psychologists and psychiatrists. Over time the counselor is likely to come in contact with any or all of those who serve the school or its constituents.

Consulting with the variety of personnel who may be interested in a given child requires discretion and responsibility by all concerned. In geographic units that provide a wide range of services, there are likely to be questions of trust and potential conflicts of jurisdiction. At the same time there is likely to be plenty of need for all who can work effectively with children or the adults in their lives. The counselor in a setting blessed with a variety of services can readily give over his contact with crisis cases and turn his attention to children's developmental needs, to self-referral, and to helping parents and teachers live more effectively with their children.

At least as often, the counselor faces another kind of jurisdictional problem, when the service a child needs is lacking and he is tempted to take on a contact that is more appropriate for another worker.

Whether the situation is one of abundance or of deprivation, there is need for communication between those involved. In both, the counselor needs guidance for his own hand in working with specific children or in obtaining outside help. The question is one of what kind of and how much help can be generated for children. Personal contact with referral resources tends to enhance the kind of mutual respect that is needed on behalf of the child. Sometimes, however, such contact with persons in related professions reveals disappointing levels of competence and adequacy, the consequence being that referrals are not made. The counselor who is hired into a situation in which referral resources are inadequate should make it one of his community obligations to seek to expand the services available to children.

SUMMARY

Consulting is the process by which those interested in the child confer about him; it is a counselor function that is complementary to counseling. Through consulting, parents can be helped to understand their children and to work with them more effectively. The counselor or the teacher may function as an advocate on behalf of the child, as a mediator between the child, his parents, and the school, or in a variety of other ways to bring the child and parent into more effective relationships. Avenues pursued include examining purposes of child behavior, planning for behavioral change, and improving parent-child communication processes.

Teacher consulting is predicated on the rationale that more effective child-teacher relationships are appropriately the concern of the counselor. The counselor may engage the teacher in a helping relationship focused on a particular child, may involve himself in curriculum consulting, or may form a variety of teacher groups intended to aid children.

In addition to his parent and teacher consulting, the counselor bears responsibility for maintaining open lines of communication between himself and the principal and between himself and the variety of persons offering services to children and parents inside and outside the school.

All consulting, regardless of those involved, is focused on assisting the child to function effectively, independently, and uniquely within his environment.

REFERENCES

Anderson, E. C. "Counseling and consultation versus teacher consultation in the elementary school," *Elementary School Guidance and Counseling, 2:* 277–285 (1968).

Auerbach, A. B. *Parents Learn Through Discussion: Principles and Practices of Parent Group Education.* New York: Wiley, 1968.

Baruch, D. *How to Discipline Your Children.* New York: Public Affairs Committee, 1949.

Berdie, R. F. "A paradox in adult-child communication," *Elementary School Guidance and Counseling, 5:* 99–103 (1970).

Brison, D. W. "The role of the elementary guidance counselor," *National Elementary Principal, 43:* 41–44 (1964).

Carlson, J. "Case analysis: parent group consultation," *Elementary School Guidance and Counseling, 4:* 136–141 (1969).

Cottingham, H. F. *Guidance in Elementary Schools: Principles and Practices.* Bloomington, Ill.: McKnight, 1956.

Crocker, E. C. "Depth Consultation with Parents," *Young Children, 20:* 2 (1964).

Dinkmeyer, D. C. *Guidance and Counseling in the Elementary Schools: Readings in Theory and Practice.* New York: Holt, Rinehart and Winston, Inc., 1968. Pp. 106–112.

————. "Elementary school guidance and the classroom teacher," *Elementary School Guidance and Counseling, 1:* 15–26 (1967).

————. "The counselor as consultant: rationale and procedures," *Elementary School Guidance and Counseling, 2:* 187–194 (1968).

———— and K. Owens. "Guidance and instruction: complementary for the educative process," *Elementary School Guidance and Counseling, 3:* 260–268 (1969).

———— and C. E. Caldwell. *Developmental Counseling and Guidance.* New York: McGraw-Hill, 1970.

Dreikurs, R. *Children: the Challenge.* New York: Duell, Sloan & Pearce-Meredith Press, 1964.

————. *Psychology in the Classroom.* New York: Harper & Row, 1957.

———— and M. Sonstegard. *The Teleoanalytic Approach to Group Counseling.* Chicago: Alfred Adler Institute, 1967.

————, R. Corsini, R. Lowe, and M. Sonstegard. *Adlerian Family Counseling.* Eugene, Ore.: University of Oregon Press, 1959.

Eckerson, L. O., and H. M. Smith. "Elementary school guidance: the consultant," in Don C. Dinkmeyer, ed., *Guidance and Counseling in the Elementary Schools: Readings in Theory and Practice.* New York: Holt, Rinehart and Winston, Inc., 1968. Pp. 112–119.

Englehardt, L., B. Sulzer, and M. Altekruse. "The counselor as a consultant in eliminating out-of-seat behavior," *Elementary School Guidance and Counseling, 5:* 196–204 (1971).

Evraiff, W., L. Falik, A. Markoff, and B. McShea. "The counseling-learning team: a model for elementary school guidance," *Elementary School Guidance and Counseling, 4:* 95–103 (1969).

Faust, V. *The Counselor-Consultant in the Elementary Schools.* Boston: Houghton Mifflin, 1968.

————. "The counselor as a consultant to teachers," *Elementary School Guidance and Counseling, 1:* 112–117 (1967).

Foreman, M. E., W. A. Poppen, and J. M. Frost. "Case groups: an in-service education technique," *Personnel and Guidance Journal, 46:* 388–392 (1967).

Franken, M. W. "A consultant role in elementary school guidance: helping teachers increase awareness of the behavior dynamics of children," *Elementary School Guidance and Counseling, 4:* 128–135 (1969).

Frankl, V. *Man's Search for Meaning.* New York: Washington Square Press, 1963.

Garry, R. *Guidance Techniques for Elementary Teachers.* Columbus, Ohio: Merrill, 1963.

Ginott, H. G. *Between Parent and Child.* New York: Macmillan, 1965.

Gordon, I. J. *Studying the Child in School.* New York: Wiley, 1966.

Grubbe, T. E. "Adlerian psychology as a basic framework for elementary counseling services," *Elementary School Guidance and Counseling, 3:* 20–26 (1968).

Hansen, J. C., and R. R. Stevic. *Elementary School Guidance.* New York: Macmillan, 1969.

Hillman, B. "The elementary school counseling process: an Adlerian model," *Elementary School Guidance and Counseling, 2:* 102–113 (1967).

Hume, K. E. "Counseling and consulting: complementary functions," *Elementary School Guidance and Counseling, 5:* 3–11 (1970).

Kaczkowski, H. "The elementary school counselor as consultant," *Elementary School Guidance and Counseling, 1:* 103–111 (1967).

Kennedy, D. A. "Use of learning theory in guidance consultation," *Elementary School Guidance and Counseling, 3:* 49–56 (1968).

———— and Ina Thompson. "Use of reinforcement technique with a first grade boy," *Personnel and Guidance Journal, 46:* 366–370 (1967).

Kratochvil, D., G. B. Jones, and L. H. Ganschow. "Helping students to help themselves," *School Counselor, 17:* 376–383 (1970).

Krumboltz, J. D. *Revolution in Counseling: Implications of Behavioral Science.* Boston: Houghton Mifflin, 1966.

———— and R. E. Hosford. "Behavioral counseling in the elementary school," *Elementary School Guidance and Counseling, 1:* 27–40 (1967).

Lee, J. M. "Is a guidance consultant needed in the elementary schools?" *Illinois Guidance and Personnel Association Newsletter,* Fall, 1963.

Mayer, G. R. "An approach for the elementary school counselor: consultant or counselor," *School Counselor, 14:* 210–214 (1967).

McClain, A. D., and K. J. Boley. "Counseling and consulting interrelationships," *Elementary School Guidance and Counseling, 3:* 32–39 (1968).

McGehearty, L. "The case for consultation," *Personnel and Guidance Journal, 47:* 257–262 (1968).

————. "Consultation and counseling," *Elementary School Guidance and Counseling, 3:* 155–163 (1969).

McNassor, D. "High priority roles for elementary school counselors," *Elementary School Guidance and Counseling, 2:* 83–92 (1967).

Medinnus, G. R. *Readings in the Psychology of Parent-Child Relations.* New York: Wiley, 1967.

Meeks, A. R. *Guidance in Elementary Education.* New York: Ronald, 1968.

Mindel, M. T. "The role of the guidance specialist in the in-service education of teachers," *Personnel and Guidance Journal, 45:* 692–696 (1967).

Muro, J. J. *The Counselor's Work in the Elementary School.* Scranton, Pa.: International Textbook, 1970.

Nelson, R. C. "Counseling versus consulting," *Elementary School Guidance and Counseling, 1:* 146–151 (1967).

———— and G. O'Connor. "A prekindergarten orientation program," *Elementary School Guidance and Counseling, 5:* 135–139 (1970).

———— and J. M. Muro. "Counselors choose counseling and consulting," *Elementary School Guidance and Counseling, 5:* 296–300 (1971).

Ohlsen, M. M. *Group Counseling.* New York: Holt, Rinehart and Winston, Inc., 1970.

Oldridge, B. "Two roles for elementary school guidance personnel," *Personnel and Guidance Journal, 43:* 367–370 (1964).

Patterson, C. H. "Elementary school counselor or child development consultant," *Personnel and Guidance Journal, 46:* 75–76 (1967).

Peters, H. J., B. Shertzer, and W. Van Hoose. *Guidance in Elementary Schools.* Skokie, Ill.: Rand McNally, 1965.

Samler, J. "Basic approaches to mental health: an attempt at synthesis," *Personnel and Guidance Journal, 37:* 638–643 (1959).

Seagull, A. "The counselor as consultant: what teachers can teach him," *Personnel and Guidance Journal, 46:* 808–810 (1968).

Shaw, M. C. "The feasibility of parent group counseling in elementary schools," *Elementary School Guidance and Counseling, 4:* 43–53 (1969).

Smith, J. M., and D. E. P. Smith. *Child Management.* Ann Arbor, Mich.: Ann Arbor Publishers, 1966.

Sorenson, M. A. "Counseling marginal students on classroom behavior," *Personnel and Guidance Journal, 40:* 811–812 (1962).

Splete, H. "The elementary school counselor: an effective consultant with classroom teachers," *Elementary School Guidance and Counseling, 5:* 165–172 (1971).

Sulzer, B., G. R. Mayer, and J. J. Cody. "Assisting teachers with managing behavioral problems," *Elementary School Guidance and Counseling, 3:* 40–48 (1968).

Toews, J. M. "The counselor as contingency manager," *Personnel and Guidance Journal, 48:* 127–133 (1969).

Van Hoose, W. H. *Counseling in the Elementary School.* Itasca, Ill.: F. E. Peacock, 1968.

Watson, D. H. "Group work with principals: implications for elementary counselors," *Elementary School Guidance and Counseling, 3:* 234–241 (1969).

Werry, J. S., and J. P. Wollersheim. "Behavior therapy with children: a broad overview," *Journal of the American Academy of Child Psychiatry, 6:* 346–370 (1967).

Whitley, A. D., and B. Sulzer. "Reducing disruptive behavior through consultation," *Personnel and Guidance Journal, 48:* 836–841 (1970).

Witmer, J., and H. F. Cottingham, "The teacher's role and guidance function as reported by elementary teachers," *Elementary School Guidance and Counseling, 5:* 12–21 (1970).

Wolfe, H. E. "Consultation: role, function and process," *Mental Hygiene, 50:* 132–134 (1966).

Zwetschke, E. T., and J. E. Grenfell. "Family group consultation: a description and a rationale," *Personnel and Guidance Journal, 43:* 974–980 (1965).

ARTICLES IN BOOKS OF READINGS

Dinkmeyer, D. C. *Guidance and Counseling in the Elementary School: Readings in Theory and Practice.* New York: Holt, Rinehart and Winston, Inc., 1968. Readings beginning on pages 106, 112, 120, 123, 128, 133, 341, 346, 355, 361.

Koplitz, E. D. *Guidance in the Elementary School: Theory, Research and Practice.* Dubuque, Iowa: William C. Brown Company, Publisher, 1968. Readings beginning on pages 238, 248.

Mills, G. D. *Elementary School Guidance and Counseling.* New York: Random House, Inc., 1971. Readings beginning on pages 177, 187.

Peters, H. J., A. C. Riccio, and J. J. Quaranta. *Guidance in the Elementary School: A Book of Readings.* New York: Macmillan, 1963. Reading beginning on page 281.

11

Coordination and Referral

A voice called, and I heard
And hearing, I replied:
It was no wandering bird
But a human voice that cried;
A lost voice in the night—   .
And do lost voices lie?
I took my self for light
And answered. Here am I.

D. S. SAVAGE:
"A Voice in the Void"

To some voices we hear we can ourselves respond. Sometimes, though we resonate to the call for help, our response is another call. We cannot always meet the need, but we can try to see that it is met.

The members of the ACES-ASCA Committee on the Elementary School Counselor[1] as well as a number of other individuals have suggested that, besides counseling and consulting, the counselor bears a third major responsibility—that of coordination. The terms *coordination* and *coordinating* are used here to mean a harmonious working together. In some ways the word *collaboration* is more precise, but in World War II it gained a rather unfortunate connotation (collaborators were those who worked harmoniously with the enemy occupation forces). The aim of coordination is to

[1] Association for Counselor Education and Supervision-American School Counselors Association Committee on the Elementary School Counselor, *The Elementary School Counselor in Today's Schools* (Washington, D.C.: American Personnel and Guidance Association, 1969).

see that, for example, one child is not the recipient of five services operating out of touch with one another while five children receive no services.

Referral may be viewed as an aspect of coordination, and certainly it is a related activity. Referral is viewed here not as an event, but as a process involving information seeking, preparing, decision making, action assisting, and follow-up.

To expand these concepts further, this chapter includes sections on coordination, the referral process, referral resources, and holding actions.

COORDINATION

Coordination is the process of relating all efforts for helping the child into a meaningful pattern. . . .

Coordination is the method used to bring into focus the school's total effort in the child's behalf, eliminating duplication of effort and insuring follow through on decisions made and policies established. This involves close working relationships between the counselor, teacher, parent, and other school and community personnel whose contacts with the child in the school situation are significant.[2]

COORDINATIVE RESPONSIBILITIES

The same paper includes the point that the counselor ". . . coordinates the organized effort of the school and community for the individual child. . . ."[3] The position taken here, however, is that so long as the counselor is satisfied that there is appropriate coordination of efforts on behalf of the child, he need not actively lead in that area. In this vein Wrenn cautions that the counselor should meet his needs for status and recognition without seeking a position of administrative leadership.[4]

The counselor need not feel either that he has a corner on the coordination-leadership market or that such leadership on behalf of a child is something he should avoid. It is often appropriate that coordinative leadership be offered by the counselor—but not always. The administrator, school psychologist, or school social worker who makes efforts to function in that capacity may be freeing the counselor to engage in his more central responsibilities of counseling and consulting. Such efforts deserve the counselor's support.

---

[2] ACES-ASCA Joint Committee on the Elementary School Counselor, "Working paper," in Don Dinkmeyer, ed., *Guidance and Counseling in the Elementary School* (New York: Holt, Rinehart and Winston, Inc., 1968), p. 104.

[3] *Ibid.*

[4] C. Gilbert Wrenn, *The Counselor in a Changing World* (Washington, D.C.: American Personnel and Guidance Association, 1962).

The ACES-ASCA Joint Committee[5] saw the counselor as *helping* to integrate school and community resources to meet the needs of children.

The counselor, whether he exercises prime leadership or not, has at least three responsibilities in coordination. (1) He keeps in touch with the services being provided on behalf of individual children to be sure that their best interests are being served; (2) he receives referrals from many sources, such as the child, parent, teacher, principal, remedial reading teacher, speech therapist, school social worker, and school psychologist, who request his direct counseling or consulting involvement with individual children or the adults in their lives; and (3) he acts as a clearing house to see that referral is made to the most appropriate person(s) or agency if he himself does not intend to cope with the problem involved.

The counselor handles these coordinative tasks without usurping responsibilities of others; he clears his efforts with appropriate individuals and keeps others informed, yet meets the emergency needs that cannot await a staffing conference and handles routine referrals that need not be processed by all who could be involved.

COORDINATIVE PROCEDURES

Coordination of services on behalf of a child can be conducted informally, with all persons involved discussing their objectives, procedures, and progress with the counselor or other designated individual. However, for maximum mutual benefit there must be some more structure than this. Most pupil personnel service staffs should be able to find a comfortable working arrangement somewhere between (a) brief reporting in a rather informal setting during bi-weekly or monthly scheduled coffee hours and (b) formal weekly half-day sessions incorporating extensive case studies.

In one small suburban district a weekly meeting involves the elementary school counselor, school social worker, school psychologist, and building principal. During successive weeks the meeting site moves until each school has been visited. Personnel change somewhat in each meeting, occasionally involving a remedial reading person or a speech and hearing person where appropriate, but always including the building principal and building counselor. Leadership is a shared responsibility. The counselor contributes primarily by naming most of the children to be considered, by consulting with teachers in order to bring progress reports to the meeting, and by discussing the progress in counseling of some of the children on the agenda. Input from other members of the pupil personnel services team varies from child to child, but all seem free to provide information, to involve themselves in the planning process, and to volunteer services as

[5] ACES-ASCA Committee on the Elementary School Counselor, *The Elementary School Counselor in Today's Schools.*

appropriate. The situation is unhurried and comfortable, and a clear expression of professional respect pervades the atmosphere.

Coordination of effort takes time, and the success of such a model of teamwork depends greatly on the time and professional commitment given it. Such a procedure, adapted to the personnel available, holds great promise for increasing the effectiveness of each team member and improving the services offered to children.

Referral and holding actions, discussed next, are among the counselor's coordination functions. He may well function as coordinator of any referrals that go beyond the services of the school, and in many cases he will need to consider involving himself in holding actions until outside referral occurs.

THE REFERRAL PROCESS:
REFERRAL TO THE COUNSELOR

Encouragement to self referral by the teacher seems an appropriate initial step in most cases, although occasionally a direct referral may be necessary. In any case, within the school building the referral process by which the teacher seeks the assistance of the counselor should be designed to facilitate easy communication. Informal contacts may be the most appropriate means of initiating teacher referral concerning elementary school students; thus, some counselors make a practice of circulating to classrooms before or after the school day, making themselves available for referral or consultation.

Where the student-counselor ratio exceeds three hundred or three hundred fifty to one, self referral may occur less frequently, the need for formalization may increase somewhat, and the use of a referral form may be indicated. Even under such circumstances the form should be brief and limited in scope so that its completion is not a major barrier. Simple referral and response forms are shown by Figures 11–1 and 11–2. For situations in which more information is needed, a more extensive form might be developed such as Figure 11–3. Counselors in Deerfield, Ill., use a checklist (Figure 11–4) to gain information about referrals.

Such devices must be supplemented by additional information where a referral is being made to the counselor by such other professional colleagues as the school psychologist. The counselor, too, when he has made the decision to refer, bears a responsibility for providing more than minimal information. When situations are complicated or have critical ramifications, it is often better that a more extensive report, such as a case study, be prepared, either by the teacher for the counselor or by the counselor for a referral resource beyond the confines of the school building.

A referral system should be simple but adequate.

WASHINGTON SCHOOL CORPORATION

REFERRAL TO COUNSELOR

Student's Name_____Grade_____Date_____

School_____Teacher_____

Nature of the problem and procedures utilized to date:

Suggestions for procedures: _____Teacher conference

                                         _____Individual counseling

                                         _____Home visit

                                         _____Individual testing

                                         _____Other (Specify)

                                         _____
                                                     SIGNATURE

FIGURE 11–1 *Referral to Counselor*

THE REFERRAL PROCESS: REFERRALS TO OUTSIDE AGENCIES

When a child's needs suggest referral to an agency beyond the school, several steps may be appropriate.

Collection of Data

1. Teachers are most often the originating sources of referrals; in any case, their general and controlled observations regarding the child may be solicited.
2. Records regarding the child may contain valuable information; a physical problem, such as diabetes or epilepsy, could be involved. A referral to the family physician and a change in medication might well alleviate the problem. Both cumulative and confidential records are checked, therefore, before outside consultation is sought.

WASHINGTON SCHOOL CORPORATION

RESPONSE BY COUNSELOR TO REFERRAL

Student's Name_____Grade_____Date_____

School_____Teacher_____

Referred by_____Date_____

Remarks:

Date, Time Suggested

Planned procedures: _____Teacher conference_____

                             _____Individual counseling_____

                             _____Home visit   _____

                             _____Individual testing_____

                             _____Other (Specify)   _____

_____
SIGNATURE

FIGURE 11–2   *Response by Counselor*

3. Parent contact, in which the parent is asked about the child's functioning at home, and in which concern about in-school behavior is expressed, may reveal that assistance has already been sought, or that concern about the behavior is or is not shared at home.

4. If the depth of the problem appears to be beyond the counselor's training, there may be little to gain from an interview process, but counselor observations may help to clarify whether the teacher's concern is warranted. Therefore the counselor may seek opportunities to observe the child in the classroom and under other circumstances.

5. Pooling of counselor and teacher information prior to further action may provide an opportunity for these professionals to plan an in-house action or to confirm the need for outside assistance.

6. Collection of data beyond that already available may be indicated. For example, a recently transferred child might have no current testing data and might be functioning poorly because of an unwise classroom assignment.

WASHINGTON SCHOOL CORPORATION

· REFERRAL TO COUNSELOR

TO: _____ SCHOOL: _____ DATE: _____

RE: PUPIL'S NAME_____ GRADE: _____

FROM: _____

In order to help me plan my approach with the child named above I should like to request that you provide whatever pertinent data you have on this form.

1. Attitude toward school:

2. Behavior in relation to teacher:

3. Behavior in relation to classmates in classroom and playground:

4. Academic achievement:

5. Special abilities, likes and dislikes, hobbies, and after school organized activities:

6. Evidence of any family problems:

7. Other observations and comments:

                                                _____
                                                  Teacher's Signature

Please complete this form by_____and return to counselor's office or box.

FIGURE 11–3 *Referral to Counselor (Longer Form)*

REFERRAL INDICATIONS

Name:_____ Born:_____ Grade:_____ Sex:_____

Date:_____ Teacher:_____ School:_____

<u>Instructions</u>: Please check mark in margin opposite those items which are representative of this child. Use a double check mark for those items which are most descriptive of him on the basis of frequency. Underline specific examples within parentheses where given.

1. Very sensitive to criticism.
2. Expresses feelings of inadequacy about self.
3. Never makes self known to others.
4. Is excessively neat or finicky about work or possessions.
5. Overconforms to rules.
6. Aggressive in underhanded ways.
7. Seeks attention excessively.
8. Very short attention span.
9. Can't work independently.
10. Shows signs of nervousness (nailbiting, crying, tics, rocking).
11. Overly preoccupied with sexual matters.
12. Daydreams.
13. Seems to fear being assertive even in ordinary ways (asking to go to toilet, defending self, making legitimate messes, joining in allowable noisy play).
14. Is receiving or recommended for speech correction.
15. Poor coordination (trouble with buttoning, tying shoes, getting shoes on correct feet).
16. Can't take turns: "me first."
17. Lacks responsibility for self: always has excuse for shortcomings.
18. Resists limits or rules in group games.
19. Tendencies toward enuresis or soiling of clothing.
20. Very messy with work or belongings.
21. Negativistic: "I won't."
22. Difficulty in handling working materials, such as crayons, scissors, paste, etc.
23. Considered an isolate in class.
24. Engages in much solitary play.
25. Displays infantile behavior (crawling, whining, clinging, sucking, chewing, mouthing).
26. Makes odd noises.
27. Makes irrelevant or inappropriate remarks.
28. Misinterprets simple statements.
29. Is disoriented in space; is confused as to directions given.
30. Shows excessive fantasy preoccupation.
31. Tendencies toward primitive hostilities.
32. Holds back in free play.
33. Antisocial tendencies (steals, lies, destroys property, bullies, defies, resists discipline).
34. Frequently tardy; frequently absent.
35. Poorly cared for before leaving for school.
36. Easily fatigued.
37. Often ill; other physical problems.
38. Feigns illness.
39. In the academic area there is evidence of underachievement in relation to ability; overachievement in relation to ability; persistent reversals of letters and/or numerals beyond first grade; lack of motivation.
40. Other (specify).

FIGURE 11-4 *Referral Checklist*

284

Preparation for the referral

1. The counselor should acquaint himself with potential referral resources within and beyond the employ of the school corporation.
2. The counselor should determine which of the possible referral resources might be of assistance in the given situation.

The referral decision

1. Parental involvement in outside referrals is vital.
2. The decision to accept referral belongs to parents of elementary school children.

Assisting the implementation of the referral, where necessary

1. Specific information should be given to parents.
2. Where necessary, facilitation of the referral (e.g., appointment making, provision of transportation) should be arranged.

Follow-up

1. The counselor should remain in contact with parents, the child's teacher(s), and frequently the child himself.
2. The counselor should also remain in contact with the agency.

An extended illustration of the referral process is presented below in the case of eight-year-old Jody Lyons.

Mr. Tanner arrived at the Elm Elementary School one Monday morning to find a note from Mrs. Stanley:

> MR. TANNER:
>   I need to talk with you as soon as possible about Jody Lyons who transferred last week. Please!
>
>   J. STANLEY

Pausing only to hang up his coat, Mr. Tanner walked immediately to Mrs. Stanley's third grade classroom.

INFORMATION SEEKING

TEACHER CONTACT Mrs. Stanley rushed to Mr. Tanner as he entered the room. "The children will be in in ten minutes. Let me tell you about Jody." She went on to describe Jody's many unusual behaviors. He could work well for eight or ten minutes at a time; then, apparently oblivious of others around him, he changed radically for a few moments. Several times he stood and yelled inarticulately. On other occasions he flung himself bodily across the several desks with which his own was grouped. Twice he climbed on top of the piano, heedless of calls to stop, jumped on the keys, rolled to the floor, and remained there silently for several moments. Following these outbursts, all occurring within the three days after his arrival at the school, he returned quietly to his desk and resumed his work, doing it quite effectively.

As the children arrived, Mr. Tanner promised immediate follow-up, a check into the previous school's records, a parent contact, and a return before lunch for a brief period of observation, plus a luncheon conference with Mrs. Stanley.

RECORD CHECKING   The transferred school record had arrived in the mail and Mr. Tanner perused it, finding it only minimally informative, perhaps the most important notation being that a confidential file had been prepared for Jody. A telephone call put him in contact with Mrs. Briggs, principal at the school from which Jody had transferred. Jody, she told him, had exhibited occasional bizarre behavior, though it was never hurtful to other children; the school had suggested a psychological referral several times since Jody had been in kindergarten, but the parents, particularly the father, had resisted the suggestion. Mr. Tanner described Jody's behaviors and found that they were similar to those observed earlier, but more severe and far more frequent. Mrs. Briggs suggested immediate parent contact, since it was her understanding that the parents had made the move to a new neighborhood to get Jody in "a better school" and away from some children who were "disturbing influences."

PARENT CONTACT   Mr. Tanner phoned Mrs. Lyons and asked to see her, indicating that Jody seemed to be having difficulty adjusting to the new school environment. Mrs. Lyons agreed to come in during the morning and seemed to be quite honestly concerned and eager to help. When she arrived, Mr. Tanner encouraged her to indicate how she saw Jody. As she talked, he found that Mr. Lyons seemed to be the one opposed to referral, that he had expected the move to "cure" the difficulties at school, but that both were concerned about Jody.

By the time the parent interview was over, Mrs. Stanley's third grade group was at recess, and Mr. Tanner asked Mrs. Lyons to observe the class at play. The two stood in the doorway, watching Jody waiting in line to engage in a four square game. Before his turn arrived, he ran from the line and tore through a rope-jumping area. He made no attempt to jump and thus was tripped as he ran through. He rolled over, picked himself up, continued to run, then stopped and walked back to the four square line. He took his place at the end of the line but the boy who had been waiting behind him called him to return to his place, which he did.

Mrs. Lyons asked for a four o'clock appointment for the following afternoon and promised to have her husband there. Mr. Tanner said that he would check with Mrs. Stanley again in the meantime.

OBSERVATION Mr. Tanner returned toward Mrs. Stanley's room to observe during the social studies period. Long before he reached it he could hear a shrill shrieking coming from the room; as he entered, Jody continued to stand in the corner and shriek at the wall. Amazingly enough, the other children made every effort to continue the social studies lesson. Soon Jody returned to his seat, picked up his book, and began to follow along—not participating, but aware—until the class was dismissed for lunch.

TEACHER-COUNSELOR INFORMATION POOLING Over lunch and again after school Mrs. Stanley and Mr. Tanner compared notes. Mrs. Stanley appeared relieved to have an opportunity to share her concerns, she was highly satisfied that Mr. and Mrs. Lyons would be involved in a conference the next day, and she was in favor of Mr. Tanner's suggestion that the child psychiatrist from Family Welfare might be brought into the case.

COLLECTION OF DATA Mr. Tanner ascertained from group testing data available in the transfer record that Jody's intelligence and achievement were well above average. Had the problem appeared to be less severe, Mr. Tanner would have sought a complete psychological report from the school psychometrist. As it was, he checked out his opinion with the psychometrist, who agreed that the Family Service psychiatrist would be the likely referral resource and that no time should be lost in making the referral.

In a situation of less urgency, a period of data collection would have ensued. Figure 11–5, a checklist for child referral utilized by counselors in Deerfield, Ill., shows the kind of information that is sought.

PREPARING

Long before the emergency with Jody arose, Mr. Tanner had prepared himself for referral situations, following two guidelines offered by Patterson:[6]

1. He had visited several in-school and community agencies in order to become acquainted with their personnel and services, and he had begun to develop a real sense of mutual respect and friendship.
2. He had ascertained that these agencies were willing and eager that he be the school contact person who would provide them information and receive their reports.

In preparing himself and Jody's parents for a referral decision, he followed three additional guidelines:

[6] Cecil H. Patterson, "Teamwork and referral," *The Counselor in the School: Selected Readings* (New York: McGraw-Hill, 1967), pp. 369–372.

CASE DATA FOR A CHILD REFERRAL

I. Identification

Name	Sex	National background
Address	Race	Family structure
Age	Religion	People in the home

II. Referral
> Person who is making referral
> Present problems and complaints leading to the referral
>> Signs of maladaptive behavior
>> If possible, trace the onset of the problem
>> Background on what led up to the referral
> Brief description of attempts to work with child on problems, if any

III. Family Background
> Parents' names, ages, occupations, places of birth
> Language spoken in the home
> Siblings--number, ages, sex (any significant data on any of the siblings)
> Other persons in the home--relations to family
> Socioeconomic background (home, apartment, trailer, etc.; size, neighborhood)
> Family relationships--climate in home, significant material on differences of opinion, responsibility for discipline--reaction to child's problems.

IV. Brief Description of the Child

V. Developmental Data
> Parental attitudes
> Birth history
> Early care--any problems in feeding, sleeping, health problems
> Early development: speech, locomotion, etc.
> Habit establishment--when, any comments made should be noted
> Initiation of ability to care for self
> Any early fears or anxieties

VI. Socialization and Emotional Description
> Relations to adults--dependent, aggressive, prefers company, etc.
> Relations to children--social status of child, plays alone or with others, friendly, aloof, leader, follower in play activities, etc.
> Acceptance of limits--to what extent? sets own limits, accepts with any particular emotional reactions, etc.
> Interests, attitudes
> Unusual drives or fears
> Any evidence of delinquency
> Usual emotional tone of child--disposition, happy, excitable, irritable, etc.

VII. School Experiences
> Admission experiences
> Progress--include present grade placement and achievement level
> Special problems in learning
> Relationships with teachers
> (General summarization of cumulative data)

VIII. Medical Background
> Illnesses
> Hospitalizations
> Special medication child taking or has taken
> Current health

IX. Previous treatment or referral reports should be attached

FIGURE 11-5 *Case Data Sheet for Referral*

3. He ascertained that no other school or nonschool personnel had been or were already working with the child or his parents.

4. He determined that in-school resources did not appear to cover the presenting problem.

5. He determined that the agency (Family Service) to which he was planning to suggest referral would consider Jody eligible for services. Either that, or he and his parents would be accepted as private clients by the psychiatrist, Dr. Kirby.

DECISION MAKING

Since referral of an elementary school student requires the consent and knowledge of the child's parents, Mr. Tanner made his recommendation to Mr. and Mrs. Lyons early in their interview. Perhaps because this contact began so early in Jody's new school career and because referral had been suggested previously, both parents seemed resigned to the need to seek additional assistance.

Mr. Tanner indicated that Dr. Kirby, the psychiatrist at Family Service, would be available to them and that the school would continue to work with them as they needed. He tried to build a reasonable picture for Mr. and Mrs. Lyons of the role the agency would play, avoiding any implication that sudden miracles would be achieved.

Because parents often tend to be alarmed by the suggestion of referral, Mr. Tanner approached the matter in an objective manner, urging referral, conveying the impression that the behavior observed was different than he usually handled in school, yet leaving to the psychiatrist the judgment as to whether the behavior should be considered unusually serious or dangerous.[7] He tried to tune in to the emotional factors and the tendency of parents to resist the suggestion of referral. He reflected the resignation that seemed apparent in the behavior of both parents and provided an opportunity for them to express their disappointment and their lack of understanding as to why Jody had these special needs.

ACTION ASSISTING

After extended discussion, during which it became apparent that the referral decision had been made, Mr. Tanner's assistance became quite specific. He gave Mr. and Mrs. Lyons a paper bearing the name, address, and telephone number of Family Service and the name of the psychiatrist to whom they were specifically referred. He asked that they let him know when they would have their first appointments, he secured a release per-

[7] *Ibid.*

[8] Glenn V. Ramsey, "The referral task in counseling," *Personnel and Guidance Journal, 40:* 443–447 (1962).

mitting him to provide information to the agency, he assured them of his continued interest in Jody and in them, and he urged them to keep in contact with him.

Had Mr. and Mrs. Lyons been more dependent in their approach to the problem or required transportation or other assistance in contacting or getting to the agency, Mr. Tanner would have given further assistance. Those steps did not seem necessary, so he followed another of Patterson's guidelines[9] and avoided "spoonfeeding" these parents. Mr. and Mrs. Lyons left, apparently grateful for the warm, yet businesslike assistance they had received, planning to make an immediate contact with Family Service.

Action assisting relating to Jody also took the form of further conferences with Mrs. Stanley. While Jody's behavior did not seem to create undue danger to other children, it was sufficiently upsetting to the classroom to warrant some consideration, if only to increase Mrs. Stanley's peace of mind. Mr. Tanner's decision to consult with Mrs. Stanley seemed particularly justified since he was not going to establish counseling contact with Jody. The severity of the problem indicated a need for more intensive counseling than could be offered in the school setting.

Conferences with Mrs. Stanley achieved two specific gains. First, Mrs. Stanley was able to express her concern and to reassure herself that she was not at fault in the development of the problem. Second, a particularly worthwhile suggestion emerged: Mrs. Stanley might suggest to Jody that when he began to feel "nervous" (his term), he had permission to go into the bookroom or the coat room adjoining the classroom and stay there until he was ready to rejoin the class. Several days after this suggestion had been made to Jody no bizarre behavior had occurred in the classroom, and the frequency of the bookroom visits had decreased considerably. The other children seemed even more ready to reach out toward Jody, although this had not previously been a problem, and Mrs. Stanley felt much less tense about Jody's continuing in her classroom.

FOLLOW-UP

The follow-up phase began with a note Mr. Tanner put on his calendar after Mr. and Mrs. Lyons left the office. The simple notation "Jody Lyons," appearing on the calendar for the following Monday, would remind him to check with Family Service to see if the Lyons family had made contact. Mrs. Lyons came in the next morning, however, to tell him that an intake interview had been scheduled for early the next week; she wanted to clear Jody's absence for that afternoon. She thanked Mr. Tanner for cutting away the red tape, saying she had expected to wait for several months before the first interview—months she felt they could ill afford. Mr. Tanner told her he was glad he had telephoned in advance if that had helped clear the way.

---

[9] Patterson, *loc. cit.*

A second step in follow-up occurred as Mr. Tanner put together a report for Family Service. He included highlights from the school record, brief descriptions of Jody's behaviors and their frequency as he and Mrs. Stanley had observed them, and a report on the use of the bookroom and its success as a way in which Jody could isolate himself when he began to feel "nervous." This he hand-carried to the agency to give to Dr. Kirby between his appointments, saying: "Tell me what you think of our attempts to help Jody so far and do let us know if you see any way in which we might facilitate his progress. For our part, we'll let you know periodically what his behavior at school is like."

The psychiatrist, obviously pleased with this evidence of school-agency rapport, said: "Yes. I'll look at this report as soon as I can. If I have any suggestions for you or the teacher I'll call or write you."

"One more thing," said Mr. Tanner, "I'd like to tell Jody that we're asking him to come here because we want to help him and that I'd like to ask him how things are going every now and then. You see, I've visited several times in the classroom and Jody knows me and knows I've talked with his parents. I'd like him to know where I stand."

"Good idea. You do that. And if there is anything we need to hear about, please call or send a note. For our part we'll keep you informed and let you know where you can help."

The third phase of follow-up began as Mr. Tanner met with Jody and his mother when she came to pick him up the following Monday. "I just want you to know, Jody, that we hope the people at Family Service can help you feel less nervous. I've suggested your parents take you there so that you can get that kind of help. But I want to check with you every now and then to see how things are going." Jody responded with a smile, yet looked puzzled. "That's OK, what I really want to tell you is that Mrs. Stanley and I care about you and want to see you get the help you need." Now the smile was ear to ear.

The next several months brought brief weekly contact between Jody and Mr. Tanner, regular contact between Mrs. Stanley and Mr. Tanner, and infrequent but meaningful contact by telephone and brief letter between the psychiatrist and Mr. Tanner. In correspondence the counselor reported on good weeks and what seemed to make the difference and bad weeks and what might have precipitated the problems.

Eventually the school became a partner in the treatment procedures. "Could Mrs. Stanley suggest that when someone does something Jody doesn't like, he tell him right then how he feels? Jody seems to just hold in his anger for a major explosion. We want to see if he can deal with it more directly." Mrs. Stanley was receptive to the suggestion and made specific use of it several times within the next few days. "Jody, why don't you tell Paul how it makes you feel when he just pushes ahead of you like that." "Jody, perhaps you'd like to say something to Francie about the way she interrupted you."

One afternoon not long afterward Mrs. Stanley came dashing into Mr. Tanner's office: "What do I do now? At recess today Jody slugged one of the boys who tried to take his turn."

"I'll check with Dr. Kirby, but I think you shout hoorah," responded Mr. Tanner.

Months later, when Jody no longer seemed to need the bookroom, and when he seemed able to control his anger where suitable and direct it appropriately otherwise, Jody was released from treatment. Mr. Tanner continued to check with Jody, with Mrs. Stanley, and with Mr. and Mrs. Lyons in order to make certain that the gains were maintained.

Following guidelines of appropriate counselor behavior such as those suggested by Patterson,[10] Mr. Tanner (1) shared with Dr. Kirby information that did not violate confidences either from Jody or his parents; (2) expected to be kept informed, but not necessarily to be appraised of details of treatment or to share confidences given by the Lyons to agency personnel; (3) expected to work cooperatively with Family Service—in this case played an important supporting role in treatment; (4) did not expect immediate change in behavior and so could understand and admit ups and downs in the general pattern of progress; and (5) showed respect for Jody and his parents and belief in their abilities to work out their problems with appropriate assistance.

REFERRAL RESOURCES

Elementary school counselors and teachers often complain about the lack of referral resources in their community. To such complaints two responses are appropriate. First, Hoyt and Loughary[11] found that in Iowa in the late 1950's secondary school counselors were uninformed about, and had not made good use of, referral resources already available. Are today's elementary school counselors or teachers doing better? There is little reason to believe that they are.

Second, the person who finds after investigation that there really is a lack of appropriate referral resources might well follow Ryden's[12] suggestion and "roll up his sleeves." Ryden's own response was to help develop a Family Service Agency. The process was long and involved: interested persons were sought; community need was investigated; community awareness was developed through radio, press, dinners, and public meetings; outside help was tapped from the Welfare Council of a nearby city; and a citizens' committee was formed. Great rewards were reaped in community

[10] *Ibid.*

[11] Kenneth B. Hoyt and J. W. Loughary, "Acquaintance with and use of referral sources by Iowa secondary school counselors," *Personnel and Guidance Journal, 36:* 388–391 (1958).

[12] A. H. Ryden, "Referral resources needed? Roll up your sleeves!" *School Counselor, 12:* 14–17 (1964).

involvement, in counselor contact with interested lay and professional persons, and in community action. Ryden cited a frontier proverb: "Cut your own wood. It will warm you twice."

Before the counselor or teacher sets out to develop new resources, however, he needs to investigate to determine whether appropriate resources already exist.

LOCATING RESOURCES

The counselor or teacher should look for assistance first among the employees of his own school corporation. Any of the following personnel may be in the full-time or part-time employment of the school district:

School nurse	Health officer
School psychologist	Consulting psychologist
School social worker	Consulting psychiatrist
School attendance officer	Remedial reading teacher
Visiting teacher	Special education personnel
Psychometrist	

The counselor should seek out these individuals to see what kinds of services they offer to the school and its children; and he should ascertain what their relationship to him and to each other is expected to be.

Under the names of the geographic subdivisions of the community, county, area, state, and nation, the white pages of the telephone directory can be most helpful in locating potential nonschool resources for referral purposes. For example, under the indicated headings in Lafayette and West Lafayette, Indiana, the following listings may be found:

Heading	*Listing*
City of Lafayette	Board of Health
County Offices	Cary Children's Home
	County Home
	Department of Public Welfare
	Health Department
Family Service	Family Service Agency
Indiana	Indiana Employment Division
	Indiana Vocational Technical College
Lafayette	Lafayette Art Center and Assoc.
	Lafayette Home Hospital
State of Indiana	Vocational Rehabilitation
Tippecanoe County	T. C. Mental Health Center
U.S. Government	Social Security Administration
Wabash	Wabash Center for Mentally Retarded
	Wabash Center Sheltered Workshop
Wabash Valley	Wabash Valley Education Center
	Wabash Valley Hospital

Universities or colleges also may offer services. For example:

Purdue University	Achievement Center for Children
	Child Development and Family Life
	Deans of Men/Women
	Psychology
	Child Psychological Clinic
	Counseling and Testing
	Psychological Services Center
	Speech and Hearing Clinic
	Student Health Service

The following listing of potential referral services, which is geographically nonspecific, suggests the range of sources from which assistance and counsel may be obtained. The listing is arranged in relevant categories:

Medical Service

Local or county mental health offices
American Branch of International League against Epilepsy
American Cancer Society
American Dental Association
American Diabetes Association
American Foundation for the Blind
American Heart Association
American Medical Association
American Public Health Association
Arthritis and Rheumatism Foundation
Association for the Blind
Cerebral Palsy Association
March of Dimes
Multiple Sclerosis Society
Psychiatric centers
State heart association
State tuberculosis and health associations

Mental Health Agencies

State and local mental health centers
County and state mental health associations
American Association of Psychiatric Social Workers
American Red Cross
Big Brothers
Family and children's agencies
National Mental Health Association
State Psychological Association

Social Agencies

Adult and child guidance clinics
Aid to the blind
Aid to dependent children
Association of the Junior League
Child guidance clinics
Child Welfare League of America
Children's Aid Society
Children's homes
Council of Social Agencies
County child welfare services
County department of welfare
Day care centers
Family Service Association
Mental retardation resources
Schools for the handicapped

While most counselors are aware at least of the kinds of services that might be available through medical, mental health, and social agencies, they often overlook the potential that exists in other areas. Service clubs and fraternal groups are often happy to help by supplying specific services volunteered by their professional members, by providing funds for the support of necessary medical or psychological treatment, or by providing transportation to the child or the family members who need help in getting to state, regional, or local agencies for treatment.

Religious agencies offer many of the same potentials as do service organizations and may also provide some of the benefits offered by youth organizations. Both religious and youth organizations may give the child or his family a feeling of status and belonging in the community as well as providing specific assistance such as day care centers so that mothers can work, and baby sitting so that treatment may be undertaken.

There are few situations that cannot be helped to some degree, directly or indirectly, by service clubs, religious agencies, or youth organizations, even if the person receiving the assistance should remain anonymous. Counselors need to be ready to seek such assistance, especially when no other help is available.

Service Clubs and Fraternal Groups

American Legion, Child Welfare Division
Amvets
Daughters of the American Revolution
Fraternal Order of Eagles
Independent Order of Odd Fellows
International Association of Lions Clubs

Kiwanis International
Knights of Pythias
Loyal Order of Moose
Optimists International
Order of Elks
Shriners of North America

Religious Agencies

Local council of churches
American Friends Service Committee
Catholic Welfare Bureau
Jewish Family Service
Lutheran Welfare League
National Council, Protestant Episcopal Church
National Jewish Welfare Board
Salvation Army
Young Men's and Young Women's Christian Association and Hebrew Association

Youth Organizations

American Junior Red Cross
American Youth Hostels
Boy Scouts of America
Boys' Club Federation
Boys' Club of America
Camp Fire Girls of America
Catholic Youth Organization
Child Study Association of America
Fraternities and sororities
Future Farmers of America
Future Craftsmen of America
Girl Scouts of America
Girl's Service League of America

Government Agencies

State departments of health
State departments of public welfare
Divisions of vocational rehabilitation
State departments of education:
    Division of guidance
    Division of special education
    Division of services for crippled children

State schools for the deaf and blind
United States Department of Health, Education and Welfare
State mental hospitals

The location of appropriate and relevant referral resources is not always easy, and sometimes no such assistance seems to be available for a particular child or his family. Some scouting on the counselor's part may turn up some services available to help the child or may show that he should alert the community to the need to provide a broader range of services. Certainly it is the counselor's obligation to become familiar with the resources that he may tap in his community, area, and state.

HOLDING ACTIONS

While the literature is replete with warnings that the counselor should not intervene in areas in which he is not competent, the reality of the matter is that many thousands of children need help, are crying out for it, and face a lengthy wait until assistance or institutionalization comes. Assistance for other children is blocked by their parents, and for still others no service is available. Many, perhaps most, of these children remain in our public schools, functioning at whatever level they can, often personally isolated but physically integrated into the regular elementary and secondary school classrooms.

In such situations the counselor should weigh the advantages and disadvantages of taking action in three areas: (1) he many wish to consider some form of assistance to the teacher, or (2) he or the teacher may attempt to reach out to the other children in the child's environment, or (3) he may attempt to assist the child himself. A fourth direction has already been discussed, that of working for the development of appropriate referral resources.

ASSISTANCE TO THE TEACHER

It may be theoretically correct to say that emotionally disturbed children should not be assigned to regular elementary school classrooms, but the fact is that they are present. Children with a variety of neuroses or psychoses are enrolled and attending. The counselor can rigidly adhere to a nonintervention policy and ignore or avoid the problem, but the teacher cannot. Perhaps the least the counselor might do is to work with the teacher.

The teacher in such instances often needs support and encouragement. Disturbed children threaten the ego of a teacher who believes he should be a teacher and counselor to all, able to cope with any problem that comes his way. If the counselor acknowledges the existence of the problem and the teacher's feelings of responsibility and guilt when he is not equipped to handle a child, this may be sufficient to sustain the teacher.

When support and encouragement fail, suggestions may help. In Jody's case, described earlier, the counselor suggested voluntary isolation of the child. Suggestions, whether drawn from the teacher or offered by the counselor, clarify the counselor's willingness to help the teacher bear the problem, clearly demonstrate counselor concern for both the teacher and the child, and may provide temporary relief in the situation. Since the training of the counselor is not suited to full functioning in such areas, it is important that he keep himself informed of behavioral changes in the child that may result from the environmental alteration and, if possible, check his procedures with a psychologist or other appropriate person.

ASSISTANCE TO THE OTHER CHILDREN IN THE CHILD'S ENVIRONMENT

When there is concern about the effect of a disturbed child on other children in his environment, help may be given to those children in several ways. Children themselves may seek out the counselor or teacher when the bizarre behavior of another child disturbs them. Fundamentally their concern may be similar to that experienced by the teacher, and they may need either to discuss their worries or make decisions on how they will approach the problem. The teacher may remind individuals or the class of the need for each child to be respected individually for his uniqueness and to be understood with humanity for his special strengths and weaknesses. The counselor may initiate individual, small-group, or classroom discussion of the treatment of the disturbed child by others and of the others by the disturbed child.

When Miss Williams realized the reciprocal nature of the other children's taunting and Grace's hostility, she decided she had to intervene. The emotional upheaval created by that sixth grade girl was amazing to behold. Grace, who was clearly misnamed, was readily provoked to strike out at others, shriek at the top of her lungs, and spew forth vile language. Her *pièce de résistance* was her threatening, or proceeding, to remove her glass eye and throw it at other children.

The strain of Grace's short stay was alleviated by the teacher's discussion with the class—an action to which Grace readily acceded, seeing it as a punishment of her classmates. In Grace's absence Miss Williams raised the following questions:

> On the basis of her actions, what feeling does it seem that Grace has about herself?
> On the basis of the class actions, what feelings about yourselves seem to be shown by the class members?

Does the class want the situation to remain as it is?

For what changes can class members take responsibility?

What changes seem necessary on Grace's part?

Does it seem likely that changes can be made by the class or by Grace?

If the class doesn't really feel Grace will change, do they feel any change can occur?

The situation as you see it, then, is entirely controlled by Grace. Grace controls your behavior. Is that correct?

Some of you now see that Grace has a problem and she does not seem likely to change. Can you plan changes in your own approach here?

What do you expect the consequences of such changes to be?

It is possible for children to consider the reciprocal nature of their unspoken contract with a class member and to plan ways of breaking into the circle. Or perhaps the most positive outcome may be the conclusion that each child has special needs and should be accepted as he is.

ASSISTANCE TO THE CHILD

Jeannie, described more extensively elsewhere,[13] an eleven-year-old, was clearly unloved, and at times her behavior was clearly bizarre. Institutionalization was an imminent occurrence for this child who had created a fantasy world far more exciting than her real world. Until then, though, Jeannie *would* be heard. She stopped people on the streets, physically restrained younger children, and continuously sought out adults to regale them with her fascinating and grandoise tales, Prince Charming episodes, sexual fantasies, stories of ownership far beyond her means, and description of other exploits.

The psychiatrist with whom she was meeting recognized the impossibility of curbing her fantasy verbalizations, and insisted she remain in school for her own well-being until she could be removed from the home. Parents of other children and teachers in the school, however, were not so certain of the appropriateness of that recommendation.

Early in the school year in which I began work as counselor, Jeannie sought me out. The impossibility of "turning her off" soon became apparent. Although my impulse was to remain totally within the bounds reinforced in my training, it became apparent that I could not do so without rejecting Jeannie completely. I offered her, therefore, a contract with reasonable limits, which she accepted.

---

[13] Richard C. Nelson, "The process response and the limited contract in counseling," *Second All Iowa Elementary Guidance Conference* (Cedar Falls: State Department of Public Instruction and University of Northern Iowa, 1968), pp. 32–41.

THE LIMITED CONTRACT   The counseling contract encompassed two limits. First, we agreed upon two forty-minute after-school sessions per week. Second, since the topic of family relationships created the greatest agitation, and since those were the meat of her psychiatric explorations, these would be eliminated from the discussion.

An immediate consequence was that Jeannie felt obvious relief. Someone had agreed to listen. She did not have the same press to seek out an individual with whom to share her fantasies. She did not have to fear the rejection of her listener—an experience that she must have had thousands of times.

THE OUTCOME   No remarkable remission was produced by this contract, at least not in Jeannie's behavior. Jeannie railed at the world, described her fantasies, and ignored the counselor's reality-checking and comments on her imagination. Nonetheless she came to accept the time limits, even noted that the time was up after hearing it stated in the first few sessions. Family references occurred infrequently, and a gentle reminder was sufficient to terminate them—curbing Jeannie's tendency to curse loudly and create a noise problem in the quiet building after school. No one, passing to a parent conference, a play rehearsal, or an athletic practice or event, thought a child was being tortured.

Jeannie was institutionalized later that year—a decision based on her need for medication, constant attention, and removal from the home. Follow-up seems to have established that this drastic step helped bring stability and reality into Jeannie's life.

Limited-contract counseling may be defined as: "Temporary . . . counseling offered to a counselee who might otherwise be out of contact with the counselor during the period of the contract, and limited on the recommendation of the counselor to dealing with areas within which an appropriate counselor-counselee relationship can be maintained."[14]

The limited contract is not directed toward ascertaining causes or providing a therapeutic relationship. If possible, it should have a foreseeable limit, so that extensive counselor time is not taken by counselees who cannot be expected to be helped in the school setting; and the hand of the counselor should in some measure be directed or reinforced by a psychologist or other person suitably trained to deal with the child. Limits should be set as early as possible in the relationship and adjusted as the situation is clarified.

The counselor should ask himself these questions:

1. What can I do for this child?
2. Is there some contribution that my personality, training, and

_____
[14] *Ibid*, p. 39.

schedule will realistically permit me to make to this child's well-being?

3. What areas of discussion can I handle and what behavior on the part of the child can I reasonably tolerate within the school setting, for his sake and mine?

4. Using the answers to the above questions as a guide, what limits do I need to set?[15]

The child who is disturbed, yet must function in the elementary school setting, is first of all a human being. He may well need the aid of a counselor. The disturbed child who is treated as worthy of help may come to relate more effectively to others as he is given evidence that others wish to relate more effectively to him. Occasionally in such cases a spontaneous remission occurs. Limited-contract counseling may facilitate this occurrence.

The counselor is not given *carte blanche* here to offer unlimited services to every disturbed child. Occasionally and selectively he may wish to give limited aid to some child who needs it, while primarily serving the larger public. The child does not need a two-session contact with an uneasy counselor, only to be shunted aside to another referral source, further convinced that his problem is helpless. Careful assessment should be made of the situation and of the priorities involved in the counseling schedule before any contract is offered. In most cases the counselor may elect not to act; in a few he will find it a profitable venture. The limited contract, in sum, should be used only after careful consideration and effective tactical planning.

SUMMARY

Coordination is needed in counseling and related services to minimize duplication and offer effective help to all who can be served. While the counselor may or may not function in a coordinating capacity, it is important that some appropriate individual accept this responsibility.

Referral is a process rather than an event; it involves information seeking, preparing, decision making, action assisting, and follow-up. Referral resources may be available within or outside the school system and may encompass a wide range of potential services—at times invaluable ones. Counselors often are unaware of the resources available to them. When appropriate resources are absent, or until they become involved, the counselor might engage in some form of holding action by working with the teacher, the other children with whom the child comes in contact, or

[15] *Ibid.*

the child himself. The limited contract in counseling may be a temporary answer for the needs of selected children.

REFERENCES

ACES-ASCA Committee on the Elementary School Counselor. *The Elementary School Counselor in Today's Schools.* Washington, D.C.: American Personnel and Guidance Association, 1969.

ACES-ASCA Joint Committee on the Elementary School Counselor. "Working Paper," in Don Dinkmeyer, ed., *Guidance and Counseling in the Elementary School.* New York: Holt, Rinehart and Winston, Inc., 1968. Pp. 99–105.

Arbuckle, D. S. "Counselor, social worker, psychologist: Let's 'ecumenicalize,'" *Personnel and Guidance Journal, 45:* 532–538 (1963).

Bowman, R. K., and D. G. Zimpfer. "The community-team approach to referral in the secondary school," *School Counselor, 14:* 110–115 (1966).

Diedrich, R. C. *Guidance Personnel and other Professionals.* Guidance Monograph Series, Boston: Houghton Mifflin, 1968.

Hahn, M. E. "Let's integrate and not build psychological ghettos," *Journal of Counseling Psychology, 13:* 21–28 (1966).

Hill, G. E. *Staffing Guidance Programs.* Guidance Monograph Series, Boston: Houghton Mifflin, 1968.

————. *Management and Improvement of Guidance.* New York: Appleton-Century-Crofts, 1965.

Hoyt, K. B., and J. W. Loughary. "Acquaintance with and use of referral sources by Iowa secondary school counselors," *Personnel and Guidance Journal, 36:* 388–391 (1958).

Mattick, W. E., and N. A. Nickolas. "A team approach in guidance," *Personnel and Guidance Journal, 42:* 922–924 (1964).

Nelson, R. C. "The process response and the limited contract in counseling," *Second All Iowa Elementary Guidance Conference,* Cedar Falls: State Department of Public Instruction and University of Northern Iowa, 1968. Pp. 32–41.

Patterson, C. H. "Teamwork and referrals," *The Counselor in the School: Selected Readings.* New York: McGraw-Hill, 1967. Pp. 369–372.

Pratte, H. E., and C. Cole. "Source of referral and perception of the counselor," *Personnel and Guidance Journal, 44:* 292–294 (1965).

Ramsey, G. V. "The referral task in counseling," *Personnel and Guidance Journal, 40:* 443–447 (1962).

Ryden, A. H. "Referral resources needed? Roll up your sleeves!" *School Counselor, 12:* 14–17 (1964).

Shear, B. E. "Teamwork in pupil personnel services," *Counselor Education and Supervision, 1:* 199–202 (1962).

Wellington, J. "Communication between a mental health clinic and the schools," *Personnel and Guidance Journal, 43:* 616–618 (1965).

Wrenn, C. G. *The Counselor in a Changing World.* Washington, D.C.: American Personnel and Guidance Association, 1962.

ARTICLES IN BOOKS OF READINGS

Dinkmeyer, D. C. *Guidance and Counseling in the Elementary School: Readings in Theory and Practice.* New York: Holt, Rinehart and Winston, Inc., 1968. Readings beginning on page 175 and 185.

Koplitz, E. D. *Guidance in the Elementary School: Theory, Research and Practice.* Dubuque, Iowa: William C. Brown Company, Publisher, 1968. Reading beginning on page 296.

Part Five

Supportive Aspects of Guidance and Counseling

12

Career and Life-Style Considerations

But yield who will to their separation,
My object in living is to unite
My avocation and my vocation
As my two eyes make one in sight
Only where love and need are one,
And the work is play for mortal stakes,
Is the deed ever really done
For Heaven and the future's sakes.

ROBERT FROST:
"Two Tramps in Mud Time"

To most children looking out upon the world, the prospects for life seem broad, exciting, and a bit frightening. An eagerness to reach toward the future is often tempered with anxiousness. Nearly all (30 of 32) of a randomly assigned classroom group of fifth graders, for example, said yes to the statement: "I often wonder if I'll get along well in the world when I grow up." Despite the adult tendency to view childhood as carefree, children often wonder what their lives as adults will be like.

While his occupational prospects are not the child's only concern, they often are the most obvious yardstick by which he can view his potential success in life. The importance of occupation is emphasized by the values he senses around him. "The most convincing proof in our society of having grown up is the ability to find and hold a job."[1] observes Angelino,

[1] Henry Angelino, "Developmental tasks and problems of the middle adolescent period," *Education, 76:* 226–231 (1955).

and Havighurst goes further: "In American society lifework is the most important thing about a man. He has been taught to evaluate his worth to society, and sometimes his worth in the sight of God, by the level of his occupation and the quality of his performance in it."[2]

When a child envisions the totality of his way of life, he comes to consider life work as of great importance. When he also considers such matters as his use of leisure time, the kind of neighborhood in which he will live, and the kind of family he might have, he is envisioning his life style and anticipating his adult living patterns.

The life style he anticipates for himself and the specific work he considers he might be able to do are important to the child and deserve consideration by the elementary school teacher or counselor. These persons need to be well informed regarding children's needs, career development theory, and ways in which needs may be met and desires implemented. Explorations of life style, career, and advanced education are appropriate activities of the counselor and teacher; they provide legitimate and desirable means of putting the adult and child into relevant communication with each other; and they provide unique and meaningful developmental guidance opportunities.

This chapter will examine (1) the reasons for exploring life style, career, and educational opportunities for elementary school children; (2) activities consistent with career development theory that are designed to meet children's needs; (3) teacher and counselor roles in developing concepts related to adult living patterns; and (4) sources of further information. (The term "adult living patterns" is used in this chapter to include life style, career, and educational considerations in the lives of adults.)

REASONS FOR EXPLORING ADULT LIVING PATTERNS IN THE ELEMENTARY SCHOOL

Why is it worthwhile to take valuable time to explore life style, career, and educational opportunities with children of elementary school age? This books assumes that such exploration (1) contributes positively to children's knowledge and attitudes, (2) serves several purposes consistent with legitimate objectives of elementary education, and (3) is consistent with career development theory.

[2] Robert J. Havighurst, *Human Development and Education* (New York: McKay, 1953), p. 129.

CONTRIBUTING TO CHILDREN'S KNOWLEDGE AND ATTITUDES

Exploration of adult living patterns can contribute to children's knowledge and attitudes in several ways. Nelson[3] sees at least five important contributions:

1. CHILDREN MAY BE HELPED TO DEVELOP A SENSE OF PERSONAL WORTH   Unlike rural children of another era, who knew that they contributed through planting, harvesting, milking, and related activities, and unlike urban children of another era, who knew that they contributed through necessary chores or through early entry into the labor market, today's urban children and many children on mechanized farms have no clear concept that their lives make a present contribution or that they will ever be responsible contributors within the adult world. The world of work is as remote and abstract as are any alternative means for gaining a personal sense of meaning. Guided exploration of career, life style, and educational opportunities may help the child to gain a clearer concept of his own potential and his personal worthwhileness.

2. CHILDREN MAY BE HELPED TO DEVELOP A FEELING THAT THEY HAVE A PLACE IN THE SOCIETY   Many children come to the elementary school with no feeling that they have or ever will have a place in our society. Unfortunately, the school may help develop a negative self-concept in children who are not academically quick. School helps children learn who they are. They may learn that they are valued, that we are pleased to have them around, and that we have positive expectations for them; or they may learn that they are tolerated and that we don't expect much of them, now or ever. Exploration of adult living patterns should show every child that there is a place for him—in truth many places for him—that he can make a contribution, and that his work will be valued.

3. CHILDREN MAY BE HELPED TO SEE HOW ADULTS ACHIEVE THE PLACE THEY HAVE   Children become aware of adults in their jobs at a point in time. They may have no idea that the business executive has filled a number of positions on the way to his present situation or that the brick-layer has worked through several jobs as well as the helper-apprentice-journeyman sequence. The child may come to imagine himself in careers

[3] Richard C. Nelson, "Opening new vistas to children through career exploration," *Needed Concepts in Elementary School Guidance* (Report of the Eighth Annual All Ohio Elementary School Guidance Conference, Columbus, Ohio: State Department of Education, Division of Guidance and Testing, 1969), pp. 13–24.

that seem rather remote if he understands the educational and work sequence that leads to them.

4. CHILDREN MAY LEARN THAT SUCCESS IS A PERSONAL MATTER RELEVANT TO A TOTAL LIFE STYLE   Their concept that jobs are important should be expanded so that children see success in life in a more total and more personal way. Avocation, recreation, family situation, and vocation are intertwined in the individual's view of successful living. Explorations of the lives of a number of adults may clarify both the process of achieving success and the degree to which a sense of success is derived from occupation and from other aspects of life style.

5. CHILDREN WHO ARE BEING RAISED IN THE ABSENCE OF A WORKING-ROLE MODEL (MALE OR FEMALE) MAY BE HELPED TO BUILD POSITIVE ATTITUDES ABOUT THEMSELVES AND THEIR POTENTIAL FOR SUCCESS IN OUR SOCIETY   Children growing up in lower socioeconomic environments may lack a view of themselves as potential wage earners in our society. The problem may be more crucial for boys in many families, since the visible working people are more often female, and the school itself is largely staffed by females. A subsequent section will deal with the "how" of life-pattern exploration, but certainly inroads can be made by involving males.

Younger elementary school children, according to Kaback[4] and Gunn,[5] exhibit an openness to a variety of career and life-style considerations and a refreshing unawareness of social status. It seems appropriate to try to develop an awareness of careers before the narrowing process begins.

Figure 12–1 represents the career broadening and narrowing process for one individual. If the solid figure represents the usual pattern of developing awareness followed by narrowing to a choice or a sequence of choices, then the dashed figure denotes the potential for development of considerably greater awareness before the narrowing to an eventual choice. Horizontal lines A and B represent the point of greatest openness and awareness. The hypothesis is that broader exploration slightly delays the beginning of the career narrowing process, permitting openness to last somewhat longer, but with eventual choice occurring on the average at about the same point in time. This is an extremely individual matter that remains relatively unresearched; nonetheless, it is assumed to be advantageous for individuals to have a broadened base from which to make selections in careers, in life styles, and in educational opportunities.

[4] Goldie Ruth Kaback, "Occupational information for groups of elementary school children," *Vocational Guidance Quarterly, 14:* 163–168 (1966).
[5] Barbara Gunn, "Children's concepts of occupational prestige," *Personnel and Guidance Journal, 42:* 558–563 (1964).

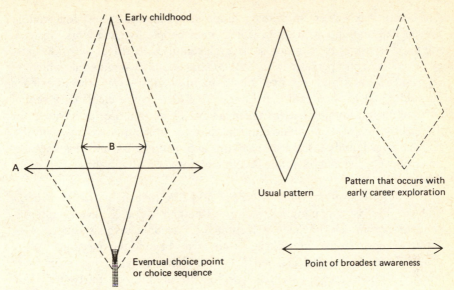

FIGURE 12–1 *The Career Broadening and Narrowing Process*

ACHIEVING OBJECTIVES OF ELEMENTARY EDUCATION

Kaye[6] believes that a career exploration project helped a group of elementary school children toward three goals of good teaching: critical thinking, respect for people and the work they do, and broader understanding related to the world about them.

Three related points are made by Nelson.[7] First, the exploration of adult living patterns injects the elementary school into a very meaningful, ongoing process. Children relate themselves to nearly every occupation to which they are exposed; they are engaged in a serious process of inclusion and elimination of whole vistas of occupations on the basis of their assumed similarity to other liked or disliked occupations. Inferential guidance along these lines is potentially inherent in every observed action and utterance related to careers: the child is equally alert to the "do-you-want-to-grow-up-to-be-a-garbage-collector" question and the air of respect given the doctor. Thus *guidance is given to children;* undoubtedly it can be handled more adequately through organized career, life-style, and educational exploration.

Second, such exploration is consistent with accepted learning theory. Learning is assumed to proceed best from the familiar to the unfamiliar, and from the immediate to the distant. The focus on school helpers

[6] Janet Kaye, "Fourth graders meet up with occupations," *Vocational Guidance Quarterly, 8:* 150–152 (1960).

[7] Nelson, *op. cit.*

and community helpers in primary grade social studies is best followed by further exploration into ways in which other people live and work. Instead, the child is asked to leap across several centuries to travel with the early explorers or the persons who settled our country—material which is repeated three, four, or five times in the subsequent social science curriculum. It is often said that things are added to the elementary school curriculum but nothing is ever taken away. There is more justification for the exploration of adult living patterns than for much that we do in health, science, social studies, English, spelling, and arithmetic—and this exploration may be meaningfully integrated with any or all of those curricular areas.

Third, exploration into career and life style helps children comprehend life as a continuous reality extending through several interdependent phases. Dean Helen Schleman of Purdue University suggests to young women that they view their lives in terms beyond the question: "What should I do until I get married?" Current data suggest that even most married women have a potential working life of thirty to thirty-five years or more. Girls and boys alike need to be helped to see life as an unfolding pattern, involving perhaps general education, recreational-avocational-vocational exploration, education that may or may not affect vocational or avocational avenues, entry jobs, more enduring jobs, promotions or lateral moves, career and life-style commitments, and retirement life styles. Children need to know that people can find life's meaning in a great variety of ways and that they themselves are and will be seekers for that meaning.

CONSISTENCY WITH CAREER-DEVELOPMENT THEORY

Bugg,[8] in a review of various career-development theories, concludes that the elementary school should provide (a) counseling for self-understanding and personal development and (b) a well-developed, broadly based, general program involving occupational information, as essential contributions to young people in making their eventual career decisions. He notes that lack of knowledge restricts such decisions.

Bugg's review, which considers the theories or constructs of Bordin, Ginzberg, Holland, Hoppock, Roe, Super, and Tiedeman and O'Hara, indicates that the work of each may be inferred to support early career exploration. This consensus appears to be the major message of each of these theories insofar as they concern elementary school children. No attempt is made here to discuss each comprehensively; however, the reader is indeed encouraged to explore Bugg's article and the works by the various authors just mentioned. (See bibliography.)

[8] Charles A. Bugg, "Implications of some major theories of career choice for elementary school guidance programs," *Elementary School Guidance and Counseling, 3:* 164–173 (1969).

As an example, Super's career-development theory makes essentially the following points:[9]

1. People are individuals.
2. Their individuality fits them for a number of occupations.
3. Each occupation requires characteristic traits and abilities but has a wide tolerance for individual differences.
4. Preferences and self-concepts change with time and experience.
5. A series of stages in career development may be predicted. These include growth, exploration, establishment, maintenance, and decline.
6. Career pattern is affected to some extent by socioeconomic level, ability, personality, and opportunity.
7. Career development can be guided partly by facilitating maturation and partly by aiding in reality testing and self-concept development.
8. Vocational development is a process of developing and implementing a self-concept and results from compromise between what is desired and what is possible.
9. The process of compromise involves role playing and role testing.
10. Work and life satisfactions are related to the degree to which the individual finds outlets for his abilities, interests, personality traits, and values in work and a work environment that he considers appropriate and congenial.

Existing vocational development theories are criticized by Arbuckle, whose concern is the assumption that the individual is a creature of destiny rather than a creator of his destiny: "The stress on prognosis, prediction, and the matching of a child's abilities to someone else's plans, implies a high level of the imposition of one human on another. It is restrictive. The implication is that one is bound by one's boundaries, and that the taking of a chance, the risking of possible failure in doing something to challenge those boundaries, is to be avoided at all costs."[10] Arbuckle suggests that children be helped to understand that they always have some freedom of choice no matter what the restrictions on them may be.

In his discussion of career development, Simons supports an existential viewpoint, noting: ". . . everyone who fails to shoulder his responsibility of self-discovery may be alienated from his work no matter how significant that work is in the eyes of society."[11] Work equals success only

[9] Donald E. Super, "A theory of vocational development," *American Psychologist, 8:* 185–190 (1953).

[10] Dugald S. Arbuckle, "Occupational information in the elementary school," *Vocational Guidance Quarterly, 12:* 81 (1963–1964).

[11] Joseph B. Simons, "An existential view of vocational development," *Personnel and Guidance Journal, 44:* 606 (1966).

when it brings happiness, Simons asserts; perhaps a better equation, though, is: *Work equals success only when it brings meaning to the life of the individual.*

Possible conflict between the positions of Simons and Arbuckle and those of vocational development theorists does not seem to be crucial to elementary school guidance. Certainly all of these positions lend support and provide a rationale for the inclusion of broad career exploration in the elementary school curriculum and the guidance program.

To what extent should early career choice be encouraged? Nelson[12] makes three points that are relevant to this question: (1) stability of vocational choice is not nearly so important as the maturing of a vocational choice; (2) long-term goals involving a total life style are more important than a specific and early choice; and (3) outside pressures toward choice are often quite severe, and so perhaps the guidance program ought to contribute in the elementary school by encouraging children to remain open to career possibilities.

Dimick and Huff note that this pressure on individuals does not necessarily emerge in the high school or college: "Tommy, a twelve-year-old sixth grader, is being pushed to choose a vocational path by his upward-bound parents and their adult friends. 'What are you going to be when you grow up?' 'What track are you going to follow in junior high school?' All of these are innocent enough questions in themselves but constitute a glimpse of the kind of pressures Tommy is confronted with."[13] The what-are-you-going-to-be-when-you-grow-up question is met intermittently by children even in their preschool years. It would appear that the child is sufficiently bombarded with the choice question at home, so that elementary school efforts in career development ought to encourage exploration rather than choice.

To what extent is there a fantasy stage in vocational development? Ginzberg[14] writing of stages of vocational development, uses the term "fantasy stage" to characterize the development of elementary school children. Since "fantasy" strongly suggests instability, one may question the value of exploring careers during such a period. Certainly fantasy *is* present, but whether this term is appropriate as a general description of the degree of vocational maturity remains in doubt.

Strong stresses the stability of interest-in-general, stating: "If, for example, 'vocational interest' is defined as 'the occupation an individual

[12] Richard C. Nelson, "Early versus developmental vocational choice," *Vocational Guidance Quarterly, 11:* 23–27 (1962).

[13] Kenneth M. Dimick and Vaughn E. Huff, *Child Counseling* (Dubuque, Iowa: William C. Brown Company, Publishers, 1970), p. 187.

[14] Eli Ginzberg, "Toward a theory of occupational choice," *Occupations, 30:* 491–494 (1952).

likes best now,' then the conclusion must be drawn that vocational interests are unstable. . . . But if 'vocational interest' is defined as 'the sum total of all interests that bear in any way upon an occupational career" then we find surprising stability, certainly among adults, and as far as we have been able to judge, also among young men of college age and presumably among still younger people."[15]

Nelson[16] points out that "fantasy" might appropriately be paired with "choice" but not with "stage," since he believes too much substantial development occurs for this term to be appropriate during the elementary school years. He criticizes the emphasis on choice as an encouragement to fantasy: *"We are asking the wrong questions!* Judging the vocational maturity of children by asking *only* what career they plan to pursue is as relevant as judging the emotional maturity of children by asking who[m] they plan to marry."[17]

Research by Hansen and Caulfield[18] suggests that fathers held a higher ideal occupational level for their sons of elementary school age than did the boys for themselves, yet both were similar in their rankings of occupations. Distance from choice alone, then, may be sufficient to produce whatever fantasy exists, and since choice is distant, even if raters would consider it realistic, it is nonetheless done in fantasy. Clearly it seems inappropriate in the elementary school to emphasize choice or to evaluate vocational development on the basis of choice.

It seems preferable, and an encouragement to elementary school career-development experiences, to characterize preadolescence as an "exploratory period" regarding vocational development and to devote attention to vocational maturity rather than to choice. At a National Vocational Guidance Association symposium[19] vocational maturity was concluded to be a matter of dealing with the vocational development tasks appropriate for one's age, and of the adequacy with which one is handling these tasks.

The explorativeness of elementary school children is a clear justification for the inclusion of career development in the curriculum—only semantics have been called into question here. Certainly vocational development theory, its positing of irreversibility and continuity, and its relatedness

[15] Edward K. Strong, Jr., *Change of Interest with Age* (Stanford, Calif.: Stanford University Press, 1931), pp. 3–4.

[16] Richard C. Nelson, "Knowledge and interests concerning sixteen occupations among elementary and secondary school students," *Educational and Psychological Measurement, 23:* 741–754 (1963).

[17] Richard C. Nelson, "The world of work in the 'fantasy stage' of development," *Elementary School Guidance and Counseling, 2:* 223 (1968).

[18] James A. Hansen and Thomas J. Caulfield, "Parent-child occupational concepts," *Elementary School Guidance and Counseling, 3:* 269–275 (1969).

[19] Vocational development: an approach to vocational guidance" (symposium presented at NVGA section on vocational counseling, American Personnel and Guidance Association Convention, St. Louis, 1958). (Mimeographed.)

to self-concept, provides much of the rationale for exploratory activities with elementary school children. Let us now consider the processes that are relevant to this exploration.

PROCESSES OF EXPLORING ADULT LIVING PATTERNS

This section will consider the processes of exploring life style, careers, and educational opportunities. A brief discussion of each activity is accompanied by whatever description or rationale may be called for. First, however, we consider the whole matter of presentation style.

PRESENTATION STYLE

If explorations of life style, careers, and educational opportunities are handled in ways that are lifeless, dull, and stylized, a seriously damaging negative message may be conveyed. In a work on which much of this section is based, Nelson[20] calls for another style of presentation:

1. THE EXPLORATION OF ADULT LIVING PATTERNS SHOULD BE ACTION ORIENTED   "Children are action oriented. Only in the elementary school do children sit with hands folded, talk in whispers, raise their hands, and walk in lines to get a drink of water, use the toilet, or enter or leave a building. Children are wondrously active otherwise. Many have almost unbounded energy, many could talk the Mona Lisa out of her secret, and many could play an active game almost from the time the sun comes up until it goes down. They sleep hard, eat hard, play hard, and some of them even take the drudgery they are given and work hard, though I'm not sure I know why."[21] Activity, not drudgery, is clearly called for.

2. CHILDREN'S QUESTIONS PROVIDE A VALUABLE BASIS FOR EXPLORATION   What do children want to know? How can their eagerness for experience and exploration be channeled without dampening their enthusiasm? Their questions must be heard, jotted down, and the list expanded as new ideas emerge. A sketchy list that comes from enthusiastic children is probably better than a comprehensive list that might have been prepared by a writer in the field of career development.

3. WIDE-RANGING EXPLORATION SHOULD BE STRESSED RATHER THAN DECISION MAKING AND PLANNING   The question about plans

[20] Nelson, "Opening new vistas to children through career exploration," pp. 13–14.

[21] *Ibid.*, p. 5 .

as a grown-up faces many children every time an interested adult or relative comes into view. The child learns to say something to satisfy the curious. There is a danger that meaningless answers will lead to meaningless commitments, yet this activity does have the advantage of clarifying to the child that his future is a matter for some serious attention. The styling of activity in the elementary school should not perpetuate this choice-oriented exercise, but should provide for children's exploration of broad life views.

4. EXCITEMENT RATHER THAN PRODUCTION SHOULD BE THE OBJECTIVE OF EXPLORATION INTO THESE REALMS Neither notebooks, nor essays, nor memorization should intervene in any way that spoils the enthusiasm of children for exploring adult living patterns. If those products emerge out of children's eagerness, all well and good; otherwise full attention should be given to process.

5. LETTER GRADES, TESTING, AND COMPARATIVE EVALUATION SHOULD NOT BE INTRODUCED INTO THIS EXPLORATION IN THE ELEMENTARY SCHOOL "Certainly at least once, perhaps four or five times in the elementary school life of a child, a six or eight week block of time can be devoted to an experience for its own sake. Call it social studies, encourage a good deal of speaking on the part of children and call it English, pin whatever label you desire on it, but don't pull up the seeds constantly to see how they are growing—don't let it go the way of all curricular matters and teach for a test and then assign a grade."[22] It can't be stressed too strongly that evaluation of a traditional sort can be a "kiss of death" on the enthusiasm of children for what should be an exciting set of experiences.

Another approach to style is suggested by Hoppock[23] in his statement of purposes for career exploration, some of which are recast here in order to include life-style and educational exploration. In this approach, counselors and teachers should style their presentations to achieve the following purposes:

To encourage the degree of security the child feels in the strange and interesting world outside the home.
To encourage the child's curiosity by helping him to learn the things he wants to learn and to enjoy learning them.
To extend the child's horizons so that he may begin to envision a wide range of ways to find satisfaction and meaning in his life.

22 *Ibid.*, p. 6.
23 Robert L. Hoppock, *Occupational Information* (New York: McGraw-Hill, 1967), pp. 351–354.

To encourage wholesome attitudes toward all useful work, toward all styles of life that provide satisfaction, and toward all educational endeavors that expand the opportunities or satisfactions of an individual.

To begin developing a broad base of information on which future decisions may be built.

If career, life-style, and educational explorations are action oriented, if they are based on children's questions, if they are focused on wide-ranging exploration rather than choice, if they are developed in ways that generate excitement, if letter grades and extensive evaluation are avoided, and if appropriate purposes undergird these exploratory efforts, there is no reason to expect anything less than enthusiastic and eager involvement by children in this venture into the adult world.

LIFE-STYLE EXPLORATION PROCESSES

For an individual, life style is more than career, more than avocation, more than leisure activities, more than social and family interaction pattern—yet it includes all of these things. For one adult the pinnacle is a camping vacation, for another his work, for another a night with his family, for another a business deal, and for many it is any genuine human interaction. Children need to understand these things. How can they be helped to do so?

One approach is through interviews with a wide range of parents and other persons in which more than "job" is discussed. Some relevant questions would be: What makes you feel important? Needed? What makes you see your life as meaningful? What do you do when you can do anything? What would you like to do if you had a great deal of leisure time? What kinds of vacations do you take? What kind would you like to take? What do you read? How important has schooling been to you? Are you satisfied with the amount and kind of education and training you have? Would more make a difference? What kind of difference? How important is your home life to you? What changes would you make in your home life if you could?

Autobiographies and biographies often suggest the range of activities engaged in by well-known and significant people.

Teacher-pupil or counselor-pupil planned units provide excellent exploration opportunities.

The whole gamut of creative activities—such things as building displays, drawing, writing compositions or plays or news stories, taking photographs, producing films, videotapes, and the like—can bring depth, color, and realism to the expression of life-style concepts.

Other specific ideas have been suggested by various authors:

Round-table discussions involving life style.[24]

Interviews with desirable role models, especially for disadvantaged children.[25] If this procedure is utilized, a reasonable ratio of blue-collar to white-collar workers should be included. Anyone cannot be anything, but everyone can be something.

Discussions oriented around questions such as: Artists are. . . . The most important thing for me about my job will be. . . . The most important thing for me about my life will be. . . .[26]

Visits by older children (or reports by classmates) with hobbies and avocational pursuits and discussion of their relation to work and the satisfactions they could bring outside of work.[27]

Discussion in small groups of the hypothetical life of a classmate—plan a week for him including class, study, leisure, family, paid and unpaid tasks.[28]

Discussion of the source of major friendships in the life of an adult. Gross[29] indicates that they do not come primarily through work.

Preparation of articles or newsletters for parents and teachers regarding work attitudes and job satisfactions, occupations and life style.[30]

Matthews[31] suggests ·that girls be given specific help to examine their inner feelings and needs, to gain respect for their own decision-making power, and to realize that they may fulfill their lives in many ways.

CAREER EXPLORATION PROCESSES

As with life style, career exploration may involve curricular units, art work, composition, filming, interviewing, and biographies and auto-

[24] Lewis A. Grell, "How much occupational information in the elementary school?" *Vocational Guidance Quarterly, 9:* 48–53 (1960).

[25] Ira M. Bank, "Children explore careerland through vocational role models," *Vocational Guidance Quarterly, 17:* 284–289 (1969).

[26] John L. Holland, "Explorations of a theory of vocational choice. Part I: Vocational images and choice," *Vocational Guidance Quarterly, 11:* 232–239 (1963).

[27] Daryl Laramore and Jack Thompson, "Career experiences appropriate to elementary school grades," *School Counselor, 17:* 262–264 (1970).

[28] Ross G. Braland and William L. Sweeney, "A differential approach to vocational counseling in junior high," *School Counselor, 17:* 260–262 (1970).

[29] Edward Gross, "A sociological approach to the analysis of preparation for work life," *Personnel and Guidance Journal, 45:* 416–423 (1967).

[30] Goldie Ruth Kaback, "Occupational information in elementary education: what counselors do—what they would like to do," *Vocational Guidance Quarterly, 16:* 203–206 (1968).

[31] Esther Matthews, "Career development of girls," *Vocational Guidance Quarterly, 11:* 273–277 (1963).

biographies. Rather than reiterating many of the same ideas, this section will expand the range of activities.

Kaback[32] suggests a number of stimulating activities for elementary school children:

Explore the jobs of people who work in the school.

Build a folder about men and women at work.

Investigate jobs in business on the routes to school.

Role-play the route money takes from one worker or employer to another.

Consider surnames that suggest vocational roles (e.g., Taylor, Smith, Baker) or that are congruent with careers (e.g., Goldstein—jeweler, Robinson—pet shop owner).

Explore the variety of occupations represented in the activities of a housewife (e.g., nurse, chauffeur, baker, seamstress, buyer, gardener, custodian).

Examine in-class occupations (e.g., librarian, milk distributor, gardener, custodian).

Arrange for children to accompany their parents or other workers to their jobs.

Consider the relationship of each school subject to a variety of jobs.

Trace the occupational routes followed by famous people and several people who are available locally.

Examine the changes in several jobs over time.

Act out a variety of career roles.

Bring in an Urban League worker to discuss work and the racially different worker.

Arrange for a Peace Corps returnee to discuss his adventures.

Laramore and Thompson[33] extend the list as follows:

Dream and pantomime about adult jobs.

Bring in upper grade children to explain part-time jobs.

Write a personal resume examining one's own skills.

Arrange for a worker to carry out his job in the back of the classroom.

Advertise personal skills in a school newspaper.

Nelson suggests encouraging children to prepare occupational briefs, having children videotape or audiotape interviews with workers, and filming workers at their jobs. He also states:

[32] Kaback, "Occupational information for groups of elementary school children."

[33] Laramore and Thompson, *op. cit.*

Boys need to be exposed to men who are employed if they are to aspire to work. This exposure might include professional workers, but it should stress the breadth of our world of work. Girls need to be exposed to women in a wider range of occupations than the typical teacher, nurse, secretary range which stifles and limits thinking. Try a female doctor, taxi driver, office manager, gemologist, factory worker, etc. Black children need to see members of their race, both male and female, who are engaged in a variety of work activities. Try a Negro lawyer, parking lot attendant, accountant, skilled tradesman, etc. If parents can illustrate the range of occupations desired for a given group of children, well and good. If not, the resources are still out there. Parents can give and receive a great deal in such ventures, but the children are the greatest gainers.[34]

Several writers present other suggestions:

Visit and explore the full range of jobs within a given industry.[35] Identify the key persons to a worker on his job. Start, for example, with a news carrier; his responsibilities are to customer, superiors, other news carriers, and, since this is his "second job," to teachers.[36]
Include occupational guessing games and riddles, and supply occupational material for slow readers.[37]
Regarding specific careers, use interview and discussion to relate such considerations as special interests, personality characteristics, aptitudes, training requirements, availability of employment opportunities, and methods of applying and interviewing.[38]
Explore want ads; build a library section and display that has a career focus.[39]

Bank suggests building the concept that all work has dignity and requires constructive attitudes. He quotes a custodian: "By being a building cleaner, you have to learn to do your best, be on time, and cooperate with others. This is important in whatever job you do."[40]

[34] Nelson, "Opening new vistas to children through career exploration," p. 21.

[35] Grell, *op. cit.*

[36] Gross, *op. cit.*

[37] Willa Norris, *Occupational Information in the Elementary School* (Chicago: Science Research Associates, 1963).

[38] Braland and Sweeney, *op. cit.*

[39] Kaback, "Occupational information in elementary education: what counselors do—what they would like to do."

[40] Bank, *op. cit.*, p. 287.

Tennyson and Monnens[41] stress the need to supplement elementary school reading texts, since they distort reality by focusing on professional, service, and agricultural occupations.

Kaback[42] has developed a list of questions, "Investigating Jobs in Our Community," for use with elementary school children as they explore occupations and interview workers. This list may be used to check whether significant areas are being omitted; however, no elementary school group should be compelled to consider all of these questions in relation to a number of jobs. The topics included are:

1. The number of different jobs in existence.
2. The number of people employed in each job.
3. The nature of the work done.
4. Whether a particular job is expanding or declining.
5. Whether it is indoor or outdoor work.
6. Whether or not it is seasonal.
7. The educational and training requirements, kind and length.
8. The route to getting a particular job.
9. Age requirements.
10. Physical requirements.
11. Hours per week.
12. Opportunities for advancement.
13. Earnings.
14. Whether union or other membership is required.
15. Vacation time allotted.
16. Whether or not there are health insurance and retirement or pension plans.

EDUCATIONAL EXPLORATION PROCESSES

The literature seems to offer few suggestions on the building of knowledge and the enhancing of attitudes about education as a pursuit. Children may advantageously learn to view education as more than formal schooling; in point of fact it is for some people a continuous lifelong process. Dole[43] suggests separating educational and vocational considerations, since they are not synonymous.

Children tend to be aware of high schools, colleges, and universities. They need to become aware of:

[41] W. Wesley Tennyson and Lawrence P. Monnens, "The world of work through elementary readers," *Vocational Guidance Quarterly, 12:* 85–88 (1963–1964).

[42] Goldie R. Kaback, "Occupational information in elementary education," *Vocational Guidance Quarterly, 9:* 55–59 (1960).

[43] Arthur A. Dole, "Educational choice is not vocational choice," *Vocational Guidance Quarterly, 12:* 30–35 (1963).

Junior colleges

Technical institutes

Business schools

Hospital nursing education program

Special schools for barbers, beauty operators, stewardesses, etc.

Vocational training programs through the public school system

Industry on-the-job training programs

Cooperative education programs

Apprenticeship programs

Special education opportunities through the U.S. Armed Services, through Civil Service, and through other government-sponsored programs

High school equivalency programs

Adult educational programs

Recreation and skills courses through YMCA and YWCA, public schools, recreation and parks departments, and colleges and universities.

Awareness of the breadth of potential educational opportunities may help to motivate children who do not see college or university education in their future. It may also help children to understand that there are many routes to personal satisfaction. Stress should be placed on the breadth and variety of opportunities and the many doors they tend to open.

Activities designed to build such concepts overlap with investigations of careers and life styles. Major avenues include visiting, requesting literature through the mail, using films and making video- or audiotapes, inviting former and present students and staff members, and attending cultural or educational events in the educational setting.

Educational opportunities may also be examined in several other ways. Among these, first, classroom groups may explore the employment possibilities opened by a particular educational program. What present and future occupations and life satisfactions become available if, for example, one completes a training program in secretarial skills, business management, teaching, plumbing, operation of business machines or heavy equipment, domestic service, or home economy? Teachers, counselors, or visitors familiar with such programs can undoubtedly tell of the vistas they open. The domestic servant who works on an ocean liner, the receptionist who works surrounded by glamour and excitement, the machinist who has traveled all over the world with his company, and the home economist who has been employed by a radio station to help with consumer education, may find deep personal satisfactions in the ways they spend their working hours.

Second, elementary school children may be helped to explore the avenues open to an individual who shows an affinity for a particular elementary school subject—math, science, English, health, social studies, music, art, or physical education. What are the relationships between interest in science or English, for example, and employment? What can one do with ability and interest in math, music, or physical education? What are the avocational and vocational outlets for people with these abilities and interests? Teachers, counselors, or visitors who are informed about these relationships can help show elementary school children that the possessor of a highly particular interest or ability may still have broad horizons open to him. A person with a scientific-mechanical bent may one day be a businessman who "putters," a mechanical engineer, an assembly-line worker or efficiency expert, a laundromat owner-operator, or a self-employed household-equipment repairman, and whichever avenue he takes has the potential for producing meaning and satisfaction in his life.

Third, elementary school children may be helped to understand that within the life of an individual any particular educational interest may deepen personal meaning. Of what use—it is often asked—is English to a mechanic, foreign language to a bookkeeper, art to a secretary, or knowledge of social studies to a truck driver? Teachers, counselors, and visitors can help develop the concept that life pleasures may depend directly on such variety. The mechanic may seek out a dramatics or public speaking course and find great satisfaction after working hours in performing in civic theater. The secretary may build on her public school art education and spend her spare time in painting. The truck driver may become a Civil War buff who studies the time of Lincoln and Lee and who delights in visiting the sites he has read about. Each may feel the pull of two interests in his or her life that complement each other and together increase personal meaning.

Fourth, emerging from the point above, children need to know that apparently unrelated educational strengths may enhance a career. When the job of shop foreman opens, the person offered it may not be the best machinist—but the effective machinist who also can write a meaningful report, keep records, and work with other men in a position of leadership. When a construction firm contracts to help build a dam in the Near East, the heavy equipment operators asked to go first are likely to be those who have command of the English language and have shown some affinity for foreign languages, who interact effectively with a variety of other individuals, and who are more than minimally aware of the social sciences. There is a need for technical writers, people proficient in specialized scientific or industrial knowledge and capable of expressing themselves clearly in writing, and there is a need for high-level executives who understand both the business and technical end of an industry. Thus job satisfaction may ultimately depend on the adaptability and breadth of an individual's education.

The exploration processes sampled above should suggest the great range of approaches that inventive counselors and teachers may wish to consider in developing their own units or programs. We next consider the division of responsibility in dealing with such activities.

TEACHER AND COUNSELOR ROLES IN EXPLORING ADULT LIVING PATTERNS

Because exploration of adult living patterns is a very meaningful curricular experience in which all children may participate, it seems appropriate for interested teachers to become fully involved. Extensive participation by the counselor, however, may mean neglect of counseling and consulting responsibilities.

The counselor might find his place in this area through:

1. Stimulating the interest of teachers.
2. Consulting with teachers.
3. Conducting in-service workshops with interested teachers.
4. Demonstrating with classes—for example, for all of the interested teachers at one grade level. (Use of videotaping would mean that not all would have to be present, and the demonstration could be reviewed and discussed later.)
5. Supplementing teacher efforts.
6. Counseling children individually and in small groups relative to their concerns about adult living patterns.
7. Making arrangements for visits and visitors. (In a school in which several teachers are working on career-related projects, for example, the counselor might well function as a clearinghouse for visits and visitors, arranging to combine them where possible and appropriate. For much of this work the counselor could use time available after the children have left the building.)
8. Purchasing supplies, monographs, texts, and so on to get maximum dollar value and avoid duplication.

Regarding teacher involvement:

There is no need for this to be a year-long project, and there is no need for every teacher no matter how uninterested to be involved in the program. It would be far better for teachers to exchange classes, one teaching arithmetic for a term while the other handles a unit on careers. It would be better that two, three, or four grades be omitted from the program and that children be exposed to this kind of material in a way which builds upon previous learnings. Teachers who get "turned-on" by such activity will find this a meaningful way to come into significant contact with children.[44]

While the counselor might strive to restrict his activities, there is no reason for the interested teacher to do so. For him, the full range of the processes and activities are appropriate—subject to minimal grade-to-grade coordination to avoid subjecting children to extensive repetition.

Hoppock sounds a caution involving a responsibility for both teacher and counselor:

> The teacher's response to the child's expressed occupational choice may help to determine the child's attitudes toward different occupations. If the teacher regards some occupations as preferable to others, he will probably be unable completely to conceal his own feelings. He should, however, be acutely aware of the fact that whenever he does reveal his feelings, he thereby risks substituting his own values for the values of the child. The substitution may not always be desirable. The teacher who has never thought much about his own attitudes toward different occupations may do well to examine himself with care to see how frequently his prejudices are showing and whether or not any of them should be revised.[45]

In summary, counselors and teachers working cooperatively can complement one another's efforts in exploring adult living patterns—the counselor offering stimulation, demonstration, and support, and the teacher working with one or more classes. While either can function independently, cooperative participation seems much more likely to achieve the goals sought.

SOURCES RELATED TO THE EXPLORATION OF ADULT LIVING PATTERNS

Both teacher and counselor may need materials. This brief section considers some of the sources that may be used in the exploring of adult living patterns.

School staff and service personnel are a natural source for elementary school exploration into adult living patterns. Teachers, counselors, administrators, cooks, bus drivers, custodial staff members, secretaries, and nurses have much potential in terms of their own career histories and their inventiveness in exploring their life patterns.

Members of the community at large, including persons engaged in business, industry, distribution of goods, agriculture, and elected and ap-

[44] Nelson, "Opening new vistas to children through career exploration," pp. 22–23.

[45] Hoppock, *op. cit.*, p. 348.

pointed offices, provide, except in small rural communities, an extensive available resource.

Vocational Guidance Quarterly, the journal of the National Vocational Guidance Association, includes in each issue a listing of current occupational literature. An annual booklet is distributed by the American Personnel and Guidance Association, 1607 New Hampshire Avenue, N.W., Washington, D.C.

Government publications available through the U.S. Government Printing Office, Public Documents, Washington, D.C., or directly through the U.S. Department of Labor, provide valuable material. *Occupational Outlook Handbook* is an excellent source which undergoes revision every two years; it describes a large number of occupations and discusses trends related to each. While it is not designed to be read by elementary school children, it could be read by many, and it would provide valuable information for teachers and counselors. A companion publication, *Occupational Outlook Quarterly*, provides even more current information on new developments in the occupational world. The U.S. Department of Labor periodically reissues the *Dictionary of Occupational Titles*, a ponderous but valuable standard resource for use by teachers, counselors, and others, which classifies, defines, and briefly discusses many thousands of occupations.

Science Research Associates has issued many worthwhile career-oriented materials that might be useful to the counselor or teacher. Examples include:

1. *Our Working World*, by Lawrence Senesh, a series of texts focused on careers and economic education.
2. *Occupational Information in the Elementary School*, by Willa Norris, a 1963 book devoted to processes and sources appropriate to elementary school career exploration.
3. *What Could I Be?* by Walter Lifton, a 1960 source for exploring occupational goals of middle and upper grade children. A teacher's manual is also available.
4. *A Book About Me*, by E. S. Jay, is an instructional source that gives children an opportunity to look at themselves and at the same time provides much information about children to teachers and counselors.
5. *Widening Occupational Roles Kit* includes a great many junior guidance briefs, a teacher's manual, pupil workbooks, and a small number of filmstrips oriented toward career exploration.
6. *Focus on Self Development*, by Judith Anderson and others, is designed to encourage the elementary school child to become more aware of his surroundings, himself, ways in which he interacts with his environment, and how he is received and perceived by others.

Guidance Associates has developed a number of films and filmstrips relevant to elementary school guidance and to career development in particular.

SUMMARY

Children are aware of the adult world about them. It engages their interests, sparks their curiosity, and to some extent may worry them. Exploration of the adult world by elementary school children contributes to their understanding and is consistent both with objectives of elementary education and with assumptions of career-development theory. If exploration is to be incorporated in the elementary school it should be oriented around activities, based on questions relevant to children, focused on exploration rather than choice, conducted so as to generate excitement rather than product, and evaluated in ways that do not dampen enthusiasm. Exploration processes should consider life style, careers, career patterns, and educational experiences that enhance the individual and bring meaning into his life.

The counselor and teacher both have important tasks in exploring adult living patterns, the counselor focusing on supportive activities and the teacher focusing on educative activities. Sources of materials are important, but the emphasis is on inventive leadership and teacher- or counselor-pupil planning in exploring adult living patterns. This exploration is a significant means by which teachers and counselors can relate to children and the world about them.

REFERENCES

Angelino, H. "Developmental tasks and problems of the middle adolescent period," *Education*, 76: 226–231 (1955).

Arbuckle, D. S. "Occupational information in the elementary school," *Vocational Guidance Quarterly*, 12: 77–84 (1963–64).

Asbury, F. A. "Vocational development of rural disadvantaged eighth grade boys," *Vocational Guidance Quarterly*, 17: 109–113 (1968).

Bank, I. M. "Children explore careerland through vocational role models," *Vocational Guidance Quarterly*, 17: 284–289 (1969).

Barbe, W. B., and N. S. Chambers. "Career requirements of gifted elementary children and their parents," *Vocational Guidance Quarterly*, 11: 137–140 (1963).

Bordin, E. S., B. Nachmann, and S. J. Segal. "An articulated framework for vocational development," *Journal of Counseling Psychology*, 10: 107–117 (1963).

Braland, R. G., and W. L. Sweeney. "A differential approach to vocational counseling in junior high," *School Counselor, 17:* 260–262 (1970).

Bugg, C. A. "Implications of some major theories of career choice for elementary school guidance programs," *Elementary School Guidance and Counseling, 3:* 164–173 (1969).

Davis, D. A., N. Hagan, and J. Strouf. "Occupational choice of twelve-year-olds," *Personnel and Guidance Journal, 40:* 628–629 (1962).

Dimick, K. M., and V. E. Huff. *Child Counseling.* Dubuque, Iowa: William C. Brown Company, Publisher, 1970.

Dole, A. A. "Educational choice is not vocational choice," *Vocational Guidance Quarterly, 12:* 30–35 (1963).

Ginzberg, E. "Toward a theory of occupational choice," *Occupations, 30:* 491–494 (1952).

Goodson, S. "Occupational information materials in selected elementary and middle schools," *Vocational Guidance Quarterly, 17:* 128–131 (1968).

Grell, L. A. "How much occupational information in the elementary school?" *Vocational Guidance Quarterly, 9:* 48–53 (1960).

Gross, E. "A sociological approach to the analysis of preparation for work life," *Personnel and Guidance Journal, 45:* 416–423 (1967).

Gunn, B. "Children's conceptions of occupational prestige," *Personnel and Guidance Journal, 42:* 558–563 (1964).

Hansen, J. C., and T. J. Caulfield. "Parent-child occupational concepts," *Elementary School Guidance and Counseling. 3:* 269–275 (1969).

————, and R. R. Stevic. *Elementary School Guidance.* New York: Macmillan, 1969.

Havighurst, R. J. *Human Development and Education.* New York: McKay, 1953.

Heisler, F. "An elementary school background for vocational guidance," *Elementary School Journal, 55:* 513–516 (1955).

Herr, E. L., D. D. Dillenbeck, and J. D. Swisher. "Content and preparation strategies relative to pre-college guidance and counseling," *Pre-Service and In Service Preparation of Counselors for Educational Guidance.* ACES-ASCA Monograph. Washington, D.C.: American Personnel and Guidance Association, 1970.

Hill, G. E., and E. B. Luckey. *Guidance for Children in Elementary Schools.* New York: Appleton-Century-Crofts, 1969.

Holland, J. L. "Explorations of a theory of vocational choice. Part I: Vocational images and choice," *Vocational Guidance Quarterly, 11:* 232–239 (1963).

————. "A theory of vocational choice," *Journal of Counseling Psychology, 6:* 33–45 (1959).

Hoppock, R. *Occupational Information.* New York: McGraw-Hill, 1967.

Isaacson, L. E. *Career Information in Counseling and Teaching.* Boston: Allyn and Bacon, 1966.

Kaback, G. R. "Occupational information in elementary education:

what counselors do—what they would like to do," *Vocational Guidance Quarterly, 16:* 203–206 (1968).

———. "Occupational information for groups of elementary school children," *Vocational Guidance Quarterly, 14:* 163–168 (1966).

———. "Occupational information in elementary education," *Vocational Guidance Quarterly, 9:* 55–59 (1960).

Kaye, J. "Fourth graders meet up with occupations," *Vocational Guidance Quarterly, 18:* 150–152 (1960).

Laramore, D., and J. Thompson. "Career experiences appropriate to elementary school grades," *School Counselor, 17:* 262–264 (1970).

Lawton, R. "Life space counseling," *Personnel and Guidance Journal, 48:* 661–663 (1970).

Lehner, G. F., and E. A. Kube. *The Dynamics of Personal Adjustment.* Englewood Cliffs, N.J.: Prentice-Hall, 1955.

Leonard, R. S. "Vocational guidance in junior high: one school's answer," *Vocational Guidance Quarterly, 17:* 221–222 (1969).

Lifton, W. M. "Vocational guidance in the elementary school," *Vocational Guidance Quarterly, 8:* 79–81 (1959–60).

Matthews, E. "Career development of girls," *Vocational Guidance Quarterly, 11:* 273–277 (1963).

Nelson, R. C. "The world of work in the 'fantasy stage' of development," *Elementary School Guidance and Counseling, 2:* 222–224 (1968).

———. "Opening new vistas to children through career exploration," *Needed Concepts in Elementary School Guidance,* pp. 13–24. Report of the Eighth Annual All Ohio Elementary School Guidance Conference. Columbus, Ohio: State Department of Education, Division of Guidance and Testing, 1969.

———. "Knowledge and interests concerning sixteen occupations among elementary and secondary school students," *Educational and Psychological Measurement, 23:* 741–754 (1963).

———. "Early versus developmental vocational choice," *Vocational Guidance Quarterly, 11:* 23–27 (1962).

Newman, M., "Pre-high school vocational counseling," *Vocational Guidance Quarterly, 6:* 6–8 (1957).

Norris, W. *Occupational Information in the Elementary School.* Chicago: Science Research Associates, 1963.

Perrone, P. A. "Values and occupational preferences of junior high school girls," *Personnel and Guidance Journal, 44:* 253–257 (1965).

Roe, A. "Early determinants of vocational choice," *Journal of Counseling Psychology, 4:* 212–217 (1957).

Simons, J. B. "An existential view of vocational development," *Personnel and Guidance Journal, 44:* 604–610 (1966).

Strong, E. K. *Change of Interest with Age.* Stanford, Calif.: Stanford University Press, 1931.

Super, D. E. "A theory of vocational development," *American Psychologist, 8:* 185–190 (1953).

———. "Consistency and wisdom of vocational preference as indices of vocational maturity in the ninth grade," *Journal of Educational Psychology, 52:* 35–43 (1961).

————. *The Psychology of Careers.* New York: Harper & Row, 1957.

Tennyson, W. W., and L. P. Monnens. "The world of work through elementary readers," *Vocational Guidance Quarterly, 12:* 85–88 (1963–64).

Theobald, R. *Free Men and Free Markets.* New York: Clarkson Potter, 1963.

Thompson, A. S. "Developmental stage and developmental needs at the junior high school level," *Personnel and Guidance Journal, 39:* 116–118 (1960).

Tiedeman, D. V. "Decision and vocational development: a paradigm and its implications," *Personnel and Guidance Journal, 40:* 15–21 (1961).

———— and R. P. O'Hara. *Career development: choice and adjustment.* New York: College Entrance and Examination Board, 1963.

"Vocational development: an approach to vocational guidance." Symposium presented at NVGA section on vocational counseling, American Personnel and Guidance Association Convention, St. Louis, 1958. (Mimeographed.)

Wellington, J. A., and N. Olechowski. "Attitudes toward the world of work in elementary school," *Vocational Guidance Quarterly, 14:* 160–162 (1966).

Wood, H. "Occupational information for junior high school youth—a symposium: Introduction," *Personnel and Guidance Journal, 39:* 115 (1960).

ARTICLES IN BOOKS OF READINGS

Dinkmeyer, D. C. *Guidance and Counseling in the Elementary School: Readings in Theory and Practice.* New York: Holt, Rinehart and Winston, Inc., 1968. Readings beginning on pages 307, 313, 319, 328, 331.

Hansen, J. C. *Guidance Services in the Elementary School,* APGA Reprint Series. Washington, D.C.: American Personnel and Guidance Association, 1971. Readings beginning on pages 123, 125, 135, 144, 153, 161.

Koplitz, E. D. *Guidance in the Elementary School: Theory, Research and Practice.* Dubuque, Iowa: William C. Brown Company, Publisher, 1968. Readings beginning on pages 103, 114, 121, 126, 132, 136, 139, 148, 271, 277.

Mills, G. D. *Elementary School Guidance and Counseling.* New York: Random House, Inc., 1971. Readings beginning on pages 159, 169.

Peters, H. J., A. C. Riccio, and J. J. Quaranta. *Guidance in the Elementary School: A Book of Readings.* New York: Macmillan, 1963. Readings beginning on pages 119, 123, 128, 135, 139.

13

The Organization of the Guidance Program

To perform a function of some complexity requires the making of thoughtful arrangements of many sorts, the selection and direction of essential personnel, the marshaling of materials, the co-ordination of energies. Such activities are components of the organizing and administrative process.

PERCIVAL W. HUTSON: *The Guidance Function in Education*

The organization of the guidance program may be viewed in terms of a district or in terms of a single school. Counselors may work in pairs or alone in a single school or in more than one school, isolated from other pupil personnel workers; they may function as part of a team of pupil personnel workers; they may owe allegiance primarily to the principal, or they may report directly to a Director of Guidance or Pupil Personnel Services Director. Teachers may carry the entire load of elementary school guidance services, they may be functioning members of a pupil personnel team, or they may work with a building counselor or share the services of a counselor during his time in the building.

Great advantages may accrue to the school district in which several counselors and other pupil personnel workers function as a team, their efforts coordinated by a pupil personnel services director. Central planning and central budgeting can give leadership and security to team members. Each can benefit from the insights and skills provided by other members of the group, and children and teachers can gain through the pooling of resources.

Since a great many school districts lack the benefits of such team-work, and because all teachers and counselors must bear some responsibility for decision making and priority setting in the guidance program within their own school building, the material in this chapter is focused upon organizing within the school. Thus, where coordinative responsibility is centralized, some adaptation of the suggestions made herein may be necessary.

Questions of priority, such as the relative emphasis to be given to group work or work with individuals, career and life-style exploration, and consulting responsibilities—have been considered throughout this text. Ultimately the individual must make these decisions out of his personal philosophy and the needs he observes. Instead of reiterating these points, we invite the reader here to consider some of the purposes, strategies, and processes involved in guidance-program organization.

THE PURPOSES OF ORGANIZATION

In this age of high educational costs and conservative budgeting, the guidance program must be developed to accomplish the philosophical objectives set for it: (1) to clarify the needs of children, (2) to encounter the needs that can reasonably be met through the school, and (3) to facilitate the development of a school environment that contributes to meeting children's needs.

In this chapter these ends are restructured and considered from a different perspective. The guidance program may be organized (a) so that it has impact on the school, (b) so that it involves the personnel of the school, (c) so that outcomes are clearly concentrated upon, (d) so that effectiveness is achieved, and (e) so that special needs are met.

ORGANIZING FOR IMPACT UPON THE SCHOOL

The guidance program should be expected to have an impact upon the school, the students, the staff members, and some home environments. Several strategies may be used to maximize these impacts.

1. APPROPRIATE STRATEGY FOR MAXIMIZING THE IMPACT OF THE GUIDANCE PROGRAM REQUIRES THE EXAMINATION OF EXISTING SERVICES Often the counselor who is developing a new guidance program, and who initiates a survey concerned with existing guidance procedures and activities, finds that there is much to build upon.

Mr. Alton, counselor at Central School, found that a second grade teacher has used an extensive unit on community helpers, the fourth grade teachers have regularly scheduled individual achievement-test interpretation sessions, an upper grade physical education teacher has used free periods to discuss nutrition, weight, diet, and exercise problems with individuals or groups of children, and individual teachers occasionally or incidentally have incorporated a great variety of one-to-one and classroom group activities designed to develop social values and personal awareness.

The report based on Mr. Alton's informal survey resulted in an expansion of existing services, since the teachers involved became aware of several good ideas and adapted them freely for their classes, and the procedures themselves were reinforced and refined as a result of the recognition given them. The extension of the program through the addition of the counselor, then, expanded previous attempts, and there was no inclination to terminate guidance activities and to relinquish all title to them to the counselor.

2. IT IS STRATEGIC TO BASE THE GUIDANCE PROGRAM ON INFORMATION REGARDING THE NEEDS OF CHILDREN   These can be explored through questionnaires or more personalized contacts.

Miss Fullerton, a half-time counselor in a large elementary school, found that in one school year she saw 30 percent of the students, another 25 percent would like to have talked with her, and over 90 percent of all students surveyed indicated that they saw a clear need for a counselor. The bulk of the problems children presented included brother-sister conflicts, difficulties with friendships, concerns over school work, not getting along well with parents, mother-father conflicts, poor self-concept, getting into trouble, needing someone to show understanding, wanting information about growing up, and unhappiness. Portions of transcribed interviews clarified the impact of needs on individual children and indicated the varieties of concerns they encountered.

3. IN ORDER TO MAXIMIZE HIS IMPACT, THE GUIDANCE COUNSELOR OR TEACHER MAY SEEK TO FUNCTION AS AN AGENT OF CHANGE   Those involved in guidance need to make conscious evaluations regarding the need for change within the school, to examine the role that each can play in producing that change, and to project the likely consequences of entering into that process. This is to say that if the change-agent role is to be assumed, it should be assumed after deliberation.

The guidance committee in Westville began to compare notes on the pressure felt by children in the departmentalized fifth and sixth grades. Although the topic was initiated by Mrs. Seamon, the counselor, as a result of concerns raised by children in counseling, the nurse and the teachers on the committee contributed heavily to the discussion. The eventual outcome was a series of sweeping changes, introducing flexibility in scheduling, reducing the number of letter-graded subjects, designating specific nights for teachers for the assigning of homework, and encouraging meaningful teacher-pupil planning in classwork and homework.

4. MAXIMUM IMPACT OFTEN REQUIRES MOVING OUT OF THE CONFINES OF THE GUIDANCE OFFICE OR THE CLASSROOM   The counselor or teacher who sees a problem in the school setting or a child's life does not wait until it is laid at his doorstep, but tactfully, yet aggressively, concerns himself with the matter at hand, functioning within legal and other reasonable limits.

Mr. Somers moved beyond the confines of his office by developing classroom group contact with the children of the primary grades, by clarifying the process of self-referral, and by taking small groups of children to his office for further discussions regarding counseling. These actions were designed to produce a sense of trust and convey a feeling of interest.

Mrs. Zimmer reached beyond her classroom in an inner-city school where the children seemed to feel that no one cared for them. She asked one parent, with whom she seemed to have a warm relationship, if she might arrange a coffee for a group of the mothers. This began a series of informal discussions over coffee that were rotated into different homes and that eventually included mothers of all of the children in the classroom. A second outcome was that a continuing group began to meet informally, focused on how parents could effectively help children, on how the school could work more effectively with the children, and upon child-rearing practices.

5. MAXIMUM IMPACT DEPENDS MORE ON DIVERSITY THAN ON UNIFORMITY IN ELEMENTARY SCHOOL GUIDANCE PROGRAMS   All too often in school districts that have several elementary schools or employ several elementary school counselors, the guidance program from school to school is "carbon-copied." Hill[1] points out that variety in programs and roles may represent appropriate adaptation to the observed needs in particular schools. Walz and Miller[2] suggest that variety in organization and activity is not only advisable, but necessary in terms of the children's needs and the counselor's skills.

---

[1] George E. Hill, "Agreements in the practice of guidance in the elementary schools," *Elementary School Guidance and Counseling, 1:* 188–195 (1967).

[2] Garry Walz and Juliet Miller, "School climates and student behavior," *Personnel and Guidance Journal, 47:* 859–867 (1969).

In the large inner-city school in which Mrs. Smith teaches, the guidance program functions primarily through activity clubs, many of which have a pre-vocational emphasis. The counselor in another school, Mr. Lewis, finds his personality well suited to working with teachers; he feels most reinforced when his activities lead to positive change in general classroom atmosphere. By contrast, Miss Heck finds her greatest satisfaction in small-group and individual counseling, yet maintains good communication with teachers and parents.

6. THE PROGRAM THAT ACHIEVES STRONG IMPACT IS GENERALLY CHARACTERIZED BY INNOVATION Often the obvious approaches have already been used, and only an innovative approach will succeed. Gelatt[3] asks for daring, imaginative approaches that may cut across traditional professional identities. Newer, fresher thinking is called for by new times and the active, involved children who are gracing our schools.

One innovative approach might involve Festinger's[4] theory of cognitive dissonance—the theory that when cognitive elements are inconsistent the person will take steps to eliminate the inconsistency. Children experience dissonance when the responses they expect do not occur and they frequently adjust their behavior and attitudes in response to the dissonance felt. Thus, the child who expects attention for disruptive behavior but who is ignored may learn to adjust his own behavior in order to get attention. Interesting evidence of cognitive dissonance has been demonstrated when students who were induced to make public statements inconsistent with their feelings resolved the dissonance by changing their perceptions—by coming to agree with their public statement. An innovative guidance program may achieve its ends through exploring the application of cognitive dissonance theory or in other unique ways.

Moon and Wilson[5] describe an experience in which a heterogeneous group of fifth grade children helped groups of first grade children who were having difficulty adjusting to the school environment. Data collected on members of the fifth grade group showed significant gain in reading achievement as well as growth in self-discipline and cooperative classroom functioning, presumably as a result of the responsibilities they were given and the insights they developed.

7. THE SCHOOL GUIDANCE PROGRAM, DESIGNED TO ASSIST STUDENTS TO LIVE IN A DEMOCRATIC SOCIETY, CAN APPROPRIATELY FUNC-

---

[3] H. B. Gelatt, "School guidance programs," *Review of Educational Research, 39:* 140–153 (1969).

[4] L. Festinger, *A Theory of Cognitive Dissonance* (New York: Harper and Row, 1957).

[5] Mozetta Moon and Doris Wilson, "Teacher-counselor cooperation: building self concepts and confidence in children," *School Counselor, 17:* 364–366 (1970).

TION TO HELP YOUNG PEOPLE BECOME INVOLVED IN THE DECISION-MAKING PROCESS   It is time to offer children feedback on their values and attitudes toward the school and its functioning, rather than dealing exclusively in "needs" in the abstract. Carey put it this way: "Counselors who really want students to get a share of the power, and who believe in an individualized approach to human needs, ought to ask themselves whether they take their ideals seriously."[6]

A teacher who was "at her wit's end" with a highly active, resistive, nonacademic class discussed her problem with Miss Olsen, the counselor, who encouraged her to have a truly open discussion with her students. At the teacher's request the counselor was present and involved when things bothering teacher and class were discussed frankly; all present were genuinely encouraged to express themselves. The discussion cleared the air, gave the students a chance to experience respect as adults willingly heard them and communicated honestly with them, and helped the teacher and the students to set expectations for the future functioning of the classroom.

8. THE GUIDANCE PROGRAM THAT HAS EXTENSIVE IMPACT IS CHARACTERIZED BY CONSIDERATION OF THE SCHOOL AND CLASSROOM CLIMATE   Walz and Miller[7] concluded that individual student success is at least partly a function of the school climate and its support of the individual's values and needs. They suggest also that school environments that are open and that encourage student autonomy may be expected to meet less student resistance. One may infer that counselor and teacher support of an open climate, giving encouragement to student autonomy, is most appropriate. Stone and Shertzer,[8] in this vein, call for "reasoned militancy" by the counselor within his school setting. Certainly, evaluation of the impact of the school and classroom climate upon the students' morale, self-concepts, and skill acquisition might well be expected of the elementary school counselor or teacher.

ORGANIZING FOR INVOLVEMENT

Another way of looking at the organization of the school guidance program is in terms of involvement. Even the counselor who does nothing but see children for the five hours of the school day can use some portion of the remaining three hours to create involvement. Even the busy teacher who

[6] Richard W. Carey, "Student protest and the counselor," *Personnel and Guidance Journal, 48:* 185–191 (1969).

[7] Walz and Miller, *op. cit.*

[8] Shelley C. Stone and Bruce Shertzer, "The militant counselor," *Personnel and Guidance Journal, 42:* 342–347 (1963).

is concerned about the guidance implications of educational practices and who worries about the unmet needs of children can find time, if the priority is high enough, to involve himself and others in the guidance program. The guidance program can be organized to involve the administrative leadership, teachers, students, parents, and support personnel.

INVOLVING ADMINISTRATIVE LEADERSHIP

Many counselors make themselves available to administrative personnel for any task, then complain that their training and expertise are misused. From the outset, the employment interview, the counselor must have some clear concepts of the appropriate functions he might perform, and he must seek the support and involvement of the administrator in carrying out these functions. While adaptation to the needs of the children and the situation is essential, the counselor who suggests that he will do "whatever is needed" may long have to contend with the tasks assigned to fill his time by the school administrator. He owes better than that to himself, to the administrator, and to those whom he wishes to serve.

If the counselor is to have the impact he might wish, he must seek to share with the administrators and the teachers the task of shaping curriculum and program to meet the needs of children. The counselor cannot be a spectator in curricular and program matters.

Meeks[9] points out that the administrative leadership of the school and the corporation must be fully aware of the guidance program, since they are responsible for interpreting the guidance program to the school board and to the community, they are obligated to give the guidance program direction through the administration of the total educational policy, and they must evaluate the effectiveness of the program in terms of its contribution to the total education effort. The counselor bears a reciprocal responsibility to make certain his efforts are understood. This point seems especially appropriate in the light of the 1963 survey by McDougall and Reitan,[10] which suggests some discrepancies in evaluation; e.g., administrators place low value upon counseling practicum and high value upon prior teaching and a learning orientation, whereas many counselors and counselor educators take the opposite position.

Hill and Luckey[11] indicate that the school administrator should

[9] Anna R. Meeks, *Guidance in Elementary Education* (New York: Ronald, 1968).

[10] William P. McDougall and Henry M. Reitan, "The elementary counselor as perceived by elementary principals," *Personnel and Guidance Journal, 42:* 348–354 (1963).

[11] George E. Hill and Eleanore B. Luckey, *Guidance for Children in Elementary Schools* (New York: Appleton-Century-Crofts, 1969).

have several expectations of his counselor. It might be excellent involvement strategy for the counselor to suggest these to the administrator, as follows:

Expect of your counselor—

1. a careful statement of the purposes of guidance activities and the functions of the school counselor.
2. an organized effort to examine the impact of the school upon the children within it and to build general staff awareness of the impact of the total educational effort.
3. a professional attitude, effective preparation, and growth.
4. an effort to enrich and extend his education.
5. a reciprocal expectation that the administrator will exemplify good human relations, good citizenship, and effective leadership.

Hoyt[12] takes a slightly different tack. His suggestions, related specifically to the secondary school counselor, may readily be adapted for the elementary school; he tells the administrator and teacher to expect the counselor to exhibit a professional career commitment to education, some specialized skills, a willingness to reach out to the teaching and administrative staff members as well as to students, a concern for the welfare of every student, and a striving to increase professional competence.

INVOLVING TEACHERS

An advantage accruing especially to the counselor assigned to a single building is that he can contact teachers informally and briefly innumerable times during the course of the school year. He can feel free to initiate and receive contacts from teachers before the school day begins, in the halls, in the teachers' room, over coffee, in social contexts, and through scheduled appointments. He can thus involve teachers very readily in the guidance program. When he wishes to extend and organize this involvement further he may work with teachers on special projects or curriculur activities, such as a career conference, a life-style exploration program, or a mental health unit. Two additional ways, briefly explored here, are the creation of a guidance committee and in-service education, both discussed more extensively in Chapter 10.

The guidance committee can serve in many ways. It can help to develop the guidance program, it can guide the hand of the counselor by assisting in the development of priorities, it can be an idea-generating body through such procedures as brainstorming, it can help to plan evaluative and data-gathering procedures, and it can bring the counselor together with an interested group of teachers. More than creating involvement for

[12] Kenneth B. Hoyt, "What the school has a right to expect of its counselor," *Personnel and Guidance Journal, 40:* 129–133 (1961).

its own sake, the guidance committee appears often to be a vital cog in the wheel of guidance. If interested persons serve on the guidance committee there is a reasonable likelihood that the program will receive support, that at least those on the committee will increase their involvement in guidance activities, and that supportive attitudes regarding the guidance program will radiate from those involved.

In-service education, preferably informal and voluntary, may also be used for creating teacher involvement. The counselor would do well to build support for such activities by providing useful bulletins and brief in-service presentations during faculty meetings and the like. If in-service activities are supported and organized by a guidance committee, if they are based on needs for information by staff members, and, where appropriate, are used for in-service education credit, there is every reason to expect appropriate involvement by those who volunteer.

In each of the past three years Mr. Teague has conducted an in-service workshop with a small group of teachers, numbering from four to eight, focusing on child study and the use of informal measures, interviews, and similar procedures in understanding children. As one result he has been requested by teachers to conduct a workshop on classroom climate during the next series of preschool sessions.

The imagination and inventiveness of the counselor and the teachers are the only real limit on teacher involvement in guidance. Jaffe and Reed[13] suggest, as a further step, that counselors can involve teachers and administrators alike by providing feedback on how students perceive what is happening in the school setting.

INVOLVING STUDENTS

There are many ways in which students can be involved in the organization of the guidance program. Hopefully all activities involving students help at least indirectly to shape the program. Greater direct opportunities occur when students can indicate their own needs, when they are invited to describe the way they see the school in relation to meeting those needs, and when they participate directly in the shaping of the guidance program or the total program of the school.

Surveys can be useful, and selected interviews can increase their value in clarifying student needs, but the counselor who wishes total involvement moves beyond this level. Jaffe and Reed and Carey suggest that much more intensive activity by counselors is appropriate in helping

---

[13] Arthur Jaffe and Alice Reed, "Involving the turned-on generation through structured rapping," *Personnel and Guidance Journal, 48:* 311–315 (1969).

students become involved: "When young people feel their opinions and ideas are recognized as important and valuable, and when they are given freedom to express these opinions and to help effect changes, they have no need for violent demonstrations to protest their impotence."[14]

Carey[15] suggests that the counselor (1) sponsor local studies on what students are experiencing, (2) recognize the students' desire for a piece of the power and help them obtain it, (3) become active in the tailoring of programs designed to meet the needs of students *now*—not in a remote future, (4) oppose nongenuine and patronizing attempts to involve students, and (5) be personally committed to sharing power within the system.

If effective functioning in a democracy is to be a true goal of the educative process, involvement in decision making must not await the senior or junior high school. The elementary school must share the responsibility for the sense of noninvolvement that young people demonstrate in many ways. Even at that level dissatisfaction is being evidenced more clearly. By and large, though, elementary school children can be readily convinced that school personnel care for them and are willing to involve them in significant ways. A student panel, either functioning as part of the guidance committee or advising it, can provide specific evidence of the interest of the counselor and guidance-oriented teachers in involving students in their educational planning.

The concerned counselor or teacher needs to see that the views of large numbers of children are involved in the development of the guidance program, and he must demonstrate that the program is not for the disturbed few. The program needs, in short, to be expansive enough so that the conclusion drawn in Oldridge's[16] study is forever inappropriate; he found that the control group gained more than a counseled group and indicated that the negative reaction received by students because they were singled out and given special attention may have contributed to this finding. It is a testable hypothesis that guidance programs that involve large numbers of students, and especially those that involve children in guidance program and educational planning, do not suffer from similar stigmatization.

INVOLVING PARENTS AND COMMUNITY MEMBERS

Perhaps citing the need for parent and community involvement in the guidance program is sufficient here. Inventive counselors and teachers will see innumerable ways in which parents and community members may

[14] *Ibid.*, p. 315.
[15] Carey, *op. cit.*
[16] Buff Oldridge, "Two roles for elementary school guidance personnel," *Personnel and Guidance Journal, 43:* 367–370 (1964).

be encouraged to engage in preschool and in-school orientation groups,[17] in discussion groups, in service activities that meet the needs of individual children or children's groups, and in precareer exploration. Such involvement has both educative and public relations possibilities, helping to dispel the impression that the school is an unfeeling educational factory. Purposeful action by the counselor, the teachers, and the guidance committee is needed in many communities in order to change this impression.

INVOLVING SUPPORT PERSONNEL

Counselor activity may be effectively supplemented through the use of support personnel, often referred to as paraprofessionals or sub-professionals. The American Personnel and Guidance Association[18] suggests that support personnel, whose employment requires a lower financial outlay, can contribute to the guidance effort by performing supportive activities under supervision. Nelson[19] recommends that support personnel be involved in disseminating information, in activities related to testing, in observing and collecting data regarding individual children, in small-group activity as observer and co-worker, and in conducting brief follow-up interviews and other structured interviews designed to alert the counselor as to whether new problems are arising.

The use of support personnel allows for greater counselor impact across a larger student population, permits the involvement of community members who are familiar with the local environment, and releases counselor time for activities of highest priority; thus, it seems like an excellent way in which to extend services. The guidance program needs the support of all who can be of help to children.

ORGANIZING FOR OUTCOMES

Besides impact and involvement the guidance program needs to be organized for outcomes. Considered briefly here, this topic is explored further in Chapter 15 on research and trends in elementary school guidance.

Organizing for outcomes requires that hunches about meeting problems be stated clearly, that procedures to be used be specified, and that

---

[17] Richard C. Nelson and Gladys O'Connor, "A pre-kindergarten orientation program with children and their parents," *Elementary School Guidance and Counseling, 5:* 135–139 (1970).

[18] American Personnel and Guidance Association, Professional Preparation and Standards Committee, "Support personnel and the counselor: their technical and non-technical roles and preparation," *Personnel and Guidance Journal, 45:* 857–861 (1967).

[19] Richard C. Nelson, "Support personnel in elementary school guidance," *Elementary School Guidance and Counseling, 2:* 303–307 (1968).

observations be organized so that the degree of success can be determined. Counselors, teachers and others encounter problems, develop hunches as to how they might alleviate those problems, set about building a program for dealing with the problems, and gather evidence periodically to see whether the program is working. This process may be developed individually or related to groups of children.

Mr. Kelly, in dealing with Ellen, a third grader, learned that her mother had left home and would soon be starting divorce proceedings. He hypothesized that the girl had a need to express affect and to work through her own limited understanding of the problem and her part in it. He provided opportunity for that expression and watched to see how the opportunity to express affect was used; he also kept in touch with the teacher in order to ascertain whether classroom behavior was being adversely affected by the problem or by his attempts at alleviation.

Miss Stevens decided to try an unstructured group experience for boys who stood extremely low in sociometric standing. She combined those boys with others of high sociometric standing and felt very pleased to observe, in later activities, the incidence of inclusion of the boys of low standing.

Neither counselor in these examples collected data or formalized hypotheses, but both conducted an investigation that could have been scaled into an exciting and worthwhile piece of research. As it is, neither counselor has any definitive basis for deciding whether or not the processes utilized effected desired changes. One of the most critical needs in the field of elementary school guidance is that of building the research that evaluates the procedures utilized with children, and it is incumbent on those functioning on the front lines of elementary school guidance, teachers and counselors alike, to help to build this research. The question stem: "I wonder what would happen if . . ." often implies both a hypothesis and a methodology. Many guidance workers develop such questions innumerable times each year. More often these hunches should be carried to researchers so that the answer is more effectively explored.

Organizing for outcomes requires effective record keeping and data collection. One article[20] related to record keeping in elementary school counseling suggests that the counselor keep three kinds of records: (1) informal notes designed for his own recall and prepared in a personalized shorthand; (2) reports on selected children to be filed in the school record, designed as communication with teaching personnel, not revealing of confidential material, yet indicating ways in which the child might be reached;

[20] Richard C. Nelson, "Record keeping in elementary school guidance," *Elementary School Guidance and Counseling*, 3: 126–130 (1968).

and (3) confidential file reports, completed on those few children for whom extremely sensitive information should be available but under conditions of appropriate security.

Information other than counseling reports that may help in clarifying outcomes of counseling or guidance procedures should include the obvious: e.g., achievement, intelligence, and attendance data. In addition, for specific purposes other appropriate data may be collected: observations, sociometric responses, sentence-completion materials, questionnaires, attitude surveys, and assessments of classroom and school climate.

Organizing for outcomes, then, requires preplanning and allows for testing of the hunches that occur to the counselor or teacher. It depends in part on periodic collection of general data and on selected supplemental data. Counselors and teachers have a great deal to contribute in organizing for outcomes and assessing the extent to which these outcomes are achieved.

ORGANIZING FOR EFFECTIVENESS

If the school guidance program is to achieve the outcomes, the impact, and the involvements sought, some attention should be given to organizing for effectiveness. Points to be considered include the location of the counselor's office, the physical facilities to be made available, and the extent of financial and clerical support.

LOCATION OF THE COUNSELOR'S OFFICE

In the planning of a new building or the remodeling of an old one, the location of the counselor's office must be considered. Counselors often express a preference for isolation from the principal's office—at least to the extent that loud voices related to disciplinary action, or a child's crying over a personal concern, cannot be heard from one office to the other. To that extent separation and soundproofing seem desirable. At the same time the tendency for the counselor to create his own sphere and separate himself from the center of activity of the school seems inappropriate.

One idea, adapted from a school layout in Columbus, Indiana, is to locate the counselor's office adjacent to a teacher's lounge and an active, free-flowing, well-used learning center, as shown in Figure 13–1. The flow of traffic makes it easy for students and teachers to be in contact with the counselor and for the counselor to mix easily with those with whom he wishes to work.

It would appear that no hard and fast rules should be set, but that the counselor should be located near the center of action so that he may be acquainted with children and readily available to other staff members.

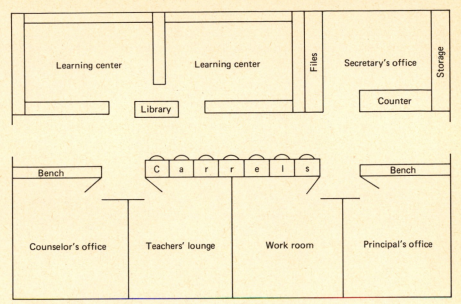

FIGURE 13–1 *Location of the Counseling Office*

PHYSICAL FACILITIES FOR COUNSELING

Minimal standards for a counseling office should include audio-privacy, comfort, attractiveness, sufficient size to accommodate either individual counseling or small groups of children, a shelf or two for the display of play media, and adequate ventilation, heating, and cooling. These standards can often be met by the conversion of a storage area, the adapting of a classroom, or the closing off of a dead-end hallway. When a facility is being converted or newly developed, however, consideration should be given to the development of a counseling center rather than the counseling office.

The need for in-service education of the counselor, the potential inherent in the counseling internship and the off-campus counseling practicum, the possibility of employing support personnel, and the opportunity to involve children as co-counselors with other children should encourage the development of facilities that provide space for more than one counseling activity and for observation. When arrangements permit observation, the counselor can obtain more effective consultation; can engage with children, other counselors, support personnel, and counselors-in-training in a wide variety of experiences; and can share selected experiences with other staff members to enhance their effectiveness in working with children. Two facilities that provide for observation and the involvement of more than one counseling activity are shown in Figure 13–2.

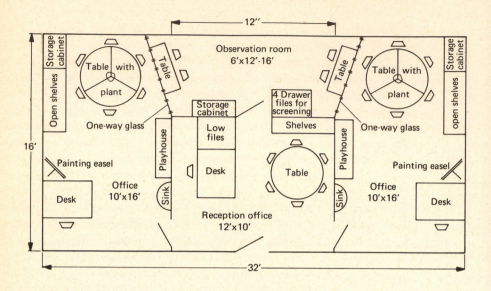

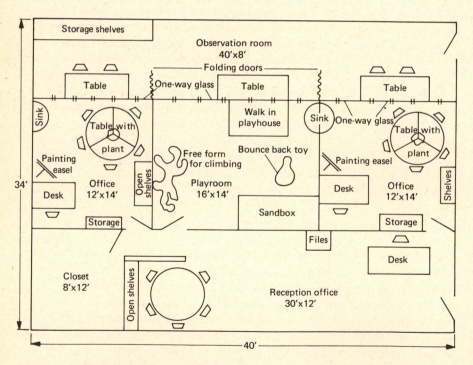

FIGURE 13-2 *Elementary School Counseling Centers* (Redrawn from Richard C. Nelson, "Physical facilities for elementary school counseling, *Personnel and Guidance Journal, 45*: 554–555 (1967). Reproduced by permission.)

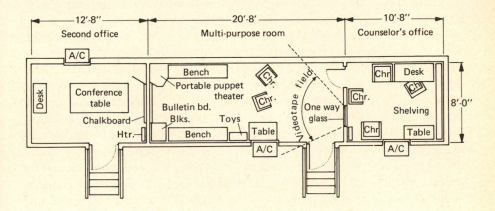

FIGURE 13–3 *Mobile Home—Elementary School Guidance Center* (Redrawn from Robert D. Myrick and William Haldin, "Making room for an elementary school counselor," *Elementary School Guidance and Counseling, 4:* 284 (1970), by permission.)

Myrick and Haldin have accepted the same principles and incorporated them into a mobile home as a counseling center (Figure 13–3).

The individual offices presented in either Figure 13–2 or 13–3 could provide a satisfactory counseling facility if finances or space were insufficient for the development of a more extensive arrangement, but the opportunities offered by an observable counseling center should not be readily dismissed.

BUDGETARY AND CLERICAL SUPPORT

If the guidance program is to develop and reach beyond the limits of four walls, some allowance must be made for materials and clerical assistance. On a pupil personnel budget that allows $300 to $500 per counselor above salaries, it is possible to purchase play media, consumable art supplies, career and mental health development materials, and a limited number of filmstrips or films designed to generate group and classroom discussion. Materials in this area are proliferating, requiring careful buying. At the same time, the costs of worthwhile and new materials are rising, so that the amount suggested may prove inadequate.

In many schools clerical support is one of the weakest links in the chain of guidance. Unless the school secretary or some other person is made available to help, many opportunities are lost. Reports are needed if insights gained are to be passed on to the teachers or to referral resources; written communications with teachers, parents, and children are needed if the follow-through phase of counseling is to be adequately handled; much of the in-service education and involvement of teachers can be handled through paperwork; career development and mental health exploration require planning, letter writing, arranging for visits and visitors, and material preparation and distribution; if the guidance program involves testing there may be needs for letter writing, clerical checking, scoring, preparation of reports and recording of data; and the whole area of public relations suggests the preparation and distribution of informative materials to the various publics—teachers, administrators, children, parents, other educational personnel, and the community at large. Much of the work involved in these activities can be handled by clerical personnel, and some of it might well be turned over to support personnel. If it continually requires the action of the counselor, he is being blocked from other activity that demands his time, and perhaps succumbing to the temptation to become a high-paid clerk.

A sensitive counselor, even if he serves several schools, works out of broom closets and a briefcase, and has no particular budgetary or clerical support, can conduct an effective guidance program. However, if the aims of the program are important, certainly they may be better achieved and evaluated given desirable circumstances and adequate support.

ORGANIZING AROUND SPECIAL NEEDS

It is possible and in many cases desirable to organize the guidance program around special needs, such as those for prevocational exploration, education related to sex, drugs, alcohol, or tobacco, or interethnic or interracial communication.

THE NEED FOR VOCATIONAL EXPLORATION

The guidance program in the school setting in a low socioeconomic environment where there are large numbers of unemployed parents and families on welfare might well place considerable focus on prevocational exploration. Every effort might be made to help children to develop the concept that the world does have a place for them, that they can succeed vocationally at least to the extent of providing for themselves, and that if they should find that impossible, assistance may be obtained. Exploration of the work done by their neighbors and parents, and explorations into other possible avenues may build healthy and desirable work attitudes.

THE NEED FOR EXPLORATION INVOLVING SEX, DRUGS, ALCOHOL, OR TOBACCO

Many guidance programs, because of criticisms through newspapers and other media, avoid the areas of sex and drug education, and some avoid considering alcohol and tobacco. There is some logic in avoiding areas that arouse controversy, especially where the guidance program is on shaky grounds in its early development stage. Yet guidance must function in the real world, dealing with the genuine problems and concerns of children. These issues are relevant and worthwhile and affect the emotional lives of many children; however, they could easily absorb a disproportionately large measure of the counselor's time. The individual counselor must decide whether or not he will engage himself in one or more of these concerns based on the children's needs he perceives in his school setting.

For the individual who does decide to involve himself, four suggestions seem appropriate:

1. The counselor or teacher should make certain that his actions in areas of controversy have administrative awareness and support.
2. Such concerns should be handled, if possible, so that the counselor's effectiveness is not impaired by his association with them. For example, if the counselor is involved in the drug problem or sex education, he may seek to invite respected authorities to work either with teachers or directly with children.
3. Such concerns should not occupy so much time that the counselor can no longer meet the needs of individual children, whether or not they are affected by the specific problem.
4. Beyond any general presentation, the discussion of such topics should involve primarily those children concerned. The counselor should demonstrate willingness to engage in follow-up discussions on an individual basis or with small groups of concerned children, preferably as a result of self-referral.

Unquestionably the counselor has a responsibility to children in need when the focus of their need is a matter of controversy. Unquestionably also, the counselor who sees need for general exploration in the school regarding sex education or information involving drugs, alcohol, or tobacco has a responsibility to request development of such a program. However, until or unless his education clearly makes him the most appropriate individual to convey such information and until or unless he makes a commitment to engage in an activity that many consider to be curricular in nature, it remains his personal decision whether or not he will immerse himself in coping with one or another of these special needs.

ORGANIZING FOR RACIAL AND ETHNIC IMPACT

When a counselor or teacher functions in a mixed racial or mixed ethnic setting, he may well bear a responsibility to make some effort for intergroup communication. Especially in areas in which sudden population changes are occurring and in areas in which court-ordered integration is being instituted, it seems quite necessary for the counselor or teacher to become involved. It may be less crucial but equally appropriate for the counselor or teacher who functions with, say, an all-white, all-black, all-Chicano, all-Lutheran, or all-Catholic population to accept some responsibility regarding interracial and/or interethnic communication for his constituents.

Perhaps the first step in taking responsibility is self-examination. Prejudices, patronizing attitudes, expectations of superior or inferior performance are often subtle, yet obvious to children. The counselor or teacher who finds he cannot see the personal worth and the positive potential of a given group of children probably should not be working with children at all, but certainly he should not put himself in the position of trying to open communication lines between groups—at least not until he has sought genuine and extensive communication himself with the group or groups of which he is not a member. Among the attitudes that need to be developed, Siegel[21] points out, great stress should be placed upon developing a view of members of a cultural, racial, or ethnic minority as individuals.

Williams and Byars warn that sudden changes in attitudes and achievement of minority youth should not be expected: "Teachers and counselors in integrated schools should not assume that integration will magically ameliorate all the self-doubt and self-hate produced by years of racial discrimination. It may be extremely difficult to upgrade the academic achievement of the disadvantaged Negro child without first providing an atmosphere in which the child can more fully discover and respect himself. The problem is of such a magnitude as to warrant a concerted attempt to train prospective teachers and counselors in the mechanics of self-theory and methodology of changing self-esteem."[22] Just as the child of a minority group will change slowly, the majority group needs to be exposed to sustained efforts over long periods of time designed to develop positive attitudes.

[21] Betty Siegel, "Counseling the color conscious," *School Counselor, 17:* 169–170 (1970).

[22] Robert L. Williams and Harry Byars, "Negro self esteem in a transitional society," *Personnel and Guidance Journal, 47:* 124 (1968).

The ideas presented below, drawn basically from three "Issues and Dialogue" columns in *Elementary School Guidance and Counseling*,[23,24,25] are some concrete suggestions of activities designed to promote racial and ethnic communication. For fuller exploration the reader is directed to the articles themselves.

In a school in which integration is about to occur, a guidance committee could plan a program for attitudinal development. Films and filmstrips may or may not be used, but the focus should be on discussion to develop understanding, to anticipate problems, to handle introductions, to smooth difficult moments.

Interschool visits prior to integration could be beneficially arranged. Exchange ideas (see below) could be utilized.

In schools with a limited racial or ethnic mix an exchange program with another school could be instituted, including art work, musical programs, compositions, and exchange visits.

Exploration of the music, dancing, and related artistry and handicrafts of minority groups could be helpful in developing positive attitudes.

Some curricular attention could be given in any educational setting to heroes and contributors to our culture from minority groups.

Efforts could be made to interpret history of this country in terms of its meaning to minority groups: westward expansion and the Indian; why Mexicans remember the Alamo; slavery as a historical tragedy; paternalism and womanhood; religious freedom and persecution; limitations on career development of minority-group members.

Within the multiracial, multiethnic classroom, every attempt could be made to distribute helping tasks and rewards on a rotating basis; otherwise race, color, religion, brightness and cooperativeness may be too influential in the assigning of tasks.

Another direction within the classroom could be experimentation with the feelings of prejudice—for example, excluding all children with blue eyes or freckles from oral participation for a half day. The ensuing discussion of the feelings engendered could be extremely valuable.

[23] Richard C. Nelson, Maryruth K. Nivens, and Helen D. Smith, "The individual and racial understanding," *Elementary School Guidance and Counseling, 4:* 142–145 (1969).

[24] Richard C. Nelson, Helen D. Smith, and Maryruth K. Nivens, "The group and racial understanding," *Elementary School Guidance and Counseling, 4:* 211–214 (1970).

[25] Richard C. Nelson, Marjorie Kinnan, and Doris Jefferies, "Racial understanding revisited," *Elementary School Guidance and Counseling, 5:* 59–63 (1970).

Where there is conflict between or among ethnic or racial groups, the parties to the conflict could be brought together to talk out their differences and to work through their difficulties.

On an individual basis such evidences of outreach as a smile, a gentle touch, a kindly word of praise or positive expectation could well do more than all other measures to convey a sense of caring to the child, whether he is of a minority group or not.

Another powerful demonstration of personal outreach is the valuing of a child for what is unique in him, perhaps his way of standing up for his rights, perhaps the way in which he throws himself into an activity, or perhaps his independence. These are traits that are valuable, but that seem seldom to be reinforced in the school setting.

Much can be done to develop communication among various racial and ethnic groups; the ideas listed above are but a sampling. Certainly the minority-group members' perceptions of the guidance program need to be positive perceptions based on genuine exchanges initiated by counselors and concerned teachers and developed out of well-considered attempts to build communication. Russell[26] indicates that the image the black student in particular has of guidance in the secondary school has been created by counselors and must be changed by counselors. One may hypothesize that there are fewer negative images to contend with and that image change is more readily secured in the elementary school—if counselors and teachers make efforts to create genuine interaction and communication opportunities.

SUMMARY

The organization of the guidance program is shaped by the strategy adopted by the teachers and the counselor; its impact depends partly on the decision of those involved whether or not to function as change agents. Additional factors that affect the impact of the guidance program include the extent to which the program is based on awareness of existing services; the degree to which the program is based upon needs of children; whether the program reaches beyond office and classroom confines; the willingness of those involved to incorporate unique and innovative activities; and the courage possessed by the organizers to involve children in decision making and to examine the school and classroom climate.

The guidance program should be organized so as to achieve maximum involvement of administrative leaders, of teachers, of students, of parents and community members, and of support personnel. In a true

[26] R. D. Russell, "Black perceptions of guidance," *Personnel and Guidance Journal, 48:* 721–728 (1970).

sense the guidance program depends heavily on extensive involvement both as a public relations measure and as a means of mobilizing the best help for children. Further, the guidance program should be organized so that outcomes may be ascertained; this requires research, assessment, record keeping, and data collection. Organizing for effectiveness also requires that the guidance office or suite be located near the center of action in the school, and that adequate facilities, a reasonable budget, and clerical assistance be provided.

School guidance programs may be organized on still another basis —to meet special needs: examples include vocational exploration; sex, drugs, alcohol, tobacco; and racial and ethnic communication.

Clearly the outcomes achieved by a guidance program will in large measure be based on the extent to which they are sought through organization.

REFERENCES

American Personnel and Guidance Association, Professional Preparation and Standards Committee. "Support personnel for the counselor: their technical and non-technical roles and preparation," *Personnel and Guidance Journal*, *45:* 857–861 (1967).

Arbuckle, D. S. "Does the school really need counselors?" *School Counselor*, *17:* 325–330 (1970).

Aubrey, R. F. "The legitimacy of elementary school counseling: some unresolved issues and conflicts," *Personnel and Guidance Journal*, *46:* 355–359 (1967).

Carey, R. W. "Student protest and the counselor," *Personnel and Guidance Journal*, *48:* 185–191 (1969).

Dinkmeyer, D. C., and C. E. Caldwell. *Developmental Counseling and Guidance: A Comprehensive School Approach*. New York: McGraw-Hill, 1970.

Faust, V. *Establishing Guidance Programs in Elementary Schools*. Guidance Monograph Series, Boston: Houghton Mifflin, 1968.

Festinger, L. *A Theory of Cognitive Dissonance*. New York: Harper & Row, 1957.

Frost, J. A., and J. M. Frost. "An evolving elementary school guidance program and on-going research projects," *Elementary School Guidance and Counseling*, *2:* 121–126 (1967).

Gelatt, H. B. "School guidance programs," *Review of Educational Research*, *39:* 140–153 (1969).

Goldman, L. "IRCOPPS: a report of progress," *Personnel and Guidance Journal*, *45:* 402–406 (1966).

"Guidance Assistants Project: A Summary Report." Deerfield, Ill., 1968. (Mimeographed.)

Hill, G. E., and E. B. Luckey. *Guidance for Children in Elementary Schools*. New York: Appleton-Century-Crofts, 1969.

————. *Staffing Guidance Programs.* Guidance Monograph Series, Boston: Houghton Mifflin, 1968.

————. "Agreements in the practice of guidance in the elementary schools," *Elementary School Guidance and Counseling, 1:* 188–195 (1967).

Hoyt, K. B. "What the school has a right to expect of its counselor," *Personnel and Guidance Journal, 40:* 129–133 (1961).

Jaffe, A., and A. Reed. "Involving the turned-on generation through structured rapping," *Personnel and Guidance Journal, 48:* 311–315 (1969).

Kaplan, B. A. "The new counselor and his professional problems," *Personnel and Guidance Journal, 42:* 473–478 (1964).

Koeppe, R. P. "Issues in initiating the services of an elementary school counselor," *Elementary School Guidance and Counseling, 1:* 41–46 (1967).

Lorimer, J., and J. Haddad. "Pupil personnel services in the elementary school," *Personnel and Guidance Journal, 47:* 975–978 (1969).

McCreary, W. H., and G. Miller. "Elementary school counselors in California," *Personnel and Guidance Journal, 44:* 494–498 (1966).

McDougall, W. P., and H. M. Reitan. "The elementary counselor as perceived by elementary principals," *Personnel and Guidance Journal, 42:* 348–354 (1963).

Meeks, A. R. *Guidance in Elementary Education.* New York: Ronald, 1968.

Moon, M., and D. Wilson. "Teacher-counselor cooperation: building self-concepts and confidence in children," *School Counselor, 17:* 364–366 (1970).

Myrick, R. D., and W. Haldin. "Making room for an elementary school counselor," *Elementary School Guidance and Counseling, 4:* 281–286 (1970).

Nelson, R. C., and G. O'Connor, "A pre-kindergarten program with children and their parents, *Elementary School Guidance and Counseling, 5:* 135–139 (1970).

————, M. Kinnan, and D. Jefferies. "Racial understanding revisited," *Elementary School Guidance and Counseling, 5:* 59–63 (1970).

————, H. D. Smith, and M. K. Nivens. "The group and racial understanding," *Elementary School Guidance and Counseling, 4:* 211–214 (1970).

————, M. K. Nivens, and H. D. Smith. "The individual and racial understanding," *Elementary School Guidance and Counseling, 4:* 142–145 (1969).

————. "Record keeping in elementary school guidance," *Elementary School Guidance and Counseling, 3:* 126–130 (1968).

————. "Support personnel in elementary school guidance," *Elementary School Guidance and Counseling, 2:* 303–307 (1968).

————. "Physical facilities for elementary school counseling," *Personnel and Guidance Journal, 45:* 552–556 (1967).

Oldridge, B. "Two roles for elementary school guidance personnel," *Personnel and Guidance Journal, 43:* 367–370 (1964).

Peters, H. J., B. Shertzer, and W. Van Hoose. *Guidance in Elementary Schools.* Skokie, Ill.: Rand McNally, 1965.

Reinhertz, H., and C. L. Griffin. "The second time around: achievement and progress of boys who repeated one of the first three grades," *School Counselor, 17:* 213–218 (1970).

Russell, R. D. "Black perceptions of guidance," *Personnel and Guidance Journal, 48:* 721–728 (1970).

Siegel, B. "Counseling the color conscious," *School Counselor, 17:* 169–170 (1970).

Stone, S. C., and B. Shertzer. "The militant counselor," *Personnel and Guidance Journal, 42:* 342–347 (1963).

Strowig, R. W., and S. E. Sheets. "Student perception of counselor role," *Personnel and Guidance Journal, 45:* 926–931 (1967).

Vance, B. "The counselor—an agent of what change?" *Personnel and Guidance Journal, 45:* 1012–1016 (1967).

Vontress, C. E. "Cultural barriers in the counseling relationship," *Personnel and Guidance Journal, 48:* 11–17 (1969).

Walz, G., and J. Miller. "School climates and student behavior: implications for counselor role," *Personnel and Guidance Journal, 47:* 859–867 (1969).

Williams, R. L., and H. Byars. "Negro self esteem in a transitional society," *Personnel and Guidance Journal, 47:* 120–125 (1968).

ARTICLES IN BOOKS OF READINGS

Dinkmeyer, D. C. *Guidance and Counseling in the Elementary School: Readings in Theory and Practice.* New York: Holt, Rinehart and Winston, Inc., 1968. Readings beginning on pages 40, 54, 64, 71.

Koplitz, E. D. *Guidance in the Elementary School: Theory, Research and Practice.* Dubuque, Iowa: William C. Brown Company, Publisher, 1968. Readings beginning on pages 49, 86, 262.

Mills, G. D. *Elementary School Guidance and Counseling.* New York: Random House, Inc., 1971. Readings beginning on pages 219, 226, 263, 286.

Peters, H. J., A. C. Riccio, and J. J. Quaranta. *Guidance in the Elementary School: A Book of Readings.* New York: Macmillan, 1963. Readings beginning on pages 159, 247, 258, 266.

14

Counselor Selection and Education

How can a child be properly educated by one who has not been properly educated himself? But where is such an extraordinary mortal to be found?

JEAN JACQUES ROUSSEAU: *Emile*

If genuineness, self-actualization, and personal meaningfulness are object-tives for counseling, they are also objectives for counselors as persons. While we cannot expect to locate or educate large numbers of "extraor-dinary mortals," we may be able to help ordinary mortals to achieve an extraordinary portion of genuineness in themselves, and meaningfulness and self-actualization in their lives. The typical pattern of random admission to counselor education programs and superficial course-to-course involve-ment seems almost antithetical to those objectives, though there do seem to be some real attempts at improvement. The improvement appears to depend largely on program flexibility and on selection that is related to projected outcomes.

This chapter deals with the selection of counselor education candidates, counselor preparation programs, the continued growth of the counselor, and counselor certification.

SELECTION OF COUNSELOR EDUCATION CANDIDATES

Counselor education candidates cannot realistically be expected to be paragons of virtue, above every temptation, and without flaws. They do need to be relatively stable, secure individuals who embody qualities of warmth, genuineness, openness, and sensitivity to others—and in whom these qualities may be developed. Unfortunately, we cannot measure these characteristics with much confidence. Nonetheless, since many sources have recommended personal attributes for the counselor, it seems appropriate to consider them.

PERSONAL ATTRIBUTES

The 1966 ACES-ASCA (Association for Counselor Education and Supervision-American School Counselors Association) Report[1] suggested that the counselor needs these personal qualifications:

Courage to bring about change
Valuing of individuals
Initiative
Sensitivity to the feelings of children and adults
Academic ability
· Emotional stability
Competence in human relations
Depth and variety of interests

Dimick and Huff suggest that the counselor should become a model: "The counselor who is willing to unstintingly share himself with others and who is willing to let himself be known is one who can foster similar behavior in others by his own behavior."[2] Such an expectation implies a selection criterion: can the counselor candidate be expected to function as a model?

Whether providing a model or demonstrating openness or sensitivity is taken as a criterion, measures would be desirable to help us distinguish the potentially effective from the potentially ineffective counselor. While McDaniel[3] concluded that instruments are of limited value in counselor selection, and Danielson[4] found no evidence of a distinct elementary school counselor personality, Jansen, Robb, and Bonk[5] found

---

[1] ACES-ASCA Joint Committee on the Elementary School Counselor, "Report (Tentative)," *Personnel and Guidance Journal, 44:* 658–661 (1966).

[2] Kenneth M. Dimick and Vaughn E. Huff, *Child Counseling* (Dubuque, Iowa: William C. Brown Company, Publisher, 1970), p. 210.

[3] Sarah W. McDaniel, "Counselor selection: an evaluation of instruments," *Counselor Education and Supervision, 6:* 142–144 (1967).

[4] Harry A. Danielson, "Personality of prospective elementary school counselors: implications for preparation," *Counselor Education and Supervision, 8:* 99–103 (1969).

[5] David G. Jansen, George P. Robb, and Edward C. Bonk, "Characteristics of high-rated and low-rated master's degree candidates in counseling and guidance," *Counselor Education and Supervision, 9:* 162–170 (1970).

differences between high- and low-rated master's degree candidates that suggest potential selection factors. Counselors who were rated higher by an instructor in an evaluation seminar in knowledge of counseling theory, knowledge and use of test data, and counseling skill, were younger and more intelligent, were more sociable, stable, and less ego-involved (more objective) according to scores on the Guilford-Zimmerman Temperament survey, and were more open and permissive according to scores on the Minnesota Teacher Attitude Inventory. The replication of such a study is made especially difficult by the inclusion of instructor judgment; nonetheless, it suggests that the counselor selection process may be enhanced by the use of measures such as those suggested above, and by the development of even more specific measures.

Shertzer and Stone[6] observe that selection research findings are generally inconclusive and often conflicting. Certainly continued research effort in this direction is needed.

TEACHING EXPERIENCE

The question of teaching experience as a selection factor relevant to the elementary school counselor is a real "can of worms." On the one hand, it is often a necessity for certification, teachers and often counselors themselves consider it essential, and the basic pool of counselors comes largely through the ranks of teachers. On the other hand, certification laws are subject to change, many counselors and counselor educators quarrel with the validity of the requirement, and it may be argued that softening this regulation would afford a larger pool from which counselors might be selected.

Arguments favoring the teaching requirement have been summarized by Ricker:[7] (1) the counselor who has taught has shown a commitment to education, (2) the fact that the counselor has taught facilitates his acceptance by the faculty, and (3) the counselor who has taught understands better the teacher-student relationship. Wilson[8] has confirmed that a sample of teachers and counselors favor the experience requirement.

The counselor does indeed need sensitivity to the problems of the teacher and awareness of the practical difficulties that may emerge in the pupil-teacher relationship. However, alternative plans for developing this sensitivity and awareness are both possible and necessary. One reason for

[6] Bruce Shertzer and Shelley C. Stone, *Fundamentals of Guidance* (Boston: Houghton Mifflin, 1966).

[7] George A. Ricker, "Must counselors have taught?" *School Counselor, 17:* 40–46 (1969).

[8] Lynn E. Wilson, "Teaching experience: counselor and teacher opinions," *Counselor Education and Supervision, 8:* 148–150 (1969).

alternative procedures is suggested by Huff[9] in a dialogue that should be read by those who support the teaching requirement. His point is that other professions do not require entry into another field before one can enter his chosen field. The awareness of such a barrier may drive many capable individuals from the ranks of counseling, since so many years are consumed in preparation for teaching, obtaining teaching experience, getting counselor training, and meeting the advanced certification requirement imposed by many states.

A second point is that some demands of teaching may build habits that are antithetical to a number of philosophical counseling positions. For example, the teacher is expected to provide structure, his authority may be shared, but it must be present, his style may well be one in which he is a presenter and questioner, and he has a clear evaluative mandate. None of these descriptions may fit the counselor. A third reason for considering alternatives to teaching experience is offered by Gazda *et al.*,[10] who noted that those who question the teaching requirement have at least as much evidence to support their hypothesis as do those who point to surveys of administrators or allege that counselors who have teaching experience "get along better" with school personnel. Peterson and Brown[11] studied counselor self-reports and concluded that matched pairs of counselors who had and who had not taught experienced significant differences in acceptance favoring teaching, but that those differences had largely disappeared in eight weeks.

Because so much heat is generated over this issue, any alternative to the teaching requirement must be designed so as to orient the prospective counselor thoroughly to the total school setting. Certainly the internship in counseling should be considered an alternative to teaching; and certainly this is a viable and reasonable alternative if well organized for exposure to the total school environment. Ricker[12] suggested that unexperienced counselors-in-training intern for part of a year with a master teacher and for part of a year with a master counselor. As another alternative, the counselor-in-training could function as a teacher aide for a half year (or semester) and finish out the term as a counselor aide or intern. Because of the dearth of definitive research data in this direction, this remains a fruitful field for experimentation and research. With the coopera-

[9] Vaughn E. Huff, "The millstone of teaching experience," *Personnel and Guidance Journal, 44:* 192–194 (1965).

[10] George M. Gazda, H. M. Clements, J. A. Duncan, and C. L. Martin, "Response sets of neophyte counselors," *Counselor Education and Supervision, 6:* 151–156 (1967).

[11] Bettie H. Peterson and Duane Brown, "Does teaching experience matter?" *Personnel and Guidance Journal, 46:* 893–897 (1968).

[12] Ricker, *op. cit.*

tion of school districts and certification officers, comparative studies of experienced counselors with and without teaching experience may help to clarify the facts of the matter. As Brown and Peterson point out: "The school counseling profession finds itself in the awkward position of having a requirement which it cannot defend or attack on any but emotional grounds. The resolution of this dilemma should be a major goal of the profession."[13]

SELECTION FOR OUTCOMES

Not much research exists to shed light on the matter of selection criteria. One interesting area of exploration—a direction for future research —has been implied by Danielson.[14] Can the profession specify outcomes sought and select and train prospective counselors so as to achieve those outcomes? Danielson looked at personality profiles of elementary school counselors and concluded that their patterns of needs appeared to be compatible with personal counseling objectives. However, their patterns seemed to be incompatible with responsibilities demanding dynamic group leadership or requiring skillful staff and curriculum management in the interests of children. Thus, the counselors surveyed seemed better equipped for individual counseling than for group work, consulting, or developing of intergroup relations. This suggests that there may be a personality profile that would suit the client-centered counselor, another that might suit the behaviorist, a third for the existentialist, and so on. Until the returns are in, however, perhaps at least the counseling style promoted in a given counselor education program and the personality of the individual might be examined for their congruence.

The selection problem is further complicated by another factor: the outcomes sought by the administrator and the community may well be discordant with the personal style of the counselor or the style promoted in the counselor education program. Johnston[15] found that there was no significant relationship, for example, between practicum grades and administrator evaluations of counselors.

At the very least, these disparities suggest needs for (1) greater agreement on the goals and purposes of counseling and (2) research on counselor selection and outcomes. Further, for the individual interested in counselor preparation, there is a need for self-examination, for program

---

[13] Duane Brown and Bettie H. Peterson, "The teaching experience prerequisite for the school counselor: an examination," *School Counselor, 16:* 20 (1968).

[14] Harry A. Danielson, "Personality of prospective elementary school counselors: implications for preparation?" *Counselor Education and Supervision, 8:* 99–103 (1969).

[15] Joseph A. Johnston, "Practicum and on-the-job ratings of school counselors," *Personnel and Guidance Journal, 45:* 16–19 (1966).

examination, and for examination of job expectations to clarify whether there is sufficient agreement among objectives.

THE SELECTION PROCESS

The standard process by which counselors apply and are selected to participate in a counselor education program involves a paper application, evidence of academic competence submitted in the form of graduate and/or undergraduate transcripts and test results, references attesting to the competence of the individual to undertake graduate study, and, where possible an interview. Generally the most discriminating device is that of undergraduate grades. Dimick and Huff[16] have offered some suggestions for improving upon these limited samplings: (1) relationship qualities should be assessed, perhaps through psychological measures, through depth interviews with close associates, through arrangements for trained raters to observe potential candidates in an ongoing T-group setting, or through feedback from children who have worked with the individual for an hour or so in a specific situation; (2) assessment should be made of the curiosity and originality of counselor candidates through testing or by setting up situations that place some demands upon these qualities; and (3) cognitive flexibility and psychological openness should be assessed through paper-and-pencil devices and simulated counseling situations. Certainly these suggestions would move the counselor selection process well beyond the present state of the art.

Assessed along with the abilities suggested above might be competence in expression, both written and oral. The counselor is a public relations man, at least for his own program. He must be capable of articulating his ideas—about counseling, himself, his experiences, and his value system. It does the counseling profession little credit to be represented by inarticulate individuals—and the preparation program cannot reasonably be expected to fill this need. Thus, it is a selection concern.

The shortage of staff time for more complex selection processes can be alleviated by broadening of the staff concept. Graduate students would doubtless be gratified to have the opportunity and to be trusted to advise the faculty in such matters. A student assigned to conduct an interviewee through the interview and experiential process and to act as host on campus would be in an ideal position to collect opinions of children and others, to assess nonintellective factors, and to make recommendations to the faculty selection committee. While those who guide each counselor education program must consider its own capacity and philosophy in developing selection procedures, certainly many universities and colleges involved in counselor preparation can greatly improve the implementation of their philosophy in the selection process.

16 Dimick and Huff, *loc. cit.*

COUNSELOR PREPARATION PROGRAMS

The outcome sought in counselor preparation is an individual who is genuine and self-actualized, who lives a meaningful life, who can be a stable, warm and secure, yet challenging force in the lives of children, and who is well informed about children, their needs, and ways of producing change in their lives. To insure some of these attributes, selection factors must be relied upon; for others, course work may help; for still others, self-examination experiences seem necessary. Counselor education programs that offer none but didactic experiences place too much reliance on fortuitous selection and accept too little responsibility for producing growth in the counselor as a person. Unfortunately, this description appears to apply to a high percentage of programs.

Through experimental programs and through federally funded institutes and workshops, counselor educators have had opportunities to develop creative models that do not place total dependence on standard course programs, but that rely extensively on integrated group experiences focused simultaneously on intellectual growth and personal awareness. Yet, certification and university requirements continue to function as barriers to creative programs. The prospective counselor-in-training should be as much concerned with how his program will be structured and how nonintellective factors will be considered in it as with the credits he will accumulate. Counselor educators should strive in every way to incorporate into their standard programs the style sampled through institute and experimental programs. In sum, this is a challenge to make counselor education programs more personally relevant than the counselor-trainee now finds them.

Ohlsen[17] states this challenge in terms of objectives, seeing the following as essential:

1. Increased knowledge of human behavior; techniques of appraisal of the impact of the home and school upon the child; counseling theories and practices; research literature about elementary school counseling, child development, and learning; and assistance in applying this knowledge in implementing his role as an elementary school counselor.
2. Assistance in gaining self-understanding, utilizing his strengths, and correcting or compensating for weaknesses that may interfere with his effectiveness.
3. Increased understanding relative to counselor ethics.

[17] Merle M. Ohlsen, "An appraisal of a program for the professional preparation of elementary school counselors," *Elementary School Guidance and Counseling, 2:* 15–32 (1967).

4. Increased competency in helping teachers to identify and describe the children with whom they wish assistance and to discuss the feelings that are engendered by these pupils.

5. Improved competency in using test and nontest data with teachers so that children are better understood and with children so that they better understand themselves.

6. Increased knowledge of guidance services so that the counselor may make appropriate selections and may assist his teaching colleagues to become effective in their involvement in guidance.

7. Assistance in recognizing and developing the counselor's own professional leadership potential.

8. Assistance in applying his knowledge of research methodology and statistics so that he may understand and conduct guidance evaluation and research.

The counselor education program should have at least three foci: (1) the counselor as a person, (2) the child, and (3) counseling and supportive services. Roach and Wehrly[18] call for distinguishing this program from the secondary school counselor education program; Meeks[19] suggests it be focused on counselor competencies; and Eckerson suggests it be focused on the counselor as a catalyst for change. She states: "The elementary school counselor working as a catalyst for change could have profound influences on education that must not fail—as it has consistently done in the past—to build positive self-concepts in all children, especially slow learners."[20]

Thus, the breadth of the challenge is great, and the number of considerations to be included make a two-year counselor preparation program a necessity. The American Personnel and Guidance Association has long recognized this need, and gradually counselor certification requirements are being updated to demand the two years of preparation.

PROGRAM INCLUSIONS

Nelson, looking at the design of counselor education programs, has listed thirty-five kinds of learning—intended as courses and portions of courses:

Definition of guidance
The development of the guidance movement
The helping relationship

[18] A. J. Roach and B. L. Wehrly, "Differentiated preparation for elementary school counselors," *Counselor Education and Supervision, 9:* 220–221 (1970).

[19] Anna R. Meeks, *Guidance in Elementary Education* (New York: Ronald, 1968).

[20] Louise O. Eckerson, "In support of a loosely defined role for the elementary school counselor," *Elementary School Guidance and Counseling, 4:* 85 (1969).

Ethical considerations in guidance and counseling
The child and mental health
The child and his self-concept
Family pressures and guidance
Societal pressures and guidance
Educational pressures and guidance
Understanding behavior dynamics and purposes
Role of the elementary school counselor
Theories of counseling
Implications of counseling theories for elementary school students
Techniques in counseling elementary school children
Facilitating verbalization with young children in counseling
Implications of play in counseling young children
Counseling with play media
Group guidance procedures
Group counseling with children
Supervised counseling with elementary school children
Consulting with parents, teachers, and others
The elementary school-aged child
Child development
Individual appraisal
Tests and measurement
Identification of children with special problems
The curriculum and guidance
Learning theory
Vocational and educational understandings for elementary school children
Application of vocational development theory for children
Community resources
Referral resources
Facilities necessary for the elementary school guidance program
Trends in elementary school guidance
Research in elementary school guidance and counseling[21]

There are, of course, a great many ways in which the above topical inclusions may be implemented. Based on a survey of needs perceived by teachers and principals, Muro and Oelke[22] have proposed the following course titles:

Principles and Techniques of Guidance
Introduction to School Guidance Services
Group Guidance
Educational and Occupational Information

[21] Richard C. Nelson, "The preparation of elementary school counselors: a model," *Counselor Education and Supervision, 6:* 199 (1967).
[22] James J. Muro and Merritt C. Oelke, "Guidance needs in the elementary school—cue to the preparation of counselors," *Counselor Education and Supervision 7:* 7–12 (1967).

Introduction to Counseling
Group Counseling
Counseling Practicum
Individual Appraisal
Psychology of the Retarded Child
Psychology of the Exceptional Child
Psychology of Childhood
Psychology of Learning
Behavior in Children
Planning the Elementary School Curriculum
Elementary School Administration
School and Community
Graduate Internship or Graduate Apprentice Teaching
Methods of Research
Descriptive and Inferential Statistics

The Muro-Oelke program obviously could not be compressed into a single year of college or university work, but would offer much direction for a two-year program. Some course areas might be combined, and a course in consulting with parents and teachers, for example, might be added in many programs, along with work in mental hygiene or child development. Certainly each state and counselor preparation program, if it is to be creatively designed, needs flexibility to meet needs and set directions of its own. Thus, program conceptualizations such as those discussed above should be considered primarily as points of departure.

EXPERIENCE IN COUNSELING

The importance of experience in counseling makes worthwhile a few suggestions about the design of the counselor education program.

Experience in counseling is advantageously incorporated early and intermittently or continuously throughout the counselor education program through prepracticum, through experiences involved in course work, through practicum, and through the counseling internship.

Experience with children using scheduled interviews and brief get-acquainted interviews should gradually give way to actual counseling experiences.

Direct experience with children is advantageously supplemented by a variety of simulation and micro-counseling opportunities giving the counselor opportunities to encounter a variety of children's concerns and styles of functioning.

Counseling experience should provide opportunities for the counselor to try out new behaviors so that he is not limited to habitual patterns of interaction.

Where at all feasible, opportunities for counseling experience and simulation should take place in blocks of time especially designed to remove the teacher or other employed person psychologically from his employment responsibilities.

Counseling experience is advantageously organized if it provides simultaneous opportunities for genuine self-examination and examination of the counselor's emerging personal counseling style. Counseling experience at least in part is advantageously scheduled in a school setting in which extensive use is made of videotaping; this gives the counselor extensive reality-checking opportunity and places a minimal demand upon the counseled child to adapt to a new environment.

The extent of the counseling experience is advantageously designed to be both intensive and extensive: intensive in that it affords the counselor-trainee much opportunity to function in a counseling capacity and to develop a personal counseling style, and extensive in that it affords experience under supervision in group counseling and in consulting with parents and teachers, particularly where this may be relevant to the needs of the individual child in counseling.

Aubrey[23] suggests several ways in which the off-campus practicum experience may be made meaningful. Included are specific designs for the orientation of the counselor; ways in which the first week might be spent—exploring, visiting, meeting children and teachers, and looking over records; ways in which the second week might best involve the counselor-trainee in counseling with children under supervision; and bases for periodic reevaluation of the counseling experience. In addition, among his several organizational suggestions he includes: focus on one student for an intensive case study; involvement of the counselor in staff, teacher, and parent conferences; scheduling of full-time experience where possible; integral involvement of the school and university supervisor in the planning and development of the practicum; heavy reliance on observation and taping; weekly seminar on campus; and the utilization of some aspect of the practicum experience as a research project.

Further exploration of the counseling practicum has been provided by Haseley and Peters[24] as well as others, and the use of simulation experiences has been discussed by several writers including Delaney.[25] Suffice it to say here that the cumulative effect of all counseling experiences

[23] Roger F. Aubrey, "Elementary school counseling practicum: some suggestions for experiences and expectations," *Counselor Education and Supervision, 7:* 13–19 (1967).

[24] Luther L. Haseley and Herman J. Peters, "Practicum: on-campus and off-campus," *Counselor Education and Supervision, 5:* 141–147 (1966).

[25] Daniel J. Delaney, "Simulation techniques in counselor education: proposal of a unique approach," *Counselor Education and Supervision, 8:* 183–188 (1969).

in the counselor education program—the prepracticum, the experiential aspects of counseling courses, the practicum, and the internship—should be designed to provide extensive opportunities for the counselor to gain some experience of himself as counselor and to develop his counseling style.

SELF-EXPLORATION EXPERIENCES

There are several ways of meeting the need of the counselor-in-training for self-exploration experiences. From time to time at Purdue University, for example, we have used various combinations of the following procedures.

> Individual counseling
> Small-group work—process groups—meeting over the period of a semester or a year
> Involvement in self-examination in conjunction with the Group Procedures course
> Weekend retreats or workshops using Encountertapes or related procedures

The position taken here is that, among educational experiences for counselors, self-exploration is equally as important as didactic experiences and counseling practice experiences.

Accent in this exploration may suitably be upon discovering strengths, emphasizing growth, and providing positive experiences. Dimick and Huff[26] suggest that "basic growth groups" of ten to fifteen persons be organized; that members of these groups share a learning context; that they meet to develop their effectiveness in interpersonal relationships; that with the support and encouragement of the group they emphasize development of new ways of behaving; and that they consider as objectives the achievement of greater trust, greater capacity to love and to accept love, greater empathy, greater congruence, and greater interdependence.

The counselor who has experience in the joys of self-discovery, and of being valued for himself, is much more capable of aiding children to experience these same joys, to develop their own sense of meaning, and to appreciate or develop their own genuineness as persons. It is self-evident that the kind of education that leads to such self-discovery and growth does not, or should not, terminate with formal counselor training.

THE CONTINUED GROWTH OF THE COUNSELOR

Exploration of counseling and guidance content, supervised counseling, and self-exploration are important both to the introductory

[26] Dimick and Huff, *op. cit.,* pp. 226–231.

education of the counselor and to his continued growth. The responsibility for growth beyond the counselor education program should be assumed by the individual himself, by the corporation for which he is employed, and by the university or college that educated him—or which functions in his vicinity. Hill[27] extends this listing to include everyone in the school and in the community. Unfortunately, this multiple division of responsibility too often results in little or no action.

The individual counselor may continue to grow by subscribing to and reading literature in his own and closely related fields. He may become active in national, area, statewide, and in-state counseling organizations, demanding of himself and others intensive, relevant participation. He may bring together small groups of counselors, either within or beyond his employing school corporation, for the discussion of literature, the mutual discussion of counseling audiotapes and of counseling problems, or further self-exploration. He may write up and share with other counselors his procedures and his practices, subjecting them to the critical review of his peers, and contributing them to the professional literature in appropriate form. He may offer or agree to participate with counselor trainers, supervisors, or other counselors in appropriate research activities—or he may initiate such activities and seek help in their execution where necessary. He may seek consultation with psychologists, social workers and other appropriate resource persons within and beyond the employ of his school corporation to obtain help and to contribute to others in intellectual development, in working to increase counseling effectiveness, and in self-exploration. The counselor is, in a real sense, limited only by his own motivation in continuing his growth.

Officials in the school corporation can contribute to the counselor's continued growth by facilitating, encouraging, or providing for some of the experiences described below. Certainly counselors and the appropriate officials (e.g., director of counseling services, supervisor or assistant superintendent for pupil personnel) should participate jointly in planning the counselor's in-service education and development. Counselor needs may also be met within the corporation through case conferences involving appropriate individuals, and through the focusing of conferences, workshops, or resource persons on particular ways in which the counseling and guidance program might develop. Continued counselor growth may also be stimulated through the use of videotaping. Examining his counseling by himself, with other counselors, with a guidance director or supervisor, or with a resource person can contribute both to counseling effectiveness and to personal growth.

Counselor effectiveness is much more a process than an achieve-

---

[27] George E. Hill, *Staffing Guidance Programs* (Guidance Monograph Series, Boston: Houghton Mifflin, 1968), chap. 4, "Staff Induction and Growth in Service."

ment at a point in time. Although many school corporations make no provision for it, the continued growth of the counselor is essential to his continued effectiveness. The school corporation may contribute to this goal of continued growth basically to the extent the goal is valued.

Counselor educators should share some responsibility for the continued development of counselors in their vicinity. The provision of night and summer courses may help, but these alone are not sufficient. Workshops and conferences focused on new and innovative ideas, on counseling effectiveness, and on self growth, offer appropriate extensions into other realms. However, fruitful ways must be found to get counselor educators into the schools, so that they may experience the particular school environment, and so that their comments and suggestions may be clearly relevant. It is easy for the counselor educator to draw inappropriate inferences when he attempts armchair diagnosis. It is equally easy for the counselor to discount a difficult suggestion as inappropriate when he feels his situation is not understood. When the counselor educator is on the scene, aware, participating, trying out his notions, demonstrating them, and checking against reality, his ideas necessarily achieve greater credibility.

In one instance, in which Purdue University counselor educators provided on-site supervision in a series of visitations, responses to a questionnaire resulted in several interesting findings. Visits were made to elementary school counselors between the second and third summers of their participation in a guidance and counseling institute funded under the National Defense Education Act and Education Professions Development Act, 1967–1969. The report[28] about this experience, which was designed to extend and expand the practicum experiences of the previous summer, indicated that the mean rating on a 1-to-9 scale regarding the overall worth of the visitations was 7.7, and 21 of 29 members responding rated this item either 8 or 9. Counselors responded positively also to the question as to whether they had gained in personal understanding—7.6 with 15 responses of 8 or 9. The lowest mean response (4.5) was to a question regarding the extent to which the counselor felt he possessed professional expertise at the beginning of the field practice year; this same item scored a 7.0 self rating at the end of the field practice. One conclusion drawn from the Purdue experience is that videotaping, the telephone, and motivation are available essentials in extending the counselor education program beyond the degree program and into the school site.

The counselor may involve others in the community in contributing to his continued growth if he values the contribution sufficiently and if he sets aside time for the purpose. A doctor and an addict may contribute much by discussing the drug problem with the counselor and his

[28] Richard C. Nelson, "Implementing the on-site supervision model" (paper presented at American Personnel and Guidance Association Convention, New Orleans, 1970).

colleagues. Parents may help by throwing light on the pressures experienced by children in schools. A variety of persons may help the counselor to understand the community and its effects on children.

The counselor himself, his supervisors, counselor educators, and community members all have a potential for input into the continued growth of the counselor.

COUNSELOR CERTIFICATION

Counselor certification is intended to provide suitably trained counselors with evidence of that training and to prevent unqualified individuals from functioning as counselors. While such objectives are highly desirable, real difficulties lie in the way of their effective implementation. Too much flexibility may result in the certification of unsuitable individuals; too much rigidity may discourage or eliminate some very effective individuals or stifle innovative counselor education practices. Too much state control may result in stereotyped programs largely unsuited to the development of a fully functioning counselor; too much university control through endorsements may result in too-liberal policies. Selection to a counselor education program, which is not generally stringent, may be tantamount to life endorsement of a counselor. Out of this maze of difficulties have developed a diversity of counselor certification practices.

Dudley and Ruff[29] note that individual states may or may not:

1. differentiate counselors as to level—elementary or secondary (less than half differentiate);
2. provide provisional certification (over half do);
3. provide a permanent certificate (most do);
4. require a master's degree (nearly all do);
5. require more than a master's degree (a few do);
6. demand teaching experience of from one to three years (most do);
7. require nonteaching work experience (over half do);
8. issue certificates through the state board of education (most do);
9. reciprocate with other states (most do not).

Such diversity, both in procedural matters and course requirements, calls for action on the part of counselors, counselor educators, and such

[29] Gerald Dudley and Eldon E. Ruff, "School counselor certification: a study of current requirements," *School Counselor, 17:* 304–311 (1970).

professional organizations as American Personnel and Guidance Association to bring some order out of this chaos. As standards are changed to reduce random variability, every attempt should be made (1) to encourage the development of counselor education programs that exhibit flexibility, that permit experimentation, and yet that demand responsibility, (2) to allow for unique and innovative attempts at meeting special needs, and (3) to allow for the development of alternative ways to meet requirements —e.g., a well-designed internship as a substitute for teaching experience, or the institute model of intense experience as a substitute for a collection of specific courses. The genuineness and individuality of counselors and counselor educators, their creativity and innovativeness, should not be sacrificed to certification regulations. Such regulations should be developed so as to reduce the likelihood that poorly educated counselors will staff guidance programs, yet attention must be given to questions of meaningfulness, flexibility, and relevance. Certification must become a servant; it may now be a master.

SUMMARY

This chapter emphasizes counselor selection and education processes intended to increase the likelihood that children will be exposed to knowledgeable, sensitive, warm individuals. Much research is needed before definitive selection criteria can be set forth, yet selection must be considered a vital factor in providing children with the best persons to help them. Attempts need to be made to assess whether the prospective counselor possesses suitable personal attributes and an adequate experiential background—which may or may not include teaching experience. A larger concept of staff, including graduate students themselves, may help in selection by assessing the effectiveness of the aspiring counselor in situations with other adults and children.

Preparation programs that contribute most to the counselor's development give attention to intellectual growth, to a variety of experiences intended to develop counseling skill, and to self-exploration—the counselor as a person. Continued growth of the counselor is considered a responsibility of the individual himself, of supervisory or administrative personnel in the employing district, of counselor educators, and to some extent of other community members.

In the area of counselor certification there is a clear need for development of flexible, yet demanding standards that show some greater degree of uniformity from state to state. More innovation, experimentation, and research are called for in counselor selection, counselor preparation, in-service work with counselors, and counselor certification.

REFERENCES

ACES-ASCA Joint Committee on the Elementary School Counselor. "Report (Tentative)," *Personnel and Guidance Journal, 44:* 658–661 (1966).

Aubrey, R. F. "Elementary school counseling practicum: some suggestions for experiences and expectations," *Counselor Education and Supervision, 7:* 13–19 (1967).

Boy, A. V., and G. Pine. "Strengthening the off-campus practicum," *Counselor Education and Supervision, 6:* 40–43 (1966).

Brown, D., and B. H. Peterson. "The teaching experience prerequisite for the school counselor: an examination," *School Counselor, 16:* 17–20 (1968).

Carkhuff, R. R., and C. B. Truax. "Training in counseling and psychotherapy," *Journal of Consulting Psychology, 29:* 333–336 (1965).

Danielson, H. A. "Personality of prospective elementary school counselors: implications for preparation?" *Counselor Education and Supervision, 8:* 99–103 (1969).

Delaney, D. J. "Simulation techniques in counselor education: proposal of a unique approach," *Counselor Education and Supervision, 8:* 183–188 (1969).

Dimick, K. M., and V. E. Huff. *Child Counseling.* Dubuque, Iowa: William C. Brown Company, Publisher, 1970.

Dudley, G., and E. E. Ruff. "School counselor certification: a study of current requirements," *School Counselor, 17:* 304–311 (1970).

Eckerson, L. O. "In support of a loosely defined role for the elementary school counselor," *Elementary School Guidance and Counseling, 4:* 82–86 (1969).

Gazda, G. M., H. M. Clements, J. A. Duncan, and C. L. Martin. "Response sets of neophyte counselors," *Counselor Education and Supervision, 6:* 151–156 (1967).

Hansen, J. C., and G. D. Moore. "The off-campus practicum," *Counselor Education and Supervision, 6:* 32–39 (1966).

———— and ————. "The full-time—part-time debate: a research contribution," *Counselor Education and Supervision, 8:* 18–22 (1968).

Haseley, L. L., and H. J. Peters. "Practicum: on-campus and off-campus," *Counselor Education and Supervision, 5:* 141–147 (1966).

Higgins, R. E. "Preparing the elementary school counselor," *Report of the Seventh Annual All Ohio Elementary School Guidance Conference.* Columbus, Ohio: State Department of Education, Division of Guidance and Testing, 1968. Pp. 36–44.

Hill, G. E. *Staffing Guidance Programs.* Guidance Monograph Series, Boston: Houghton Mifflin Company, 1968.

————. "Doctoral preparation in the field of elementary school guidance," *Elementary School Guidance and Counseling, 4:* 197–202 (1970).

————, and D. F. Nitzschke. "Preparation programs in elementary school guidance," *Personnel and Guidance Journal, 40:* 155–159 (1961).

Huff, V. E. "The millstone of teaching experience," *Personnel and Guidance Journal, 44:* 192–194 (1965).

Jansen, D. G., G. P. Robb, and E. C. Bonk. "Characteristics of high-rated and low-rated master's degree candidates in counseling and guidance," *Counselor Education and Supervision, 9:* 162–170 (1970).

Johnston, J. A. "Practicum and on the job ratings of school counselors," *Personnel and Guidance Journal, 45:* 16–19 (1966).

McDaniel, S. W. "Counselor selection: an evaluation of instruments," *Counselor Education and Supervision, 6:* 142–144 (1967).

Meeks, A. R. *Guidance in Elementary Education.* New York: Ronald, 1968.

Muro, J. J., and M. C. Oelke. "Guidance needs in the elementary school—cue to the preparation of counselors," *Counselor Education and Supervision, 7:* 7–12 (1967).

Nelson, R. C. "The preparation of elementary school counselors: a model," *Counselor Education and Supervision, 6:* 197–200 (1967).

————. "Implementing the on site supervision model." Paper presented at American Personnel and Guidance Association Convention. New Orleans, 1970.

Ohlsen, M. M. "An appraisal of a program for the professional preparation of elementary school counselors," *Elementary School Guidance and Counseling, 2:* 15–32 (1967).

Peterson, B. H., and D. Brown. "Does teaching experience matter?" *Personnel and Guidance Journal, 46:* 893–897 (1968).

Phillips, W. "The professionalization of elementary school counselors," *Elementary School Guidance and Counseling, 4:* 87–94 (1969).

Ricker, G. A. "Must counselors have taught?" *School Counselor, 17:* 40–46 (1969).

Roach, A. J., and B. L. Wehrly. "Differentiated preparation for elementary school counselors," *Counselor Education and Supervision, 9:* 220–221 (1970).

Shertzer, B., and S. C. Stone. *Fundamentals of Guidance.* Boston: Houghton Mifflin, 1966.

Wehrly, B. L. "Elementary school counselor preparation programs in the United States," *Elementary School Guidance and Counseling, 4:* 203–210 (1970).

Whiteley, J. M. "Counselor Education," *Review of Educational Research, 39:* 173–187 (1969).

Wilson, L. E. "Teaching experience: counselor and teacher opinions," *Counselor Education and Supervision, 8:* 148–150 (1969).

ARTICLES IN BOOKS OF READINGS

Koplitz, E. D. Guidance in the Elementary School: *Theory, Research, and Practice.* Dubuque, Iowa: William C. Brown Company, Publisher, 1968. Readings beginning on pages 76, 320, 328, 333.

Patterson, C. H. *The Counselor in the School.* New York: McGraw-Hill, 1967. Readings beginning on pages 163, 170, 179, 182, 188, 200.

15

Research and Trends

Know then thyself, presume not God to scan,
The proper study of mankind is man.
ALEXANDER POPE: "Essay on Man"

Serious questions are being raised today about the effectiveness of counselor services in the elementary school; and at the same time enthusiasts are implying that elementary school counseling and guidance may be a panacea for everything from the dropout problem to warts. Muro[1] puts this discrepancy into focus by pointing out a considerable lag between speculation and evidence. At present both unbridled pessimism and optimism are out of place. There is enough support, if ingested, to quiet those who are close to giving up the attempt to work in elementary schools, and there is plenty of evidence to sober those who are unrealistically enthusiastic.

Certainly, counselors and teachers have not set standards high enough for themselves, have not clarified their goals sufficiently, and have not been rigorous in ascertaining whether what they were doing has made any difference to children. Public support for elementary counseling programs is growing, but so is the quest for accountability. Only if the accumulated evidence begins to appear somewhat more positive in the future can those interested in the field, in good conscience, continue to seek support.

[1] James J. Muro, *The Counselor's Work in the Elementary School* (Scranton, Pa.: International Textbook, 1970).

Ryan and Gaier observe that well-meaning counselors need to set forth on journeys that have destinations: "From the data presented here, one of the most salient conclusions that emerges is the almost complete lack of concerted effort by the counselors in the system to accomplish anything specific. Theirs was counseling effort without defined objectives."[2] This chapter will encourage all those who do anything in the name of guidance and counseling to define objectives for at least some of their actions, to seek means to ascertain whether or not these objectives are achieved, and to determine whether or not their actions make a difference. This challenge is intended for counselors, teachers, administrators, supervisors, and counselor educators, not exempting the present writer.

THE NEGATIVE RESEARCH EVIDENCE

Kranzler[3] reviewed several research studies and concluded that either (a) counseling is effective and evaluation methods are ineffective, (b) evaluation methods are effective and counseling is useless, or (c) counseling affects some children positively and others negatively. Mayer, Kranzler, and Matthes[4] reported a control-experimental attempt to affect peer relations and found no significant differences. After determining that consulting with teachers equaled counseling in its ineffectiveness, Kranzler[5] observed that consulting is more efficient if not more effective, but that leaving children alone is still more efficient. Lewis[6] reinforced the conclusion that neither counseling nor consulting was effective in improving the sociometric standing of third grade children. Alper and Kranzler[7] compared client-centered and behavioral approaches and concluded that neither approach helped children to reduce out-of-seat behavior. This study, these

---

[2] Doris W. Ryan and Eugene L. Gaier, "Student socio-economic status and counselor contact in the junior high school," *Personnel and Guidance Journal, 46:* 471 (1968).

[3] Gerald D. Kranzler, "Elementary school counseling: an evaluation," *Elementary School Guidance and Counseling, 2:* 286–294 (1968).

[4] W. A. Matthes, G. D. Kranzler, and G. R. Mayer, "The relationship between the client's perceptions of counselor behavior and change in the client's behavior," *Elementary School Guidance and Counseling, 2:* 179–186 (1968).

[5] Gerald D. Kranzler, "The elementary school counselor as consultant: an evaluation," *Elementary School Guidance and Counseling, 3:* 284–288 (1969).

[6] Michael D. Lewis, "The effects of counseling and consultation upon the sociometric status and personal adjustment of third grade pupils," *Elementary School Guidance and Counseling, 5:* 44–52 (1970).

[7] Theodore G. Alper and Gerald D. Kranzler, "A comparison of the effectiveness of behavioral and client-centered approaches for the behavioral problems of elementary school children," *Elementary School Guidance and Counseling, 5:* 35–43 (1970).

authors concluded, has demonstrated "one more time that talking to children in the privacy of the counselor's office is largely a waste of time, no matter what the counselor's theoretical orientation."[8] Perhaps this is too modest a conclusion, since these studies were based on approaches to individual children and to their teachers; a further-reaching conclusion at this point would be that no approach has been established to be valuable. Seidman[9] lent further support to this conclusion in demonstrating that child-development consulting did not influence student achievement.

Along with the evidence that casts doubt on the value of the counselor's work, research offers reasons to question some fundamental assumptions made by many counselors. Acceptance of the counselee is often valued as therapeutic; however, Matthes, Kranzler, and Mayer[10] found a significant positive relationship between the acceptance level in counseling and the frequency of inappropriate social behavior in children, suggesting that fifth and sixth grade students did not consider other ways to improve peer relations because the counselor accepted the behavior that had caused their low sociometric status.

Self-disclosure is often valued as therapeutic. Leventhal and Kranzler[11] found no relationship between the amount of personally relevant material offered by the child and the amount of constructive personality change. A related process, catharsis—the talking through of personally relevant emotional material—is also considered valuable by many counselors. Nighswander and Mayer[12] reviewed extensive literature and concluded that catharsis leads to unnecessary and undesirable aggression.

The theory of cognitive dissonance offered by Festinger[13] has intrigued many counselors. Basically it suggests that (1) if an individual can be induced through mild pressure to do something or say something contrary to his beliefs or his self-concept, he will change his beliefs or his self-concept in the direction of the statement or the act; (2) mild pressure or reward is more effective than either no pressure, no reward, high pressure,

---

[8] *Ibid.,* p. 41.

[9] Eric Seidman *et al.,* "The child development consultant: an experiment," *Personnel and Guidance Journal, 49:* 29–34 (1970).

[10] Matthes, Kranzler, and Mayer, "The relationship between the client's perception of counselor behavior and change in the client's behavior."

[11] Richard B. Leventhal and Gerald D. Kranzler, "The relationship between the depth of intrapersonal exploration and constructive personality change in elementary school children: an exploratory study," *Elementary School Guidance and Counseling, 3:* 12–19 (1968).

[12] James K. Nighswander and G. Roy Mayer, "Catharsis: a means of reducing elementary school students' aggressive behaviors?" *Personnel and Guidance Journal, 47:* 461–466 (1969).

[13] L. A. Festinger, *A Theory of Cognitive Dissonance* (New York: Harper & Row, 1957).

or high reward in producing change; and (3) if the action or statement is observed and accepted by people who are important to the individual, it is more likely to produce self-concept or behavioral change than if it remains private. Mayer and Cody[14] and Mayer, Rohen, and Whitley[15] spelled out how this theory might specifically apply to elementary school counseling; then Mayer *et al.*,[16] applied it in an experimental design. Counseling with or without public commitment proved ineffective in influencing school anxiety, teacher-pupil relations, or sociometric status.

Directed in many ways specifically to the matter of concern here, the studies cited above are well designed, well executed, and in many cases superior to those that appear in the next section. However, conclusions that counseling be discarded seem premature, both because findings from other studies suggest other conclusions and because even negative evidence is spotty at best.

THE POSITIVE RESEARCH EVIDENCE

Kranzler, Mayer, Dyer, and Munger,[17] in the only study from that group that has yielded positive and significant results, found differences favoring an experimental group of fourth grade counseled children; these differences were maintained over a seven-month period. Stormer[18] utilized a combination of counseling, teacher group work, and parent meetings and found that underachievers in grades three to five decreased in general anxiety and that parent-child relations were less strained among those in the experimental group. Anderson[19] found that fourth graders who were counseled individually improved in self-concept, while a teacher-consultation treatment affected self-concept significantly for sixth grade children.

[14] G. Roy Mayer and John J. Cody, "Festinger's theory of cognitive dissonance applied to school counseling," *Personnel and Guidance Journal, 47:* 233–239 (1968).

[15] G. Roy Mayer, T. M. Rohen, and A. D. Whitley, "Group counseling with children: a cognitive-behavioral approach," *Journal of Counseling Psychology, 16:* 142–149 (1969).

[16] G. Roy Mayer *et al.,* "The use of public commitment and counseling with elementary school children: an evaluation," *Elementary School Guidance and Counseling, 5:* 22–34 (1970).

[17] Gerald D. Kranzler, G. R. Mayer, C. O. Dyer, and P. F. Munger, "Counseling with elementary school children: an experimental study," *Personnel and Guidance Journal, 44:* 944–949 (1966).

[18] G. Edward Stormer, "Milieu group counseling in elementary school guidance," *Elementary School Guidance and Counseling, 1:* 240–254 (1967).

[19] Ethel C. Anderson, "Counseling and consultation versus teacher-consultation in the elementary school," *Elementary School Guidance and Counseling, 2:* 276–285 (1968).

Findings from a study by Schmieding,[20] involving children who had failed one or more subjects, revealed that counseled children had significantly higher academic achievement and better teacher-pupil relationships, while noncounseled children tended to worsen in both respects.

Several studies involving group work yielded positive findings. Hansen, Niland, and Zani[21] used upper sociometric children as models for lower sociometric children and found that the target children gained significantly in sociometric status. Tosi, Swanson, and McLean[22] utilized group counseling with nonverbalizing elementary school children and found that the experimental group increased significantly in unsolicited· verbal responses. In another experiment in which Crow[23] utilized structured aural, structured visual, and unstructured group experience, significant gains for the combined groups were registered on the criterion of emotional expansiveness. Gribbons[24] tried another structured approach and observed gains for eighth graders in self-awareness; in accuracy of abilities, values, and interests; and in possession of information on educational and vocational topics. Stetter[25] fed back results of the Mooney Problem Checklist to junior high school students and found that the discussion of personal problems led to reduced anxiety. An unstructured, permissive group experience organized by Seeman[26] resulted in significant gains in reading over a control group for an experimental group of children with social-emotional disturbance. Moon and Wilson[27] involved fifth grade children in giving reading assistance to younger children and found gains for the involved fifth graders. Duncan and Fitzgerald[28] held parent conferences when

[20] Orville A. Schmieding, "An investigation of efficacy of counseling and guidance procedures with failing junior high school students," *School Counselor, 14:* 74–80 (1966).

[21] James C. Hansen, T. M. Niland, and Leonard P. Zani, "Model reinforcement in group counseling with elementary school children," *Personnel and Guidance Journal, 47:* 741–744 (1969).

[22] Donald J. Tosi, Carl Swanson, and Pat McLean, "Group counseling with nonverbalizing elementary school children," *Elementary School Guidance and Counseling, 4:* 260–266 (1970).

[23] Mary Lynn Crow, "An investigation of structured aural, structured visual, and unstructured group counseling techniques with elementary school children" (Denton, Texas: North Texas State University, 1970. Mimeographed.)

[24] Warren D. Gribbons, "Evaluation of an eighth grade group guidance program," *Personnel and Guidance Journal, 38:* 740–745 (1960).

[25] Richard Stetter, "A group guidance technique for the classroom teacher," *School Counselor, 16:* 179–184 (1969).

[26] Julius Seeman, "Child therapy in education: some current trends," *Education, 74:* 493–499 (1954).

[27] Mozetta Moon and Doris Wilson, "Teacher-counselor cooperation: building self-concepts and confidence in children," *School Counselor, 17:* 364–366 (1970).

[28] L. Wendell Duncan and Paul W. Fitzgerald, "Increasing the parent-child communication through counselor-parent conferences," *Personnel and Guidance Journal, 47:* 514–517 (1969).

children entered junior high school and found that those children whose parents were counseled were significantly better in attendance, grade-point, dropout, and disciplinary statistics. Parents also remained more involved throughout the three-year period of the study.

In the area of support for counseling a number of studies had interesting findings. Nelson's[29] study involved interviews in twenty different schools with counseled and noncounseled children and their parents. Significantly more children who had been seen by counselors, as well as their parents, viewed the counselor as a past and future source of help. Also, counseled children were more positive than noncounseled children about the school and the counseling program. Bender,[30] Brown and Pruett,[31] and Kornick[32] found increased support for the counseling and guidance program by teachers over time as counselors worked with them. This finding was also a part of the outcome in studies by Lewis[33] and Mayer *et al.*;[34] in both of these cases teacher perceptions improved for the group of children who were subjects of consultation, while perceptions became more negative for the group of children who were only counseled.

Individualized action on the part of counselors dealing with specific children's concerns has also yielded some positive data. Myrick[35] reported success with an effeminate boy, Kennedy and Thompson[36] with a child with an attention problem, and Kennedy, Thompson and Cress[37] with a child having difficulties in social interaction.

The optimist can look at the present section and find much support. The pessimist can look at the previous section and find reason to leave the field. Perhaps the realist concerns himself with how to proceed in the future.

[29] Richard C. Nelson, "Fourth and final technical report on the institute for counseling and guidance" (Lafayette, Ind.: Purdue University, 1970).

[30] Don Bender, "Counseling, consulting, or developmental guidance: toward an answer," *Elementary School Guidance and Counseling, 4:* 245–252 (1970).

[31] Duane Brown and Rolla F. Pruett, "The elementary school teacher views guidance," *School Counselor, 14:* 195–203 (1970).

[32] Joseph Kornick, "An analysis: impact of an elementary school counselor on teachers' perceptions of the counselor's role and function," *Elementary School Guidance and Counseling, 4:* 188–196 (1970).

[33] Michael D. Lewis, "Elementary school counseling and consultation: their effects on teachers' perceptions," *School Counselor, 18:* 49–55 (1970).

[34] Mayer *et al.*, "The use of public commitment and counseling with elementary school children: an evaluation."

[35] Robert D. Myrick, "The counselor-consultant and the effeminate boy," *Personnel and Guidance Journal, 48:* 355–361 (1970).

[36] Daniel A. Kennedy and Ina Thompson, "Use of reinforcement technique with a first grade boy," *Personnel and Guidance Journal, 46:* 366–370 (1967).

[37] Daniel A. Kennedy, Ina Thompson, and Joanne Cress, "A behavioral approach to consultation in elementary school guidance," *School Counselor, 15:* 220–223 (1968).

DESIGNS FOR THE FUTURE

The researcher must have a free hand to choose his own path through the elementary guidance and counseling maze. To help him in choosing new paths, however, several suggestions are offered below. Any researcher, counselor, or teacher wishing to stray from these guidelines may, of course, find the exploration fruitful; those looking to avoid well-worn blind alleys, however, may find the suggestions useful. It may be impracticable to attempt to incorporate all of these ideas in any one study.

Do ask significant questions. The researcher, Hosford and Briskin suggest, needs to ask himself whether the results of his study will affect what individuals do in working with children. They criticize existing research: "Too often the independent variable is labeled 'counseling' and the dependent variable (the objective of counseling) is some personality test score. This situation is not unlike the medical patient who receives 'doctoring' for severe abdominal pains, but whose cure is measured by a test on attitudes toward medicine."[38] Thoresen[39] supported this criticism and called for greater clarity of goals in counseling. Thus, questions must be both specific and worth answering.

Do include multidimensional approaches to children. When a child arouses concern in the mind of the counselor and teacher, he is likely to receive counseling, he may be placed in a group experience, teacher and counselor may confer, and counselor and parents may get together. This design is developed because the counselor or teacher believes that a combination of approaches may be best for the child. In research, too, while isolating the critical procedure may become a most desirable objective, the first question is: can we help this child? At present it seems highly desirable to compare multidimensional counseling and related activities to a variety of single activities (compare counseling, group work, parent consulting, *and* teacher consulting to each or any of these procedures taken separately). The whole may indeed be greater than the sum of its parts. This point is developed further in the three items below.

Don't isolate target children. A number of studies involving individual and group counseling may have achieved nonsignificant results because they did not "take along" other children either as models or as allies in the process of change. Barclay speaks of the mysterious-stranger phenomenon: "The elementary school counselor should function as an integral part of the elementary curriculum rather than a visiting dignitary who mysteriously appears and summons children to meet with him. . . .

[38] Ray E. Hosford and Alan S. Briskin, "Changes through counseling," *Review of Educational Research, 39:* 189 (1969).

[39] Carl E. Thoresen, "Relevance and research in counseling," *Review of Educational Research, 39:* 263–281 (1969).

The inferences become clear to all the students in the class and a maladaptive response can easily generalize both to the student so singled out and to the elementary counselor."[40]

Three recommendations: (1) when group experiences are arranged for target children, nontarget children should generally be included, (2) target children should be selected where possible by a randomized drawing from a pool of self-referred children, and (3) when target children are involved, nontarget children should also be involved in counseling. Caution must be observed lest children become isolated; children may come to resent even the self-referred child who gets to see the counselor once or twice every week while their appointment is continually deferred.

Do consider subculture needs. Potential need differences are evident in different cultures involving race, ethnic background, or socioeconomic levels; however, in building his design the researcher needs to be aware of still more subtle subcultural needs. Tulkin, Muller, and Conn[41] observed sex differences relevant to this point; girls with a high need for approval tended to be most popular, while boys with the same need tended to be least popular. Thus getting a boy to try harder to succeed with his peers may mean that he succeeds less. Ringness[42] found that academically nonsuccessful bright children had a greater need to affiliate than to achieve, as compared to their bright, successful counterparts. Thus, again, social pressures may thwart counselor efforts; lower-achieving, popular, bright boys may consider it feminine to change their tactics.

Walz and Miller[43] have also addressed this question. In their review of literature on classroom climate they found that some student groups tend to affiliate *because* they are not congruent with the school climate, and these writers suggest that penetrating such groups may be extremely difficult for the school counselors. They note that ". . . counselor effectiveness can be thought of as a function of the appropriateness of the counselors' behavior to the needs of different student subgroups."[44]

Suggestions for the researcher: (1) anticipate possible subgroup problems; (2) select target children from among those indicating interest in obtaining assistance; (3) deal directly with the matter of subgroup differences in designing studies.

[40] James R. Barclay, "Effecting behavior changes in the elementary classroom: an exploratory study," *Journal of Counseling Psychology, 14:* 246 (1967).

[41] Steven R. Tulkin, J. P. Muller, and L. K. Conn, "Need for approval and popularity: sex differences in elementary school students," *Journal of Consulting and Clinical Psychology, 33:* 25–29 (1969).

[42] Thomas A. Ringness, "Affective differences between successful and nonsuccessful bright ninth grade boys," *Personnel and Guidance Journal, 43:* 600–606 (1965).

[43] Garry Walz and Juliet Miller, "School climates and student behavior: implications for counselor role," *Personnel and Guidance Journal, 47:* 859–867 (1969).

[44] *Ibid.,* p. 864.

Do include the teacher when counseling. In studies by Lewis[45] and Mayer *et al.*,[46] teacher-pupil relations have been observed to improve during consulting and deteriorate during counseling. One may hypothesize that, left to his own imagination, the teacher may be drawing negative conclusions about children seen over time in counseling when he receives no feedback; *or* the teacher's negative feeling about the lack of feedback may rub off onto the child. Some form of limited teacher feedback may be necessary for the benefit of the child. This might, for experimental purposes, be limited to (1) checking with the teacher on progress, (2) making generalized positive statements about the child—e..g, "John seems to be making good progress in counseling," or (3) making both kinds of contacts.

Do continue counseling research. Children seem to feel tremendous press to be heard. Opportunities offered for counseling children of elementary school age are readily snapped up. Although some of the literature suggests that it makes no difference, children seem to feel it does. Most counselors feel the same way. There is clear need to continue researching whether counseling makes any positive difference. A few of the criteria that may be used are frequency of positive self-referent statements in counseling, self-control related statements in counseling, and positive attitudes toward school after counseling. (Criteria are discussed in detail in the next section.)

Do consider the problem of increased awareness and its effect on criterion measures. One outcome occasionally observed in counseling is an increase in the number of problems checked by children and an increase in the negative direction on personality profiles. While it may be hypothesized that counseling has, in fact, worsened conditions for a child, it is also possible that (a) the child is allowing into his perceptive field more awareness of himself and his difficulties, or (b) he is more willing to share with others the concerns that he has—is expressing himself more genuinely. Longitudinal studies may show whether counseled children do increase in problem awareness for some time, then experience a decrease in problem frequencies as counseling helps them in coping.

Do design for prevention. The elementary school counselor often contends that his job involves the prevention of problems; Hosford and Briskin[47] note, however, that very little research has been done to ascertain such results. Longitudinal studies on target groups of predelinquent children or on children who are potential school dropouts, for example, may help to answer this kind of question. Data need to be obtained also on the

[45] Lewis, "Elementary school counseling and consultation: their effects on teachers' perceptions."

[46] Mayer *et al.*, "The use of public commitment and counseling with elementary school children: an evaluation."

[47] Hosford and Briskin, *op. cit.*, pp. 189–207.

successes of children involved in elementary school developmental counseling.

Do attempt longitudinal measurement. As suggested above, longitudinal research is an important concern in counseling. For example, developmental effort with children entering adolescence may not materialize in attitudinal differences during the next week or several weeks, but short boys and heavy or early-maturing girls may exhibit different attitudes toward themselves and others as these differences are accented further in adolescence. Counselors and teachers are attempting to influence a great variety of attitudes and behaviors; they need to examine over time whether they are achieving the objectives they intend.

Do include a number of counselors and/or teachers and a number of children. There is a point of diminishing returns in including many hundreds of children and many dozens of adults in any research activity. Since levels of significance are related to the numbers of cases—that is, the same finding may be statistically significant if based on one hundred cases and not if based on thirty cases—it doesn't take a sophisticated researcher to understand that large numbers greatly increase the chance of significant differences or significant relationships that may be meaningless. On the other hand, existing elementary school counseling and guidance research has often relied upon too few children per subgroup to expect positive returns. Cooperative efforts in research are needed so that any target group may become large enough to demonstrate real and significant differences or relationships after treatment if they exist.

Do specify treatment procedures. Too many research studies suffer from lack of specificity in the planning and/or the description of the treatment procedures used. A treatment cannot be replicated—and it should be if the process has proved to be of value—unless the procedures are thoroughly described. "Counseling" is not a sufficient description, nor are "consulting," "coordination," "behavioral counseling," or "Adlerian family consultation." The Matthes, Kranzler, and Mayer[48] study cited earlier, which indicated that counselor acceptance led to reinforcement of inappropriate social behavior, may or may not have included counselor confrontation of inappropriate counselee behaviors and assumptions; the reader does not know—yet it seems essential to an understanding of the outcome. And this research is more specific in this regard than most other studies. The point is that counselors need to think through the procedures they believe will effectively counter a given problem, specify these, and check them out against some criterion, whether or not they are conducting a formal research investigation.

---

[48] Matthes, Kranzler, and Mayer, "The relationship between the client's perception of counselor behavior and change in the client's behavior."

Do consider individual gains or target-group gains. Thoresen states: "The counseling investigator is typically not seeking significant group mean differences or group average gains compared to mean changes expected in some comparable untreated group. The counseling researcher is more typically interested in change in some individual performance. He seeks to make predictions, explore causal relationships or accurately describe individual behaviors."[49] Certainly Thoresen is correct in principle, but in fact too much energy does seem to be devoted to establishing mean differences and mean relationships. The counselor or teacher might well concentrate on producing change in individuals or a small target group; if he wishes to test the effectiveness of specific procedures across a large group, he might, as suggested previously, enlist the cooperation of others in the field in his research efforts.

Do enlist the Hawthorne effect. The Hawthorne effect, produced when adults or children perform because they know they are involved in a research activity, is often carefully factored out of a study. Stormer[50] suggests that elementary school programs should try to accentuate this effect in the interests of children. If better attitudes or conditions will result when children or the adults in their lives know that they are involved in an experiment, then at times it may be wise to let them know.

Do use appropriate criteria. Criterion measures for elementary school guidance and counseling present a genuine problem—one that has had its effects upon previous research. The next section discusses criteria in some detail.

Do follow hunches and test them out. The section after the next one considers involvement in research. In general, practitioners are in the best position to plan and execute meaningful research, but often they are most hesitant to try. Counselors and teachers need to examine their hunches, looking for objective ways to answer the question: What changes have my actions produced? Many sources of technical help appear to be available; thus, less hesitancy seems to be in order.

CRITERIA

The criteria against which elementary school counseling or any other guidance activity may be appropriately evaluated should be as relevant as possible to the activity designed. This caution is by no means always followed. For example, many studies have utilized sociometric measures, which might be expected to reflect group interaction changes,

---

49 Thoresen, *op. cit.,* p. 269.
50 Stormer, *op. cit.*

as criteria to evaluate introspective individual counseling. A number of other measures might more appropriately be related to such counseling.

Table 15–1 lists and describes ten criteria and indicates appropriate usage. This is simply a sampling from among hundreds of criteria that may be useful in counseling and guidance research.

Inventories used with elementary school children, it should be noted, often result in negative findings. One may hypothesize that on a variety of measures increased self-awareness may lead to an increase in negative self-statements. Therefore, in Table 15–1 it is suggested that a simple pre- and posttesting design may be inadequate to reflect positive growth for elementary school children on such measures. Designs should allow for more than one posttesting in order to determine whether negative self-statements are maintained. A valid research question is whether children who increase in negative self-statements or inventories during counseling are observed to function over time less effectively than those who do not.

Sociometric measures as typically administered reflect best the status and movement of children in the upper sociometric stratum within a classroom. They do not adequately reflect movement among children in the lower stratum, nor do they reflect greater group unity. Therefore, Table 15–1 presents two alternative procedures. First, the child may indicate all those toward whom he feels friendly, a procedure that does not allow him to indicate the intensity of his feeling as does first choice, second choice, and so on; or, second, he may distribute stars or use a similar procedure to indicate how friendly he feels toward individuals in the class. This latter procedure is currently under investigation at Purdue University.

Obviously, the matter of selecting criteria by which to evaluate counseling is not a simple matter. Considerable creative energy may be used in the development of new measures. Whether newly developed or preexisting measures are used, three questions should be answered in selecting criteria: (1) Will the findings from the anticipated use of this measure make a difference to the way counselors or others handle their counseling and guidance responsibilities? (2) Is this criterion as relevant and as closely related as possible to the objective sought and the treatment procedure planned? (3) Can it be demonstrated that this criterion is reliable and valid in the kinds of circumstances in which its use is planned?

INVOLVEMENT IN RESEARCH

Perhaps it may seem questionable, when so many elementary school guidance and counseling studies have been undertaken and have proven inconclusive, for the counselor or teacher who is unsophisticated in matters

Table 15-1 SOME USEFUL CRITERION MEASURES

Measure	Description, explanation, example	Primary use
1. Positive self-referent, other-referent statements.	Either within or beyond counseling, tallies are made of numbers of positive self and "can do" statements, or statements valuing others. Tape analysis or observation may be used.	Self-referent relates to individual counseling, other-referent to group counseling, consulting. Target group should be those with low self-other view.
2. Semantic differential	Paired adjectives are used on a scale of 1–3, 1–5, etc. Pairs may be focused on individual self view, view of individual by others, or his view of others. Example: Good 1 2 3 4 5 Bad	If focus is self view—individual counseling. If view of or by other children—group counseling. If view of or by adults—consulting.
3. School attendance	Record kept of absences before and after counseling.	Individual counseling—those in poor attendance.
4. Inventories	Locus of control, self-concept, personality measures. Should be used in a design that includes more than one posttesting.	Individual counseling.
5. Sentence completion	Incomplete sentences allow an unstructured response. Useful, but difficult to score.	Individual counseling.
6. School/classroom climate	Attitudes toward the school, its environment, the classroom, the teacher may be assessed in a variety of ways.	Depending on its focus and relevance to treatment it may relate to any guidance process.

7. Sociometric measures	A. Children may be asked to list in order children within the classroom who are their three best friends or those with whom they would like to work or play.	Group counseling focused on high sociometric students.
	B. Children may be asked to circle names of *all* those whom they consider their best friends, etc.	Group counseling. Secondary—individual counseling.
	C. Children may be asked to indicate both the number of children whom they favor on a criterion and the intensity. This may be done by giving them a number of stars equivalent to the number of children in the classroom to place by names of children on a class list.	Group counseling.
8. Behavioral observation	Frequency or duration of behaviors may be observed. Base rate of verbalizations, self-assertive behaviors, sharing behaviors, or target nonverbal behaviors, etc., of children or adults may be compared to posttreatment observations.	May be related to any treatment. Observations may be taken within or outside of counseling in the most relevant setting.
9. Trait ratings	May be applied to self, to peers, or by adults to children. Ratings should relate to treatment.	May be related to any treatment.
10. Academic growth	Growth on achievement measures is relevant when the target group is underachieving and the treatment relates to academic considerations.	Teacher consulting. Occasionally to individual or group counseling.

of research design, population sampling, selection of criteria, and analysis of data to be encouraged to engage in research. An important reason for such encouragement emerges from the recent concern for accountability; counselors who cannot provide supportive data may find that their support dwindles. Unless hard data clarify that counseling makes a difference, there is little reason to expect that counseling programs will continue to expand even at the present modest rate. Flashy, new educational inventions may siphon away existing tax dollars unless objective evidence can be cited to support guidance services.

The second reason for encouraging the counselor and teacher to engage in research is that practitioners should be and often are able to ask the most relevant questions. In order to shape these questions into an effective research design and to plan and conduct an objective study, the practitioner may need to arrange for research consulting either within the school district or through a university or other agency. This is not an insurmountable problem. Research personnel are increasing in number, and computers, often used at only from one fifth to one half their capacity, could generate in a matter of seconds all the answers available from a complex collection of data.

Arbuckle puts it this way:

> The counselor must become involved in research, not on a grandiose scale, but simply to gather some implications about the effects of what he and several of his colleagues are doing. What if the counselor starts to see several girls who have been chronic disciplinary cases? What if some small groups are organized for children who are doing poorly in a certain subject? What if the parents of several children who have been tight and tense in class are seen once a week by a counselor? What if a counselor becomes a member of a team trying to make more meaningful the educational experience of several classes in ninth grade earth science? What if a counselor in one school tries to organize the parents so that they can help to develop a curriculum for their children in grade five? These are fairly routine counselor tasks, and there is no real reason why the counselor cannot have a valid answer to the question, "Just what happened as a result of these various counselor activities?"[51]

The third reason for encouraging the counselor and teacher to engage in research is that they have the best access to the children about whom they feel concern. They know the population and its problems. They can see that in the process of inquiry the humanness of the child is protected.

Critical steps in formulating many research studies are presented below in the form of a hypothetical illustration.

[51] Dugald S. Arbuckle, "Does the school really need counselors?" *School Counselor, 17:* 330 (1970).

1. ASK A QUESTION   Mrs. Jackson had a hunch and formulated it as follows: What would happen if I placed some of the shy children who are ignored by others in some situations in which they might function as leaders with other children?

2. READ   The most relevant study, that by Barclay,[52] suggested that suitable activities might (a) demand the cooperation of all members of a group within a classroom, (b) restructure existing cliques, (c) be non-threatening to low-status children, and (d) exclude the possibility of ridicule for failure.

3. PLAN A PROCEDURE   Mrs. Jackson decided to use the socio-drama design suggested by Barclay. She planned that twice weekly for five weeks she would set aside an hour for preplanned sociodrama presentations and discussions. The leadership role of the target children was to be low-key. Each was to introduce the role-play activity in his small group, select a part for himself in which he might have a chance to try out some new behavior, and open the discussion of how the roles would be distributed and played. Other key involvement for these children was to be arranged as it became feasible.

4. SELECT A POPULATION   Sociometric data collection had shown that seven of the twenty-seven children in the classroom were either not chosen at all as one of the first three choices of others in the classroom under three different conditions (sit with, play with, work with) or were chosen once only as a third choice. One of these seven children was judged to be highly aggressive and was not included in the target group. Mrs. Jackson selected three names randomly. Half of the classroom members were to be sociodramatists for five weeks while the others functioned as observer-evaluators; therefore the three who were chosen were to become leaders for five weeks, while the others were part of the observer group.

5. SELECT A MEASURE   Mrs. Jackson developed the plan to tally all unsolicited verbal expressions by the six target children for three days under a variety of conditions. Each day she planned to have a group discussion in which two of the children would be included. A similar data-collection period was to follow the five-week experiment. A teacher's aide was to record the tallies.

6. SEEK RESEARCH CONSULTATION   With her plan jotted down and the group tentatively selected, Mrs. Jackson discussed her idea with Miss Grayson, Director of Elementary Education for the school district. Miss Grayson suggested several minor modifications and raised several procedural questions that led to a tightening up of the plan. The one major

---

[52] Barclay, "Effecting behavior change in the elementary classroom: an exploratory study."

alteration suggested was that since base-rate data could be collected, they would function as a substitute for a control group. Therefore, pairs of these children might be randomly assigned as co-leaders for the duration of the experience, and all of the children might benefit simultaneously. Miss Grayson suggested that follow-up sociometric data also be collected.

7. COLLECT DATA   Prior to the beginning of the sociodrama experiment, Mrs. Lewis, a teacher's aide, tallied unsolicited verbal contributions by the six target children. These were found to average 2.2 per day per child.

8. INSTITUTE THE TREATMENT   Despite some scheduling problems and interruptions, the sociodrama activities were instituted. All six children willingly and somewhat fearfully participated.

9. COLLECT FOLLOW-UP DATA   Unsolicited verbal responses and sociometric follow-up data were collected.

10. SEEK ASSISTANCE IN ANALYSIS OF DATA   Miss Grayson analyzed the two basic pieces of data and found significant pretest-posttest differences.

> Target children before treatment—sociometric selections: 3
> Target children after treatment—sociometric selections: 9
> Target children unsolicited verbal responses prior to treatment: $N = 13$, mean $= 2.2$
> Target children unsolicited verbal responses after treatment: $N = 49$, mean $= 8.2$

The illustration above, although hypothetical, does illustrate the major considerations in developing a research study. It demonstrates that research design is primarily a matter of effective planning. Counseling and guidance research directed toward the needs of particular children *is* within the range of capabilities of most counselors and teachers. It is often said that whatever is worth doing is worth doing well. It is also worth the attempt to determine whether or not it has been done well.

Research conducted by practitioners will have to be a trend of the future in elementary school counseling and guidance, if the field is to survive to full maturity. Other trends in the offing are considered in the next section.

TRENDS IN ELEMENTARY SCHOOL COUNSELING AND GUIDANCE

A number of trends seem to be emerging in elementary school counseling and guidance. Judgment (as to the nature and importance of a present or past development), speculation (as to directions of future development), and perhaps some wishful thinking characterize many discussions of trends. It is likely that judgment, speculation, and wishful thinking are generously mixed in the paragraphs that follow, which are offered tentatively as possible trends in elementary school counseling and guidance.

TREND TOWARD HUMANIZING THE GUIDANCE EFFORT

Much of the development of guidance at the secondary school level has occurred in response to Sputnik, or in order to assist young people in selecting and entering colleges and careers, or in order to take advantage of existing testing technology. Some of it, of course, occurred because educators became aware of the need to humanize the efforts of the school. In elementary schools there has been less need for full-blown programs focused on testing, colleges and careers, or the need for scientists. This has not necessarily meant greater human concern, as counselors, to some degree emulating their secondary counterparts, have concerned themselves overmuch with nonpersonal activities. They have spent too much time keeping cumulative records, meeting the guidance-for-all-children objective, or dealing with needs of children as seen primarily by adults. Nonetheless, counselors do seem to be growing more comfortable with the idea of humanizing the guidance program and ultimately of helping to humanize the school.

This trend, if it may be called such, is an important one. Children exist too much of the time in a world that is predesigned and proscriptive. Teachers and counselors need to be involved in drawing out and sustaining children's efforts to be individuals, functioning uniquely and genuinely within their world. Changes in school settings may well start with changes in counseling and guidance program.

TREND TOWARD EXPANSION OF SERVICES

Nationwide surveys by Van Hoose and Vafakas[53] and Van Hoose and Kurtz[54] have established that elementary school guidance programs are growing steadily and that local funding is being used increasingly to support these programs. During 1966–67, 3837 elementary school counselors were functioning in the schools of this nation as against 6041 during 1968–69. While 22 percent of programs were funded locally in 1966–67, local support had increased to 36 percent in 1968–69. Projecting this steady, rapid

[53] William H. Van Hoose and Catherine M. Vafakas, "Status of guidance and counseling in the elementary school," *Personnel and Guidance Journal, 46:* 536–539 (1968).

[54] William H. Van Hoose and Sister Marie Kurtz, "Status of guidance in the elementary school: 1968–69," *Personnel and Guidance Journal, 48:* 381–384 (1970).

development as a trend for the future, Phillips[55] suggested that elementary school counseling will be more widely instituted, better staffed, and better funded year by year.

TREND TOWARD RELEVANCE

Like their counselors, Carey has suggested, students "want an education that is sensitive to the individual needs of students in a modern society."[56] While Carey's entire commentary might relate to the secondary school or even the college, the elementary school seems to call for the same relevance. Relevance, as Carey[57] sees it, demands the following trends:

1. A trend away from the view that the student has the responsibility for making his education relevant.
2. A trend away from the idea that a rule is a rule, and right or wrong it must be obeyed.
3. A trend away from school rules designed for the convenience of educators and toward a limiting of rules to those that provide essential controls.
4. A trend away from the view that students "never had it so good," and an awareness of youth discrimination.
5. A trend away from the view that we have adequate processes to bring about needed changes in laws and institutions.
And, especially important:
6. A trend away from the view that counselors can sit in their offices as "listeners" and expect to meet the guidance needs of young people.

Carey continued with a call for counselors: to sponsor local studies on what students are in fact experiencing in their schools; to recognize student desire for a piece of the power; to tailor programs to meet the present needs of students rather than hoping to meet these needs as a by-product; to combat attempts to create student involvement that is merely patronizing or illusory; and to be committed to sharing power with students within the system.

Relevance has been a concern of many elementary school guidance programs since their inception. While the concept of relevance may need expansion, it is nonetheless something of a trend in elementary school guidance and counseling. Hopefully this trend will continue to develop.

[55] Wallace Phillips, "The professionalization of elementary school counselors," *Elementary School Guidance and Counseling, 4:* 87–94 (1969).

[56] Richard W. Carey, "Student protest and the counselor," *Personnel and Guidance Journal, 48:* 185 (1969).

[57] *Ibid.,* pp. 185–191.

TREND TOWARD MORE EFFECTIVE COUNSELING EFFORT

Nelson,[58] in an APGA convention paper, listed more effective counseling as a primary direction for the future. There is a need for, and perhaps a trend toward, a view of counseling as integrally concerned with relationships and with processes or techniques. This is a trend away from emphasizing either the relationship or the technique to the exclusion of the other.

TREND TOWARD STATESMANSHIP

Elementary school counseling and guidance programs no longer seem quite so much to be isolated problem-solving agencies functioning down the hall away from the centers of action. Concerned counselors and teachers seem to show a bit more willingness to lead the way in meeting children's needs, in restructuring the atmosphere in the school, and in producing curricular change. Statesmanship, rather than trend-following or reinforcing of the status quo, seems to be increasing, as well it ought to if counseling and guidance programs are to have appropriate impact.

TREND TOWARD EXPERIMENTATION

Mayer *et al.,*[59] have called for "maximum experimentalism" in elementary school counseling and guidance. Research and evaluation are clearly on the increase, as evidenced by the frequency of reports in journals. Certainly this is a trend of vital importance if elementary school guidance programs are to become maximally effective—and if they are to survive.

TREND TOWARD DIVERSITY AND UNIQUENESS

Although most elementary school guidance programs have more of the common than of the unique, experimentalism does exist, and there is a related trend toward the design of programs specifically for the setting and for the strengths of the counselor. Many may lament this lack of unity; however, until more definitive research data establishes the effectiveness of particular approaches, the present writer is inclined to support creative, considered development of new approaches and creative utilization of existing procedures. Perhaps one of the greatest hopes for the future of

[58] Richard C. Nelson, "The emerging role of the elementary school counselor: the counseling role" (paper read at the American Personnel and Guidance Association Convention, Dallas, Texas, 1967).

[59] Mayer *et al.,* "The use of public commitment and counseling with elementary school children: an evaluation."

elementary school guidance and counseling arises from this trend toward diversity and uniqueness.

TREND TOWARD MULTIDIMENSIONAL APPROACHES

A trend appears to be developing for the counselor to rely less on a single approach with selected children. More often counseling is supplemented by teacher-consulting, the child is included in a group experience, and his parents are involved in discussions of the concern. Attempts are made to provide an outlet for his concerns, and his home and school environment are altered; all this is done, for example, so that he may begin to see himself as being more capable than he has acknowledged. Less commitment to a single approach is freeing the counselor to deal more realistically with children's needs.

TREND TOWARD ACCOUNTABILITY

A demand for accountability is growing as the costs of education continue to escalate. Tax dollars are limited, and the public rightfully demands evidence that services offered are doing what they purport to do. As guidance programs increase in number and scope in elementary schools, and as taxation problems increase, it must be expected that such programs will face demands for proof of effectiveness at the risk of loss of financial support. The greater public support will come when formal research evidence is supported by local evaluation, when data concerning number and kinds of concerns effectively encountered are available, and when teachers, parents, and children see the program as being so vital that it must continue even in the face of financial crisis.

TREND TOWARD UTILIZATION OF TECHNICAL RESOURCES

Computers, teaching machines, educational television, and other media are producing a gradual revolution in the classroom. As counselors and teachers become more sophisticated in the effective use of technical resources, this revolution will reach beyond the sketchy developments of the present and affect every aspect of the educational world. Guidance programs will be altered and—hopefully—improved through use of these resources.

One especially useful medium, videotape recording, will be utilized more extensively by counselors in training in self-examination and in simulation; by counselors in examining their own effect in counseling; and by teachers, and perhaps counselors with teachers, in examining classroom environment and procedures. Franken[60] has utilized videotape recording and playback with teachers, focusing attention on classroom work and counselor-teacher consulting. Certainly the use of such devices holds much promise for improving the effectiveness of the guidance program, if the media are not permitted to detract from the humanizing mission of the program.

TREND TOWARD INTEGRATION OF EFFORT

Teachers, counselors, school psychologists, social workers, and others seem to be integrating more of their efforts on the behalf of children. Teachers and counselors especially are coming to see the need as the teacher acknowledges his own effect upon children and as the counselor realizes the need for involving himself in curricular matters. Teachers know more about guidance, Phillips[61] suggested, and they are coming to expect more from counselors and from themselves. Hopefully, neither will accede meekly to suggestions by the other; rather, in line with these changed expectations, counselors and teachers will sit down together and plan creative approaches to children's difficulties. Certainly, as Leiter[62] pointed out, a true integration of effort should involve counselors, teachers, parents, other professionals, and community members.

TREND TOWARD SERVING TARGET GROUPS

The counselor and teacher who accept the concept of guidance for all children are increasingly coming to realize that their efforts, if they are to be evaluated, must focus in some measure on particular children. Successful guidance effort may lead an aggressive, hostile child to channel his actions toward leadership, a shy child to become more aggressive, a tense, achievement-oriented child to accept a lower academic standard for himself, an underachiever to make academic strides, a sociometric leader to realize that his efforts toward popularity are blocking other evidences of his worth, or a low sociometric child to find ways to communicate more effectively with his peers. It is difficult for a single measure or group of measures to reflect the growth experienced by each of these children. To some extent the progress made by one member in one direction may be

[60] Mary Weiking Franken, "A consultant role in elementary school guidance: helping teachers increase awareness of the behavior dynamics of children," *Elementary School Counseling and Guidance, 4:* 128–135 (1969).

[61] Phillips, *loc. cit.*

[62] Sarah Leiter, "There is no tomorrow," *Report of the Seventh Annual All Ohio Elementary School Guidance Conference.* (Columbus, Ohio: State Department of Education, Division of Guidance and Testing, 1968), pp. 49–55.

canceled out by the gain of another member in an opposing direction. At least part of the guidance effort, then, should be focused on specific children or groups of children, should be designed to meet their special needs; and should be evaluated against appropriate criteria. The trend toward serving target groups does not automatically cancel out the attempt of the counselor to be accessible to all children; it should mean, on the contrary, that his work will tend to have both breadth and focus.

TREND TOWARD IMPROVED COUNSELOR PREPARATION

A trend toward improved counselor preparation is developing in at least four ways. (1) Preparation programs are incorporating some of the advantages of an institute model—an intensive, integrated experience in which the group itself is a factor in the learning of its members. (2) Emphasis is shifting away from counselor preparation as a totally didactic adventure capped by a practicum, to a personalized program focusing at least in part on the counselor as a person. (3) Technological progress, primarily involving the use of videotape and simulation, is providing new opportunity for counselors-in-training to understand how they function in counseling. (4) As counselor educators focus research attention on the processes of counseling and supervision, a tentative experimental atmosphere is pervading the counselor education program. It is to be hoped that this trend toward improved counselor preparation will continue.

TREND TOWARD IMPROVED IN-SERVICE EDUCATION

Educators willingly acknowledge that teacher and counselor education really "commence" when the student leaves the campus; nonetheless, very little is done by counselor educators, teacher educators, or supervisors to upgrade the skills of teachers and counselors who are on-the-job. It may be pretentious and premature to call a few recent efforts in this direction a trend, but the matter certainly deserves some attention as future developments are considered. Beginning teachers and counselors in particular appear to be very willing to acknowledge their need for in-service assistance—especially help specific to their circumstances. The Purdue NDEA-EPDA attempt to provide in-service support and direction for counselors beginning new jobs met with great enthusiasm,[63] and similar sponsored in-service education programs have been enthusiastically endorsed. When these functions are taken together with the number of counselors who are observed seeking practical assistance at regional, state,

[63] Nelson, "Fourth and final technical report on the institute for counseling and guidance."

and national conventions, and the number who spend their time evenings and summers taking courses beyond those required for certification, the nucleus of a trend may be observed. Certainly this is a fruitful area of future exploration and development.

The trends in elementary school guidance and counseling are hopeful. Growth and increased effectiveness seem almost inevitable; however, elementary school counselors hold a public trust that is not only precious but fragile. Counselors must meet the demand for evidence of their effectiveness head on. If they can do this, the future looks extremely bright.

SUMMARY

On the negative side of the ledger, some sincere students of elementary school counseling and guidance have concluded from research evidence that one-to-one counseling is a waste of time and that leaving children alone is as effective and far more efficient. Consulting with teachers has produced changes in teachers' opinions, but not necessarily in their behaviors or the behaviors of their students. Behavioral counseling, child-development techniques, consulting, and psychotherapeutic efforts have proven no more successful. Several assumptions of counseling have been seriously questioned. Acceptance by the counselor has been related to inappropriate social behavior by the child; no relationship has been found between self-disclosure and constructive personality change; catharsis may be related to an increase in aggression; and cognitive-dissonance theory has not yet been established as a theoretical basis for producing change in the behavior of children in counseling.

On the positive side, some studies have related counseling to sociometric and self-concept gains. Multidimensional approaches (milieu counseling involving individual counseling, teacher group work, and parent meetings) have been successful in producing positive growth. Children who have failed subjects have been helped in both achievement and teacher-pupil relationships. Group counseling has been related to improvement in the sociometric standing of children, to increased verbalization by nonverbalizing children, to emotional expansiveness, to self-awareness, to reduced anxiety, and to improvement in reading. Counseled children and their parents have come to see the counselor as a source of past and future assistance. Individually prescribed treatment has been related to gains for children with a variety of individual problems.

In order to avoid some of the research problems characterizing past studies, several suggestions have been made regarding designs for the future. Significant questions need to be asked; multidimensional approaches need to be compared to single approaches; isolation of target children needs to be avoided; subcultural needs should be considered; teachers should be given feedback even when the primary treatment is individual counseling; further research needs to be directed toward an examination of counseling in order to ascertain what benefits children receive, if any; the effect of increased awareness on outcome criteria must be examined; preventive counseling designs need to be developed and tested; longitudinal measurement must supplement short-term efforts; in relation to most existing studies, numbers of counselors, teachers, and children need to be increased so that nonsignificant data are not an inevitable artifact of the sample; treatment procedures must be more adequately described; individual and target-group gains must be given as much consideration as gains in group means; the Hawthorne effect should be capitalized upon; appropriate criteria must be used; and more of the hunches of counselors need to be tested out.

Criterion measures must be selected or developed for their relevance to the treatment and the needs of the sample. Sociometric data may be more reasonably influenced through group counseling than through individual counseling, for example, since these data reflect effects on groups. A variety of criterion measures are categorized according to the primary use to which they might be put.

The counselor and teacher are urged to participate in research because of the increasing call for accountability, because practitioners know the questions they want to have answered, and because they have access to children. Several steps in the development of a research design have been suggested. Further development of the field of elementary school guidance and counseling depends in large measure on the extent to which practitioners can establish that their work makes a difference in the lives of children.

Trends in the field appear to be developing in the following areas: toward humanizing the guidance effort, toward expansion of services, toward relevance, toward more effective counseling effort, toward statesmanship, toward experimentation, toward diversity and uniqueness, toward multidimensional approaches, toward accountability, toward utilization of technical resources, toward integration of effort, toward serving target groups, toward improved counselor preparation, and toward improved in-service education.

The prospects for growth and development in elementary school counseling and guidance are extremely bright. Continued expansion, however, is somewhat dependent upon (1) research evidence that guidance services make a difference and (2) continued development in the present positive directions. The future of elementary school counseling and guidance is in our hands.

REFERENCES

Alper, T. G., and G. D. Kranzler. "A comparison of the effectiveness of behavioral and client-centered approaches for the behavioral problems of elementary school children," *Elementary School Guidance and Counseling, 5:* 35–43 (1970).

Anderson, E. C. "Counseling and consultation versus teacher-consultation in the elementary school," *Elementary School Guidance and Counseling, 2:* 276–285 (1968).

Arbuckle, D. S. "Does the school really need counselors?" *School Counselor, 17:* 325–330 (1970).

Barclay, J. R. "Sociometry: rationale and technique for effecting behavioral change in the elementary school," *Personnel and Guidance Journal, 44:* 1067–1076 (1966).

———. "Effecting behavioral change in the elementary classroom: an exploratory study," *Journal of Counseling Psychology, 14:* 240–247 (1967).

Bender, D. "Counseling, consulting, or developmental guidance? Toward an answer," *Elementary School Guidance and Counseling, 4:* 245–252 (1970).

Brown, D., and R. F. Pruett. "The elementary teacher views guidance," *School Counselor, 14:* 195–203 (1967).

Carey, R. W. "Student protest and the counselor," *Personnel and Guidance Journal, 48:* 185–191 ·(1969).

Carlson, G. D. "An experience in group counseling," *School Counselor, 14:* 116–118 (1966).

Cianciolo, P. J. "Children's literature can effect coping behavior," *Personnel and Guidance Journal, 43:* 897–903 (1965).

Cottingham, H. F. "Research voids in elementary school guidance," *Elementary School Guidance and Counseling, 1:* 218–239 (1967).

———. "National-level projection for elementary school guidance," *Personnel and Guidance Journal, 44:* 499–502 (1966).

Crow, M. L. "An investigation of structured aural, structured visual, and unstructured group counseling techniques with elementary school children." Denton, Tex.: North Texas State University, 1970. (Mimeographed.)

Doyal, R. N. "The development and evaluation of an inventory for rating elementary school counseling in grades 5 and 6." Unpublished doctoral dissertation, Purdue University, Lafayette, Ind., 1970.

Duncan, L. W., and P. W. Fitzgerald. "Increasing the parent-child communication through counselor-parent conferences," *Personnel and Guidance Journal, 47:* 514–517 (1969).

Feldhusen, J. F., J. E. Thurston, and J. J. Benning. "Sentence completion responses and classroom social behavior," *Personnel and Guidance Journal, 45:* 165–170 (1966).

Festinger, L. *Theory of Cognitive Dissonance.* New York: Harper & Row, 1957.

Franken, M. W. "A consultant role in elementary school guidance:

helping teachers increase awareness of the behavior dynamics of children," *Elementary School Guidance and Counseling, 4:* 128–135 (1969).

Frost, J. A., and J. M. Frost. "An evolving elementary school guidance program and ongoing research projects," *Elementary School Guidance and Counseling, 2:* 121–126 (1967).

Gage, N. L., ed. *Handbook of Research on Teaching.* Skokie, Ill.: Rand McNally, 1963.

Gamsky, N. R. "Action research and the school counselor," *School Counselor, 18:* 36–42 (1970).

Gordon, I. J. "Action research improves an aspect of elementary school guidance," *Personnel and Guidance Journal, 37:* 65–67 (1958).

Gribbons, W. D. "Evaluation of an eighth grade group guidance program," *Personnel and Guidance Journal, 38:* 740–745 (1960).

Gutsch, K. U., and W. D. Bellamy. "Effectiveness of an attitudinal group approach as a behavior determinant," *School Counselor, 14:* 40–43 (1966).

Hansen, J. C., T. M. Niland, and L. P. Zani. "Model reinforcement in group counseling with elementary school children," *Personnel and Guidance Journal, 47:* 741–744 (1969).

Hosford, R. E., and A. S. Briskin. "Changes through counseling," *Review of Educational Research, 39:* 189–207 (1969).

Kennedy, D. A., and I. Thompson. "Use of reinforcement techniques with a first grade boy," *Personnel and Guidance Journal, 46:* 366–370 (1967).

————, I. Thompson, and J. Cress. "A behavioral approach to consultation in elementary school guidance," *School Counselor, 15:* 220–223 (1968).

Kornick, J. "An analysis: impact of an elementary school counselor on teachers' perceptions of the counselor's role and functions," *Elementary School Guidance and Counseling, 4:* 188–196 (1970).

Kowitz, G. T., and N. G. Kowitz. "Elementary school attendance as an index of guidance needs," *Personnel and Guidance Journal, 44:* 938–943 (1966).

Kranzler, G. D. "Elementary school counseling: an evaluation," *Elementary School Guidance and Counseling, 2:* 286–294 (1968).

————. "The elementary school counselor as consultant: an evaluation," *Elementary School Guidance and Counseling, 3:* 284–288 (1969).

————, G. R. Mayer, C. O. Dyer, and P. F. Munger. "Counseling with elementary school children: an experimental study," *Personnel and Guidance Journal, 44:* 944–949 (1966).

Langford, L. M., and O. W. Alm. "A comparison of parent judgments and child feelings concerning the self adjustment and social adjustment of 12-year-old children," *Journal of Genetic Psychology, 85:* 39–46 (1954).

Leiter, S. "There is no tomorrow," *Report of the Seventh Annual All Ohio Elementary School Guidance Conference,* pp. 49–55. Columbus, Ohio: State Department of Education, Division of Guidance and Testing, 1968.

Leventhal, R. B., and G. D. Kranzler. "The relationship between the depth of interpersonal exploration and constructive personality change in elementary school children: an exploratory study," *Elementary School Guidance and Counseling, 3:* 12–19 (1968).

Lewis, M. D. "The effects of counseling and consultation upon the sociometric status and personal adjustment of third grade pupils," *Elementary School Guidance and Counseling, 5:* 44–52 (1970).

———. "Elementary school counseling and consultation: their effects on teachers' perceptions," *School Counselor, 18:* 49–55 (1970).

Matthes, W. A., G. D. Kranzler, and G. R. Mayer. "The relationship between the clients' perceptions of counselor behavior and change in the client's behavior," *Elementary School Guidance and Counseling, 2:* 179–186 (1968).

Mayer, G. R., D. L. Beggs, N. Fjellstedt, J. Forhetz, J. Nighswander, and R. Richards. "The use of public commitment and counseling with elementary school children: an evaluation," *Elementary School Guidance and Counseling, 5:* 22–34 (1970).

——— and J. J. Cody. "Festinger's theory of cognitive dissonance applied to school counseling," *Personnel and Guidance Journal, 47:* 233–239 (1968).

———, G. D. Kranzler, and W. A. Matthes. "Elementary school counseling and peer relations," *Personnel and Guidance Journal, 46:* 360–365 (1967).

———, T. M. Rohen, and A. D. Whitley. "Group counseling with children: a cognitive-behavior approach," *Journal of Counseling Psychology, 16:* 142–149 (1969).

McCandless, B. R. *Children: Behavior and Development.* New York: Holt, Rinehart and Winston, Inc., 1967.

McCreary W. H., and G. Miller. "Elementary school counselors in California," *Personnel and Guidance Journal, 44:* 494–498 (1966).

McDougall, W. P., and H. M. Reitan. "The elementary counselor as perceived by elementary principals," *Personnel and Guidance Journal, 42:* 348–354 (1963).

Moon, M., and D. Wilson. "Teacher-counselor cooperation: building self-concepts and confidence in children," *School Counselor, 17:* 364–366 (1970).

Muro, J. J. *The Counselor's Work in the Elementary School.* Scranton, Pa.: International Textbook, 1970.

Myrick, R. D. "The counselor-consultant and the effeminate boy," *Personnel and Guidance Journal, 48:* 355–361 (1970).

Nelson, R. C. "Fourth and final technical report on the institute for counseling and guidance." Lafayette, Ind.: Purdue University, 1970.

———. "The emerging role of the elementary school counselor: The counseling role." Paper read at the American Personnel and Guidance Association Convention, Dallas, Texas, 1967.

Nighswander, J. K., and G. R. Mayer. "Catharsis: a means of reducing elementary school students' aggressive behaviors? *Personnel and Guidance Journal, 47:* 461–466 (1969).

Oldridge, B. "Two roles for elementary school guidance personnel," *Personnel and Guidance Journal, 43:* 367–370 (1964).

Phillips, W. "The professionalization of elementary school counselors," *Elementary School Guidance and Counseling, 4:* 87–94 (1969).

Pintner, R., and J. Lev. "Worries of school children," *Journal of Genetic Psychology*, *56:* 67–76 (1940).

Ray, R. S., D. A. Shaw, and J. A. Cobb. "The work box: an innovation in teaching attentional behavior," *School Counselor*, *18:* 15–35 (1970).

Reinhertz, H., and C. L. Griffin. "The second time around: achievement and progress of boys who repeated one of the first three grades," *School Counselor*, *17:* 213–218 (1970).

Ringness, T. A. "Affective differences between successful and non-successful bright ninth grade boys," *Personnel and Guidance Journal*, *43:* 600–606 (1965).

Ryan, D. W., ad E. L. Gaier. "Student socio-economic status and counselor contact in the junior high school," *Personnel and Guidance Journal*, *46:* 466–472 (1966).

Schmieding, O. A. "An investigation of efficacy of counseling and guidance procedures with failing junior high school students," *School Counselor*, *14:* 74–80 (1966).

Seeman, J. "Child therapy in education: some current trends," *Education*, *74:* 493–499 (1954).

Seidman, E. *et al.* "The child development consultant: an experiment," *Personnel and Guidance Journal*, *49:* 29–34 (1970).

Stetter, R. "A group guidance technique for the classroom teacher," *School Counselor*, *16:* 179–184 (1969).

Stormer, G. E. "Milieu group counseling in elementary school guidance," *Elementary School Guidance and Counseling*, *1:* 240–254 (1967).

Thoresen, C. E. "Relevance and research in counseling," *Review of Educational Research*, *39:* 263–281 (1969).

Tiegland, J. J., R. C. Winkler, P. F. Munger, and G. D. Kranzler, "Some concomitants of underachievement at the elementary school level," *Personnel and Guidance Journal*, *44:* 950–955 (1966).

Tosi, D. J., C. Swanson, and P. McLean. "Group counseling with non-verbalizing elementary school children," *Elementary School Guidance and Counseling*, *4:* 260–266 (1970).

Tulkin, S. R., J. P. Muller, and L. K. Conn. "Need for approval and popularity: sex differences in elementary school students," *Journal of Consulting and Clinical Psychology*, *33:* 35–39 (1969).

Van Hoose, W. H., and Sister M. Kurtz. "Status of guidance in the elementary school: 1968–69," *Personnel and Guidance Journal, 48:* 381–384 (1970).

———— and C. M. Vafakas. "Status of guidance and counseling in the elementary school," *Personnel and Guidance Journal*, *46:* 536–539 (1968).

Walz, G., and J. Miller. "School climates and student behavior: implication for counselor role," *Personnel and Guidance Journal*, *47:* 859–867 (1969).

ARTICLES IN BOOKS OF READINGS

Dinkmeyer, D. C. *Guidance and Counseling in the Elementary School: Readings in Theory and Practice.* New York: Holt, Rinehart and Winston, Inc., 1968. Readings beginning on pages 367, 371, 378, 385, and 391.

Koplitz, E. D. *Guidance in the Elementary School: Theory, Research and Practice*. Dubuque, Iowa: William C. Brown Company, Publisher, 1968. Readings beginning on pages 289, 296, 302, 310, 351, 355, and 361.

Litwack, L., R. Getson, and G. Saltzman. *Research in Counseling*. Itasca, Ill.: F. E. Peacock, 1968. Readings beginning on pages 276, 292, and 376.

Peters, H. J., A. C. Riccio, and J. J. Quaranta. *Guidance in the Elementary School: A Book of Readings*. New York: Macmillan, 1963. Readings beginning on pages 209, 214, 218, 224, 229, and 241.

Index